The Counter-Revolution

Doctrine and Action

1789-1804

JACQUES GODECHOT

Translated from the French by Salvator Attanasio

PRINCETON UNIVERSITY PRESS

PRINCETON, NEW JERSEY

Published by Princeton University Press, Princeton, New Jersey
In the United Kingdom: Princeton University Press, Guildford, Surrey

Originally published in France as *La Contre-Révolution*:
Doctrine et Action, 1789–1804 by Presses Universitaires
de France, Paris. Copyright © 1961, Presses Universitaires de France.

LCC 70-159820
ISBN 0-691-00788-8 pbk.

Printed in the United States of America
by Princeton University Press, Princeton, New Jersey

First Princeton Paperback printing, 1981

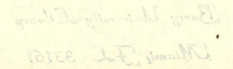

CONTENTS

v

INTRODUCTION

The biggest gap in the history of the French Revolution is, paradoxically, the history of the counter-revolution.
—Alfred Cobban, *Times Literary Supplement*, January 6, 1956

Historians generally, and those of France in particular, have dealt very inadequately with the history of the counter-revolution.

Why is this so? Those generally referred to as historians of the Left have been interested primarily in the study of the revolutionary movement and the ideas of the "patriots." Historians of the Right, fewer in number, have in most cases written works of an apologetic character; eulogizing the counter-revolutionaries. Moreover, these historians, often recruited outside the universities, have been deficient in methodology and in preparation. Consequently, in France the works on the counter-revolution are both scarce and of inferior caliber.

Two works deal with the counter-revolution as a whole. One by Emmanuel Vingtrinier, entitled *La Contre-Révolution*, was published in 1924.[1] Unfortunately, it was never completed because the author died after publication of the first two volumes, which leave off at 1791. In them Vingtrinier focused primarily on the political activity of the counter-revolutionaries and their conspiracies, but he totally neglected their ideology.

The other work is that by Louis Madelin, *La Contre-Révolution sous la Révolution*, which appeared in 1935.[2] This covers the period between 1789 and 1815. It is a superficial study and, moreover, again devoted exclusively to political movements, with no mention of the counter-revolutionary ideology.

1. (2 vols., Paris, 1924).
2. (Paris, 1935).

vii

Thus, on the French side there is not much in the way of comprehensive works. Several valuable studies, however, have been published elsewhere. I shall cite, in particular, that of Paul H. Beik, entitled *The French Revolution Seen from the Right, Social Theories in Motion, 1789–1799*,[3] published in 1956. This has not yet become the object of much comment, even in France, but it is a valuable book and perhaps the only one that deals thoroughly with counter-revolutionary ideology.

Why are there so few studies of this ideology? In my opinion, it seems likely that historians of the counter-revolution thought the counter-revolutionaries had no ideology, that they simply wanted to restore things as they had been in 1789. But this apparently was not so. On reading the works of the counter-revolutionaries themselves we discover, in fact, that these authors professed a doctrine or, more precisely, several doctrines, and that very few of them thought in terms of restoring the Old Regime without changing anything in it. The doctrinaires of the counter-revolution were for the most part revolutionaries in their own way. In this study, we shall begin by examining the principal counter-revolutionary doctrines.

It must not be thought that the counter-revolution was limited to France. In a book entitled *La Grande Nation*,[4] I tried to show that the Revolution was a general phenomenon, which began around 1770, lasted until around 1850 and spread to the entire West. The American historian, R. R. Palmer, has resumed this argument with greater vigor and more proofs valid for the period from 1770 to 1790.[5] This interpretation, which differs from the one normally accepted, is closer to the viewpoint Fernand Braudel has so rightly described as that of "the long duration."[6]

If, accordingly, the Revolution was "western" and not only "French," and it lasted eighty years and not ten, the counter-revolution also spread throughout the West during the same period. Indeed, it is strange that the most original theorists of the counter-revolution are not Frenchmen, but an Englishman—Burke, a Swiss—Mallet du Pan, and two Germans—Rehberg and Gentz.

As early as the Genevan revolution of 1768 the theorists of the counter-

3. *Transactions of the American Philosophical Society*, Philadelphia, 1956, new series, vol. 46, part I. Republished (New York, 1971).
4. (2 vols., Paris, 1956).
5. R. R. Palmer, *The Age of the Democratic Revolution*, Vol. I: *The Challenge* (Princeton, N.J.: 1959).
6. Fernand Braudel, "Histoire et Sciences sociales: La longue durée," *Annales* (*E.S.C.*), 1958, pp. 725–753.

revolution appear on the scene; it is they who have Rousseau's *Contrat social* burned in the public square by the public executioner. Two or three years later American "loyalists" oppose the Revolution that was not only to create the United States, but also to bring the world major innovations in the political and social order: they have their own theoretical justifications.[7] In Great Britain at the time of the troubles of 1782–84, in Holland during the revolt of 1783–87 and in Belgium during the revolution of 1787–90 authors again appear who sought to set up a counter-revolutionary doctrine in opposition to the revolutionary ideology. But more often than not these first counter-revolutionary doctrines had as their objective the particular revolution which had occasioned their expression. It was only later, after 1790, that the awareness set in that the Revolution was spreading to half Europe and that the revolts that had been set off in America, Ireland, Holland, Belgium and Switzerland were of the same nature as those which had taken place in France. The theorists of the counter-revolution, then, broadened their point of view; they no longer fought the Revolution in this or that country, but the Revolution as such, and they formulated counter-revolutionary theories of universal value. Among these theorists, many had already composed works relating to specific past revolutions, for example the Englishman Burke, the Swiss Mallet du Pan and the German von Schlötzer.

Counter-revolutionary action, like the doctrines, found the chance to manifest itself from 1768 to 1790. And it had recourse to a method we shall often see employed subsequently: appeal for assistance abroad. The English used German mercenaries, Hanoverians and Hessians, to fight against the American insurgents. In 1782 the Genevan oligarchs called to their aid the troops of Zurich and Berne, of the kings of Sardinia and France, who enabled them to crush the revolution. Similarly, in 1787 the "stathouder" of the United Provinces, William V, could recover his throne thanks to the military intervention of England and Prussia, and three years later the counter-revolution was to triumph in Belgium and the Liège district thanks to Austrian and German troops. These foreign troops were sometimes supported by the émigrés; for example, the loyalist émigrés of the United States—in proportion to the population more numerous than the French émigrés—played an important role in the struggle against the American Revolution. Among the methods employed

7. C. H. Van Tyne, *The Loyalists in the American Revolution* (New York, 1902); V. L. Parrington, *Main Currents in American Thought* (3 vols., New York, 1927–30).

by the counter-revolution before 1790, only the great peasant insurrections do not yet appear.

Thus in 1790 the counter-revolution was already endowed with the elements of a doctrine and possessed most of its means of action. It would be interesting to study the counter-revolution from around 1770 because we would then be able to give a more complete outline of its history. However, that is not the intention here, first because the problem has already been discussed by R. R. Palmer,[8] secondly, and above all, because the present work is the product of a series of lectures delivered in 1958–59 before candidates for the *agrégation*, whose program included the period extending from 1789 to 1804. This explains the chronological limits imposed, which do not coincide with the natural breaks of history. The counter-revolution began twenty years before 1789 and lasted well beyond 1804. However, the period included between these two dates is undoubtedly the most characteristic of its history. It was then that theorists elaborated the great counter-revolutionary doctrines which were to be applied later, in the course of the—provisional—triumph of the counter-revolution between 1815 and 1848, and which were to become the breviary of counter-revolutionaries in all western countries until the publication of the works of Charles Maurras and of the doctrines inspired by fascism. It was also during this period that the struggle assumed its most diverse and dramatic forms: peasant insurrections, urban riots, strife between espionage networks. What appears in both the doctrines of the counter-revolution and the struggles to which they lead is one whole aspect of the civilization of yesteryear.

This book is by no means intended as a definitive work; but I have the feeling that it fills a gap and I hope that it will give rise to new studies capable of revitalizing a fascinating subject which has been overly neglected by historians.

8. *Op. cit.*

PART I:

DOCTRINE

Note: In the original French text, bibliographical citations were given at the opening of each chapter. For this edition, these have been transferred to a separate section at the back of the book, pp. 388–396. As in the French edition, the bibliographical notes begin at Chapter II, since Chapter I contains such information within the text.

The Origins of the Doctrines of the French Counter-Revolution

Contrary to general belief, the origins of the French counter-revolutionary doctrines stretch far back into the past. Indeed, we can link these doctrines to three great currents of thought that developed throughout the course of the eighteenth century but whose sources can be traced back to the seventeenth century. We shall call the first of these three currents historical conservatism, or the doctrine of historical rights; the second, the doctrine of enlightened despotism; and the third, the doctrine of integral absolutism.

1 / Historical Conservatism

The principal authors who demanded that France should return to those former institutions she had supposedly forgotten lived at the end of the seventeenth century or at the beginning of the eighteenth. They were notably Fénelon, Boulainvilliers, and the duc de Saint-Simon. It is not our intention to analyze the work of these authors in detail, but we cannot avoid the task of showing how they were at the fountainhead of this stream of thought.

Fénelon, as is known, was appointed by Louis XIV as tutor to the duc de Bourgogne. He wrote various works for his pupil, in particular *Les Aventures de Télémaque*, which already outlines the model commonwealth, the perfect commonwealth, ruled by a prince assisted by the nobles of the country. *Télémaque*, however, unfolds in an unreal utopian setting, whereas Fénelon also wrote works of a much more precise character.

The book *Télémaque* displeased the entourage of Louis XIV, and as a result Fénelon was twice disgraced, first in 1695, and again in 1710. He was banished to his diocese at Cambrai and it was there that, among other works, he wrote *Les Remonstrances à Louis XIV sur certains points de son administration, L'Examen de conscience sur les devoirs de la royauté*, followed by a *Supplement, Les Plans de gouvernement concertés avec le duc de Chevreuse pour être proposés au duc de Bourgogne*, and the *Mémoires sur la guerre de Succession d'Espagne*.

In these different works Fénelon refers constantly to a "constitution of the kingdom." This constitution is not one that must be drawn up by making a clean sweep of the past. Rather, it is a constitution that already exists, an unwritten constitution, one that gathers together the ancient customs. France must return to this former constitution, which imposes upon the king precisely defined duties, limits his absolute power, grants a large measure of power to the nobles and organizes the participation of the nobility in the governing of the kingdom.

Fénelon also has very clear and distinct ideas as regards administration. France should be governed by a hierarchy of assemblies. At the base, assemblies or diocesan Estates General which, in a word, correspond to the present-day general councils of departments; above these, provincial estates grouping several dioceses; and finally, in Paris, the Estates General of the kingdom, which would meet regularly every three years and which, obligatorily, would vote all taxes. No tax could be levied without the authorization of the Estates General.

Yet, Fénelon is by no means a democrat; he does not wish to abolish the orders. This whole hierarchy of assemblies is to be made up of chambers, each chamber being composed of the members of an order. There are to be three chambers in each assembly: a chamber of the nobility, a chamber of the clergy and a chamber of the Third Estate or the commoners.

Fénelon did not provide a justification for demanding the maintenance of orders and chambers and a return to this traditional constitution. This justification was to be supplied by Boulainvilliers, as well as by a lesser known author, Le Laboureur.

Boulainvilliers, in 1727, published *Lettres sur les anciens parlements de France qu'on nomme Etats généraux*, and, in 1732, *Précis historique de la monarchie française*, as well as *Essai sur la noblesse*. At about the same time Le Laboureur wrote *Histoire de la pairie*, but it was not published until later, in 1740.

These two authors attempt to justify the existence of the orders and the privileges enjoyed by the first two orders, and especially those of the nobility. In their view, the nobles are the descendants of the Franks who defeated the Gauls or the Gallo-Roman population. After this victory, exercising the right of victors, they confiscated the lands, subjected the vanquished to forced labor (*la corvée*) and reduced them to serfdom. As a result of the victory the nobles therefore enjoy privileges, feudal dues.

Accordingly, it is proper to maintain the pre-eminence of the nobility, which is justified by the victory of the Franks. It is not possible to abolish feudal dues because these dues were paid to the nobility by the peasant serfs as the price of their manumission, which took place in the twelfth and thirteenth centuries. Finally, the nobles, as descendants of the victorious Franks, ought to participate in the governance of the State much more than they did at the time Boulainvilliers and Le Laboureur were writing, that is, at the beginning of the age of Louis XV when, practically speaking, the administration was in the hands of the ennobled bourgeois.

The duc de Saint-Simon, renowned for his *Mémoires*, shares the same beliefs. He deeply deplores that Louis XIV has excluded the nobles from the governance of the State. Saint-Simon figured among those who, after the death of Louis XIV, urged the regent once more to entrust the government to the nobility, grouped in councils. This system, called "*polysynodie*," failed after five or six years and there was a return to the traditional administration. The nobles of the sword showed themselves incapable of efficient administration, and it became necessary again to entrust the principal administrative posts to masters of petitions (*maîtres de requête*), and to the judges of parlement, that is, to members of the newly sprung-up nobility of the robe (*noblesse de robe*), sons or grandsons of ennobled bourgeois.

But why exclude the nobility of the robe from governing the State?

The doctrines of Boulainvilliers and Saint-Simon were useful as justifications for the pre-eminence of the nobility of the sword. But the nobles of the robe claimed that there was no reason to discriminate against them. One of the most ardent champions of the robe was Montesquieu.

Montesquieu, as we know, wrote several very celebrated works. But it is above all in *L'Esprit des lois* that he develops the idea of the necessity of the participation by the nobility of the robe, that is, of the members of the parlements, in the governance of the State. *L'Esprit des lois* enjoyed an extraordinary success. In fact, this book in certain respects shows a liberal spirit. Montesquieu, with apparent impartiality, outlines the advantages and disadvantages of the different forms of government. *L'Esprit des lois* is first of all an excellent treatise on the political sciences, perhaps the best treatise of this type to be published in France in the eighteenth century. It sets forth the various types of government, and their degeneration. The republic, on the one hand, and the monarchy, on the other, are good forms of government, but they are susceptible to deterioration; the republic can transform itself into despotic demagoguery and the monarchy into tyranny.

In fact, the work as a whole is intended to eulogize what Montesquieu calls "monarchy." This ideal monarchy is a limited monarchy. The king governs but the powers are separate. Montesquieu borrowed the idea of separation of powers from the English political theorist, Locke. Locke distinguished several separate powers. Montesquieu believes that there should not be more than three powers in an ideal monarchy: the executive power, the legislative power and the judicial power.

The executive power is entrusted to the king, but there is a legislative power which will be turned over to the nobility. Finally, the judicial power is the prerogative of the parlements. We must not overlook the fact that Montesquieu was the first president of the parlement of Bordeaux, and that in defending the parlements, he was defending his personal situation.

Montesquieu is by no means opposed to the maintenance of the three orders; on the contrary, he warmly approves of this distinction, for in his view, each type of government has a "motive force." For the republic, the motive force is virtue; for the monarchy, it is honor. Now honor cannot be brought into play unless a nobility exists whose role is to defend the country's honor and familial honor as well.

So Montesquieu upholds the division of France into three orders. Only he does not restrict the nobility exclusively to the military nobility descended from the victorious Franks. He rapidly passes over the reasons for the superiority and privileges of the nobility, and approves, moreover, of the fact that the nobility of the sword enjoys privileges justified by the victory of the Franks over the Gauls; but he believes that the monarchy has evolved. In contrast to Boulainvilliers, who wants to see the monarchy return to a primitive state—which had never existed, save in his mind—Montesquieu considers that things have changed. If the nobility of the sword has been the only order to enjoy the privileges justified by the victory of the Franks, the nobility of the robe has been taking shape gradually during the evolution of the monarchy and it too possesses rights, notably, the right to govern; it is therefore logical that it too should have its share of privileges. Montesquieu approves of privileged persons being exempted from certain taxes in exchange for the specific services they render the monarchy. He approves of feudal dues being maintained because they represent the price of the manumission of the serfs.

But he also approves of the king's being able, in consequence of the general evolution (Montesquieu is an evolutionist), gradually to suppress the seigniorial courts of justice by exercise of the right of redemption. Montesquieu thinks that it is necessary to compensate the proprietors, and if he acknowledges that feudal dues can be abolished, he considers their redemption obligatory.

Thus, in contrast to his predecessors, Montesquieu formulated a coherent program of social conservatism. He maintains the monarchy as it existed at the beginning of the seventeenth century, before Richelieu, but he tempers absolute monarchy by calling for the participation of the Estates General, divided into orders, and of the parlements. He preserves feudal rights while acknowledging that they can be redeemed. He retains the autonomy of the provinces and cities with their privileges. He is satisfied with the social hierarchy. Hence, the great success of *L'Esprit des lois* is not surprising. One finds it in all the libraries—even those of persons who were to be the fiercest champions of the Revolution, the Jacobins, and Montagnards, as well as on the shelves of the conservatives.[1]

The influence of *L'Esprit des lois* can be discerned in the great majority of revolutionary institutions. But we must not forget that it also contained a moderate conservative doctrine. The work was likewise the basis of Napoleonic institutions. From Montesquieu, Napoleon was to take specifically the idea of "intermediary bodies," which were to be graduated between the sovereign and the mass of the population in order to bind the prince to the people. We find Montesquieu's doctrine in the Charter of 1814. Thus, Montesquieu was in the forefront in the development of revolutionary and counter-revolutionary doctrines alike. And among the

---

1. On the influence of Montesquieu in the United States, see the excellent study by Paul M. Spurlin, *Montesquieu in America, 1760–1901* (New Orleans, La., 1940). My colleague at Toulouse, M. Dupuis has studied the influence of Montesquieu in Spain.

first French counter-revolutionaries—those who expounded their ideas at the time of the convocation of the Estates General in 1789—many cited Montesquieu.

In particular, even before the convocation of the Estates General, one man is notable for involving Montesquieu, and also Boulainvilliers and Fénelon, in order to formulate a doctrine of social conservatism, namely, the comte d'Antraigues. D'Antraigues played a considerable role in the whole history of the counter-revolution, often a very mysterious role, on which we shall try to shed more light.[2] He was born in 1753 in Montpellier. His father came from a family originally Swiss and Protestant but which had become Catholic and French. The comte's father was sixty when the child was born, but his mother was only seventeen. She was the daughter of the intendant of Languedoc, comte de Saint-Priest, an affiliation which was to play a considerable role in the comte's extremely checkered career.

The comte d'Antraigues exhibited extraordinary intelligence in his very early years, but he also showed signs of a difficult character and his family rid itself of him by packing him off to Versailles as a member of the Royal Guard at the age of fourteen. But he was not very happy in this élite corps and two years later he transferred to the carabiniers. He soon abandoned the military life, thereafter reformed his character, and in 1778 and 1779 set out on a protracted journey. He left for the Orient and Egypt, returning to France by way of Poland and Germany. For ten years, from 1779 to 1789, he remained almost without interruption in the village of Antraigues living off his revenues, which amounted to 40,000 livres, a considerable sum for that time. (The bulk of these revenues consisted of feudal dues, which explains the comte's future attitude.) The great agitation of 1789 supervened, provoked by the announcement of the convocation of the Estates General, and d'Antraigues immediately published a pamphlet entitled *Mémoires sur les Etats généraux*,[3] which achieved extraordinary fame.

The essential aim of these *Mémoires* was to oppose the designation of deputies to the Estates General by the estates of the province of Languedoc.

---

2. See below, Chapter X. On the comte d'Antraigues, cf. Léonce Pingaud, *Un agent secret sous la Révolution et l'Empire* (Paris, 1893; see preferably the second edition of 1894).
3. (Avignon, 1788).

In 1614, in the *pays d'Etats*,* and notably in Languedoc, the provincial estates had elected deputies to the Estates General. D'Antraigues demands that the deputies of Languedoc now be chosen by all the electors, as in the other provinces. But this is not the pamphlet's only aim. We find in it many general ideas on the form the monarchy ought to assume, ideas not inspired solely by Montesquieu because d'Antraigues had also read Rousseau. Thus the work appeared to be democratic and even "republican," which was one of the reasons for its success. But if one examines these *Mémoires* more closely it becomes clear that d'Antraigues was, in fact, very far from a belief in democracy.

The pamphlet appeared democratic because d'Antraigues conceded that the king was not necessary and declared that kingship was not "of divine right." He adopted the theory of the "social contract," according to which the king ruled in consequence of a "contract" concluded with the people by his distant predecessors. But if the king is not of divine right, he can be dethroned and the nation can conclude a contract with another person.

Accordingly, d'Antraigues approves the idea of a constitutional monarchy. However, he believes that in a country as large as France, no other type of regime except the monarchical is conceivable. And here d'Antraigues joins with Rousseau, who also believed that a republic was possible only in small countries such as the Swiss cantons and the states of classic antiquity.

Subsequently we see d'Antraigues following the ideas of Boulainvilliers, Le Laboureur and Saint-Simon, arguing that the nobility must play the foremost role in the State because the nobles are descended from the Franks who conquered Gaul.

The Estates General form one of the fundamental institutions of the kingdom. The king convoked them from the beginning of the fourteenth century and the monarchy has degenerated since it ceased to convoke them, that is, since the beginning of the seventeenth century. D'Antraigues spiritedly criticizes the "royal despotism" (an expression taken from Saint-Simon) which was established in France from the time of Richelieu, and especially of Louis XIV, onwards. He declares that in this viewpoint he follows "the illustrious Montesquieu" and that what is required is a monarchy tempered by a legislative power belonging to the Estates

---

* Provinces attached to the kingdom in the post-feudal period and retaining their representative estates—Trans.

General or, at the worst, to two assemblies, as in England: a House of Lords and a House of Commons.

As regards the judicial power, he holds entirely to the ideas of Montesquieu. He demands that the parlements and venality of offices be maintained because only venality of offices can assure the independence of the magistrates.

Finally, d'Antraigues maintains that the Third Estate cannot but adhere to these ideas and support the nobility in its claims. We must not forget that this pamphlet appeared in 1788, that is, at the time of what has been called the aristocratic revolution, when the nobility was in revolt against acts of the royal power which it considered arbitrary. At that particular moment it was the nobility that demanded an overthrow of the organization of the kingdom. Now, during this period the members of the Third Estate applauded the action of the nobility of the sword against the absolute power—one has only to recall the "Day of Tiles" at Grenoble or the uprisings at Rennes. To a certain extent the comte d'Antraigues's opinion could appear justified.

Thus, d'Antraigues thinks that the Estates General will bring about the triumph of the program of the nobility, with the help of the clergy and of the Third Estate. In exchange, he thinks that the nobility could give up its fiscal privileges. He approves the notion of equality of taxation and recognizes the existence of a certain number of abuses, "of vain and odious privileges," contrary to the general interest.

Such was the position of d'Antraigues in 1788, a position that subsequently would undergo further development. We shall see the comte, little by little, draw closer to the doctrine of enlightened despotism and then to that of integral absolutism.

2 / Enlightened Despotism

The ideas of Boulainvilliers, Fénelon and Le Laboureur had not been received without criticism in France. The Third Estate had been displeased to see the privileges of the nobility glorified to such an extent and some authors took upon themselves the task of replying to the theorists of the rights of the nobility.

Abbé Dubos figures in the first rank of the defenders of the Third Estate. He published *Histoire critique de l'établissement de la monarchie française*,[4] in which he refuted the theory of the victory of the Franks,

4. (Paris, 1743).

and in any case tried to show—and his demonstration was pertinent—that the nobility was not of Frankish origin. The majority of the nobles in the order of nobility of the sword, he said, could not trace their ancestry further back than fourteenth century. He also tried to show that the privileges of the nobility consisted of usurpations, either of the rights of the king or of those of the people.

In the course of French history, declared Dubos, the bourgeoisie and the king had been united since the thirteenth century in their struggles against the privileges of the nobility. This was true enough. Accordingly, abbé Dubos views the theories based upon the superiority of the nobility as groundless and so concludes in favor of the necessity of a union between the bourgeoisie and the king against the nobility.

He feels, however, that the bourgeoisie as a whole is not capable of participating in the government. Confidence must be reposed in the king, who will choose his councillors from among the most enlightened elements of the French people and, as much as possible, from among the bourgeois.

Another theorist of enlightened despotism was the marquis d'Argenson, a great lord, nobleman of the sword, intendant and minister of foreign affairs. In 1737 he wrote *Considérations sur le gouvernement ancien et présent de la France*.[5]

In the *Considérations*, d'Argenson glorifies the Capetian dynasty. He shows that the kings have been the architects of the people's happiness. It was the kings who freed the serfs despite the lords, it was the kings who forced the lords to grant charters to the communes. The kings, therefore, have always desired the happiness of the people, and it is proper that this state of affairs should continue, as is possible if the kings are "enlightened."

This doctrine of enlightened despotism was propagated by a number of *philosophes*, for example by Mably, in his *Parallèle des Romains et des Francs*, published in 1740, and above all by Voltaire. There is nothing surprising in this: Voltaire, as we know, had been engaged as a councillor by Frederick II, king of Prussia, and had thus naturally become a partisan of enlightened despotism.

Voltaire extolled this regime in many works, but most notably in a reply to Montesquieu's *L'Esprit des lois* entitled *Commentaire de 'L'Esprit des lois.'* In this commentary Voltaire refutes Montesquieu and tries to show the dangers inherent in the parlements. Indeed, Voltaire fought

5. The work was not published in Paris until 1764.

vigorously against the parlements, writing extremely virulent pamphlets against some of them, particularly that of Toulouse in connection with the Calas affair.

Voltaire considers that the nobility enjoys all kinds of usurped rights. It is therefore necessary to make an attempt to reduce these rights, but he does not go so far as to demand suppression of the nobility. Moreover, he exhibits great hostility to the Church—not to religion in general but to the clergy. Voltaire is anti-clerical, but he believes that "A religion is necessary for the people," and he himself professed one. He demands, of course, fiscal equality, the abolition of all fiscal privileges, although he approves of redemption of feudal dues.

In a general way, we can say that the whole group of Encyclopedists was in favor of an enlightened despotism rather than of a truly democratic regime, or even of a monarchy tempered *à la* Montesquieu.

Another group of political thinkers, the physiocrats, tried to provide a legal base, as it were, for this enlightened despotism. They concerned themselves primarily with economic problems, particularly rural ones, but in their opinion—and no doubt they were correct—the reforms which they urged could be realized in the economic domain only by a very strong power, properly counseled, and assisted above all by physiocrats. They formulated a doctrine that is known as the doctrine of "legal despotism," that is, the doctrine of a certain kind of absolutism, limited not by natural law but by positive law.

We shall not dwell at length on the ideas of these advocates of enlightened despotism, but it is necessary to draw attention to one of those who tried to apply them, Calonne.

Calonne was controller-general of finances, that is, prime minister in effect, from 1783 to 1789. He was the son of a president of a parlement and had himself at first been a magistrate, and later intendant at Metz and Lille. Called to the administration of finances by the king upon the queen's advice because of his great elegance and charm, Calonne was very soon forced to propose to the king a plan of reforms similar to that formulated by Turgot (one of the physiocrats), or by Necker. But Calonne's scheme went much further.

The plan was submitted to an assembly of notables, chosen in the main from the clergy and the nobility of the sword or of the robe. This was a grave error, indicating a total lack of psychological understanding, for Calonne had not taken into account the fact that the nobles of sword and robe were much more favorably disposed toward the system of tempered monarchy, appealing to the parlements or to councils of nobles, than to enlightened despotism.

And so the assembly of notables rejected Calonne's plan, whereupon he left for England, becoming it is said the first émigré of the French Revolution. But we can find Calonne's ideas clearly formulated in the scheme that he had recommended to the assembly of notables, as well as in several pamphlets written in England.[6]

Being intelligent and perspicacious, Calonne considers that the revolution which is in the offing in France can be avoided if the king, exercising his full authority, will himself draw up a projected constitution. This constitution should establish a regime in which the king would preserve a good many of his powers but yield a great part of the legislative power to two chambers as in England, a House of Lords and a House of Commons, that would meet periodically. The king would abolish fiscal privileges and leave the chambers free to vote taxes.

The king should also create administrative assemblies in all the provinces and grant Frenchmen essential civil liberties, individual freedom, freedom of the press and freedom of assembly.

Without these reforms there will be a revolution, according to Calonne. He thinks that the tempered monarchy as recommended by Montesquieu is henceforth impossible because of the turbulence of the nobility, who have rejected the plans presented to the assembly of notables. Moreover, the absolute monarchy as it previously functioned could endure no longer. If Calonne's plan were to be rejected, France would fall either into despotism and dictatorship, or into anarchy. Calonne concluded his counsel thus: "Above all, respect the throne, for you do not have enough character to be republicans and the first step you take towards primitive liberty will plunge you into slavery."

3 / Integral Absolutism

Alongside these two currents of thought is a third, which aims at the maintenance of the system of absolutism without great changes, at best by modifying as little as possible the institutions and organizations of the State.

There had already been some theorists of integral monarchical

6. See especially *Lettre adressée au roi par Monsieur de Calonne*, February 9, 1789, and *Seconde Lettre adressée au roi*, April 5, 1789.

absolutism; Bossuet, no doubt, had been the most characteristic of this group of thinkers.

Bossuet's *Discours sur l'Histoire universelle* had been an apologia for absolutism as it existed under Louis XIV. He had continued this apologia in his book entitled *La Politique tirée de l'Ecriture sainte*, as well as in his *Cinquième Avertissement aux protestants.*

Bossuet's doctrine had been put into practice by Louis XIV, and Louis XV had tried to put it into effect once more. The declaration made by this monarch to the Paris Parlement on March 3, 1776, speaks for itself:

> It is in my person alone that the sovereign power resides whose essential character is the spirit of counsel, of justice and of reason. It is from me alone that my Courts derive their existence ond their authority. The plenitude of this authority that they exercise only in my name remains always in me. It is to me alone that the legislative power appertains, without dependency and without division. It is through my authority alone that the officers of my Courts proceed not to the formation, but to the registering and promulgation of my law, and that they are permitted to present remonstrances to me, which is the duty of good and faithful councillors; the entire public order emanates from me. I am its supreme guardian, my people is but one with me, and the rights and interests of the nation, which some have the effrontery to treat as a body separated from the monarch, are necessarily united with mine and rest exclusively in my hands.

This is still the philosophy of Louis XIV: *L'Etat, c'est moi.*

On the eve of the Revolution one theorist of integral absolutism, Jacob Nicolas Moreau, emerged; he was little known and we can say that he has been rescued from obscurity thanks to the work of Paul H. Beik.

Moreau was a native of Bourgogne and belonged to the very petty nobility of the robe; practically speaking, he was a bourgeois. He occupied the post of historiographer of France, which had been the appanage of some illustrious men—Boileau, Racine, Voltaire—and was archivist at the Dépôt des Chartes, a function equivalent to that of director of the National Archives.

At the request of the dauphin (father of Louis XVI, Louis XVIII and Charles X), Moreau, in 1764, drew up a kind of manual of absolute monarchy, under the title *Leçons de morale, de politique et de droit publique puisées dans l'histoire de notre monarchie ou nouveau plan d'étude de notre histoire de France rédigées par les ordres, d'après les vues de feu Monseigneur le Dauphin pour l'instruction des princes, ses enfants.* Undoubtedly scholars have been wrong not to scrutinize Moreau's works more closely inasmuch as they had a great influence on three kings of France. Moreover, Moreau was so pleased with his little manual that he decided to transform it into a larger work of twenty-three volumes, of which only twenty-one were printed; the last two volumes could not be published because the Revolution intervened. The title of this larger work was *Principes de morale, de politique et de droit public puisés dans l'histoire de notre monarchie.*

Moreau in his works assumed the defense of integral absolutism and his ideas were to enjoy practical success in that the comte de Provence, the future Louis XVIII, chose him as first councillor.

Moreau, like Bossuet, considers that the Holy Scriptures, the Bible and the dogmas of the Catholic Church must be immune to all discussion and must form the basis of all political doctrines. The Church must not persecute; nevertheless, it cannot approve of the multiplicity of cults. As for other faiths, Moreau allows only private worship. "The Church has the right to manifest a just and reasonable intolerance," he writes. He consents to the extension of civil rights to Protestants, but nothing more.

He thinks the king definitely has the right to have the press kept under surveillance. It is in the king's interest to prevent the printing or the circulation of bad books. But he is not an advocate of violence. Burning bad books serves no useful purpose; what is needed is to produce a greater number of good books which will drive out the bad.

The royal power, according to Moreau, is limited only by the natural law, which he identifies with the divine law, that which can be derived from the Scriptures; it is this law that he calls the fundamental law of the State.

Thus the royal power entails both legislative and executive authority. Moreau distinguishes, however, between legislation and the legislative authority that belongs to the king. Legislation, for its part, is limited not only by the fundamental law and the divine law, but also by human reason. Herein lies a certain concession on Moreau's part to philosophic ideas, to reason.

In terms of the historical development of the monarchy, Moreau rallies to the ideas of abbé Dubos and not to those of Boulainvilliers. He considers that it is the king's task to fashion the happiness of the French people; that ever since its existence the Capetian dynasty has contributed to this happiness, and that the king definitely has the right to limit the powers of the nobility. Moreau, of course, is in favor of preserving the orders. Indeed, he is very much opposed to the idea of equality.

In 1787, at the time of the meeting of the assembly of notables, Moreau published *Exposé historique de nos administrations populaires, aux plus anciennes époques de la monarchie française*, in which he formulated a kind of theory of French institutions, a theory which led him to reject suppression of the parlements. And in February of 1789 he published an *Exposition et Défense de la constitution monarchique de la France*, in which he elaborated his ideas.

From these different pamphlets, it can be seen that Moreau formulated a number of criteria on the validity of law. Law is the expression of the general will, he asserts, but he does not exactly define how this will is to be expressed. It must be applied to all the subjects, or at the very least, to all the members of a same order. It must be made in the interest of the governed and not of the governors. And it must have been deliberated upon in such a way that the subject derives advantages from it, and that it does not injure his interests. The law must be written and registered according to established customs and in an unalterable manner; it must also be made public.

It is very interesting to see this champion of integral absolutism expressing certain criteria applicable to law, criteria drawn from the writings of the *philosophes* or publicists of the eighteenth century.

Moreau is not opposed to the convocation of the Estates General, but he thinks the Estates will be useful only if they give the king a means of dispensing with them in the future. He is opposed to the periodic convocation of the Estates General or of legislative assemblies. And he is opposed to the suppression of the parlements, as we have said. He believes, in fact, that the parlements form one of the great traditional forces of the State and must be re-established. Finally, Moreau is in favor of the king's broadening the composition of his council by summoning members of the nobility of the robe and of the parlements to assist him.

Thus, the reforms demanded by Moreau are minimal; yet we cannot say that this theorist of integral absolutism wished to maintain the Old Regime intact.

From this review of the three doctrines dominating French conservatism in 1789, we can conclude that no author was a champion of the status quo. All proposed reforms, thus confirming that the counter-revolutionaries, in their way, were also revolutionaries.

CHAPTER II

The Reaction to the

Revolution of 1789

Three groups of people, whose ideas we shall set forth here, reacted in different ways to the Revolution in 1789: the first group included the king and his entourage. In fact, the king outlined a program of reform which will be studied in the first part of this chapter.

In the Constituent Assembly we can distinguish what, from the end of 1789, was called the right party, later the Right. This in turn can be divided into two factions: the moderate Right, which accepts some reforms, and an intransigent or extremist Right, which rejects nearly all the proposed reforms but which, nevertheless, is not as totally reactionary as is often believed.

1 / The Royal Program

The royal program is contained in four documents: on the one hand, the three addresses delivered at the opening of the Estates General on May 5, 1789; on the other, a royal Declaration of June 23. The addresses of May 5 were delivered by the king, the keeper of the seals, and the director-general of finances, Necker, in that order.

The royal address had been very carefully prepared. Ten drafts of it have been preserved. Admittedly, it was not drawn up by Louis XVI, but by his ministers; Necker himself had prepared a first rough draft. The minister of foreign affairs, Saint-Priest, and the keeper of the seals, Barentin, also had a hand in it. Thus it had been the object of extremely meticulous preparation. The king had retained in particular the recommendations made by Necker and Montmorin, but he had modified them under the influence of the queen, Marie-Antoinette, who had been consulted at considerable length by her husband.

This address is rather insipid. The king begins by discussing the State debt—the fundamental reason for the convocation of the Estates General—but quickly passes on to the "exaggerated" desires for innovation. Thus he rejects fundamental reforms, or structural reforms, as we would call them. He suggests to the Estates General that they concern themselves with economies to be effected and with ways and means of re-establishing order in the financial sphere. The king believes that his people are faithful, that they are attached to the monarchy, whose fundamental principles cannot be subjected to discussion. Finally, he concludes by expressing the hope that agreement and unity may reign in the Estates General. It was, in short, a very disappointing address. The deputies had been expecting a great program of reforms; the king had proposed practically nothing.

As soon as he had finished, Barentin, keeper of the seals, took the floor. In the royal entourage, Barentin represented the faction that was opposed to any sweeping reforms, whereas Necker, the director-general of finances, was in favor of reforms.

Barentin, however, did not express his personal views in his address. He had amended his violently anti-reform outlook by accepting a certain number of reforms. This we know because a draft of Barentin's address, which had been sent to the king on April 19, 1789, has been preserved and it differs from the one delivered. No doubt Barentin modified his speech at the suggestion of the king and Necker.

Although he was personally hostile to any concessions, Barentin accepts equality of taxation. He believes the Estates General should be allowed to deliberate on freedom of the press, on public safety—which implies a reform of judicial procedure—and even on the administration of justice; on *lettres de cachet*—which implies their probable suppression—on criminal legislation—which supposes the abolition of torture—and on civil proceedings, which he thinks should be simplified.

Nonetheless Barentin insists upon "the maintenance of ranks," that is, of the hierarchy between the social classes, and of the privileges of the first orders of the State. He concedes that the nobility can be made more "open" than it has been, so that access into it can be facilitated. But he fiercely defends the privileges of the nobility and the special status that distinguishes it from the Third Estate. Lastly, he appeals to the clergy to reconcile the opposing interests of the different orders, and concludes, like Louis XVI, with an appeal for union and a eulogy to national unity.

Necker's address is in contrast to the two previous ones. Whereas those delivered by the king and Barentin were short, indeed too short, Necker's was exceedingly long and very boring. It was so long that Necker was unable to read it in its entirety himself and had to call upon an aide to replace him halfway through. Moreover, three-quarters of the speech dealt exclusively with technical matters, larded with figures and hardly likely to bring Necker the goodwill of his listeners or even to retain their interest, all the more so because it was read in a monotone.

But if we disregard the form of this address and the inordinately lengthy section devoted to the organization of finances, certain proposals for reform remain. Necker alludes to a more equitable division of taxes so that, like Barentin, he seems ready to grant fiscal equality. He alludes—and one wonders why—to the possible abolition of the slave trade. Obviously this was a question of some weight, but beside all the others being posed in France in 1789 it was not of the first importance.

He also alludes to a transformation of the Estates General into a Legislative Assembly, but what he has in mind is not exactly defined. It seems that his preferences lay in a regime inspired by England, with an upper chamber in which the members of the nobility and the upper clergy would sit and a lower chamber composed of the deputies of the commoners. But he does not say whether this Legislative Assembly was to be periodic, nor when it was to meet. Nor does he give any indications—and for this he has been most severely criticized—on the method of voting in the Estates General. Should it take place by head or by order? This was the great debate at the time, yet Necker says absolutely nothing about it. He, too, concludes with an appeal for unity, as had the king and Barentin before him.

These addresses, all too vague, provoked a major crisis, which lasted from May 5, 1789, to the following June 20. It was ended by the session held at the Tennis Court, the oath that followed it, and the meeting of the orders with a view to the formation of a national Constituent Assembly.

The king did not accept the Constituent Assembly or, rather, did not want to accept it, so he convoked the three orders in a second royal session on June 23, 1789. This session was brought to a close by Mirabeau's celebrated dramatic utterance: "We are here by the will of the people and only the power of bayonets can drive us out." But it is generally forgotten that in this session the king had laid down, and in great detail this time, a program of reforms which unquestionably he had not adopted on May 5, but which he had to put into effect very swiftly between June 20 and 23, in order partially to satisfy the demands of the Third Estate, and to escape the domination of an Assembly that was becoming more and more revolutionary.

This program of reforms constitutes the royal Declaration of June 23. In establishing it, Louis XVI had followed the advice of the famous journalist Rivarol, who said: "If one wishes to avoid the horrors of a revolution, one must will it and make it oneself." Later De Tocqueville was to write in *L'Ancien Régime et la Révolution*: "A great king would have accomplished this revolution not only without losing his crown, but also having greatly increased his power." Perhaps if Louis XVI had persisted, he might have been able to make a "royal revolution." But he did not go beyond this Declaration of June 23 and made no attempt either to disperse or to win over the revolutionary deputies.

The royal declaration had been prepared under very painful circumstances that should not be overlooked. The dauphin, eldest brother of the future Louis XVIII, had died that month. The court had come to Marly, near Versailles, to go into mourning. Thus the declaration had been drawn up in the bosom of a family disconsolate because it had sincerely loved the dauphin, whose birth had been so eagerly awaited.

Necker had drawn up a draft which accepted a great number of the demands of the Third Estate, but which provided for their actualization by stages. Necker was a "reformist"; he accepted major reforms, but by degrees. His text was submitted to the council. But the keeper of the seals, Barentin, supported by the comte d'Artois and the comte de Provence, the king's two brothers, as well as by Marie-Antoinette, had the draft modified. It was thoroughly and retrogressively recast. Many of the reforms that Necker proposed were eliminated, depriving the Declaration of June 23 of both breadth and passion. It was not capable of making the deputies of the Third Estate retract their revolutionary will.

It is an interesting document, nevertheless, because it contains a program, Louis XVI's, which was to become that of the princes after their emigration.

Overall, the Declaration of June 23 may be said to preserve the ideas expounded by Moreau, discussed in the previous chapter. The king affirms, first, that he is the common father of all his subjects, that he wishes the happiness of all, but that he is the defender of the rights of the kingdom, which it is his duty to uphold. Then he touches on the burning question of the vote and proposes a compromise that was hardly likely to attract many adherents: the verification of credentials would take place separately, but in the event that one of the excluded deputies protested, his case would be examined in general assembly with a vote by head. If one of the orders contested the decision by two-thirds of the votes, the king would make the final decision—a compromise that might have been acceptable in a more peaceful period, but could only be rejected in time of trouble.

The king then accepted the vote by head on matters of general interest. Voting by order, however, would be continued on certain reserved affairs, which he listed: the "ancient and constitutional rights" of the three orders (the form of constitution to be given in the next Estates General), feudal and seigniorial properties and the honorific privileges—notably the feudal dues, whose abolition was demanded. The king was of the opinion that the clergy could make some sacrifices in order to restore finances, but nothing affecting religion could be changed without its approval; this by definition presupposed the maintenance of tithes because it was exceedingly improbable that the clergy would renounce them on its own responsibility.

Such is the restrictive part of the declaration, but it also contains a constructive part. The king agrees that taxes and loans must have the prior consent of the Assembly that will succeed the Estates General, and acknowledges the right of the Assembly to vote the allocation of funds among the various public services, including those for maintaining the court, that is, the pensions.

He consents to fiscal equality, individual liberty and freedom of the press. He approves the creation of provincial estates throughout the whole of France, but these will have to continue to be composed of the representatives of the three orders, with a double representation for the Third Estate. This was a far cry from the demands of the latter.

The king, moreover, envisages sweeping reforms in the administration of the Crown domain, in the administration of finances and, particularly, of the excise tax (*la gabelle*). He announces an overhaul of the administration of justice and of customs duties, abolition of the royal *corvée* for the construction of roads, and suppression of mortmain, that is, of the last vestiges of serfdom.

But he presented these concessions as a maximum program, not subject to further discussion, and he concluded his address on this menacing note:

"If you abandon me in so excellent an enterprise, I alone will effect the welfare of my people." This was tantamount to saying, "I will proclaim the dissolution of the Estates and effect reforms by my authority alone, drawing inspiration from enlightened despots."

If we study these plans for reform closely, we cannot escape the impression that they would have led swiftly to the establishment of a constitutional monarchy with two chambers. But they would not have wrought any deep social transformation. No doubt honorific seigniorial rights would have been abolished and seigniorial dues redeemed, but this would not have been accomplished swiftly. At any rate, the nobility would have been preserved with a part of its privileges.

A program of this sort might perhaps have been well received in 1774, when Louis XVI ascended the throne, or even in 1787; but in 1789 it was too late.

Such was the fundamental basis for the program of the counter-revolution in France. Certain quite remarkable individuals, however, added to it or watered it down and figured for a longer or shorter period as its leaders.

2 / The Leaders of the Moderate Right: Cazalès and Montlosier

Cazalès had been elected deputy to the Estates General by the nobility of Rivière-Verdun, near Toulouse. He was thirty-two in 1790, tall, fat and an extremely good speaker. He was the son of a councillor in the parlement of Toulouse and his nobility was of recent vintage.

Cazalès had been greatly stirred and grieved by the events of June, 1789, and, above all, by those of July. After the taking of the Bastille he left Versailles and set out towards the frontier in an attempt to emigrate. But he finally gave up this plan and returned to take a seat in the National Assembly.

He immediately made his presence felt in the Assembly, first because of his impassioned eloquence and later because of his fundamental integrity. He was a man alien to compromise, the Incorruptible of the Right.

Physically, his obesity and perhaps too his habits gave him an air of negligence; he looked a little like a demagogue of the Right. His fierce devotion to his ideas involved him in many duels, among which was the famous *affaire d'honneur* with Barnave in August of 1790. Barnave suffered a light injury on the forehead but the two men remained on intimate terms, as the following exchange between them on that occasion attests. Cazalès said to Barnave: "I would be inconsolable if I were to kill you, but you are giving us a lot of trouble and I would like to keep you off the rostrum for a spell." To which Barnave replied: "If you kill me, I'll have successors on the rostrum, but if I kill you, we shall all die of boredom because we shall be forced to listen to one of your associates."

Cazalès remained in the Assembly until the end of the session, then emigrated to Coblenz, where he was ill received. Disappointed, he returned to France, where he remained until August 10, 1792. Then he set out for a third time and enlisted as a soldier in the army of the princes, after which he went to England where he became the friend of Fox, leader of the Whigs, that is, the liberals.

Cazalès had been one of the first to raise his voice, and vehemently, against verification of credentials in common and against the vote by head. In his view the nobility was, and must remain, the first order of the nation and the people must be contained "within the just limits of the constitution," that is, must be prevented from rising higher in the social scale. The nobility must guide the people. Cazalès showed himself hostile to what he called "abstract constructions," the constructions of the *philosophes*, and by so doing, perhaps, he pointed the way to the English counter-revolutionary theorists we shall study later. It is also possible that he was one of the first to read Burke's *Reflections*, but we have no proof of this.

Cazalès does not deny that the Estates General or the Constituent Assembly has a role to fulfill. But for him the Assembly's role is to write, to draw up the constitution of the kingdom as it exists, not to create one on the "tabula rasa" of former institutions. What must be done is to commit to writing the old customs and the old traditions, rather than the principles of the *philosophes*.

Like all theorists of historical conservatism, Cazalès thinks that the constitution must include an Estates General, but with three separated orders, voting in isolation and discussing their affairs privately with the king.

If this constitution is not committed to writing and another, based on innovations, is adopted, it will lead to the violation of all the old funda-mental rights. Cazalès concedes that in this case Frenchmen, who care about their rights, are duty-bound to emigrate, bringing with them their goods and chattels. Notions of nationalism or patriotism are altogether foreign to him.

In some of his works and speeches, Cazalès recognizes the sovereignty of the people, but not the sovereignty of the Assembly. The Assembly must restrict itself to a definite task. Above all, he believes that the royal authority of the king is higher than that of the Assembly. The king's authority, in fact, is based upon 800 years of continuous exercise—still another idea that we shall come upon again in Burke. Only the people could break the royal will, and they would have to do this unanimously, which is manifestly impossible.

Cazalès approves of a degree of separation between the legislative and executive powers, but he thinks the executive should possess a part of the legislative power. The executive also holds the judicial power. In his view, magistrates ought to be appointed by the king, not elected.

Moreover, he professes a great admiration for British institutions, and calls himself the "leader" of the opposition, using the English word. He would have welcomed the transformation of the Estates General into an assembly on the English style, with an upper House of Lords and a lower House of Commons.

He protests against the division of citizens into active and passive. Here we see the birth of a theory that was later to develop among the "Ultras," leading them to think that universal suffrage would be more favorable to a strong if not absolute royalty than a restricted suffrage, because most partisans of constitutional monarchy were recruited from among the bourgeoisie.

On the whole, therefore, Cazalès does not emerge as an advocate of integral absolutism; he espouses that trend which favored historical rights. In fact, he is a moderate counter-revolutionary. Cazalès did not accept the decisions of 1789, and he was to like the Constitution of 1791 even less. But he was in favor of reforms which, perhaps, went further than the royal program of June 23, 1789.

Although Montlosier is very difficult to classify, we have placed him in the same group as Cazalès. He is a "moderate independent."

Born in December, 1757, Montlosier was elected a substitute deputy to the Estates General. He entered that body in September of 1789 and immediately took his seat on the Right, yet leaned toward those who were called *monarchiens* ("monarchicals")—the partisans of a constitutional monarchy with a strong executive power.

Unlike Cazalès, Montlosier expressed his ideas primarily in books. In 1791 he published two works bearing characteristic titles: *De la nécessité d'opérer une contre-révolution en France* and *Des moyens d'opérer la contre-révolution.*

Montlosier had read the principal authors of the traditionalist school: Saint-Simon, Boulainvilliers. Like Cazalès, he approves a certain number of reforms. He accepts the idea of administrative reorganization, the division of France into departments of approximately equal size. To a certain extent, he even approves the Civil Constitution of the Clergy; he is against any political role for the Church, but disapproves of some stipulations of this text, in particular the abolition of monastic religious orders.

It is necessary, in his view, to rely upon force to destroy the evil that the Constituent Assembly has created and to return to principles he thinks more sound. He is one of the first counter-revolutionaries to consider the power of ideas insufficient and to believe it necessary to have recourse to force, to the army.

When, however, the support of this force became available, the issue was not to be the restoration of the institutions of 1789, but the introduction of necessary and reasonable reforms. What reforms? Montlosier expounded them in a third work, *Essai sur l'art de constituer les peuples*, which appeared in 1790. In it he shows, first, that the Revolution was perhaps not caused by a conspiracy or even by the financial crisis; rather, it was the result of the intellectual exchanges among various social classes and peoples. This was a very interesting idea which had not been formulated often at that time: that intellectual exchanges and even economic and commercial exchanges can, in fact, generate revolutions.

It must be noted that Montlosier also thought that a bad constitution was not necessarily a cause of revolution. He points out that peoples endowed with good constitutions have also had revolutions and, consequently, he arrives at an idea developed by certain modern historians, especially from Karl Marx onwards: that the causes of an economic order can trigger revolutions.

Another very interesting idea developed by Montlosier is that the division of humanity into nations, such as existed in 1789, is not definitive. An equalization of these nations will eventually be achieved and one day, perhaps, instead of various constitutions governing diverse peoples, there will be but a single constitution, valid for all mankind.

These ideas show that Montlosier had reflected and meditated on the Revolution of 1789. To him it was caused by a whole series of factors and, above all, by the national character of the French as shaped by the monarchy under the kings who succeeded one another on the throne.

Consequently, those primarily responsible for this Revolution are the kings of France. But the monarchical institutions also provoked it. If the French rise in revolt, it is because the institutions have deteriorated. Therefore they must be improved, but Montlosier, like Cazalès, rejects the notion that such improvements can be ushered in by an abstract constitution. According to him, it is necessary to go back to the old constitution of France—still Boulainvilliers' idea.

In order to re-establish this constitution, Montlosier begins with the individual. Like Cazalès, he recognizes the sovereignty of the people and natural rights; nevertheless, he considers that only the proprietors—and here he parts company with Cazalès—can usefully exercise their rights as citizens. As a result, he accepts the distinction between passive and active citizens.

The rights of the citizen have been exercised to the present in the Estates General, which have functioned only moderately well. Nothing, however, prevents their improvement and transformation into a bi-cameral legislature with an upper house for the lords and a lower house for the commons. These legislative chambers will vote on taxation.

Montlosier, like Cazalès, is opposed to the separation of powers. The king must possess the three powers: executive, legislative and judicial. The assemblies will have only a part of the legislative power and the courts a part of the judicial power.

He thinks the social hierarchy must be maintained. The orders must be preserved, while at the same time arranging possibilities for the Third Estate to accede to the nobility. As a counterpart, however, he sanctions the expulsion from the nobiliary order of any individual whose way of life does not conform to the rules governing it. He writes that in his view the son of a tradesman, of a merchant, can never be a real nobleman: nobility includes heredity, a certain ancientness of lineage. He does not go so far as to maintain that only those are nobles whose nobility dates back to the Crusades; he knows that nine-tenths of the nobility is made up of the ennobled. But he thinks that elevations to the rank of nobility should be rare and gradual.

Montlosier dwells at length on the role that the family should play in the State. This is interesting because it is an idea that we shall find cropping up again with many counter-revolutionary theorists. In his view the family is truly the fundamental unit of French society. In contrast to the *philosophes* and Jean-Jacques Rousseau, who see only the individual, he believes that the family should play a vital role, with the help of religion taught in its bosom. But Montlosier himself was not religious; he was an atheist and had been influenced by the *philosophes* of his time, particularly Voltaire. Like Voltaire, he affirms that religion is necessary for the people because it keeps them within proper bounds, whereas enlightened, educated individuals can think what they please.

Thus Montlosier appears to us as a moderate, a "monarchical"—one who accepts a certain form of constitutional monarchy.

3 / *The Comte d'Antraigues, Abbé Maury and Mirabeau-Tonneau*

Next to Cazalès and Montlosier, other deputies represented the extreme counter-revolutionary Right. We shall study three of them, the comte d'Antraigues, abbé Maury and Mirabeau-Tonneau.

We have already discussed the comte d'Antraigues in the preceding chapter and mentioned that at the time of the elections to the Estates General he had brought out a work that made him appear more liberal than he actually was. D'Antraigues was elected deputy by the nobility of the Vivarais, but immediately thereafter he shed all that was liberal in his ideas. After arriving in Versailles, he transformed himself into an almost total defender of absolutism. This has been called the "conversion" of d'Antraigues. He expounded his ideas in a great number of speeches delivered to the Estates General up to December, 1789, and later in brochures or pamphlets published in France or abroad. For in February, 1790, he left France to avoid arrest after he had been compromised in the counter-revolutionary plot of the marquis de Favras, and abroad he led an adventurous and, at times, mysterious life to which we shall return later.

As early as May 11, 1789, in the chamber of the nobility, d'Antraigues delivered a violent speech against voting by head, and on May 28 he gave another in which he called for a return to "the constitution of our fathers"; finally, on June 25, he made a third in which he totally adhered to the royal Declaration of June 23 and demanded, in particular, the maintenance of all feudal dues—hardly surprising inasmuch as the bulk of his revenues came from such dues.

Nevertheless, on August 3, 1789, d'Antraigues rallied to the article of the Declaration of Rights which guaranteed private property. He saw in it a certain pledge given to the social order and subsequently he was to insist upon the necessity of defending property.

Such are the speeches. What do we find in his pamphlets? First of all, the fundamental idea that democracy is not good for France. This is taken from Rousseau who, as we know, approved of democracy for small republics, but not for large countries. D'Antraigues considers that the traditions of France require the monarchy and that the monarchical form itself cannot allow profound political transformations. He approves of two chambers, one of which is an upper chamber, and, of course, he is in favor of the king's exercise of the absolute veto, which he thinks indispensable. Finally, he wants to preserve orders and privileges.

Abbé Maury is considered the principal orator of the Right in the Constituent Assembly and also an able counter-revolutionary theorist. He was the son of a cobbler of Valréas; therefore he was a commoner, and his ancestors were Protestants who had converted to Catholicism only at the time of the revocation of the Edict of Nantes. Maury had pursued his studies at Avignon. He arrived in Paris in 1765 and achieved a name for himself in the literary salons, being elected to the Académie française in 1785. By 1789, therefore, he was a man whose value and merits had been recognized.

Maury had himself elected to the Estates General by the clergy of Péronne, a town with which he had no connection, and he played the same role in the chamber of the clergy as that of Cazalès or d'Antraigues in the chamber of the nobility. He tried to prevent parish priests from joining ranks with the Third Estate, and defended the procedure of voting by order and the old traditional constitution of the kingdom.

He enjoyed a great success because he was a remarkable orator with an encyclopedic memory and a great facility with words. He spoke without notes. He was extremely brilliant and very violent and he shook the rostrum so vigorously that on several occasions he almost broke it.

It has been said that abbé Maury was not a man of conviction, that he was merely ambitious; his subsequent career, in part, provides justification for those who, like Alphonse Aulard, have supported this point of view. Maury, in fact, had obtained the election to the Académie française, and later a cardinal's hat, by intrigue. Aulard considers that he was driven solely by ambition. As to this, it seems that some reservations are in order. The American historian Paul Beik, who has examined abbé Maury's speeches in great detail, thinks that we can extract a coherent program from them.

Maury is an advocate of a quasi-absolute monarchy, with the Estates

General meeting only every five years, for a brief period, and restricted to the exclusive task of voting taxes. Like the king, he consents to the abolition of fiscal privileges and *lettres de cachet*, as well as to the free circulation of grains. But he is for maintenance of the absolute veto and is opposed to any sweeping social reform. He protested vehemently against the degrees of August 4 which abolished feudal dues, and against the admission to rights of citizenship of Jews and actors, who possessed no rights under the Old Regime.

Maury gave proof of very great tactical skill. He knew better than anybody how to turn their own arguments against the democrats, and tried to prove to the Left that it was precisely the democrats who were the greatest foes of freedom because they were exponents of the omnipotence of the Constituent Assembly, an omnipotence that negated individual freedom.

He believed, or affirmed, that the Revolution was born of a conspiracy and that the deputies of the Left did not represent the will of the people. He charged that the Left included in its ranks a great number of speculators, shady financiers who subsidized the rioters during the revolutionary *journées*.

In short, abbé Maury formulates a program whose limit seems to be the Declaration of June 23. But, unlike the king, he has the advantage of expounding this program with great flair, eloquence and much oratorical skill. Unquestionably Maury was one of the fiercest defenders of the privileges of the Right and he emerges as one of the leaders of the counter-revolution in 1789 and 1790.

We shall conclude this survey with a brief discussion of Mirabeau-Tonneau, a deputy hostile to any concessions whatsoever, even those proposed by the Declaration of June 23.

Boniface, vicomte de Mirabeau, was the brother of comte de Mirabeau, the famous orator, but whereas the comte de Mirabeau sat on the Left, the vicomte took the Right. The comte was corpulent, the vicomte obese, hence his nickname, "*Tonneau*" (barrel). Born in 1754, he rapidly showed himself to be a problem child, so the family, to get rid of him, packed him off to the Order of Malta. But within a short time he was expelled for misconduct and insubordination. Thereupon he enlisted in the army and went through the American campaign. Upon his return, after having lived for a time in his château at Limousin, he was elected deputy of the nobility of Haut-Limousin in March, 1789.

Like his brother, he was a good writer and a wit, but these are practically the only things they had in common. The vicomte was a braggart, unquestionably courageous, a frequent duelist; but he was not a genuine theorist. He made himself in some fashion the champion of the absolutism of the Old Regime, opposed to any concessions whatsoever. He is the man who defended the counter-revolution at swordpoint or on the rostrum, but counter-revolution with a return to absolutism as it existed in 1788.

He enjoyed a measure of success at the Assembly because of his witticisms and practical jokes. One day he scaled the rostrum in order to chase his brother from it. On another occasion he mounted it wearing his sword, which he then broke across his thigh, saying that he had no further use for the weapon since the Assembly had taken away the king's power by withdrawing from him the absolute veto and by obliging the deputies to take an oath to the constitution and not to the sovereign. At other times, the delegates witnessed even more picturesque but less edifying scenes staged by him when he appeared at the Assembly drunk.

Finally, he achieved notoriety through the incident that took place at Perpignan. He was, in fact, a colonel and commanded the regiment of the Touraine infantry quartered at Perpignan. In June of 1790 the vicomte went off to Perpignan to establish contact with his regiment, which was beginning to be won over by revolutionary ideas. He failed to put down a mutiny and suddenly quit Perpignan, taking away the "cravats," that is, the tassels of the flagstaffs. Under the Old Regime, army regulations and tradition stipulated that a regiment could not go into battle formation if its banners were not ornamented with tassels. Their removal somehow was tantamount to dissolution of the regiment.

The disappearance of the tassels was noticed the day after the colonel's departure, and immediately a search was organized. Finally his pursuers caught up with him at Castelnaudary where he was forced to give back the tassels, which earned him a second nickname, "Mirabeau-Cravates."

At most, Mirabeau-Tonneau or Cravates, an integral partisan of the Old Regime, accepted equality of taxation; he was opposed to any sweeping reform.

His position was to become untenable very quickly and he emigrated as early as August 3, 1790. He settled in Germany, where he created his own legion because he got along no better with the princes than he had with the deputies. The Mirabeau Legion or Black Legion, however, never even had an opportunity to fight because at the beginning of the war, on September 15, 1797, Mirabeau-Tonneau died, in circumstances which remain mysterious. There was talk of apoplexy, of a duel, or of an accident while riding horseback. Among the representatives of the counter-revolution he was one of the most picturesque characters, as well as the one most attached to absolutism.

Such were the leaders of the Right in 1789 and 1790. We have seen their ideas. Only Mirabeau-Tonneau favored the integral maintenance of the Old Regime. They accepted more or less developed reforms—the reforms that were to constitute the program of most of the French counter-revolutionaries after 1789.

CHAPTER III

Some French Theorists of the Counter-Revolution: Rivarol, the Comte Ferrand, Sénac de Meilhan, and the Abbés Barruel and Duvoisin

The Rightist deputies in the Estates General were not the only ones to outline a doctrine of counter-revolution. Outside the Assembly, a swarm of journalists, pamphleteers, scribblers of all sorts drew up drafts of constitutions and governments in which the royal power was restored. Most of these drafts were rather lacking in ideas and their influence remained limited. Among this mass of theorists we shall focus only on five writers whose notoriety surpassed that of their rivals: Rivarol, the comte Ferrand, Sénac de Meilhan, and the abbés Barruel and Duvoisin.

1 / Rivarol

Rivarol is incontestably one of the most famous French counter-revolutionary writers. He is also without question the wittiest, though not the most profound.

Antoine de Rivarol, descendant of a family of Italian origin—the Rivaroli—that settled in Nîmes at the beginning of the eighteenth century, was born on June 26, 1753, in Bagnols-sur-Cèze. After brilliant studies in his native city, then in Bourg-Saint-Andéol and at the seminary of Avignon, he gave up his intention of becoming a priest and left for Paris. There he quickly achieved renown as a habitué of salons, dilettante, idler, wit, brilliant conversationalist and specialist in puns and offensive epithets. His sister Françoise came to join him in Paris; married to a certain baron de Beauvert, she was to become the mistress of Dumouriez.

From 1779 onwards, Rivarol wrote in *Le Mercure*, and published brochures and pamphlets. The most famous of these is the *Dissertation sur l'universalité de la langue française*, which in 1784 earned him a prize from the Berlin Academy that he shared with Professor Schwab of Stuttgart. Following this success, Rivarol was named a member of the Berlin Academy.

At the beginning of the Revolution he founded, with abbé Sabatier de Castres, the *Journal politique national*, which appeared rather irregularly until November, 1790. At the same time he published anonymous, but easily identifiable articles in the *Actes des apôtres* and other newspapers of the Right, such as the *Journal royaliste* and the *Chronique scandaleuse*. In 1790, he issued a *Petit Dictionnaire des grandes hommes de la Révolution, par un citoyen actif, ci-devant Rien*.

All these brochures and articles make amusing reading. In them, Rivarol, with unprecedented violence, attacks the men who made the Revolution. He uses any weapon to hand, especially slander and calumny. But it is difficult to discern a coherent doctrine in the midst of all this virulent condemnation.

It is certain that, in 1789, Rivarol hoped for reforms. He made public declaration of his shock at the discrepancy between the brilliance of French thought and the dullness of the government. "This throne is eclipsed in the midst of the Enlightenment." But he believed that philosophy and politics were two different sciences, the former being the science of the absolute, the latter of the relative. He would have welcomed a revolution made by the king without consultation with the Estates General:

> From the day when the monarch consults his subjects, sovereignty
> is as though suspended. There is an interregnum. . . . When peoples
> cease to esteem, they cease to obey. A general rule: peoples whom
> the king consults begin with vows and end with wills of their own. . . .
> If one wishes to avoid the horrors of a revolution, one must will it
> and make it oneself; it was too necessary in France not to be inevitable.

He accepted the royal Declaration of June 23, in the drafting of which he had collaborated, as a program for this revolution. He went even further, and demanded the abolition of all the privileges of the nobility and of the clergy, subscribing to a bi-cameral system. But the king, he felt, should be granted absolute veto power. Hostile to abstractions, Rivarol criticized the Declaration of the Rights of Man violently but brilliantly; it is possible that Burke drew the inspiration for the book which he published in 1790 from Rivarol's articles.

Under the Legislative Assembly, Rivarol proposed to La Porte, intendant of the civil list and an important distributor of secret funds, that he (Rivarol) be called to the court to advise the king. La Porte received him coldly. Nevertheless, Rivarol addressed several memoranda to Louis XVI and to Marie-Antoinette and may have been received by them. He advised them to rely on the people rather than on the nobility or the bourgeoisie. He had the idea of a "popular monarchy," which was to be taken up by others—notably the Ultras after 1815: "The king will not become king of France again save by giving proof to France that he no longer wishes to be the king of noblemen." At the time of the invasion, in 1792, he wrote a *Lettre à la noblesse française* in which he tried to point out to the émigrés the futility of their enterprise: the people would certainly not follow them. However, in June of 1792 he himself emigrated. After a sojourn in Belgium, Holland and England, he settled down in Hamburg in 1795, where he wrote *Traité de la souveraineté du peuple*, published by his brother after his death in 1831. This treatise on popular sovereignty seems to have been thoroughly recast and cannot be considered as truly representing Rivarol's thought; on the whole, the argument here seems rather threadbare and contrasts with the celebrity of the author, whose reputation outran his actual merit.

2 / The comte Ferrand

Although the comte Ferrand was a minister under the Restoration, he is undoubtedly less well known than Rivarol. His work, nevertheless, is of a more solid character. Born on July 4, 1751, he came from a family belonging to the nobility of the robe. In 1770 he became a member of the Paris Parlement, where in the following year he opposed Maupeou's reform and then, in 1787, that sponsored by Lamoignon. But this opposition did not lessen his attachment to the king and he left France in December, 1789, as soon as the degradation of the royal power was obvious to him. Later, he was to enlist in the army of the prince de Condé.

The first of his works is *Essai d'un citoyen*, published at the beginning of 1789. In this *Essai*, Ferrand, in general, seems to profess ideas akin to those expounded by the comte d'Antraigues in 1789: he wants a return to the old constitution of France. The only difference is that Ferrand is more interested than d'Antraigues in what he calls the lower classes, the peasants and artisans.

He is in favor of some reforms that would restore France to her traditional constitution, whose natural development had been interrupted by absolutism. Liberty which, he affirms, is "a natural right, the key to both individual and social happiness," meets with his approval. But liberty has three essential aspects: property, which means the freedom of every individual to possess what he can acquire; personal security, which is the freedom of movement; and freedom of thought.

As regards equality, Ferrand reduces it to equality of taxation and tries to show that freedom is best assured in a monarchy, in which the executive power can act very swiftly, rather than in a parliamentary regime, in which it is necessary to go through all sorts of cumbersome machinery before an order is finally executed.

Ferrand advocates the separation of powers, as described by Montesquieu, but it is not to be an absolute separation. Executive power is entrusted to the king, but the king also participates in the legislative power which he shares with a bi-cameral assembly, a house of lords and a house of commons. Judicial power is to be exercised by the parlements.

On the whole, Ferrand's doctrine is close to that of Montesquieu; it is manifestly influenced by the philosophical doctrines in the air at the time, since Ferrand does not exclude a discussion of freedom or equality but avoids touching on religious problems. He himself certainly was not much of a believer, nor much of a practicant.

Ferrand dwells, above all, on the old constitution of France; it was this constitution, he says, by which the Franks in the forests of Germany were governed and here he draws a comparison between the constitutional evolution of France and England.

In England the old constitution, that of the Angles and Saxons, had been able to develop freely because the country's political and strategic situation allowed it to do so. The country's isolation left it free of worry about defense, so that the three powers were strengthened in reciprocal interaction, and the outcome was the constitutional harmony so admired by Montesquieu.

In France, on the contrary, the old constitution had been abandoned for both geographical and strategic reasons: on the one hand the climate, which was more varied—obviously Ferrand has read *L'Esprit des lois*—on the other, the population of France, which was much larger than that of England even in the eighteenth century, and made a strong government essential. But military problems played the most decisive role: the need to defend extremely long land frontiers and an extended coastline simultaneously. All these factors led France to reject her old constitution for a time, and to adopt an absolutist regime. Thus the separate evolutions of France and England are the result of certain vital innate qualities.

Ferrand thinks that France must return to her old constitution, but without copying English institutions because she simply cannot disregard the problems posed by climate and population. Accordingly, a constitution must be drafted that is truly French and that links up with the old constitution of the country, taking geographical factors and strategic requirements into account. Ferrand traces the broad lines of this constitution: an Estates General divided into two, instead of three, chambers, which would meet every three years, vote by order but maintain the parlements with their right of remonstrance. The Estates General would deliberate fiscal laws, loans and important changes in the basic laws of the State. On the other hand, the king would be empowered to draw up judiciary laws as well as general and local administrative laws, and to promulgate these subjects to approval of the parlements. If the parlements formulated remonstrances, the king must take account of them.

Thus Ferrand ends up with a kind of synthesis between British institutions on the one hand and the so-called old French constitution on the other, which had never existed except in the imagination of the eighteenth-century theorists of political science.

He continued to write after his emigration in September, 1789, publishing numerous pamphlets on the Revolution; *Lettre d'un commerçant à un cultivateur sur les municipalités*, *Lettre à mes concitoyens*, *Les Conspirateurs démasqués* and, finally, *L'Etat actuel de la France* (1790).

In all these pamphlets, Ferrand defines his ideas on the new institutions of France precisely. He believes, first of all, that Rousseau was right to affirm that a republic was possible only in small countries: the small states of antiquity or the Swiss cantons. A democratic regime and, *a fortiori*, a republic are not viable in a country the size of France, where only a monarchy with a strong executive power for the promulgation and execution of laws is conceivable.

Ferrand returns to the problem of the separation of powers. In *Essai d'un citoyen*, as we have seen, he approved of such a separation; but he renounced it in 1790. Now he believes that the king must share in the three powers, possessing all the executive power and a part of the legislative and judicial power. He also renounces the idea of an Estates General divided into two chambers, deciding that it is necessary to adhere to the traditional division into three chambers, corresponding to the three orders.

And he opposes the division of French citizens into active and passive

as decreed by the Constituent Assembly in 1790. He feels that the traditional grouping into three orders must be maintained, each order being
subdivided into classes. The traditional hierarchy cannot be dispensed
with in France. French society must form a kind of pyramid, the apex of
which is the king, with the peasants, artisans and bourgeois forming its
base. Ferrand thinks the social hierarchy is necessary in order to assure
a proper harmony between the classes because the people live on the rich.
It is the rich—this idea was very widespread at the time—who make it
possible for the people to work, who commission the artisans to make
things for them, who buy from the peasants.

Ferrand concedes that equality had existed initially, as described by
Rousseau, but that it had existed only "in the state of nature." In an
organized society, equality no longer exists save before the law, which has
Ferrand's blessing. Social equality, he believes, is a chimera.

Finally, in his pamphlet entitled *Les Conspirateurs démasqués*, Ferrand
introduces an idea destined for fruitful development: that of the causes
of the Revolution. For him, the Revolution originated not so much in the
abandonment of the traditional constitution of France and the installation
of absolutism, as in the existence of conspiracies, hence the title, "The
Conspirators Unmasked." These conspiracies are born of the ambition of
certain men, such as the duc d'Orléans, Necker, Lafayette, and several
others. This idea of a conspiracy was to be taken up again by other
theorists of the counter-revolution whom we shall study in later chapters.[1]

Such were Ferrand's ideas. They established a constructive doctrine of
historical conservatism that was to influence the great counter-revolutionary theorists—Joseph de Maistre, Bonald and Chateaubriand. Through
them, it would play an important role in the institutions of the French
constitutional monarchy in the nineteenth century, as well as in those of
the traditional monarchies restored in the different countries of Europe
in 1814.

3 / Sénac de Meilhan

Sénac de Meilhan was the son of a personal physician to King Louis XV.
In 1789, he was fifty-three, hence well on in years. He had been a *maître*

---

1. Bernard Fay in his book *La Grande Révolution* (Paris, 1959) has set forth the
   idea that the principal cause of the Revolution was a plot inspired by the duc
   d'Orléans.

des requêtes in the council of the king, then intendant in three provinces: first La Rochelle, then Provence and finally in the province of Hénaut. He had also been employed at the Ministry of War in the time of Saint-Germain.

Contemporaries considered Sénac de Meilhan a very able, intelligent, pleasant person, well launched in literary circles. A would-be poet, he had written verses in his youth and had been one of Voltaire's friends.

On the eve of the Revolution he published two works in which he showed himself quite skeptical about the worth of the Old Regime: in 1786, *Les Considérations sur le luxe et les richesses* and, the following year, *Les Considérations sur l'esprit et les moeurs*.

Like Ferrand, Sénac emigrated very swiftly. As early as 1790 he went off to London and, later, he traveled all over Europe. He reappeared in Germany, Aachen, Venice, then in Poland and Russia, where he tried to enter the service of Czarina Catherine II. Finally, he was to return to Germany and live in Hamburg; he died in Vienna in 1803.

His ideas on the counter-revolution are expounded principally in a small book entitled *Des principes et des causes de la Révolution française*, which he published anonymously in London in 1790, but it was an anonymity easily exposed.

In this work Sénac shows himself at once as a nationalist—if one may employ this term to characterize the ideas of an eighteenth-century author—and an empiricist. He hoped that his book would trigger broad discussions. His ambition, as he himself wrote, was to be the "Montesquieu of the Revolution": he wanted to explain the Revolution by the great principles of political science. He made a great effort to reconcile his admiration for the *philosophes*—he was, after all, a man of the Enlightenment—and for the Encyclopedists, the economists and the physiocrats with his idea that the statute of France should be modified as little as possible.

He believed that historical evolution had shown that Enlightenment and, in general, science must be the privilege of the upper classes, of the richest and most intelligent classes, and that religion, on the other hand, must be left to the people: an idea that Voltaire had already developed when he said that religion was necessary for the people. This is also close to Rivarol's argument.

Sénac concedes that the Enlightenment was responsible for the Revolution because it had been spread so widely; it had not been confined to those capable of understanding it and drawing the proper conclusions from it. The Enlightenment was wrongly interpreted by people poorly prepared to accept it, and it is they who have made the Revolution.

He is the disenchanted spectator of this Revolution, not believing in its success. He thinks that history, or "the lessons of history," as he puts it, will restore the monarchy to France, and he reinstates ideas formulated by Polybus and developed by Montesquieu: supposedly, there is a historical cycle; democracy gives birth to demagogy, monarchy to tyranny, etc. Thus for Sénac, the Revolution in France is but an element in an eternal cycle. Consequently, one should not be overly concerned, one should not take sides or commit oneself excessively to struggle against it, because the wheel will turn and the counter-revolution, bringing in its train the restoration of the monarchy, will inevitably succeed the Revolution.

In his book, however, Sénac de Meilhan does not spare the Old Regime criticism. To him, a certain number of abuses or disturbances and grave fiscal injustices were the hallmarks of the Old Regime, a point on which all counter-revolutionaries are in agreement. He also criticizes the Old Regime for its ministerial instability—a criticism that was often to be leveled at all French governments. He recognizes that the systematic resistance of the privileged classes to all reforms was one of the causes of the Revolution. Finally, he believes that the financial disorders which arose toward the end of the reign of Louis XV (disorders which he distinguishes from the fiscal injustices) were the immediate cause of the disturbances that beset France from 1787 to 1789.

Such are the causes of the Revolution according to Sénac de Meilhan. As can be seen, he grasped merely the external and superficial ones; for him, there were no deep underlying economic causes. In his work he makes no allusion to the situation of the peasants, to their crushing burdens, to the tithe, to feudal dues. He believes that the causes he has enumerated are enough to explain what he calls the "fermentation of minds." For the Revolution is due "to the fermentation of minds" of those who wrongly understood the Enlightenment, or who were not properly prepared to receive it and to apply its insights to the new necessities.

After thus faulting the Revolution, he tries to outline what, according to him, would be the best regime: a balanced monarchy, whose foundations would lie precisely in long experience; and, in this respect, his demonstration comes close to Burke's, which we shall discuss in the following chapter. Like Burke, Sénac de Meilhan is essentially a traditionalist and an empiricist.

France must be a traditional monarchy; all her institutions must be consecrated by long existence. Some reforms, however, must be introduced, and abuses corrected. Sénac recommends regular meetings of the Estates General, but with three chambers and voting by order; voting by head is to be resorted to only in absolutely exceptional cases.

He also feels that the bankers, those he calls "the capitalists," must be put in their place. Such persons in point of fact had become too powerful towards the end of the Old Regime and had led the monarchy to its ruin by their intrigues, their ambitions and their insane desire to enrich themselves. Finally, the parlements must be restored with their right of remonstrance, because these parlements constitute the most solid rampart of the Old Regime.

Nevertheless, Sénac was quite aware of the fact that one of the essential causes of the Revolution was the revolt of the nobles in 1787 and was, perhaps, the first person to point this out. Significantly, in this connection, he writes:

> Many of those who later were called "Aristocrats" were "Democrats" in this period. The aristocracy—the upper nobility, the clergy, great ladies and nobles of the robe—at that time demanded a change in the government. By using their influence over the nation, they sought to obtain greater consideration from the ministers. They wanted to be honored in their province, they wanted to be exempt from the dangers of exile and of the Bastille. These aristocrats are the real authors of the Revolution.

Sénac de Meilhan is one of the first to formulate this affirmation: "By their speeches and their examples, they [the Aristocrats] inflamed the minds of the people in the capital and in the provinces and later were unable to arrest or slow down the movement which they themselves had incited."[2]

Thus Sénac shows little sympathy for the nobility, which is why he can be ranked with Rivarol, Calonne and the partisans of enlightened despotism. All these men believed that the monarchy should preserve its traditional character, but that the executive power should be reinforced and that sovereigns should be counseled by philosophers, enlightened men who would be able to guide them by suggesting laws applicable to all and by furnishing them with the means with which to subdue the most rebellious and reticent classes, even the nobility.

2. *Des principes et des causes de la Révolution française* (London, 1790), pp. 78–79.

4 / *Abbés Barruel and Duvoisin*

Abbé Barruel was born in 1741, abbé Duvoisin in 1737. Thus they were contemporaries. Abbé Barruel entered the order of the Jesuits; abbé Duvoisin, who remained in the secular clergy, became canon and vicar-general of Laon. Abbé Barruel had achieved some prominence before the Revolution as editor of a journal that had a wide circulation among parish priests, *Le Journal ecclésiastique*.

He left France at the beginning of the Revolution, a little later than Ferrand and Sénac de Meilhan, in 1792. He was to return to his homeland only after the signing of the Concordat, but was still to enjoy a long career. As for abbé Duvoisin, in 1789 he was the royal censor, that is, he was in charge of examining new books; and he was also a professor at the Sorbonne. He too emigrated to England in 1792 and, like Barruel, returned to France in 1802. He was appointed bishop of Nantes and baron of the Empire. Thus these two clerics had similar careers: they emigrated early, criticized the Revolution but returned to France as early as the Consulate, under which they occupied important posts.

Barruel gave his first interpretation of the Revolution as early as 1789 in a work entitled *Le Patriote véridique, ou Discours sur les vraies causes de la Révolution actuelle*. Here, he was already formulating the fundamental ideas that he was to develop in his subsequent works, namely, that of providential action combined with the hypothesis of conspiracy as the two underlying causes of the Revolution.

The thesis of providential action was already widespread in France and many Catholic countries; it posited that the ills from which France suffered were willed by God. God deliberately produced the poor harvests, the high cost of living, mendicancy and vagrancy in order to punish France, choosing to chastise her because of her intellectual and moral decline in the eighteenth century. On the other hand, the Revolution, although it was a divine punishment, was also favored by a conspiracy of which the *philosophes* were the authors.

The king, according to Barruel, had been too generous in convoking the Estates General. Why had France been in the throes of social agitation for three years? Essentially because of fiscal injustices. When the king had remedied these injustices, the agitation would subside; it was not necessary to consult the Estates General. All the reforms, in preparation at the time the book appeared, are denounced as huge blunders.

The idea of conspiracy appears in the second part of the work, but it is not yet distinctly formulated; it was to be laid out with greater precision and clarity later, no doubt after he had read Ferrand's book, but it is already set forth here in embryo. The *philosophes*, declares Barruel, bear a very great responsibility for the outbreak of the Revolution because they placed individual interest before the collective interest. This theory was to be taken up and developed at length by all the doctrinaires of the Right. The *philosophes* have a completely erroneous idea of progress; indeed, the theory of progress as formulated by them is an "absurdity." There is no constant progress, only a material progress which is effected to the detriment of morality and religion. To abbé Barruel, a people without moral rule is bound to be plunged into misfortune. So progress cannot improve the common lot, as the *philosophes* claim in their writings. Any genuine Empire, that is, any State, needs dogmas in order to sustain the throne; without universal dogmas, such as the Catholic religion propounds, "the State has no foundation, the wicked know no constraint, and the law has no force."

Therefore, the *philosophes* deliberately launched a frontal attack on the Church and the State. But this attack, says Barruel, was relatively easy because the clergy did not put up an effective defense against the assailants. Why? Because the clergy was in a state of decadence and this decadence falls within the scope of providential action. Providence willed it thus in order to punish France for her immorality.

The decadence of the clergy derived from the bad selection of priests and, in particular, of bishops, who were too often appointed without taking into account their religious and moral qualifications. This does not mean that Barruel was for a fundamental modification of the method of nominating bishops. He rejected the method which the Civil Constitution of the Clergy was to introduce in France in 1790, and did not advocate the election of bishops; he was no "Jansenist." He was for maintaining the traditional mode of nomination of the bishops by the king and the Pope, but both sovereigns must make better choices.

Barruel also evinced great hostility toward any limitation of the prerogatives of the monarchy. The king must remain absolute; for where numbers make the law, there is no longer a king. There is, of course, the example of England, and like Ferrand and Sénac de Meilhan, he discusses the English problem by showing that England's situation differs vastly from that of France from the geographical, political and military points of view. Given her geographical position, her climate, her immense frontiers, France cannot do without absolutism.

But this absolutism must be distinguished from tyranny, because the absolute monarch nonetheless has limited power by virtue of what Barruel calls "the natural laws," which are confounded with what, under the Old Regime, were called the "fundamental laws of the State"—respect for the life of each subject, for their liberties and property. The law is the emanation of the general will, but it is the king who is made aware of this will through the intermediary of his usual councils, which are the Estates General. Barruel approves of the convocation of the latter in certain exceptional cases, but he is absolutely opposed to periodic convocations. The Estates General are to be the interpreters of the general will.

The king is the representative of God on earth, and by virtue of this authority, he is the supreme judge; accordingly, he directs the judicial power. In the domain of justice, however, the royal will is limited by divine justice, to which the king himself is subject. Here Barruel joins company with Bossuet.

As regards society, Barruel rejects the individualism of the revolutionaries. For the revolutionaries, the State is formed of a great number of individuals. For Barruel, it is formed of a whole series of families: the nation is the gathering of all the families and the king is, as it were, the *paterfamilias* of all France. This great family is divided into orders; the nobility is the first order, and the defense of the monarchy is its duty and *raison d'être*.

Barruel recognizes that the nobility has not exercised this duty; it has not defended the monarchy, or it has defended it imperfectly, and he censures the resistance of the nobles to the royal will in the years that preceded the Revolution. He contends that this resistance stemmed principally from the fact that the nobles were jealous of the bourgeois. The rise of the bourgeoisie—a consequence of the increase of its wealth and of the nation's economic development—made the nobility jealous so that it lost the sense of its rights and duties. The bourgeoisie therefore must be put back in its place. It should bear in mind that it exists only through the king, inasmuch as the king has constantly defended the bourgeoisie against the encroachments of the nobility. Here we see Barruel taking up the ideas of abbé Dubos on the development of monarchic absolutism linked to the protection of the bourgeoisie by the king. The bourgeoisie has become the auxiliary of the royal power for several centuries, but it must confine itself to this role. It must not attempt to get on a par with the nobility and, *a fortiori*, to replace it.

As for the peasants, they too have forgotten their debt of gratitude to the king. For it was the king who liberated them from serfdom and forced the lords to grant them charters.

In conclusion, Barruel states that only three types of regime are possible in France: traditional monarchical absolutism, aristocratic oppression as it existed in an indeterminate Middle Ages or democratic anarchy. France, having rejected monarchical absolutism, is seesawing between aristocratic oppression and democratic anarchy. In fact, these three possible regimes deprive the French of any choice at all, because the country, wishing neither to founder in misfortune nor to be oppressed, has no other resort save to restore monarchical absolutism.

In 1791 abbé Barruel published *Questions nationales sur l'autorité et sur les droits du peuple et du gouvernement*, in which he dealt with problems he had not touched upon in his previous work. Here he devotes a large amount of space to the Civil Constitution of the Clergy, which has just been voted by the Constituent Assembly. He views this civil constitution as a grave error and even a heresy. The clergy alone may deal with religious problems; lay persons should not mix in questions of dogma or even in the more general aspects of religion.

From this Barruel arrives at an elaboration of the problem of authority. He tries to construct a whole theory of authority. God can command because He is the Creator; accordingly, logic demands that God should have all the powers. Man can command animals because God has given intelligence to man and denied it to the animals. But there is one difficult point that must be settled: to what extent man can command man since in the state of nature, as Barruel concedes, men are equal. He resolves this difficulty by employing the family as intermediary. Man is *pater-familias*, he raises his children; it is therefore logical that he should command his children. And a kingdom is but a gathering of families, the king the father of all families. Therefore, he has the same authority over these families as a father has over his children. So reason requires that the king have authority over all his realm and that all subjects be duty-bound to obey him.

Barruel distinguishes between authority and sovereignty. Authority can be exercised by every father of a family but sovereignty, which is authority over the whole of the country, is the prerogative of the king. The "social contract," whose existence Barruel accepts, brought man from the state of nature to the state of society. This could not be decided by the sovereignty of the people, but was concluded by the will of God.

Barruel tries to develop this theory at length by taking up Rousseau's arguments one by one and then turning them against him.

After thus demonstrating the necessity of monarchical absolutism, Barruel draws a portrait of the absolute king as an ideal type, so to speak. Such a king will govern within the limits set by the fundamental laws of the realm; in other words, he will be able to do with impunity all that these laws and God do not forbid. The fundamental laws, writes Barruel, guarantee the freedom of conscience, but he ventures no opinion on the freedom of worship or of the press. The fundamental laws also guarantee the right of property, with the reservation, however, that restrictions dictated by the general interest may be imposed upon it. The fundamental laws prescribe equality before the law, which Barruel also accepts, but he does not go beyond this point.

He then proceeds to examine the Constitution of 1791 in the light of the theories he has just developed. He considers this constitution an absurdity; virtually nothing in it relates to his ideas. He thinks that it is inapplicable, that numerous crimes will be committed on its application and that France will wallow in the bloodiest anarchy until the Bourbons are recalled to the throne as absolute monarchs. Barruel buttresses his argument by numerous references to history: England in the seventeenth century, Bohemia at the time of the Hussites, Germany at the time of Luther, France at the time of the wars of religion. In short, the Revolution can lead only to the worst woes imaginable.

In 1792, shortly before the September massacres, Barruel left France and went to England, where he became chaplain to the prince de Conti, who had been living there for some time. There he collected abundant evidence on what had just taken place in France, particularly in connection with the clergy, and this formed the material for his *Histoire du clergé pendant la Révolution française*, which is a lengthy diatribe against the Civil Constitution of the Clergy. Barruel seeks to determine why this constitution was voted and finally fixes the responsibility on very many Frenchmen but first and foremost the members of the clergy. He blames the attitude of some bishops and many priests, but the nobility also bears its share of responsibility for having passively accepted the ideas of the *philosophes*. And he also blames the bourgeoisie, as well as the parlements that had adhered to the subversive principles of the Encyclopedists. As to what he calls "the populace," it has been the dupe of the cultivated classes: "The populace wanted neither the vote by head—it did not know what that meant—nor the changes that had occurred since 1789."

In this book Barruel clearly formulates the conspiracy theory he had only roughly sketched in his first work; meanwhile, no doubt, he had read Ferrand's *Les Conspirateurs démasqués*. But this time the theory is elaborated in great detail. It was to enjoy considerable success for a lengthy period because it was repeatedly taken up again by the majority of the theorists of the Right, even up to the present day.[3]

The Revolution, therefore, was the product of a conspiracy. Says Barruel: "This Revolution had been planned for a long time in France by men who, under the name of *philosophes*, seem to have shared between them the mission to overthrow throne and altar." But now the *philosophes* are unmasked. They duped the people by establishing the constitutional monarchy in September of 1791; it has been clearly shown that this could not last because it collapsed less than a year later; as for the Civil Constitution of the Clergy, it was only a means to organize the persecution directed against the Church.

All the *philosophes* are not equally guilty. There are some who are only remotely responsible, but there are also criminals, of whom the worst are Mirabeau, Lafayette, Sieyès and Barnave; after them come those whom Barruel classifies as their disciples: Brissot, Robespierre, Danton, Marat. These criminals have destroyed the monarchy in order to create a republic and now they are about to destroy religion.

Barruel does not, however, abandon the thesis of providential intervention: the conspiracy was willed by Providence in order to punish France for her immorality and her decadence.

In general, when abbé Barruel's ideas on conspiracy are discussed, people rarely refer to his *Histoire du clergé* because he took up and developed the conspiracy theory in another work which is much better known, *Les Mémoires pour servir à l'histoire du jacobinisme*, published in Hamburg by Fauche in five volumes in 1798.

This work is divided into three parts. The first treats the anti-Christian conspiracy, the second the conspiracy against kings and the third the "conspiracy of the sophists of impiety and of anarchy," that is, the combination of the first two conspiracies. These *Mémoires*, which were to enjoy an extraordinary success, merely developed the ideas Barruel had already expounded in his previous works, notably *Histoire du clergé*. The thesis of conspiracy is now presented in a more compact, solid, distinct

3. Notably by Augustin Cochin, and most recently by Bernard Fay; see above, page 37, note 1.

and positive form. The first paragraph is sufficient to give a clear idea of its tone and thrust:

> Around the middle of the century in which we live, three men met together, all imbued with a deep hatred of Christianity. These three men were Voltaire, d'Alembert and Frederick II, king of Prussia. Voltaire hated religion because he was envious of its Author and of all those whose glory it has constituted, d'Alembert because his cold heart could love nothing, and Frederick because he had known Christianity only through its enemies.

These three are the men who hatched the conspiracy. Barruel demonstrates that everything that transpired in France since 1787 had been willed, prepared in advance, premeditated; nothing was fortuitous.

His philosophy of history was also fated to enjoy a great success. "We have seen," he writes,

> men shut their eyes to the causes of the French Revolution, we have seen those who tried to persuade themselves that any revolutionary and conspiratorial sect before this Revolution was but a chimerical sect. For such men all the evils that plague France, all the terrors that plague Europe follow upon each other and are linked one to the other merely by the simple conjuncture of unforeseen and unforeseeable circumstances. Basing our thesis upon facts and armed with proofs, we shall propose something very different. We shall state that everything in this French Revolution, including its most terrifying crimes, was foreseen, premeditated, planned, resolved. Everything was the work of the most abominable villainy.

The conspirators, of course, are the *philosophes*, but also their friends and disciples, the Freemasons. Barruel develops at great length the thesis of the Masonic conspiracy, which was to be taken up over and over again by many authors, to the present day.

As regards reforms, Barruel accepts none of them. He condemns the royal program of June 23, 1789, because the king made exaggerated concessions and so promoted the conspiracy. The monarchy must be restored along the lines of the most integral absolutism.

Thus Barruel appears as one of the teachers of the counter-revolutionary doctrine of integral absolutism. He inspired Taine in the nineteenth century, but he also inspired the whole policy of the Holy Alliance and of the system practiced by the restored monarchies from 1815 onwards in France, Spain, Italy, and elsewhere.

Very similar ideas were professed by abbé Duvoisin, a friend of Barruel. In 1789, Duvoisin had published a small book, *La France chrétienne, juste et vraiment libre*, in which he heaped censure on the religious crisis and the growing impiety. It was necessary, he declared, to return to tradition; the Church must defend herself against dangerous innovations, tolerance, freedom of the press, the materialism of the philosophers, deism, the intervention of the civil authorities in religious affairs and civil marriage. He develops a theory of the social contract similar to Barruel's and extols tradition, as Burke was to do the following year.

But Duvoisin shows a greater aversion than Barruel for the nobility. He saddles them with a large part of the responsibility for the Revolution, because it was the whole nobility, infected by the ideas of the *philosophes*, that rebelled against the king. The same applies to the bourgeoisie, from whom nothing good can be expected. Which, then, is the healthy class? It is the people, the "proletarians"—Duvoisin uses this very word. The proletarians are devoted to absolutism, they form the healthiest part of the nation.

These ideas were to gain currency in France in the nineteenth century; the Ultras around 1825 were to declare that the monarchy ought not to fear universal suffrage. The people are basically good, but the "lower classes" have been the tools and victims of the Revolution; hence intermediaries should no longer be placed between the king and the people. The king must act directly on the people; only thus will it be possible to restore the traditional monarchy.

After his emigration to London, like Barruel and indeed in the same year, 1798, Duvoisin published another book entitled *Défense de l'ordre social contre les principes de la Révolution française*. In this work, he tries to show that only the legitimate, traditional monarchy can save France. He develops anew the idea of the contract willed by God, reproducing the ideas of Bossuet, amended at times by those of Montesquieu. He asserts that the alliance between Church and State must be very firm, very solid, because only this can keep the people in obeyance and, as a result, restore happiness to France under a traditional monarchy.

Again Duvoisin clearly shows his hostility toward the nobility and the upper bourgeoisie. And here he takes up the ideas expounded by abbé Dubos: he does not believe that the nobles derive their superiority from the right of conquest. The privileges they possess are usurped, consequently no question of restoring their privileges to them is involved; on the contrary, what must be done is to restore to the king his rightful power.

The great principles which one must work hard to restore are property —which it is expedient to spread and to define with greater exactness— production, which must be stabilized, and equality before the law. It is necessary to provide instruction for the people and, above all, to enrich the people and raise their living standards. In a sentence that curiously foreshadows Karl Marx, Duvoisin writes: "The man who possesses nothing is a man without a country, it is difficult for him to support a government which keeps him in a state of humiliation and want." Thus the living standards of the people must be raised so that they will support the traditional monarchy. At the end of his book Duvoisin deals with the conspiracy. On this subject, he has the same ideas as Barruel. He alludes to the intervention of Providence, which has willed the woes that plague France; but at the time that he is writing, in 1798, Duvoisin believes the Revolution is drawing to its close: "The Jacobins can keep themselves in power only by tyranny at home and war abroad; France is on the eve of the restoration of the traditional monarchy."

The works of these five political theorists show a certain kinship. Although they are determined counter-revolutionaries, none of them is hostile to reforms. One comes upon ideas in their works that are common to them all: the hope for a Revolution accomplished from above, the desire for a constitution more or less inspired by the English model, distrust of the nobility, the idea that the Revolution was the product of a conspiracy or the consequence of providential intervention. From this common point of departure, however, these five writers eventually were to arrive at the hope of restoring a regime as akin as possible to the absolute monarchy as it functioned before 1789.

CHAPTER IV

Edmund Burke

Among all the theorists of the counter-revolution, the first whose works created an international stir was the Englishman Edmund Burke.

His *Reflections on the Revolution in France*, published in November, 1790, is a work of the highest order which enjoyed an extraordinary success throughout Europe and America. It exerted a considerable influence on the doctrinaires of the counter-revolution, not only during the period from 1790 to 1815, but for the whole of the nineteenth century and even into the early years of the twentieth.

Burke's *Reflections* offers multiple themes for thought. In contrast to abbé Barruel's thesis, it shows that the Revolution in France had not been the result of a conspiracy, but had been brought into being by the collapse of the Old Regime. Moreover, contrary to Burke's intention, the *Reflections* also proves that the French Revolution and the American Revolution are but two phases of the same western revolution. For Burke and Lafayette, who took part in both revolutions, were in a better position than any of their contemporaries to grasp the close connection between these two phases of the "Atlantic revolution." Burke's attitude to the French Revolution, moreover, illumines his feelings about the American Revolution.

For a proper understanding of his work we should know at least a little about Burke's life before the publication of this book. In fact, the book in question is not the work of a young man. Burke was born in 1729; thus he was sixty at the time of the Revolution and had a long career behind him.

In the first part of this chapter, we shall examine Burke's life up to 1790; the second part will be devoted to an analysis of the *Reflections*, and the third will deal with the reverberations that the book set off throughout the world.

1 / Burke up to 1790

Burke was born in Dublin, Ireland, in 1729, of a Protestant father and a Catholic mother. This should be noted inasmuch as scholars have sometimes attributed some influence on his ideas to his mother's religion.

Before 1789, Burke lived a very full life. He pursued his studies in Dublin at Trinity College, during which time he already became interested in French literature: it was at Trinity that he read the works of Lesage and Montesquieu. In 1750, after completing his secondary instruction, he went to London to study law. At this point he became acquainted with the works of Rousseau, in particular, the *Discours sur l'inégalité*.

Several years later, in 1758, he founded a political and literary journal, the *Annual Register*. This published critical reviews of the principal books appearing at the time. Although these reviews were not signed, most Burke specialists acknowledge that they were written, or inspired, by him; it is perhaps excessive to consider Burke as the author of them all since at best this can be only a matter of conjecture. But if Burke did indeed write them, we can know what he thought of the works of Rousseau, Voltaire, d'Alembert and Diderot.

In discussing the *Discours sur l'inégalité*, Burke extols civilization and progress and combats Rousseau's idea of the superiority of the state of nature over the state of civilization. He emerges, with Voltaire, as an optimist, against Rousseau who is a pessimist.

In his criticism of d'Alembert's *Lettre sur les spectacles*, he denounces this work's negative character. In 1762 the *Annual Register* published a review of *Emile* which is undoubtedly by Burke. Although this gives high praise to the practical nature of the education Rousseau proposes for children, it is full of reservations about the Savoyard vicar's profession of faith. At all events, characteristically enough the journal contains no analysis of the *Contrat social*, which does not seem to have engaged the attention either of Burke or of the other contributors to the *Annual Register*.

Burke made several journeys to France before the Revolution. Nothing much is known about these trips; they remain enigmas. We have information only about the journey of 1773, because Burke talks of it in his *Reflections*. At that time he visited Versailles, where he saw the court of Louis XV, who was to die the following year. For the first time he met Marie-Antoinette, then the dauphiness, sixteen, and "like the morning star, glowing with life and splendour and joy." In Paris, Burke made the acquaintance of the *philosophes*, the Encyclopedists, the economists. He remained uncharmed by the conversations he had with them and returned to England greatly mistrustful of the philosophy of the eighteenth century and particularly of rationalism, on the political as well as the religious level.

He was to maintain the relations that he had established with the French during that period, however, by dint of an extremely voluminous correspondence which was to stop only at the outbreak of the Revolution. So Burke was kept abreast of events in France by his correspondents.

No sooner had he returned to England than the first difficulties arose between Great Britain and her North American colonies. Burke was to take part in the political struggle, for in 1770 he was elected deputy and took his seat in the House of Commons.

In the House he sat on the Whig bench, that is, on the side of the liberals, and when the troubles began he showed himself favorable to the American insurgents. He delivered two very important speeches on this, one in 1774 against the taxation of the colonists, and the other the following year, 1775, on the necessity of a reconciliation with the Americans in order to avoid the secession of the colonies.

Subsequently, he intervened on different occasions in very serious matters and each time his speeches created a great stir. Thus in 1778 he spoke in favor of his native Ireland, demanding that England grant her freedom of trade, of religion and of parliamentary debate. And in 1780–81, he delivered several speeches in connection with abuses committed by certain functionaries in Great Britain.

On the whole, if we examine Burke's political activity in the House of Commons between 1770 and 1789, we get the impression of a liberal influence of an impassioned defense of the rights of the British Parliament, of a struggle against injustice in the American colonies, as well as in Ireland, in the Indies and in England proper. Although at times he was considered a fool, Burke attained the peak of fame around 1785–88, alongside such Whig party leaders as Fox and Thomas Paine. One must, however, be wary of a general impression. Burke's speeches and writings should be scrutinized more closely.

Under such scrutiny it is immediately apparent that Burke was anti-rationalist and, long before 1789, conservative. No doubt he was the advocate of a fairly liberal regime, but he favored such a regime not in the name of reason, justice, freedom or the philosophical abstractions in vogue on the continent, but for reasons of a purely practical nature.

In his great speech against the taxation of Americans in 1775, he writes: "I am not here going into the distinctions of rights . . . I do not wish to enter into metaphysical discussions. I hate the very sound of them." And in his speech on conciliation with the colonies: "Alas! alas! What power do these theoretical speculations have against facts?" Burke is first and foremost an empiricist, a realist. When the citizens of America proclaim their rights, either in the Declaration of Independence or in the declarations that precede the constitutions of the various American states, Burke says that the problem of rights has no interest for him: "The question with me is—not whether you have a right to render your people miserable, but whether it is not in your interest to make them happy."

Accordingly, when Burke fights against injustice in America, the Indies or Ireland, it is not for abstract reasons nor to defend philosophical doctrines, but to allot a greater measure of happiness to British citizens.

There is another reason why he defends the American colonists. He views these colonists as English and as British citizens; they have the right to enjoy all the privileges that the law recognizes as theirs. Therefore, he defends them in the name of tradition, of custom, of the ancient constitution of Great Britain, not in the name of a Declaration of the Rights of Man, which he considers absolutely worthless.

In his speech on reconciliation, he does not attribute the American Revolution to the influence of the *philosophes*, but to particular conditions. Burke was always to profess this opinion. For him philosophical ideas had no real influence. It was always particular circumstances that determined events, and he explained them thus: in the American colonies of the North, the Puritan religion aroused a great love of freedom among the colonists, which made them more sensible than others to the fact that the British government was unjust and violated their rights and privileges. In the colonies of the South, where the colonists were Anglican, slavery played the same role. Since the colonists of Virginia were great landed proprietors, owning "a vast multitude" of slaves who worked for them, they were more alert to the maintenance of their rights as free men, hence more sensible to the fact that these rights were being violated. Thus the American Revolution was due to the very specific, and different, circumstances prevailing in the northern and southern colonies. It also came about because the proportion of men of law was greater in the British colonies in America than in England. Thus the colonists there found many champions.

Burke thinks too that the king and the English Parliament were, in part, responsible for the revolt of the colonies because they violated the rights of the colonists, who are British citizens.

In 1777–78, when the great war between the United States—in alliance with France, Spain and Holland—and England begins, Burke is still thinking of a reconciliation, a return to the status quo; he does not take the Declaration of Independence very seriously. When the alliance between France and the United States is concluded, he still believes that it can be broken if England withdraws her troops from North America and solemnly restores to the colonists their rights and privileges. Only when the treaty of peace between the United States and England is signed does it dawn on him that secession is a fact, but he refuses to believe that it will be definitive. In his congratulatory letter to Benjamin Franklin, he is already thinking of a rapprochement between the two countries, perhaps of a reintegration of the United States of America into the British Empire. In 1788, five years after the Peace of Versailles, Burke still regretted the American secession and the thought of making an apologetic defense of the United States Constitution then being discussed never once crossed his mind. On the contrary, he was considering the possibility of a return by these states to the bosom of the British community.

Thus when we analyze Burke's speeches and the works of the period, we see that he has become the champion of tradition, of the struggle against rationalism. Burke believes that the British constitution has great value because it is based on history and not on a social contract, whose existence he denies. It is in the name of tradition that he opposes any parliamentary reform in England. In a speech prepared in 1784 but never delivered, he speaks of the "false theory of the supposed rights of man." Unquestionably Burke fought against abuses, but only because he thought they were injustices that would alter venerable historical traditions. He acknowledged that institutions could be perfected by little retouchings while leaving much of the major work to time, but he was opposed to any sweeping, radical reform.

Had he read the German philosopher Herder? Had he been influenced by what Herder calls the *Volksgeist*, the folk spirit? Herder considered that a people taken as a whole constituted a living being, endowed with a genuine collective spirit that was difficult to change. We do not know for certain whether Burke read Herder, but the similarity between his thought and that of the German philosopher must be noted. Burke believes that tradition and jurisprudence must furnish the guiding principles of states. He writes significantly: "The science of jurisprudence, which is the pride of human intelligence . . . is reason gathered in the course of the ages; it combines the principles of primitive justice with the infinite variety of human interests."

This passage comes from a speech delivered to the House of Commons on May 7, 1782, and it contains one of the fundamental features of Burke's doctrine. History must form the basis of any human institution; only the slow modifications produced in the course of time are lasting. According to Burke, any attempt at reform based on abstract philosophical principles is doomed to rapid failure. No principle can pass into custom, no law be truly accepted by the people or executed, if it is not based on a long tradition.

In his speeches Burke never appeals to reason, but always to this or that argument drawn from history. When he calls for reconciliation with the American colonies, he cites England's relations with Wales, or with certain areas within the country, like those of Chester or Durham, as examples, relations which were weakened at times but finally restored as a result of the will to reconciliation and of the respect of the historical rights of each side.

Whenever he takes the floor in Parliament, Burke always appeals to experience, to prudence. If he invokes reason, it is a reason totally different from that of the *philosophes*. This is no abstract, metaphysical reason, deduced from Cartesian logic; it is an experimental reason, drawn from the experience mankind has slowly acquired down the ages. He appeals to what he believes is "the organic unity of human societies." There is a British people, a French people, a German people, who are fundamentally different from each other, and each of them evolves according to its own law, its *Volksgeist*—a word, of course, which he never uses but which could easily be put in his mouth. Consequently, he attaches prime importance to jurisprudence, tradition and historical precedent, and attributes changes only to particular circumstances, never to general causes.

2 / *The* Reflections on the Revolution in France

Let us now examine the particular spirit in which Burke took the French Revolution. Certainly he saw no connection between the French and American revolutions. If we have said that his work proves the kinship of these revolutions, it is because he was to reason identically in order to prove that no connection whatsoever existed between the two and that they were due to specific circumstances peculiar to each.

During the first months of the French Revolution, Burke appeared to be very unmoved by it. But he was seized by a violent rage when he learned of the events of October 5 and 6, 1789, during which the people of Paris went to Versailles to fetch the king, queen and royal family to escort them to the capital where they were, in fact, kept prisoners. Burke waxed indignant over the bad treatment suffered by the royal family, and especially by Marie-Antoinette, of whom he cherished the dazzling memory of 1773 when the court's brilliance was at its height.

Of these events he exclaims: "The age of chivalry is gone. That of sophisters, economists, and calculators has succeeded, and the glory of Europe is extinguished for ever."

Burke's anger was reinforced on the occasion of the meeting of the English Revolution Society on November 4, 1789. The aim of this gathering was to commemorate the anniversary of the revolution of 1688 that had placed the House of Orange on the English throne. On November 4, 1789, the English Revolution Society held its annual assembly, this time to celebrate the 101st anniversary of this revolution. During the proceedings a dissenting pastor, Dr. Richard Price, delivered a major speech on the general theme of "The Love of Our Country," which glorified the British revolution of 1688 and compared it to the French Revolution being carried out in the name of the same liberal ideas. Other speeches were delivered to the group, all expressing enthusiasm for the French Revolution, and the meeting ended with the adoption of a resolution to send a congratulatory message to the Constituent Assembly.

Burke fell into a rage when he read an account of this meeting and vented his fury in letters to some of his French friends—Menonville, deputy to the Constituent Assembly, de Pont and Dupont (all figures we shall discuss later). He also expressed his indignation to the House of Commons, notably during the session of February 5, 1790.

The army budget was under discussion during this session. Pitt, the prime minister, declared that it was impossible to reduce the British army's budget because of the revolutions that were troubling Belgium and France at the time, the ultimate consequences of which were unforeseeable. Burke then took the floor. He replied that it was too early to determine whether the Revolution would strengthen France, as the prime minister seemed to affirm, or weaken her, as others claimed. For his part, Burke declared that France had eliminated herself from the concert of great European powers and that she would not be able to play a genuinely important role in Europe during this period. But he had no idea how long this would last. Accordingly, he felt that as a precautionary measure it was better to keep British forces in a state of readiness, and not reduce the army's budget.

Four days later, on February 9, Burke again took the floor and talked at length about events in France; he showed that France was plunged in chaos and virulently criticized the political rationalism that the Constituent Assembly apparently wanted to apply in its reforms. And he ridiculed the rights of man, which were built, he said, on abstractions.

In the course of the voting, the Tories followed Burke, who was a Whig, and for the first time the Whigs were split in two—a split that was to last throughout the revolutionary period. The Whig majority approved Burke's hostility to the Revolution, whereas the minority, headed by Fox and Paine, opposed him. Undoubtedly it was from that moment that Burke began to write his *Reflections on the Revolution in France*. The book appeared in London in October, 1790.

At the opening, the work takes the form of a letter addressed to a friend in France on the occasion of the meeting of the Revolution Society on November 4, 1789. The full title reads *Reflections on the Revolution in France and on the Proceedings in Certain Societies in London Relative to that Event in a Letter Intended to Have Been Sent to a Gentleman in Paris.*

For a long time scholars have puzzled over the identity of the person to whom the work was addressed. Prior, Burke's first biographer, in his *Life* identified the addressee as Menonville, a little-known member of the Constituent Assembly. But Burke speaks of a young man, whereas Menonville was fifty, so that scholars tended to think it unlikely Menonville could be this "young man." They have therefore looked elsewhere, and speculation turned to the man who translated the *Reflections* into French, whose name was Pierre Gaétan Dupont, a councillor in the Parlement of Paris. Burke had made the acquaintance of this Dupont—and of Menonville as well—in the course of his journeys to France and had maintained a copious and regular correspondence with him. But the same objection can be raised here: Dupont too was fifty in 1790.

In a critical study published in 1932 in the journal *La Révolution française*, Mantoux came to the conclusion that Burke's correspondent could not be either Menonville or Dupont. And the discovery of new Burke papers preserved in the Royal Archives at Windsor led H. V. F. Somerset, an assistant professor at Oxford, to demonstrate beyond any possible doubt that Burke's correspondent was called de Pont. Somerset was not able to identify this de Pont, but I have managed to help him: he was Charles-François de Pont, born in Paris in 1765, hence only twenty-nine in 1789. The identification is incontestable. De Pont was the son of Jean de Pont, who had been the intendant of Trois-Evêchés in Metz for several years. Charles-François de Pont himself, in 1789, was a councillor in the Parlement of Paris, like Dupont, and at a very young age, like all sons of the great nobility of the robe, he had been appointed solicitor-general to the parlement of Metz before going on to the Parlement of Paris.

Burke had met the de Ponts, father and son, when they journeyed to England several years before. The intendant of Metz and his son came to London and were invited to a big banquet given by the lord mayor. Burke attended the banquet, where he saw the young de Pont for the first time.

The *Reflections* addressed to de Pont have a twofold purpose: (1) To criticize French institutions and the events taking place in France; (2) To attack the British Revolution Society and similar groups that tried to compare the French Revolution of 1789 to the British revolution of 1688.

By this dual criticism Burke, for the first time, bequeaths to the counter-revolution what had not been provided by the counter-revolutionary theorists already discussed, namely, a solid, coherent program, based on a complete philosophy of history. He offers this program, not only to the counter-revolutionaries of France (they were to be those who profited from it the least), but to all those who oppose the Revolution, in Europe and in America. Burke's book, therefore, has a universal significance; it is the breviary of the western counter-revolution—a fact that is universally recognized.

The work is poorly arranged; Burke did not have a rational cast of mind. Nevertheless, we can distinguish two major parts. The first has as its point of departure the speech delivered by Dr. Price. Burke tries to show that there is a fundamental difference between the British revolution of 1688 and the French Revolution of 1789. It is a difficult task, but he succeeds. He interprets the English revolution of 1688 as a restoration, an interpretation that is not absolutely wrong, and he explains all the events of 1688 from a very conservative standpoint.

The second part is devoted to the criticism of the institutions which the French Constituent Assembly is in the process of establishing in France: executive and judicial power, military and financial organization. This criticism of the institutions is harsh, unjust and peevish.

Thus Burke's work has two aspects: on the one hand, it is a virulent and often extremely arbitrary polemic, replete with errors; on the other, a doctrinal statement. The polemic is no longer of any value. Burke was poorly informed or even distorted facts deliberately; but the doctrine still remains valid and for a century and a half it has served as a basis for all works opposed to the Revolution.

The general idea pervading the *Reflections* is that institutions constructed on a *tabula rasa*, on reason, are not lasting. The book wages a constant struggle against abstraction and individualism. In particular, Burke attacks the following ideas, which he attributes to revolutionaries. Revolutionaries, he says, want to make "a *tabula rasa* of the past" in order to construct a rational society. Burke views this as a grave error; such a regime will not be able to survive for long. Revolutionaries want to institute a secular State or, at least, a State in which the Church will have only a subordinate role; he believes such an arrangement is impossible. And revolutionaries believe that reason, the development of science, will enable mankind to make limitless progress and to secure happiness on earth; Burke does not share this belief.

Here we shall develop three points of Burke's thesis: the struggle against abstraction, the struggle against the concept of "nature" as expounded by the *philosophes* and the struggle against the "reason" of the *philosophes*.

Burke assigned a much more important place in the *Reflections* to the struggle against abstraction than he had in all his previous works. He declares that he cannot give praise or blame "to anything which relates to human actions, and human concerns on a simple review of the object, as it stands stripped of every relation, in all the nakedness and solitude of metaphysical abstractions." For him a fact, an institution, has no value except in the context of circumstances. "Circumstances (which with some gentlemen pass for nothing) give in reality to every political principle its distinguishing colour and true character. The circumstances are what render every civil and political scheme beneficial or noxious to mankind."

He refuses to do as Dr. Price demands and congratulate France upon the recovery of her freedom. Price, and de Pont, had written Burke in October of 1789 asking that he send his felicitations to France but he refused because, as he put it: "When I see the spirit of liberty in action, I see a strong principle at work; and this, for a while, is all I can possibly know of it." There are different kinds of liberties; for example, the liberty of one who has been in prison and who has escaped: ". . . Am I seriously to felicitate a madman, who has escaped from the protecting restraint and wholesome darkness of his cell, on his restoration to the enjoyment of light and liberty? Am I to congratulate a highwayman and murderer, who has broke prison, upon the recovery of his natural rights?"

Burke does not know what "liberty" in the abstract means. For him, there is the liberty of the honest man, and the liberty of the escaped thief, which he considers "noxious."

As to the rights of man, he claims that the champions of such rights "have wrought underground a mine that will blow up, at one grand explosion, all examples of antiquity, all precedents, charters and acts of parliament." The rights of man will enable the mass to lay claim to power, but Burke does not believe in the wisdom of the "mass" because it is an abstraction and its will can give birth only to abstract, inapplicable principles.

He deplores the impersonal character of the new institutions created by the Constituent Assembly. In the new constitution, "a king is but a man, a queen is but a woman; a woman is but an animal, and an animal not of the highest order." Love for the king will disappear because one has love for this or that king, for Louis XV or Louis XVI; one cannot love a constitutional king. Government therefore will no longer be possible.

He criticizes the pseudo-geometric simplicity of French institutions: "When I hear the simplicity of contrivance aimed at and boasted of in any new political constitutions, I am at no loss to decide that the artificers are grossly ignorant of their trade or totally negligent of their duty. The simple governments are fundamentally defective, to say no more of them." Burke mistrusts simplicity. For him, the complication of institutions is a much greater proof of happiness than their simplicity, which attains only an apparent and feeble unity.

Next comes the struggle against the concept of "nature" as it exists among French politicos. The word "nature" was used frequently in the eighteenth century, first by the English philosopher Locke and then by the French, notably Rousseau. Burke also employs it, but in an altogether different sense. For Locke and Rousseau, the natural is what is innate in human nature at all times and in all places; for Burke, on the contrary, the natural is the result of a long historical development, of long usage. Thus it is what is specifically precise, not what is universally applicable. This is a conception of nature diametrically opposed to that of the rationalist philosophers. Burke believes that, left to themselves, things generally find their "natural order." Consequently, the whole heritage of the past has an incalculable value because it is willed by nature, and he gives an example: the British constitution is excellent because it is the work of centuries. But it must not be thought that because it is good for Great Britain it will be good for France or Germany; it functions so well only for Great Britain. What other countries need is a constitution that is also the work of centuries.

Burke shows that the English revolution of 1688 merely sanctioned the heritage of the past by restoring royal heredity and hereditary peerage, re-establishing the ancient rules of the House of Commons. The British political system is a "natural" system because it is founded upon the experience of centuries. The political system that the Constituent Assembly proposes to establish in France is anti-natural because it is based upon an abstraction.

Burke sets great store by prejudices because they are the result of history; rational philosophy is wrong to fight against them. It is instinctive for a man to cling to prejudices. "Now what is more natural," he argues, "than instinct?" Equality is contrary to nature, since historical development has not made it manifest: "In all societies consisting of various descriptions of citizens, some description must be uppermost. The levellers, therefore, only change and pervert the natural order of things."

Burke, of course, criticizes democracy, the "law of number," as he calls it, which is anti-natural. "It is said that twenty-four millions ought to prevail over two hundred thousand. True, if the constitution of a kingdom be a problem of arithmetic. . . . The will of the many and their interests must very often differ." The many cannot have a clear notion of their interests.

He combats the idea that a *tabula rasa* must be made of the past. To do so is to "insult nature." But this does not signify that Burke is the champion of an immobile status quo. He thinks that the existing order of things can be improved, but that there is an incommensurable distance between piecemeal amelioration little by little of things as they are and total abolition in order to start again from scratch. "If circumspection and caution are a part of wisdom when we work only upon inanimate matter, surely they become a part of duty too when the subject of our demolition and construction is not brick and timber, but sentient beings, by the sudden alteration of whose state, condition, and habits multitudes may be rendered miserable." The builders of France no doubt must hail from the same country as the French gardeners, who get rid of everything that nature has created in order to construct geometric gardens; Burke vaunts the superiority of English gardeners, who respect what nature has put in place: hills, streams, waterfalls. "We [in England] have not been drawn and trussed, in order that we may be filled, like stuffed birds in a museum, with chaff and rags and paltry blurred shreds of paper about the rights of man." And he concludes with a fervent eulogy of the British constitution.

Finally, Burke does not reject "reason" but gives it another meaning. Reason is the ensemble of prejudices, whereas for the *philosophes* it is constructed by a deduction which takes no account of traditions— Cartesian reason. "Many of our men of speculation, instead of exploding general prejudices, employ their sagacity to discover the latent wisdom which prevails in them . . . they think it more wise to continue the prejudice with . . . the reason involved, than to cast away the coat of prejudice and to leave nothing but the naked reason." This idea was to be taken up by many philosophers and writers of the nineteenth century, particularly Taine, who wrote: "Prejudice is a kind of reason which is ignorant of itself," and even Maurice Barrès, who declared: "Let us don our prejudices, they keep us warm."

Thus, for Burke, reason is composed of prejudices. He also believes in the existence of a collective reason, which he defines as the traditional mode of thinking of all the inhabitants of a particular country, and this collective reason is an effective force. "Prejudice," he states, "engages the mind in a steady course of wisdom and virtue."

Such are the fundamental ideas contained in the *Reflections*. Together they form the body of a doctrine. Indeed, Burke expounds a coherent doctrine far more fully than had been formulated by the other theorists of the counter-revolution. Hence it is not surprising that his work set off a wave of extraordinary reverberations, first in England and then throughout the whole western world.

3 / *The Influence of the* Reflections

In England, the success of the *Reflections* was tremendous; the book went through eleven editions in less than a year. At Burke's death, 30,000 copies had been sold. The French Revolution, which had generally been sympathetically received in England, began to lose disciples after the publication of the *Reflections*; after the execution of Louis XVI, the number of English supporters dwindled constantly. To a great extent this may be said to be a result of Burke's work.

The British government, which at first had been favorable to the French Revolution only because it had the inestimable advantage of weakening France, began to change its attitude. The *Reflections* put an end to the ministers' euphoria and Lord Morley declared: "Burke's book divided a nation in two, it accelerated and precipitated opinion on both sides."

The Tories, whose adversary Burke had been for a long time, made a veritable cause of the *Reflections*; and some of the Whigs also accepted Burke's ideas. Only the radical minority of Whigs opposed him.

The book occasioned a host of troubles. On July 14, 1791, a great English scientist, Priestley—peer of Lavoisier, and who had at that time made similar discoveries—presided at a banquet in Birmingham commemorating the anniversary of the taking of the Bastille. As he was eulogizing the Revolution, a mob, incited by the local Tories who had read the *Reflections*, staged a demonstration in front of his house and set it afire, destroying all his scientific instruments.

Burke broke solemnly with his former friend Fox, who became the leader of the radicals, in May of 1791. The radicals, however, did not remain silent. The first response appeared one month after the publication of the *Reflections*. It was Mary Wollstonecraft's *A Vindication of the Rights of Men*, which was followed by James MacKintosh's *Vindiciae Gallicae*, a convincing refutation of Burke's work. Finally Thomas Paine published *The Rights of Man*, a book which enjoyed a huge success in France but which met with a cooler reception in England. A whole series of British poets, of course, celebrated the merits of the Revolution in verse and voiced their opposition to Burke. But their influence gradually waned.

What is the explanation for the extraordinary success of Burke's *Reflections* in a country that had created two revolutions during the seventeenth century? We can say that the England of 1790 was no longer the England of 1688; all countries change. The England of 1790 was a thriving, satis-

fied, conservative land. The England of 1688 was beginning to be undermined by an anti-religious movement that attained its apogee around
1730, whereas in 1790 England was being swept by Wesley's famous
religious "revival." This may explain why Burke's *Reflections* was well
received in a country which had undergone a considerable change.

In France the *Reflections* was rather poorly received, even by the
Right. We know the reactions of a certain number of Burke's correspondents. The addressee, de Pont, for example, after receiving Burke's book,
immediately replied as follows: "I shall even confess to you that I would
have never hazarded my request had I been able to foresee what its
effect would be, and had your opinions been known to me at that time I
would have urged you not to bring them to light."[1] Dupont, the translator of the *Reflections*, later was to inform Burke that de Pont had
"gone over to democracy" and that he should take no account of his
judgment.

Nevertheless, de Pont thought that Burke, ill-informed, would change
his opinion if he saw France, and he ended his letter on an optimistic note:

> I am strongly reassured, Monsieur, by the progress of the Enlighten-
> ment that you have so cruelly attacked. I am reassured by the freedom
> of the press of which you do not talk at all, and I am convinced that
> these economists, these philanthropists, these philosophers whom you
> so harshly insult, by their writings will contribute as much to the
> maintenance of freedom and to the re-establishment of order as those
> brave paladins, those errant knights, whose absence you deplore.

The translator, Dupont, exchanged a lengthy correspondence with
Burke, which gives us a progress report on the sale of the translation. He
writes that 2,000 copies of the first edition were sold in two days. In
February, 1791, four months after publication, 10,000 copies had been
sold in Paris and 6,000 in Lyons and Strasbourg. Three editions appeared
successively. Even unauthorized editions of the book were published,
clear proof of its success.

Menonville, another of Burke's correspondents, wrote him a very long
letter in English on November 17, 1790, several days after publication of
the French translation. Menonville, a moderate deputy elected by the
nobility of Mirecourt in Lorraine, did not appreciate Burke's criticism at
all and raised numerous objections.

1. This letter has been published by H. V. F. Somerset, see Bibliographical Notes,
   p. 389.

On the whole, the *Reflections* had a good sale in France, although its success seems to have been due more to curiosity than to the publication of a considered doctrine of the counter-revolution. Only much later, after 1815, was Burke to have an influence on French counter-revolutionaries. We can say that the real heirs of Burke in France are Hippolyte Taine and Maurice Barrès; but none of the French theorists of the counter-revolution prior to 1815, not even Chateaubriand, can be considered as genuine disciples of Burke.

In Germany, on the other hand, the influence of the *Reflections* was enormous; it was praised in the many journals that appeared there and Friedrich von Gentz, whom we shall discuss later, published a translation of it in the spring of 1791 which created a considerable stir. Gentz was to become one of the theorists of the counter-revolution in Germany and to be known as the German Burke.

In Italy, Burke's influence was less widespread. Italy, like France, was too imbued with rationalism to hearken to a fundamentally anti-rational doctrine. However, an obscure Italian writer, Scrofani, praised Burke and published a pamphlet entitled *All are wrong, or Letter to My Uncle on the French Revolution*.[2] Burke's influence was felt, above all, in the kingdoms of Piedmont-Sardinia and Naples; in Piedmont-Sardinia he was much appreciated by Joseph de Maistre.

The work also caused a certain stir in Switzerland, where it was read by Mallet du Pan (studied in the next chapter), who spread several of Burke's ideas. The *Reflections* also influenced Sir Francis d'Ivernois.

In Spain it was prohibited by the Inquisition, which systematically forbade publication of works dealing with the Revolution, whether favorably or not. It was feared that through the *Reflections* Spaniards might get some idea as to what was transpiring in revolutionary France. Nevertheless the book entered the country as contraband, and was translated as early as November, 1790, by two priests of Tarragona. Several copies completed by them were sent to Barcelona and Madrid. We also know that the Spanish philosopher, Jovellanos, was able to obtain a copy of the French edition, which he read and then sent to one of his friends in Orviedo. In 1796 the Inquisition again confirmed the prohibitions of the *Reflections*.

In Russia Catherine II, old friend of the *philosophes* and patroness of Voltaire and Diderot, addressed her most ardent felicitations to Burke on his achievement.

2. *Tutti han torto, ossia Lettera a mio zio sulla Rivoluzione francese*, 1791.

In the United States the Federalists who, *grosso modo*, represented the opinion of the "Right" were enthusiastic readers of the *Reflections*. It had an influence, in particular, on Washington's secretary of the treasury, Alexander Hamilton, and on a very interesting figure, a politician and man of letters, Gouverneur Morris, who was soon to become the United States ambassador to France.

Thus the *Reflections* went around the world in the space of a few weeks. The work had a genuinely universal meaning, like the Revolution it opposed. And it provided the counter-revolution with its doctrine.

Burke did not cease his activity after the publication of the *Reflections*; he showed himself to be a fierce foe of the Revolution up to his death in 1797. To be sure, he did not change his views on nature or reason, but perhaps under the influence of the writings of abbé Barruel, he came to attribute a providential cause to the Revolution, viewing it as God's punishment for the sins of men. He also went so far as to acknowledge that the Revolution would not be easily defeated and that the State which had issued from it—the French republic—might exist "as a nuisance on the earth for several hundred years." Nevertheless, he strove with all his might to defeat it. When England entered the war against France, he wanted the British government to publish a manifesto calling upon all the countries of Europe to launch a crusade against France. Pitt refused. But from the rostrum Burke delivered vehement speeches against revolutionary France and tried to induce the prime minister to organize a combined expedition to help the rebels in the Vendée. But Pitt no longer followed Burke's advice, at least not in 1793; and when the government, in 1795, decided to aid the Vendéans and *chouans*, the propitious moment had passed.

Although Burke did not succeed in modifying the policy of the English government toward France, he was more successful in his struggle against those whom he called the "English Jacobins," that is, the radicals and democrats. He heaped calumny on them using the most contemptuous terms and treated their followers as the "swinish multitude." Toward the end of his life, in 1796, he estimated that there were 80,000 "English Jacobins"—a number which thoroughly alarmed him. It was in the wake of Burke's indictments that the prime minister took repressive measures against the British democrats and then against the Irish revolutionists. Thus Burke emerges as one of the principal champions of the counter-revolution throughout the world.

CHAPTER V

Jacques Mallet du Pan

Mallet du Pan is the author who, side by side with Burke, has had the greatest reputation outside France for doctrinal influence against the Revolution.

He has some features in common with Burke. Like Burke, he was Protestant. Like Burke, he sided with the liberals in a first phase of the western revolution, namely, the revolution in Geneva of 1781–82; Burke, as we know, had supported the liberals in the American Revolution. Again, like Burke, after having defended the liberals, Mallet du Pan later turned against the Revolution.

But here the similarities between the two men cease, inasmuch as Burke was a resolute foe of rationalism, of the philosophy of the Enlightenment, whereas Mallet du Pan, although making no secret of his hostility to the Revolution, remained faithful to the rationalist philosophy of the eighteenth century. Essentially Mallet du Pan has the temperament of a conciliator, a moderate.

1 / His Youth and Intellectual Formation

Mallet du Pan was born on November 5, 1749, in Céligny, a tiny village on the north bank of Lake Léman, about 12 miles from Geneva. Thus at the beginning of the Revolution in France Mallet du Pan was forty years old, twenty years younger than Burke.

He came from a family of modest circumstances. His father was the Calvinist pastor of Céligny, but the family was related to people who had played an important role in Geneva. The Mallets were of French origin, having emigrated from Rouen at the beginning of the wars of religion, and they had been admitted to the so-called bourgeoisie of Geneva in 1558. A number of intellectuals in the Mallet family played notable roles in various branches of knowledge. Henri Mallet (1727–1811) was a geographer; Paul-Henri Mallet (1730–1807) a historian; Jacques-Henri Mallet (1740–1790) an astronomer; and Jean-Louis Mallet, who was born in 1757 and died in 1832, wrote a very important history of the city of Geneva.

As for the Du Pans—the name of the maternal side of the family—they were of Piedmontese origin and had settled in Geneva before the Mallets, in 1486. The Du Pan family had supplied not intellectuals, but functionaries, to the city of Geneva: syndics, municipal councillors, public prosecutors. Thus the two families, Mallet and Du Pan, belonged to the patriciate of Geneva, that is to say, to that élite of the bourgeoisie which governed the city.

Mallet du Pan's father died when his son was still very young. The boy was placed in a boarding school at the collège of Geneva, then at the Académie founded by Calvin. He excelled at his studies and obtained numerous scholastic awards. One of Mallet's fellow students at the Académie was Clavière, the financier who was to become a minister in France during the Revolution.

Mallet pursued his studies in an atmosphere which must be described in order to understand his ideas. It was the period of the quarrels between Voltaire and Rousseau, quarrels that on occasion attained a marked degree of violent feeling. All the problems posed by the Enlightenment philosophy were being discussed in Geneva at that time and Mallet du Pan certainly underwent their influence.

Thus it is not surprising that at the tender age of twenty-two, in 1771, he published a work which was liberal in aspect and inspired by Rousseau's ideas, and which bore the title *Compte rendu de la défense des citoyens bourgeois de Genève adressé aux commissaires des représentants par un natif.* This requires some explanation.

The population of Geneva was divided into three categories. The first was formed of "representatives" who constituted the élite of the bourgeoisie, the patriciate. The "representatives" sat in the councils, which were the governing bodies of the city. They bore that particular title because they represented the bourgeois in the administration of the city. The "representatives" had taken a negative attitude toward the demands formulated by the other categories of the population: thus they were often also called the "negatives." The second category of the population comprised the "bourgeois," who enjoyed most of the rights of the citizen, but did not sit in the councils. Finally, the third category, the "natives," was formed by the inhabitants of the republic of Geneva, who were descendants of recent immigrants who had arrived in the seventeenth or eighteenth century. Neither these immigrants nor their descendants had been admitted to full citizenship rights; they enjoyed only a restricted part of these rights. Now the "natives" had risen in revolt against both the "bourgeois" and the "representatives" in 1766, as a result of which they had obtained a trifling concession: the compromise of March 9, 1768, had decided that each year five families of "natives" would accede to the bourgeoisie, to full citizenship. It was a poor concession, for at the rate of five families a year it would have taken many years before all the "natives" could become "bourgeois," citizens of Geneva in the full sense of the word. It had been impossible for the "natives" to obtain a more meaningful concession because the "bourgeois" had allied themselves with the "representatives" in resisting their demands.

Mallet du Pan's book is an attempt at a compromise. He tries to make the "bourgeois" and the "representatives" listen to the voice of reason by asking them to make greater concessions to the "natives." He therefore presents himself as a defender of the "natives." It is a work which is incontestably liberal, indeed democratic, in tendency. Hence it displeased the "representatives" and even the "bourgeois." The magistrates of Geneva, all of whom were "representatives" condemned the book to be torn up and burned in front of the gate of the Hôtel de Ville, the very same fate that had befallen Jean-Jacques Rousseau's *Emile* several years earlier. Mallet du Pan's book had been judged "seditious, prejudicial to the honor of the State, of the councils, of the citizens, of the bourgeois."

This condemnation led Mallet du Pan to leave Geneva for a considerable period of time; he felt uneasy in a country in which he had run into the hostility of the magistrates. On the other hand, the verdict handed down by the Genevan bourgeois had earned him the congratulations of the *philosophes* and notably of Voltaire.

It was thanks to Voltaire that Mallet was able to find employment abroad: the philosopher, in fact, gave him an introduction to the landgrave of Hesse-Cassel. So Mallet du Pan set out for Hesse, where he became professor of history and literature. He remained there only two years and in the course of his stay published a rather inferior work entitled

Quelle est l'influence de la philosophie sur les belles-lettres? There is not much to be said about it.

By 1773, however, the condemnation of the *Défense* of the "natives" had been forgotten. Mallet returned to Switzerland, married, and two years later, in 1775, published a new book entitled *Doutes sur l'éloquence et les systèmes politiques, adressés à Monsieur le Baron de B . . . chambellan de son Altesse Royale le Prince Henri de Prusse.* This work marks a change of attitude. Mallet seems to have been influenced by Linguet, the great adversary of Voltaire, and we see him evolving toward moderation.

He spent the years 1777 and 1778 in travel, visiting Italy, Piedmont, England (London) and the Low Countries (Brussels). Mallet's journey to London seems to have had a great influence on him. He was struck both by the freedom which the English regime accorded its citizens and by the political corruption that parliamentary customs entailed.

On his return to Geneva, the quarrel of "natives" versus "representatives" flared up again, and in 1782 a real civil war broke out in Geneva. It was a revolution, firmly linked to all those that broke out in the same epoch: the American, Dutch and Irish revolutions. Mallet would have liked to play the role of conciliator. He was not partial either to the oligarchy, to which his family belonged, or to democracy; so he published a pamphlet entitled *Idées soumises à l'examen de tous les conciliateurs par un médiateur sans conséquence*—a work which preached conciliation.

But the situation in Geneva was very changed compared to 1766. This time, in fact, the "natives" had obtained the alliance of the "bourgeois" against the "representatives"; together, "natives" and "bourgeois" formed a very strong party. This revolutionary party created a Committee of Revolutionary Security whose name and scope of action were quite similar to the Committees of Security formed at the same time in the United States and the Low Countries, and to those which were to appear later in Belgium and France. This committee seized power and arrested several leaders of the hierarchy. Those who had escaped arrest, the "negatives" who were still free, appealed for aid abroad—a technique that was to be brought into play in Holland in 1787 and used against France in 1791. The traditional allies of the republic of Geneva, the allies of the patriciate, in fact, were the powerful neighbors Piedmont, France and the canton of Berne. They sent troops who easily took over the city; furthermore, the revolutionaries did not put up much resistance and the invaders restored the old constitution providing for the predominance of the oligarchy. The revolutionary leaders were forced to emigrate and most of them sought refuge in France, as was the case with Clavière, former fellow pupil of Mallet du Pan. Mallet du Pan has described this revolution in the *Tableau historique et politique de la dernière révolution de Genève* (Geneva, 1783).

In this book, Mallet wanted to show that the revolution in Geneva was, perhaps, inevitable, but that it could not be considered legitimate. Two major ideas emerge here that henceforth were to dominate Mallet's work: first, the submission to what he calls the "force of things"—which Saint-Just was to repeat later—a notion which interestingly enough has been taken up by the existentialists in our own time.[1] And secondly, the idea that if things are ineluctably engendered in the wake of the "course of events," one can always attempt to reconcile adversaries, to bring opposing parties closer, and one ought not to acknowledge the legitimacy of anything acquired through force. These are the two major aspects of Mallet's thought and in his book on the revolution in Geneva, he condemns the demagoguery of the revolutionaries as much as the claims of the "negatives." He particularly reproaches the "bourgeois" for having indulged in demagoguery and having sought alliance with those whom he calls the helots of the republic of Geneva. He believes that the only legitimate solution to the Genevan troubles resides in the "golden mean" (he uses this expression) and he calls for a "wisely balanced" government.

It is curious to note that a young journalist, Brissot, who was very little known at that time, responded violently to Mallet du Pan's ideas in a book entitled *Le Philadelphien de Genève ou Lettre d'un Américain sur la dernière révolution de Genève, sa constitution nouvelle, l'émigration en Irlande, pouvant servir de tableau politique de Genève jusqu'en 1784* (Dublin, N.D.). Brissot accused Mallet of having betrayed his former ideology, which had defended the "natives."

Thus Mallet du Pan was increasingly implicated in Genevan affairs and thought it prudent, once again, to leave his homeland to escape the partisan struggles. He settled in Paris, where he found émigrés from Geneva who, for the most part, were the leaders of the revolutionaries. Here he met not only Clavière, but also Francis d'Ivernois,[2] Etienne Dumont and du Roveray.

In Paris Mallet du Pan also made the acquaintance of a famous publisher, Panckouke, who, in 1784, entrusted him with the editorship of

---

1. See the work by Albert Ollivier, *Saint-Just, ou La Force des choses* (Paris, 1954).
2. Francis d'Ivernois, like Mallet du Pan, had been a theorist of the counter-revolution but to a lesser degree.

Le Mercure de France. This journal was to publish a political chronicle, written by Mallet du Pan. As he himself put it: "From historian I became gazeteer and from author, journalist." He defined his program thus: "To support the interests of reason and humanity against the interests of force and against the despotism of habit, in legislative practice."

From 1784, the date of his arrival in Paris, until 1789, the beginning of the Revolution, he wrote a great number of articles in *Le Mercure de France.* Among them should be cited in particular those devoted to the defense of enlightened despotism and the work of Joseph II in Belgium and Austria, as well as of the grand duke Leopold of Tuscany, who was to succeed Joseph II as emperor. Mallet supported all the advocates of enlightened despotism, especially the Italians Verri and Beccaria. Thus he seems to have been well launched in the philosophical movement, or at least in the section of it that approved of enlightened despotism. Moreover, the articles devoted to Switzerland were in favor of keeping the traditional organization of the Helvetian cantons, and in the same way he criticized the American Revolution and the new institutions of the United States.

As a whole, these articles mark Mallet as a moderate, disliking excesses and intemperance, a man who is seeking for the golden mean, the middle way, and a thinker who is not systematically opposed to this or that current of thought. On the contrary, he is very open-minded, interests himself in everything and tries to avoid extreme positions. This was the fundamental attitude of Mallet du Pan when the French Revolution broke out.

2 / Mallet du Pan and the Work of the Constituent Assembly

He continued to direct the political writing of *Le Mercure de France* from 1789 to 1792, and it is in *Le Mercure* that we must look for the expression of Mallet's ideas.

In a general way we can say that he is not in favor either of the French people or the Revolution. He does not favor the Revolution because he is hostile to all great mass movements, all revolutionary disturbances, just as he had disapproved of the Genevan revolutions. He is not in favor of the French people because he has a twofold distrust of the French: that of a Calvinist, hostile to the mass of the French people, because it is Catholic; and that of a rigorist raised in the atmosphere of Genevan puritanism, who sees a France in which "execrable morals" prevail. Thus he is very pessimistic when he talks about events in France. He finds that the French tend to become too quickly inflamed over certain ideas, that they are lacking in seriousness. As early as 1787, he speaks of the "great farce being staged in the name of the king at the theater of Versailles." And again, "France, being incapable of cold deliberation, is also incapable of a free government in which each one must discuss matters with wisdom and circumspection" (1787).

He maintained a certain reserve in his political chronicles until about July, 1789; inasmuch as he was a foreigner, he thought it would be improper for him to interfere in French affairs. But from the time of the taking of the Bastille, as the pace of the revolutionary movement accelerated, Mallet no longer remained silent or even impartial. He had drawn very close to that small group of deputies in the Constituent Assembly whose members took the title *"monarchiens"* or "monarchicals."

The "monarchicals," as we have seen, were those who did not reject reforms out of hand. They favored moderate reform, believing that the Old Regime could not be restored, but that a new monarchical regime must be created, based on two chambers, with the preponderant royal power. Malouet, Clermont-Tonnerre, Bergasse and Montlosier figure among the most celebrated "monarchicals." And Mallet du Pan is considered the "guide to the policy of the 'monarchicals.' "[3] In fact he had become a great admirer of the British constitution—whose functioning he had studied on the spot in the course of his journey to England—and was reputed to be the theorist of the "two chambers."

When the Declaration of the Rights of Man was voted in August, 1789, Mallet devoted several articles to it in *Le Mercure de France*. As a whole, they constitute a concise, intelligent, aggressive, but very logical critique of the Declaration. To him, the Declaration of the Rights of Man will be valid only if it is applied in full, but in that case it will be very dangerous, because the principles expounded can go very far. He believes that it would have been better to have held fast to the Gospel, which gives the simplest, shortest and most complete Declaration of the Rights of Man by proclaiming: "All that you wish men to do to you, even so do you to them." And he adds: "A doctrine is not a law unless the law consecrates the doctrine, which becomes a positive statute, but then that could be very dangerous if all principles should become laws."

3. On the monarchicals, see especially Jean Egret's *La Révolution des notables, Mounier et les monarchiens* (Paris, 1952).

Mallet compares the Declaration of the Rights of Man with the American declarations. He notes that the American Constitution of 1789 is not preceded by a declaration: only the constitutions of some individual states include declarations and these are much more positive than the French Declaration.

These articles made Mallet instantly famous among the aristocrats and in milieux hostile to the Revolution; thenceforth he was considered one of the masters of counter-revolutionary thought.

Mallet's criticism differs greatly from Burke's. He is not opposed to the Declaration because it is a declaration of abstract, metaphysical principles, which was Burke's position. Mallet opposes it on more practical grounds, because he believes that either this Declaration will not be applied, and is therefore useless, or it will be applied, in which case it will produce an upheaval of extremely grave proportions.

The *journées* of October 5 and 6, 1789, during which the royal family was brought from Versailles to Paris by the people in revolt, alarmed Mallet. He believed that the Revolution was becoming very dangerous and could be characterized by the formula: "Believe or die!" Thenceforth he felt the pen was powerless to fight against the revolutionary movement; the latter is driven by the "force of things." "An army and not a code of law will save us," he writes. From this melancholy conclusion he was led to wonder whether the British constitution was really as good as he had believed and whether its application could be as useful to France as he had once thought. From the middle of 1790 onwards, he no longer praised the English constitution in *Le Mercure*; he devoted all his efforts to the defense of property, which he saw as threatened.

Above all, Mallet defended landed property, which he claims is coveted by what he calls the mercantile "aristocracy," that is, the mercantile bourgeoisie, the speculators. Although defending landed property, he does not praise the feudal regime. He does not say that the feudal system ought to have been maintained, but he insists upon the necessity of redeeming the feudal rights which are, in his view, a legitimate property of the nobles. The abolition of feudal rights without redemption signifies a fatal blow struck at property.

Other articles are devoted to the Civil Constitution of the Clergy. Mallet was a Calvinist, and he could have rejoiced over this civil constitution, which gave the Church of France a statute similar to that of the Calvinist Church. On the contrary, he laments it and deplores the persecutions it will set off against the members of the clergy. In one article he writes:

> Posterity will easily understand the expropriation of the clergy, the reduction of its revenues, the abolition of its privileges, the changes effected in discipline. Minds will be divided in fifty years, as they are today, on the necessity, the utility, of this reform. But what will not be viewed without a tremor of indignation is the pitiless fury with which the members of this important order are being persecuted.

On the whole, therefore, we see that Mallet is not irreducibly hostile to the Revolution, although he is one of its severe critics. He loves freedom but fears anarchy. He loves order, but dreads the dictatorship of the mob. He approves of the ends of the Revolution of 1789, but rejects the means.

The flight of Louis XVI in 1791 unleashed a first wave of terror over France. Those who were considered parties to this flight, presented moreover as a kidnapping, were hunted down, as Mallet was for this reason. He had to suspend publication of *Le Mercure* and go into hiding during the three months of June, July and August, 1791.

He did not reappear on the political scene until the Constitution of 1791 had been definitively and solemnly accepted by the king. Mallet was still skeptical about the worth of this Constitution and its duration, however, and in this he showed a clairvoyance that he never ceased to exercise until his death.

When *Le Mercure* reappeared in 1791, Mallet published two remarkable articles: "Du principe des factions et de celles qui divisent la France" and "Resumé de l'histoire politique de l'année 1791." In these articles he affirms once again the political ideal of the "monarchicals," that is, a constitutional monarchy with two chambers, one of which is a House of Lords. But he also goes into the reason for the failure of the "monarchicals." For him this lies essentially in the *journées* of October 5 and 6, 1789. It is because the king yielded in the face of rioters, and because the "monarchicals" of the Constituent Assembly yielded to the Paris mob and consented to the transfer to Paris of the governmental bodies, that they were eliminated as a political factor. And he believes that in the wake of their elimination the development of the Revolution toward the Left is inevitable. The legitimate Revolution, he says, failed, not so much because of the errors of men as because of the pressure of what he calls the social revolution, which he compares to the great barbarian invasions.

The war which broke out between France and Europe in April of 1792 dashed the last hopes of Mallet and the moderates: "We must fear a war whose inevitable result will be anarchy, or the federative Republic, or an absolute counter-revolution." The men shaping events are turning aside from Mallet's ideal, which is conciliation. They are marching towards extremes: either the dictatorship of the revolutionary extremists, or the dictatorship of those whom he calls absolute counter-revolutionists, that is, those who want to restore the Old Regime lock, stock and barrel.

Moreover, the war has plunged France into a real dilemma: "If the patriotism of the French succeeds in saving the Revolution, the war will become European." But if France is defeated, total counter-revolution will take place. Mallet would have liked to avoid these two consequences, but it seemed to him that it was impossible to prevent their happening.

He therefore decided to leave a France in which he saw that he would no longer be able to write, or even to live, freely. Before leaving he was put in touch with Louis XVI, who assigned him a mission to his émigré brothers. The mission was to urge moderation on them, to prevent them from proclaiming that their aim was the integral restoration of the Old Regime.

What were Louis XVI's intentions? Was he sincere or did he want to put his enemies on the wrong scent? This is a difficult point to determine. We know that the king did play a double game: while he was prodigal of assurances designed to reassure the French revolutionaries, in secret he incited the émigrés to action and assured them of his support. It is possible that Mallet's mission might have had one of these objectives.

Mallet was also commissioned to appear before the king of Prussia and the emperor, in order to request them to publish a manifesto in which they would declare that they had no intention of dismembering France in the event of victory, and that their only aim was the deliverance of the royal family.

Mallet du Pan left France on May 21, 1792; he passed through Geneva, and then went to Frankfurt. He was perhaps able to see the king of Prussia there, but he did not meet the emperor, who was in that city for his coronation. He did have an interview with the maréchal de Castries and explained to him the intentions of Louis XVI.[4] He had some contact with several émigrés, but was the butt of their hostility; most of them, in fact, favored an almost integral restoration, or at all events one that

4. Duc de Castries, *Le Testament de Monarchie*. Vol. II: *L'Agonie de la royauté* (Paris, 1959), pp. 343–345.

was much more complete than that dreamed of by Mallet du Pan, and they were very hostile to the "monarchicals," whom they reproached for having been the first to compromise with the Revolution. Thus the mission was a total failure and Mallet went back to Geneva, then to Berne.

3 / *The* Considérations sur . . . la Révolution de France

After having lived almost ten years in France, Mallet du Pan then returned to Switzerland and devoted himself mainly to writing a book which is the most important of his works against the Revolution, and comparable to Burke's *Reflections on the Revolution in France*. It was entitled *Considérations sur la nature de la Révolution de France*, and was published in Brussels in August, 1793. It was a violent pamphlet, written after Mallet had taken the advice of émigré "monarchicals" and of such figures as Mme de Staël, whom he had met at Coppet, near Geneva, where she had taken up residence. In the *Considérations*, Mallet fights against abstraction but he does not have the same point of view as Burke. He does not reject the Enlightenment, or rationalism. Furthermore, whereas Burke's *Reflections* was published at the end of 1790, Mallet's *Considérations* appeared three years later and the author takes account of the tempo of the Revolution. He believes that August 10, 1792, and the *journées* of May 31 and June 2, 1793, merely accentuated the social revolution that he had foreseen.

This social revolution, according to Mallet, will bring to power the irresponsible mobs, who will seize all the property of the nobility and the bourgeoisie and divide it among themselves.

However, Mallet rejects the thesis upheld by Burke and later by abbé Barruel, according to which the Revolution was caused by the *philosophes*.

It is an error to think that the French Revolution derives its origin, as is commonly said, from the spirit of philosophy, of depravity and of irreligion regnant for so long a time in France. It is a great error to attribute it to this or that form of representation in the Estates General, and it would be a further self-deception to think that a prince . . . had been the first and principal agent.

Here Mallet was alluding to the role that was often attributed to the duc d'Orléans.

The badly regulated spirit of philosophic disorders, like that of disorder in religion or, in general, the dogmatic spirit in any form, avails itself of, or takes over, revolutions but does not make them. A revolution is essentially a displacement of power, which is effected by necessity every time that the old power no longer has the strength to protect the commonwealth or the courage to protect itself . . . once power had escaped from the king's hands, the feeling set in that it belonged to whoever would succeed in seizing it for himself.

This is the great idea defended by Mallet du Pan: the Revolution took place because the Old Regime had collapsed of itself; and having collapsed, power was there for the taking. The nobility and the clergy at first had tried to seize this power in May and June of 1789. These two orders failed in their undertaking and it was the Third Estate—notably, the bourgeoisie—which seized power on July 14. But the bourgeoisie itself did not know how to preserve it; on August 10, 1792, it was eliminated in its turn and replaced by the small proprietors, the petty bourgeoisie. The latter were able to remain in power only for a few months: the revolutionary *journées* of May 31 and June 2, 1793, eliminated them also. "So," writes Mallet, "power passed into the hands of the nonproprietors." This was a highly inaccurate appraisal, as recent studies on the social structure of the "sans-culottes" have shown. In fact, these "sans-culottes" most often were small proprietors.[5] But for Mallet du Pan, the class which came to power on June 2, 1793, was composed of the starving and indigent, in short, of proletarians.

And he foresees the probable evolution of the Revolution: "The displacement of power," he says, "inevitably leads to the displacement of property, which will pass into the hands of the 'sans-culottes'; this class will become a class of proprietors which, in its turn, will preserve power to its advantage. Nevertheless, things will not necessarily evolve in this direction because there is a major unknown factor, the war."

A very interesting section of the *Considérations* is devoted to the war. Mallet believes that it has become one of the reasons for the prolongation of the Revolution. It was planned by the Jacobins, directed by Brissot, who saw in it a means to defeat the Crown, and to ruin the aristocrats and the constitutionalists. But the war, in its turn, defeated the Brissotins and

5. *Les Sans-culottes parisiens en l'an II*, by Albert Soboul (Paris, 1958), is an excellent analysis of the social structure of the "sans-culottes" class. See especially pp. 439–455.

is transforming the course of the Revolution. Mallet says: "The war abroad has therefore created this regime, which is reducing 20 million men to two professions exclusively: agriculture and the military art. The moment draws near when in France we shall see only knapsacks and bayonets; the Revolution necessarily leads to the military republic." For Mallet du Pan, as for Robespierre, the end product of the war is military dictatorship. Indeed, for him this dictatorship has already begun: "Another regime has supervened with the institution of the Committee of Public Safety . . . its influence has grown apace with the dangers, and success has perpetuated and consolidated it." And he concludes that henceforth, in France, passion will be stronger than reason. "Passions subvert the universe much more than understanding. These two despotic sovereigns, reason and passion, form plans not as a result of our wills, but of necessity and the imperious course of things." This is how Mallet du Pan attributes the march of the Revolution to the "imperious course of things."

What were the repercussions of this book? In France they were slight; the country was at war; only a small number of copies could reach the interior. But in Germany the *Considérations* had a considerable success, as great as Burke's *Reflections*. Gentz, the translator of the *Reflections*, published them in German; Fichte and Kant were influenced by them, as shown in their writings of 1794.

The *Considérations* brought Mallet du Pan to the height of fame, and as a result he was chosen as political councillor by the principal sovereigns of Europe.

4 / *Mallet du Pan's* Correspondances

Thus a new phase in Mallet's life began. After taking up residence in Berne, from 1794 to 1798, he undertook a political correspondence with the principal courts of Europe: Berlin, Turin, and London where, through the medium of Lord Elgin, he sent several memoranda to the Ministry of Foreign Affairs. But of all his correspondence, the most important is that with the court of Vienna, comprising 136 letters, from December 28, 1794, to February 26, 1798.

He also maintained a regular correspondence with the French princes, the comte de Provence and the comte d'Artois, forcing them to choose between himself and the comte d'Antraigues, who directed an important intelligence and spy network. It is quite possible that Mallet du Pan also headed a spy network; up to the present no one has been able to prove this, at least for this particular period of his life. But the situation is different, as we shall see, in 1799.

In his *Correspondance politique* with the court of Vienna, Mallet du Pan touches on numerous subjects which cannot all be examined here. We must limit ourselves to just a few of them.

First of all, the theme of peace. In 1795, Tuscany, Holland, Spain and Prussia concluded peace with France. Should the Empire, should Austria, also conclude peace? For Mallet du Pan, peace is as full of dangers as war. "It is not a paradox to assert that a premature peace or a war, pursued according to the system which has dominated up to now, offers an equal danger." He believed that in the event of peace, the principles of revolutionary France risked being spread by propaganda to neighboring countries; but if a peace was not concluded, the war too could bring these principles into the same countries. On the other hand, peace would strengthen the Convention and the Revolution; but in the event of victory, war would have strengthened them all the more and led inevitably to the military dictatorship he had foreseen in his *Considérations*.

In the *Correspondance*, Mallet also examines French Jacobinism. Inwardly he admires it for having known how to fuse all the wills of the nation into a solid union. Only Robespierre's death had considerably diminished its force. "I have an idea," he writes, "to which everything seems to subordinate itself, namely, that the Jacobins have perfectly constituted the Nation. Upon this endeavor they have lavished a marvelous artistry, to which History will have to direct its attention. It will be necessary to organize order, just as they have organized anarchy." Thus the counter-revolutionaries, when they become victors, will have to take the Jacobins as a model in the organization of nations.

As to the outcome of the Revolution, Mallet comes back to his earlier idea: it depends upon the "force of things." "France is being led by events and not by men; the latter are driven by the force of circumstances and hardly ever plan them in advance."

Among the suggestions that he submits to the Vienna court, we find above all counsels of moderation and conciliation. Extremes are to be avoided; neither Burke nor d'Antraigues's plans should be followed. And he reproaches the comte de Provence, who has taken the title of Louis XVIII, strongly for his plans and proclamations, which are very hostile to the Revolution.

In 1796 and 1797 Mallet du Pan places all his hopes on the triumph of the moderates in France, of the "Clichyans." The latter had won a majority in the elections of 1797; their triumph seemed imminent and with them the old "monarchicals" would return to power.

But the *coup d'état* of 18 Fructidor once again dashed his hopes. In the same period he also wanted to address himself to the French republicans, giving them counsels of moderation and conciliation similar to those he had sent the sovereigns of Europe. In 1796 he published a book entitled *Correspondance politique pour servir à l'histoire du républicanisme français*, in which he stated in particular: "The nefarious and bloody Revolution is finished; all that remains is to combat the philosophic Revolution, already half discredited by experience of its principles." Since the "drinkers of blood" have been eliminated, it is useless to continue to preserve a revolutionary regime. The republic is being held in place only by a minority; accordingly, it is necessary to re-establish the constitutional monarchy, which seems to be desired by the great majority of Frenchmen. Similar ideas were upheld in France at the same time by the "Clichyans" and especially by Lacretelle.[6]

After the *coup d'état* of Fructidor, Mallet was once more persuaded that his hopes had little chance of success and once more resigned himself to the "course of things." He feared the realization of the "Great Nation," that is, the European expansion of France. Actually, his prophecy was to be partially realized as early as 1798.

In January, 1798, Switzerland was invaded and soon Geneva, annexed to France, became the administrative center of the department of Léman. Mallet du Pan lost no time in leaving his country. He managed to reach Basle, then Constance, Fribourg, and finally England, where he arrived on May 1, 1798.

In the London archives I have found documents on his activity in England which prove irrefutably that Mallet du Pan was employed by the English government as the head of a spy network at the end of 1798 and 1799.[7] For this service he was paid £100 a month. However, he did not acquit himself to the full satisfaction of the government which, after several months, removed him from direction of this network and paid the arrears of his salary.

6. J. Godechot, "Les Français et l'unité italienne sous le Directoire," *Revue d'Histoire politique et constitutionnelle*, 1952, pp. 96–110 and 193–204.
7. J. Godechot, "Le Directoire vu de Londres," *Annales historiques de la Révolution française*, 1949, pp. 311–339, and 1950, pp. 1–27. The documents of the Public Record Office concerning Mallet du Pan are preserved in the Foreign Office series 27, 53, 54.

Thus in London Mallet du Pan maintained a regular correspondence with those who, whether French or English, were the agents of this network on the continent; and he wrote summaries of the information received, which he presented to the British government.

But at the same time he founded in London a newspaper similar to the one he had directed in Paris: *Le Mercure britannique*, the first issue of which appeared on August 20, 1798. It continued for thirty-six issues before vanishing from the scene in March, 1800.

Le Mercure britannique was a fortnightly review which published very lengthy articles by Mallet and his "monarchical" friends, now refugees in Great Britain, or by Swiss living in England.

The first issue contains an important study entitled "Essai historique sur la destruction de la ligue et de la liberté helvétiques." Mallet has seen all his hopes dashed, his country's freedom vanish. His tiny homeland, Geneva, which had been an independent republic, is now annexed to France. In his article he idealizes the ancient Genevan and Helvetian freedoms. We sense that he has been influenced by Burke since his arrival in Great Britain. He extols tradition and becomes the champion of what has been called "Helvetism," this myth of a montagnard, free Switzerland which was to be taken up again in the nineteenth century, notably by Sismondi.

In another article, Mallet studies the degree of influence that philosophy has had upon the Revolution. In spite of the constant successes of the Revolution and everything else that has happened, he is still resolutely attached to rationalism and the philosophy of the Enlightenment. It is not philosophy, but the wanton abuse of it, that has released the Revolution. He preserves his faith in "true equality" before the law, in "true" freedom.

But at this point Mallet was an extremely weary and sick man, although only fifty-one. His emigration and the attacks upon him from the French émigrés in favor of integral counter-revolution had worn him out. He retired from the scene, at first to Lally-Tollendal in Richmond. Soon, however, his illness worsened, and on May 10, 1801, he died, several days after Bonaparte had successfully negotiated the Great Saint-Bernard Pass, several months after the establishment in France of the military dictatorship which he had foreseen as early as 1792.

Was Mallet an enlightened reformer, as some have claimed? Or was he a defender of tradition? He is very difficult to classify. There is no doubt that to the day of his death he constantly manifested his attachment to rationalism and to the Enlightenment. But he did not believe that it was necessary blindly to abolish all traditional institutions, since many of them were useful and could be improved.

At all events, Mallet stands out as a figure distinguished by the lucidity of his intelligence and the extreme clarity, indeed the prophetic value, of his judgments on the Revolution. In terms of immediacy, however, his influence was rather weak. The group of "monarchicals" had little importance. Only later, fourteen years after his death, were they to return to power in France, at the time of the Restoration. With the Charter of 1814, they were to institute in France a regime of which no doubt Mallet du Pan would in part have approved, and for which, at all events, he had fought hard.

CHAPTER VI

The Theocrats: Joseph de Maistre and Louis de Bonald

De Maistre and de Bonald are the theorists to whom the name "theocrats" has been given because they placed God and religion at the head of the society they wanted to rebuild.

In general, Joseph de Maistre and Louis de Bonald are linked together in works devoted to political ideas; they are, as it were, the Castor and Pollux of theocracy. In point of fact, there were fairly deep differences between them but what they had in common, although they did not make each other's acquaintance until very late, was an aspiration toward a fundamentally religious society, under the guidance of God.

De Maistre and de Bonald, moreover, differed considerably because of their origins. Joseph de Maistre was not a Frenchman; born in Savoy, he was a subject of the king of Piedmont-Sardinia. Louis de Bonald was French and a native of Languedoc; he was born in Millau. But they were contemporaries: Joseph de Maistre was born in 1753, Louis de Bonald in 1754. And we can also consider as a common feature the fact that they exercised their influence preponderantly at the time of the Restoration. In the reactionary Europe of 1815 they were the oracles of the restored monarchies. Their chief works, however, appeared before 1804. Both de Bonald and de Maistre published their fundamental work—one more similarity—almost on the same date, in 1796, only a few months apart.

From 1804 onwards, they entered into a regular correspondence which, however, took place at great intervals. It was only later that they met. Thus it is pure coincidence that before 1804 we can set these two men together.

84

1 / Joseph de Maistre

Joseph de Maistre was born on April 1, 1753, in Chambéry. He was the son of François-Xavier de Maistre, who was of very recent nobility. He had, in fact, been ennobled by the king of Sardinia for his important contribution to the codification of the laws of the kingdom. The de Maistres belonged to the nobility of the robe. François-Xavier was president of the senate of Savoy, although we must not be misled by this title; the senate was not a deliberative assembly, but a high court of justice, similar to the French parlements of the Old Regime. However, de Maistre's family was not of Savoyard origin, but had emigrated from Languedoc to the duchy of Savoy in the sixteenth century. Joseph de Maistre's mother was Christine de Motz. She was an extremely pious woman, so much so that her son once said that she was an angel to whom God had lent a body.

Joseph had four brothers and five sisters. Of the brothers one became equally famous: Xavier, a writer, who achieved distinction as a novelist and essayist rather than in political philosophy.

It is certain that the political, social and economic organization and the geographical conditions of Savoy around 1753 had an influence on Joseph de Maistre's upbringing. Savoy, a country of mountaineer peasants, was deeply subject to the Church, and the priests wielded a very great influence. Furthermore, it must be recalled that from 1762 onwards, the sovereigns of Piedmont-Sardinia abolished serfdom and organized the redemption of feudal dues in Savoy. In this regard Savoy was very much ahead of France. The reform was a result of the enlightened policy of the kings of Sardinia. In 1789, feudal dues had practically all been redeemed in Savoy and serfdom completely abolished for more than twenty years.

Joseph de Maistre went to school in his home town of Chambéry and later pursued his studies at the faculty of law in Turin. As soon as he gained his degree in law, he returned to Chambéry and was nominated assistant fiscal advocate-general of the senate, that is, was attached to the magistracy.

From 1774 to 1789, he led a very tranquil existence in Chambéry, but was interested in all the great currents of thought. His most notable activity took place within Freemasonry. In fact, the important role which he played in the Savoyard Freemasons is one of the more curious features of his personality. This role has been set into bolder relief by different historians, particularly Paul Vulliaud, who has published a work on de Maistre as Freemason[1] which develops the revelations furnished historians by François Vermale's study entitled *Notes sur Joseph de Maistre inconnu.*[2] De Maistre belonged to the "Sincerity" lodge, which was divided into two sections, one consisting of the ordinary members of the lodge, the other of the especially "enlightened" members—the latter being affiliated to a secret organization of a mystical character which bore the title "College of knights, grand prophets of the Holy City."

This occult organization had been much influenced by the mystics of the time, notably Saint-Martin, the "unknown philosopher," leader of one of the most curious mystical trends in France. This point must be emphasized since in his youth, at the age of twenty-five, Joseph de Maistre was one of the principal adepts of Martinism. This did not prevent him from being an excellent Catholic. It should also be stressed that he knew how to reconcile his ardent Catholicism with his adherence to Freemasonry, despite the fact that at this time the latter had already been twice condemned by the Pope.

Of de Maistre's Catholicism, there are proofs: upon his return to Chambéry, he had become a member of the Confraternity of Black Penitents, whose task was to attend prisoners condemned to death and to keep vigil at their obsequies.

Another very revealing index of this profound Catholicism is the public act of the whole de Maistre family, which went into mourning when the Jesuit order was suppressed by the Parlement of Paris.

Thus de Maistre reconciled his adherence to Freemasonry in its most mystical aspect with a very sincere and profound Catholicism. All his life he was to consider abbé Barruel's thesis, which attributed to Freemasonry the conspiracy supposedly at the origin of the Revolution, absurd.

During these tranquil years de Maistre on several occasions went to Lyons where Saint-Martin and his disciple Willermoz exercised a very great influence: Lyons, at this time, was the true capital of French mysticism, as has been clearly demonstrated by Louis Trénard.[3]

Freemasonry, on the eve of the Revolution, can be divided into two tendencies: a universalist, reformist, democratic one, which exercised no influence on de Maistre; and a mystical, Catholic, conservative one, to which de Maistre belonged. He was an assiduous reader of Saint-Martin's basic work, *L'Homme de désir*, and in his own great book, *Les Considéra-*

1. Paul Vulliaud, *Joseph de Maistre franc-maçon* (1926).
2. François Vermale, *Notes sur Joseph de Maistre inconnu* (1912).
3. Louis Trénard, *De l'Encyclopédie au préromantisme* (2 vols., Paris, 1958).

tions sur la France, published in 1796, he was to attest that he owed much to Saint-Martin's work.

Nevertheless, up to 1789 de Maistre wrote little; at least, we do not have very much of his writing of that time. In 1775, on the occasion of the journey of the king of Sardinia, Victor Amadeus III, to Chambéry, de Maistre was commissioned to deliver an address on behalf of the senate. The ideas contained in this address are rather vaguely liberal. They deal with freedom of thought, the right of remonstrance. Yet de Maistre declares that religion is the most powerful political "spring," the true nerve of states; and he evinces hostility to the notion of freedom of the press. To the chancellery of the Kingdom of Sardinia his address appeared too liberal and he was censured for it.

In 1784, nine years later, de Maistre delivered another address devoted to a more limited subject: the vocation of the magistrate. In it he attaches great importance to the functions of the magistrate and particularly to the role of the senate, that is, of the parlements. We see de Maistre deeply imbued with the parlement-oriented doctrine developed by Montesquieu, which allots to the parlements a preponderant role in the State: "The decrees of parlements," he asserts, "must be respected nearly on par with the sacred Scriptures."

In 1789 the Revolution broke out in Paris. De Maistre was not unaffected by the emotion or the general enthusiasm it released: it seems he approved the Tennis Court Oath and the night of August 4. The abolition of feudal dues could hardly have troubled him inasmuch as it merely generalized, throughout France, what had existed in the duchy of Savoy for twenty years. Under Montesquieu's influence, it seems that de Maistre too gave thought to the transformation of the senate of Savoy, a court of justice, into a legislative assembly. But he dropped this idea very quickly.

During the months of July and August, we see de Maistre express his wish for the triumph of the "monarchicals" in the Constituent Assembly. The "monarchicals," already mentioned here, were represented in the Assembly notably by Clermont-Tonnerre, Malouet and Mounier. Their spokesman was Mallet du Pan.

Joseph de Maistre began to change his attitude as early as mid-August when the Declaration of the Rights of Man and of the Citizen was voted. He convinced himself at that time that the Old Regime had been completely destroyed, that it would never again be possible to re-establish it, and he expressed this conviction in the correspondence he maintained regularly with the baron Vignet des Etoles.

Vignet des Etoles was the minister of the king of Sardinia in Berne. The letters in which de Maistre explains to his friend that the Old Regime has definitively disappeared make him sound like a Jacobin, and Vignet mocks him. But de Maistre is convinced that the Old Regime will never be able to re-establish itself; he thinks that it must now be replaced by another regime similar but more solidly constructed, and this idea is confirmed in de Maistre's mind after his reading of Burke's *Reflections on the Revolution in France*. In fact de Maistre wrote to another correspondent, Costa de Beauregard, on January 21, 1791, in connection with Burke's book: "I don't know how to tell you to what degree Burke has reinforced my anti-democratic and anti-Gallican ideas." Thus, already in 1791 we see de Maistre abandoning his original enthusiasm for the Revolution and becoming one of its most outspoken foes.

This position, of course, was to be strengthened even further by the attitude of France to Savoy when the war between the two nations broke out in 1792. Savoy was invaded, peacefully as it happened, by the French armies in September of that year. The great majority of the Savoyard populace proclaimed the fall of the Old Regime and manifested its attachment to France by demanding integration into the republic through the vote of the "National Assembly of the Allobroges."

De Maistre felt that he could no longer remain in Savoy. In November, 1792, he left his country with his family—he had been married since 1786 to a young lady named de Morand, and had several children. Despite the inclement weather, the de Maistre family made its way through the snow-covered passes of the Alps in order to take up residence in Aosta.

A short time later, the National Assembly of the Allobroges, which was governing Savoy while waiting for ratification of the annexation by the Convention, voted a law ordering émigrés to return before January 1, 1793, under penalty of confiscation of their properties. De Maistre was in Turin at the time but his wife, learning of the law, despite the fact that she was expecting a baby the following month, returned to her property to prevent its confiscation. De Maistre followed her several days later.

He was astounded at the change that had been effected in the mind of the populace. He never imagined that the attachment of the Savoyards to revolutionary principles was so deep. He believed that one had a duty, or perhaps simply thought it prudent, to enroll in the National Guard, but he showed no great fervor. To one of his friends he wrote: "I am mounting my first guard at the Town Hall; a fine question would be to know whether I shall mount the second." Later, he refused to pay the war tax because he did not want to aid, through his contribution, France's struggle against the Kingdom of Sardinia; in fact, he continued to consider the Piedmontese and the Sardinians as compatriots. This refusal entailed vexations of all sorts, and in particular searches on his property; so he emigrated a second time. He left alone and was not to see his wife again for twenty years.

This time he turned not towards Piedmont, but Switzerland. He settled in Lausanne, where he met sundry personages who were interested in France and the Revolution, notably the skeptical, sarcastic, anti-clerical British historian, Gibbon. He engaged in very lengthy discussions with Gibbon, which were to have a profound influence on him. In Lausanne he also found his friend Costa de Beauregard and met Mme de Staël, who had left France. So he led an active political and literary life.

Moreover, de Maistre was soon appointed agent of the king of Sardinia at Lausanne and assigned a very specific twofold mission: intelligence gathering and political action. His task was to transmit to the king all the information gathered about Savoy and to countersign the passports of the Savoyard émigrés. He was also to encourage the Savoyards hostile to France and, if possible, to foment an insurrection in Savoy.

During the summer of 1793, at the time of the federalist insurrection at Lyons, when the Sardinian troops once more negotiated the passes and were positioned in the high Savoyard valleys, de Maistre secretly arranged for the passage, through Switzerland, of Savoyards and Piedmontese in civilian dress. They could thus cross over into neutral territory and so enter Savoy in order to join up with the soldiers of the regular army or provoke disturbances in the rear of the French armies. De Maistre's activity was therefore markedly counter-revolutionary. He did not limit himself to espionage and intelligence gathering, but also engaged in many literary and political activities. In fact he wrote various works, although many were not published until after his death in 1884, when the complete works appeared for the first time. Among the books published during de Maistre's lifetime, we shall discuss only two of his pamphlets printed at this time.

The first is entitled *Lettres d'un royaliste savoisien à ses compatriotes*, published in Lyons in 1793. It is de Maistre's first printed book. We can already distinguish the characteristic style, marked by an extreme purity and elegance of language, but the content is quite banal. De Maistre counsels the Savoyards to be loyal to the king, and to the king he urges clemency toward the misguided Savoyards who had adhered to France.

In the same period he also published another very curious pamphlet: *Jean-Claude Têtu, maire de Montagnol, à ces chers concitoyens du mont Blanc*. Only a small number of copies were printed in 1795, but it was reprinted in 1822. It is a work of counter-revolutionary, anti-French propaganda, written in a pseudo-peasant style, the aim being to incite the Savoyards to demand a return to the Sardinian monarchy. Some excerpts follow:

"On all our hearts weighs this sorry comedy of 1792, when a handful of rogues who called themselves the Nation wrote to Paris that we wanted to be French. You all know, before God, that it was nothing of the sort and how we were all free to say No on condition that we said Yes. . . ."

". . . In my youth I never understood why our tiny Savoy was not a province of France and how this tiny perch had been able to live for such a long time alongside a big pike without being gobbled up. But in thinking about it since, I have seen how right my deceased grandmother was when she told me, 'Jean-Claude, my friend, when you do not understand something, trust Him who makes the stem of the cherry.' "

The pamphlet ends with the promise of pardon made in the name of the king of Sardinia, apparently without his permission to do so, if the Savoyards would rally once more around their former sovereign.

At this time de Maistre also wrote a work entitled *Les Bienfaits de la Révolution française*, which was not published until a hundred years later. In this book he again takes up Burke's ideas, saying that it is absurd to believe that all men are made for freedom. The real errors of government are those made by the governed. Prejudices are fine things, they are the holiest laws. It is folly to want to remake the social pact because all governments are the result of the tacit agreement of men gathered in society, and because the real expression of their assent is founded upon the character of peoples and upon an infinite host of circumstances which it is impossible to know in their totality.

Consequently, to draw up a social pact makes no sense. The art of reform does not lie in the total overthrow of institutions, which are then to be reconstructed upon abstract and ideal theories; on the contrary, they should be bound once again to internal and hidden principles which must be discovered in history. These internal, hidden principles, which political men must discover, form the real constitution of a people. So a constitution must not be written on a "tabula rasa." It is absurd to consider that because a people does not have a written constitution it is without one.

Legislative assemblies should not deliberate on laws and constitutions, but simply respond by a Yes or No to the questions submitted to them by the government. Here we see de Maistre anticipating the Legislative Corps of the Empire, which was not to discuss the projects that were submitted to it but simply vote Yes or No.

The privileges of the aristocracy correspond to functions, and they ought not to be abolished; without these privileges the principle of honor which they represent would disappear and society would be structured on what the author calls "the odious hierarchy of wealth."

De Maistre also wrote other pamphlets and various works which have not been published, in particular the speeches of citizen Cherchemot, which were intended to lampoon the harangues, larded with platitudes, delivered by the political men of the French Revolution.

All these works, however, are but minor ones. His major work is *Les Considérations sur la France*, published in Neuchâtel in 1796 and in London in 1797. It is here that we must seek the quintessence of Joseph de Maistre's thought.

It seems evident that the title of this work was inspired by that of Mallet du Pan and by the *Considérations politiques, philosophiques et religieuses sur la Révolution française* by Saint-Martin, both of which had appeared several months before. De Maistre, however, points out that in his work religious considerations outweigh political ones.

Whereas in his previous works de Maistre expounded ideas, reflections on events in France, but no real doctrine, in *Considérations sur la France* a solidly constructed theory of counter-revolution is outlined. Its principal elements are as follows: In 1789 all the governments and nations of Europe were in a very parlous moral and religious state. The Revolution, which broke out in France and is spreading through all Europe, is the result of this moral and religious decadence. France therefore should not be punished for having made the Revolution, nor amputated territorially, because all the states of Europe are equally responsible. Peace must be built in the respect for the equilibrium of Europe. But in order for this peace to be a lasting one, a profound moral and religious restoration is necessary. And it is the elements of this restoration that de Maistre expounds.

Thus he does not demand the restoration of the Old Regime, or old regimes, such as had existed before 1789, because as he sees them, they are injurious, inadequate and responsible for the Revolution. He wants to see a new regime set up, based essentially upon religion; a "theocratic" regime.

Considérations, in fact, begins with the sentence:

> We are all bound to the throne of the Supreme Being by a chain which restrains without enslaving us. In times of revolution, the chain which binds man contracts suddenly; his field of action narrows and his means betray him. Never is Providence more palpable than when providential action replaces human action and works wholly alone. This is what we are witnessing at this moment.

And he develops his ideas on the basis of nature and reason. But like Burke, he gives these two concepts a meaning totally different from that which the philosophers of the eighteenth century attributed to them. For de Maistre, nature is the nature of man, that is, the nature of an intelligent, religious and social being. The man who lives according to nature is not at all the savage Rousseau describes; rather, he is the man who lives in society, and history alone can inform us on the nature of man. Now historically, man has always lived in societies ruled by sovereigns; monarchy, therefore, is a government in keeping with nature.

As to reason, for de Maistre, reason is not that of the philosophers. Human reason left to itself is but a brute, whose power is merely the power to destroy. Reason alone can produce only disputes. Now, it is not fitting for man to dispute over problems which he cannot solve; but he must believe. Reason, therefore, is belief, and prejudices are the fundamental elements of reason.

After thus defining nature and reason very much in Burkean terms, de Maistre enters upon the subject of constitutions. As he has already done in his pamphlets, he condemns written constitutions and declarations of rights which, in his view, are absurd, nonsensical. A constitution is the result of an imperceptible germination of an infinity of fortuitous circumstances: "The national constitution," he says, "is always anterior to the written constitution, and any good written constitution can be only the transcription of a political dogma resulting from the national reason." Thus he does not discard the written constitution, but makes the condition that it must not be based upon abstract reasoning and that it must be the emanation of the unwritten national constitution. And he adds: "The more one writes, the weaker are institutions, because one writes only to defend tottering institutions" (hence the less written, the more solid the institutions). After having thus examined the problem of institutions in general, he attacks the Constitution of Year III.

Considérations sur la France, in fact, constitutes a full-fledged attack on the Constitution of Year III. It is fascinating to compare these *Considérations* with those of the Swiss, Benjamin Constant, published in the same period but with a diametrically opposed purpose. Benjamin Constant, in that same year, had written a work entitled *De la force du gouvernement actuel de la France et de la necessité de s'y rallier*. De Maistre's book, conversely, can be said to demonstrate the weakness of the government of France and the necessity of not rallying to its support. The Constitution of Year III, he says, could be applied to any country whatsoever— actually it was to be applied in the "sister republics"—accordingly, this constitution is not a genuine one; indeed, it is the very antithesis of a constitution.

After thus condemning the Constitution of Year III, de Maistre examines the problem of the war which the Revolution is waging against Europe. For him, war is a normal thing, forming part of the life of humanity: "Blood is the fertilizer of that plant we call genius." But this war which, for the moment, is awarding brilliant victories to France, will backfire against her. For de Maistre the victory of the counter-revolution is an acknowledged certainty, requiring only an attitude of patient waiting.

In fact, Providence desires the counter-revolution. The Catholic de Maistre substitutes Providence for the Protestant Mallet du Pan's "force of things," stating: "It has been said with good reason that the French Revolution leads men more than men lead it"—a statement that compares interestingly with the thought of Mallet du Pan discussed in the previous chapter.

Providence leads men and Providence has chosen to punish France for the corruption of her mores. Once again we encounter the "providentialism" already noted in a number of theorists. The Revolution is a miracle, a supernatural event, that cannot be explained scientifically; but another miracle lies in the persistence of the Catholic faith in France and in Europe, despite the persecutions of which Catholics are the victims. This Catholic faith will ultimately triumph and prevail over its enemies. The expansion of the French Revolution in Europe has been chosen deliberately by Providence in order to put Europe in contact with the French clergy, which has been forced to emigrate. It is the émigré priests who show the other peoples in Europe what persecutions Catholicism has suffered in France; by their example, by the austere, pure and moral life they lead in exile, they are educating the other nations.

The Revolution therefore, concludes de Maistre, is a fight to the death between Christianity and philosophy: either the Revolution will conquer, after which a new religion will rise—a satanic one—or Christianity will get the upper hand (of this de Maistre has no doubt) and will establish a renovated, rejuvenated form of society, based upon theocracy. The counter-revolution will be accomplished at the hour willed by God; but it cannot fail to come.

Considérations sur la France had a great influence, especially on the émigrés. After reading it, Louis XVIII sent a gift of 50 *louis* to de Maistre and expressed the wish to see his book disseminated throughout Europe. Blacas, the favorite councillor of Louis XVIII, maintained contact with de Maistre and later, in 1817, de Maistre paid a visit to Louis XVIII in Paris.

In England, Germany, Italy and Spain the *Considérations* assumed the character of an official doctrine of the French emigration. It seemed that thenceforth the aim of the émigrés was the establishment in France of a regime more or less based upon theocracy. But in France itself the *Considérations* had little, if any, effect. Only a small number of copies could be smuggled across the frontiers into the country and few men read it.

Between 1797 and 1802 de Maistre wrote many other works which were not published until 1884, including *Etude sur la souveraineté* and *Réflexions sur le protestantisme dans ses rapports avec la souveraineté*. In the latter work, one must first of all note that de Maistre vigorously attacks Protestantism, unlike Mallet du Pan and Burke, who were Protestants. He formally condemns Protestantism which, he affirms, is an insurrection against general reason. He approves of the persecutions of Protestants by the kings of France, and he shows that results justify these persecutions. Louis XIV, who revoked the Edict of Nantes, died in his bed at the apex of his glory, whereas Louis XVI, who granted Protestants their civil rights in 1787, died on the scaffold. The persecution of Protestants, therefore, is justified.

A work entitled *Antidote du congrès de Rastadt ou Plan d'un nouvel équilibre politique en Europe* has also been attributed to de Maistre although this is contested. The work argues for a general restoration and the maintenance of the balance of power in Europe. Yet certain sentences seem to show that the author is not opposed to the unification of Italy, under the guidance of the Sardinian monarchy. For example, he says: "Piedmont must become the Prussia of Italy." Thus if this pamphlet really is by de Maistre, we would have to consider him one of the forerunners of the Risorgimento.

Between 1802 and his death in 1821, de Maistre still had a long career and wrote numerous books, perfecting his doctrine. Upon returning to Italy in 1798, he took up residence in Venice, at that time an Austrian possession. After the victory of the Austro-Russian troops in 1799, he returned to Piedmont and was appointed to an important administrative post on the island of Sardinia, and then commissioned to represent the king at the court of the czar of Russia (1802). He remained in St. Petersburg and wrote from this observatory of European politics until 1817. Among his works, three are notable: *Les Soirées de Saint-Pétersbourg*, *L'Examen de la philosophie de Bacon* and *Du pape*. The first contains a series of proposals on government, public instruction, the organization of the army and justice. The second resumes de Maistre's attacks against rationalist philosophy, and against those whom he considers its allies, the Protestants and the Jews. The third is directed against Gallicanism and thus makes de Maistre one of the champions of Ultramontanism which, in the course of the nineteenth century, was gradually to win over the whole Church of France. De Maistre also wrote an *Essai sur le principe générateur des constitutions politiques et des autres institutions humaines* in 1809, which was to be published at the time of the Restoration in 1814.[4] Here he resumed the theses already developed in the *Considérations* and in his *Etude sur la souveraineté*: the universe rests upon the "holy alliance" of politics and religion. Written constitutions are worthless; indeed, they are harmful. This work therefore was designed to combat the Charter and to support the policy of the Ultras.

After the end of his mission in St. Petersburg, de Maistre passed through Paris before returning to Chambéry. He paid a visit to Louis XVIII, but

4. See the new edition of this work by Robert Triomphe (Paris, 1958).

it turned out to be a great disappointment to him. Despite his warnings, the king had granted a Charter to France and the latter, instead of establishing a theocracy, instituted a regime which consolidated the conquests of the Revolution. Upon his return to Chambéry, de Maistre was not even appointed to an important post; he held various administrative offices of a secondary nature and died on February 26, 1821.

2 / Louis de Bonald

The other theorist of "theocracy," Louis de Bonald, was born in Millau in the Rouergue on October 20, 1754. He belonged to a noble family which had furnished numerous magistrates to the French monarchy, and he owned immense properties in the region of Millau. De Bonald pursued his studies in Paris, at first at a boarding school, later with the Oratorians at Juilly, who at that time operated one of the most famous schools in France. De Bonald wanted to be an officer and enlisted in the musketeers, an élite corps of the royal guard. But upon the dissolution of this corps in 1776, he returned to Millau and married a young lady named Guibal de Combescure. In 1787, he was appointed mayor of Millau, a post which he still held at the outbreak of the Revolution.

Initially, de Bonald seems to have been rather in favor of the Revolution. As mayor, he took the initiative on August 6, 1789, to organize a federation of the national guards of Millau, Villefranche-de-Rouergue and Rodez—the first of the federations of France.[5] De Bonald's period as mayor of Millau was very important because it gave him contact with the realities of communal administration, an experience which was to leave a deep mark on his works.

As for his plan for a federation, one may speculate on its purpose. Was he a revolutionary? The federation he proposed was certainly a result of the "Great Fear" that was spreading throughout the Rouergue region. But it is also possible that Bonald had a conservative and anti-revolutionary aim. This has not yet been clarified.

In July of 1790 de Bonald was elected member of the departmental assembly, which sat in Rodez; as a result, he had to tender his resignation

5. P. H. Thore, "Fédérations et Projets de fédérations dans la région toulousaine," *Ann. hist. de la Révolution française,* 1949, pp. 346–370.

as mayor of Millau. Then he underwent a rapid evolution, showing hostility to the reforms voted by the Constituent Assembly. As early as the end of 1791, after the vote of the Civil Constitution of the Clergy, he emigrated to Germany and enlisted in the army of the princes; after its dissolution, he settled in Heidelberg, where he read voraciously, particularly the works of Leibniz, which exerted a great influence on him.

He drew on these readings and on his meditations for his principal work, published anonymously in Constance in 1796 under the title *Théorie du pouvoir politique et religieux dans la société civile, démontrée par le raisonnement et par l'histoire*, "by M. de B . . . French gentleman."

It is an austere, ponderous, difficult work to read, in contrast to those of de Maistre, which are written in a brilliant style. It is a study which, like de Maistre's *Considérations*, furnishes the counter-revolution with a doctrine. But de Bonald's *Théorie du pouvoir*, consisting of three very abstract tomes claiming to be a complete exposition of an entire political, social and religious system, is much more voluminous than de Maistre's *Considérations*.

For the convenience of study, *Théorie du pouvoir* can be divided into four major parts, in which de Bonald studies the role of religion in the State; the place and formation of society; the place of the individual in society; and, finally, power, which is the end product of his theory. For de Bonald everything is geometric: his reasoning is mathematical and his book a veritable pyramid, whose summit is power defined.

First of all, religion. It dominates everything and is the feature that brings de Bonald close to de Maistre: "God is the author of all the states; man can do nothing over man save through God and owes nothing to man save for God."

He too is very hostile to Protestantism, with which he had been in contact because there were many Protestants in the Rouergue and in the town of Millau. "The Reformation," writes de Bonald, "divided religious society and it has brought the same disorder into political society." The Reformation therefore is the fountainhead of the Revolution because Catholic truth sustains social unity; if this social unity is broken, it is because of the rupture of religious unity.

Secondly, society. For de Bonald, as for de Maistre, society is formed when a constitution can be drawn up from its history. Accordingly, de Bonald distinguishes two forms of societies: the constituted society and the nonconstituted society. The constituted society excludes the "absurd" notion of a written constitution, unless this written constitution is the transcription of a pre-existent constitution drawn from history. A written constitution is necessary only in nonconstituted societies. These non-constituted societies are despotic, aristocratic or democratic societies. But the society par excellence, the constituted society, is the "royal, monarchical society."

There is no need to write the constitution of such a society; it imposes itself by its natural force. Political society has one constitution and religious society another, and the combination of these two constitutions constitutes civil society; both constitutions result from the nature of the beings who make up each of the two societies, "as necessarily as gravity results from the nature of bodies." Thus de Bonald condemns all written constitutions, beginning with that of the United States. He believes that the written constitution of the United States will very rapidly lead that country towards ruin.

Thirdly, the individual. The individual has only duties—no rights. He has duties toward human nature, toward society and toward God, who envelops all. The Revolution must come to a close with a Declaration of the Rights of God, which will nullify the Declaration of the Rights of Man. The right of the people to self-government is a challenge to all truth: the truth is that the people has the right to be governed.

De Bonald condemns any individualist philosophy that ends in what he calls modern society, formed of grains of sand—an image that was to influence Bonaparte, who took it up again and tried to effect an agglomeration of these grains of sand. Men must return to the ancient society, a society formed of social groups and of families. Here we note the influence of Montesquieu's "intermediary bodies," which de Bonald has transformed into social groups. The family is the original society. The first nucleus of society is a society constituted between man and man, a society which de Bonald calls domestic and which is formed of a trinity—de Bonald has a fondness for the triadic division—father, mother and child.

Families form social groups. Over the families de Bonald places the professions that group them, then the corporations that group the professions. The totality of all these social groups forms the society of production and of public conservation.

De Bonald despises men of letters. He believes they have been presumptuous in wanting to place the individual at the center of society. Society ought to be formed of numerous groups or intermediate bodies.

Finally, at the summit of the pyramid, at the summit of society, resides power.

"There is no public society except royal monarchy." De Bonald uses these two words ("royal monarchy") which, he says, do not constitute a pleonasm. And by the phrase "absolute and hereditary royal monarchy," de Bonald signifies that he excludes despotic monarchy, which knows neither restraint nor rule, and elective monarchy, which he condemns because, in fact, it means a republic and a democracy.

The royal monarchy is incarnated in power, whose characteristics are to be unique, indivisible, general, independent and absolute. Accordingly, de Bonald rejects the separation of powers, the balance of powers and mixed government, that is, constitutional government with a deliberative assembly. He calls any mixed government "political polygamy,"

> the power must be independent of the subjects, but not of the laws, because if it is independent of the laws it becomes despotic and if it is dependent on the subjects it becomes democratic. . . . The subjects must be subjected to the action of the power; if not, the subjects would be power and the power subject.

Thus de Bonald was to become the chief theorist of the Ultras, like de Maistre, after 1814. The royal monarchy must be organized according to the triadic system so dear to de Bonald: the king at the summit, at the base the subjects, and between the two the mediators, who are the ministers.

Then he poses the question, Who will prevent the power from becoming despotic, from being independent of the law? And his answer is that there is a built-in prevention in the way the laws are drawn up. In a monarchy the king makes the law but he does not make it alone. He is assisted by the councils, the mediators, the ministers, the complaints that come from the subjects and by the remonstrances addressed to him by the courts of justice. Thus the intermediary bodies, which include precisely these courts of justice and the local institutions, play a vital role, that of restraint. It is the intermediary bodies that prevent the royal monarchy from becoming despotic. Napoleon, who insisted on the importance of intermediary bodies, seems to have made careful note of all this part of the development of de Bonald's thought.

But among these intermediary bodies, de Bonald attaches particular importance to the commune, and here we see the former mayor of Millau reappearing. The commune is the principal body among the intermediary bodies; but not the urban commune, because de Bonald condemns the city, industry and industrial concentration, of which he has but a vague notion. For him the ideal commune is the rural one, the commune formed of peasants who "expect everything from God," whereas workers "receive everything from man." The rural commune furnishes the ideal framework within which the family and the social group can expand; it is directed by the notables and is the model of the constituted society. And the totality of rural communes forms the constituted society, governed by the royal, hereditary and absolute monarchic power.

Almost immediately after the publication of his book, de Bonald returned clandestinely to France and managed to re-enter Montpellier, make his way to Paris and inquire about the impact made by his book. He was acquainted with a police officer, who led him to the offices of the Ministry of Police and showed him a stack of copies of *Théorie du pouvoir* mixed higgedly-piggedly with other works of pornographic or anti-governmental character. "I ended up in really bad company," said de Bonald. In point of fact *Théorie du pouvoir* was as little known in France, at least at that time, as de Maistre's *Considérations*.

However, men like Fontanes who were to play a great role under the Empire read and meditated on *Théorie du pouvoir*. Chateaubriand also read it and, it is said, Napoleon, who brought it along with him on the Italian campaign of 1800 and ran through it while crossing the Great Saint Bernard Pass. Napoleon is also supposed then to have written to de Bonald offering to republish the book at State expense, but de Bonald, who distrusted Bonaparte, refused.

Nevertheless, de Bonald remained in France. Soon, owing to the indulgence of Napoleon, he resumed his name and again took up residence in Millau, where he was to remain until the end of his days. He published still other works, notably *L'Essai analytique sur la loi naturelle de l'ordre social* . . . , in 1797, *Du divorce considéré au XIXe siècle relativement à l'état domestique et à l'état public de la société* and *La Législation primitive considérée dans les derniers temps par les seules lumières de la raison*. As these merely repeat the ideas expressed in *Théorie du pouvoir*, there is no point in analyzing them here.

In 1808 Napoleon summoned de Bonald to the Council of the University; he refused at first but accepted in 1810. In 1814, Louis XVIII appointed him to the higher Council of Public Instruction. In 1815, he was elected deputy from Aveyron and was responsible for the abolition of the divorce law, in conformity with the book he had published. In 1823 de Bonald was appointed peer of France. During the period of the Restoration, he delivered numerous addresses and published several further works, in particular *Observations sur les "Considérations de la Révolution française de Mme de Staël"* in 1818, and in 1827 *Les Démonstrations philosophiques du principe constitutif des sociétés.* The latter was his last book. In 1830 he refused to take an oath of loyalty to the bourgeois monarchy of Louis Philippe, resigned from the peerage and kept only the title of member of the Académie française which had been bestowed on him in 1816 by an ordinance of Louis XVIII. He remained silent, faithful to his king and to his ideas. Jules Simon has said of him: "M. de Bonald never sold himself, he was never anybody's fawner, not even of his political friends; his love for legitimate power, his hatred of freedom constantly guided his whole conduct." And Lamartine declared: "He was indulgent and gentle like men who believe themselves to be the certain and infallible possessors of truth."

De Bonald died in 1840.

Clearly, de Maistre and de Bonald shared a considerable similarity because of the similarity of many points of their doctrine, theocracy. Indeed, de Maistre himself wrote to de Bonald: "I have never thought anything that you had not previously written, nor written anything that you had not previously thought." But there are distinct differences between them.

De Maistre is a brilliant writer, varied, lively. De Bonald, on the other hand, is an austere person whose works are abstract, ponderous, metaphysical. De Bonald lives outside reality, he is even a romantic. Both men deplore the fact that the Old Regime has disappeared forever and outline a new regime, whose essential features are borrowed from the Old Regime, but which nevertheless would be very different from it.

Both are very hostile to Protestantism and to the Revolution. They defend Catholicism above all else; later the monarchy exclusively; and both are deeply opposed to the primacy of the individual. They fight for the primacy of the family and of society over the individual. They create a kind of social science, a sociology of theocracy, made in the image and for the use of conservatives. This sociology is based upon pseudo-scientific reasonings because de Bonald and de Maistre constantly refer to history and to the exact sciences.

Both were to enjoy their greatest successes under the Restoration, after 1814. Their ideas had deeply influenced the émigrés and were taken up by the Ultras, to whom they seemed to represent the supreme goal of the counter-revolution.

CHAPTER VII

The German Counter-Revolutionary Theorists

In Germany, the counter-revolutionary tendencies were linked to deep currents, preceding the Revolution.

Germany in the second half of the eighteenth century, in fact, was profoundly divided between two tendencies: a rationalist one, the tendency of the Enlightenment (in German, the *Aufklärung*) and a mystical, irrational one.

Whereas in France rationalism very largely predominated, in Germany mysticism held sway in public opinion. It lay just beneath the surface, ever ready to reappear. And even before the Revolution, a German writer, Johann Gottfried von Herder, had allotted a very important place in his work to irrationalism.

1 / Herder and Möser

It is necessary here to recall several of Herder's ideas which are at the basis of German counter-revolutionary thought.

Herder was born in Prussia in 1740. He pursued his studies in Königsberg, where he attended Kant's lectures; subsequently, he became a pastor and a professor. He traveled in France, visiting Nantes and Paris. Later, he went to Strasbourg, where he became an intimate friend of Goethe.

After having been a tutor in Germany, he obtained rather inferior employment as pastor in the tiny village of Buckeburg. At that time he was in a state of total disenchantment, feeling that his merits were not being properly appreciated. But finally he obtained the more important post of superintendent of the Protestant church of Weimar, then the capital of the Enlightenment in Germany, the city where Goethe had taken up residence.

This review of Herder's life is indispensable to an understanding of his ideas. The first of Herder's two fundamental works, published in 1774 and bearing the title *Auch eine Philosophie der Geschichte zur Bildung der Menschheit* (*Another Philosophy of History for the Education of Mankind*), is directed against rationalism in historiography; the second, which comprises several volumes, is entitled *Ideen zur Philosophie der Geschichte der Menschheit* (*Ideas for the Philosophy of the History of Man*). The latter appeared from 1784 to 1791; the last volume, therefore, is contemporaneous with the Revolution.

In these works Herder reacts against the rationalism which contends that man is everywhere the same, that the person who lives in Germany, in England, in Africa, is one and the same being, from which it follows that one nation will always be similar to another. There is no originality in human groupings, it is claimed; consequently the same rules, dictated by reason, could be applied to all nations. Herder compares what he has seen in Germany with what he observed in Latvia, at the time of his sojourn in Riga, and the observations he has made in France. From this comparison he arrives at the conclusion that each group of men is in fact different from every other, that each nationality is characterized by a particular spirit, which he calls "*Volksgeist*," a difficult word to translate, but approximated by the expression "national spirit" or "national character."

So the national spirit animates the nation. Herder compares the *Volksgeist* to an animated being, a plant that grows, blooms and withers. Thus there is a life of national groupings, of "nationalities." The *Volksgeist*, says Herder, "is singular, marvelous, inexplicable, ineffable." In other words, it eludes any explanation through reason. It is as ancient as the national grouping itself, and evolves with this grouping; and its withering and death mark the end of the national grouping.

If the *Volksgeist* cannot be explained rationally, how are we to grasp it? In the phenomena of history, Herder answers, and thereby joins company to a certain extent with the explanations that were to be given by the historicists, and notably Burke.

The *Volksgeist* is expressed through language, literature, religion, the arts, customs; through the Anglo-Saxon word "folklore." It follows therefore that two nations cannot have the same *Volksgeist*, the same national culture, and that consequently the rules that are applied to one nation are not valid for another. Laws must be adapted to the spirit of each nation. Thus Herder abandons the rationalist philosophy, having subjected it to a keen criticism. He is staunchly opposed to all that rationalism, which is cosmopolite and universalist in character, asserts. In contrast, he believes in particularism.

Herder elaborates extensively on an idea borrowed from Montesquieu, namely, that man is the product of the land which he inhabits, of the climate in which he has developed and of the circumstances which have marked his life. The rationalists, he thinks, have not properly understood Montesquieu, whom they invoke so often, because they have not attached enough importance to his theory of climates. If a nationality is to flourish, it must be sheltered from external influences because these can modify the national spirit.

Consequently, when the Revolution breaks out in France Herder demands that Germany shield herself against revolutionary propaganda. He is very hostile to the idea of the free choice of populations. Revolutionary France, as we know, had proclaimed the right of the people to self-determination and, as a beginning, had applied this to the population of Avignon, which had asked for unification with France.

Herder views the free self-determination of populations as a worthless doctrine because the destiny of national groups is fixed by imperatives beyond popular modification. These imperatives are race (Herder did not formulate a theory of race, but to a certain extent he can be considered as a forerunner of modern racism), language, tradition and natural frontiers—he believes in the natural frontiers bequeathed by Providence. "It must be learned that one cannot become a man except on native ground," he writes, whence the importance of the ideas of nation, of Fatherland, which Herder elaborates at length. The greatest of human virtues, according to him, is dedicated service to one's native land. History therefore must play a preponderant role in education: it must show how the Fatherland evolved in time and, as a result, it must be essentially national, even nationalistic. Thus Herder feels that the history of the Middle Ages has not been given the weight it ought to have. In the eighteenth century, priority was given to the study of ancient and modern history. Herder redeemed the history of the Middle Ages and broadened the general concept of history. In the eighteenth century, except for a few men like Voltaire, history was perforce essentially political history. For Herder, history is a history of the totality of "culture"; it must treat of the language, customs, religion and folklore.

Thus Herder predisposed the German theorists to take a hostile stance toward the rationalism of the Revolution. His influence, however, does not explain everything; there were other theorists in Germany besides Herder and we must also bear in mind Burke's influence.

Herder wrote general works, a philosophy of history. Justus Möser wrote a history in which he applied not Herder's ideas, with which he became acquainted only later, but his own, admittedly similar.

Möser was born in Osnabrück in 1720; he died in 1794 in this same city where he had pursued his whole career. A lawyer, then representative of the city to the provincial estates, he later fulfilled the function of secretary-general of the city which, in fact, placed him in charge of administration.

He took a keen interest in the history of his tiny Fatherland and in 1780 published *Osnabrückische Geschichte* (*History of Osnabrück*). In this *History*, he showed how the community of Osnabrück, in the eighteenth century, could be explained only through its past. This was easy to maintain because at that time the institutions of Osnabrück were a tangle of customs and traditions which had been superimposed on each other in the course of the ages, without any of the new accretions supplanting the previous mores. Thus Möser showed that in Osnabrück, the freedom and equality of all the landed proprietors lay at the base of the constitution. This freedom, this equality, were explained by the ancient Germanic constitution, in which men were free and equal.

There was in Osnabrück, however, a whole hierarchy of men, lords and vassals. Möser explains this hierarchy by the evolution of Germany in the Middle Ages. All the lords had been the defenders of their subjects, which justifies the hierarchy. We find in Osnabrück a charter of the Middle Ages which grants communal liberties to the city. This city has also been a setting for the opposition between Church and State, between the bishop and his chapter, between the Reformation and the counter-reformation. Osnabrück therefore, according to Möser, is a kind of microcosm reflecting the whole of German history.

In another work entitled *Patriotische Phantasien* (*Patriotic Fantasies*) Möser expands these ideas and shows that they are valid for vaster territories, indeed, for the whole of Germany.

Like Herder, he believes that as regards a people, religion, language, institutions, law, beliefs, even the most secret customs—those which are the least expounded in books—explain the totality of behavior of a national group; he also believes in the existence of the *Volksgeist*, a national, creative spirit, which characterizes the group. Institutions, therefore, cannot be modified according to the whims of the legislator without the risk of completely transforming the national spirit, possibly even causing its destruction, and creating great disturbances.

So the statesman must above all respect historical evolution, tradition and the essential element in this tradition, which is landed property. For Möser, the strength of a state resides in the power of the institutions that regulate landed property. It is the rural class that gives the State strength and assures its continuity. But by rural class Möser understands the class of large landed proprietors, that is, in most cases nobles, or, at least, large bourgeois proprietors. The peasants are subject to these nobles and in Möser's view do not form the rural class.

Möser demands that, as far as possible, studied efforts should be made to maintain landed property. In contrast to the rationalists, who demand the abolition of the *fidei commissum*—that is, the provision of law which permits landed property to be transmitted from heir to heir without reduction in size—Möser recommends that the *fidei commissum* be made obligatory. This idea was to take root in Germany: under the Nazi regime, Hitler instituted "familial property," which was to be transmitted from generation to generation.

On the other hand, Möser is in favor of reducing the influence of commercial and economic capitalism, as well as the capitalist bureaucracy which threatens the land. He longs for a return to the institutions of primitive Germany, the Germany of free proprietors. This does not mean that he wants to see the abolition of serfdom or of the subjection of the peasants. For him, indeed, serfs and peasants subjected to feudal dues are the witnesses of an ancient epoch, the descendants of the vanquished. Accordingly, they must be kept in their present state.

When the Revolution broke out, Möser, who was a witness to it, opposed it. He considered the idea of the social contract, as expressed by Locke and later by Rousseau, erroneous. For him there was a double contract: a contract between the first occupants of the soil, free men who have become free proprietors; followed by a second contract between these first free proprietors and the newcomers. The second contract subjected the newcomers to the first occupants, and made them merchants, artisans or even serfs and slaves.

Möser condemns the work, justified by history, of the Constituent

Assembly, which suppressed all feudal dues, secularized the properties of the Church and thus abolished sacred traditions. He denounces the Declaration of the Rights of Man, believing that rights of man are a usurpation. The mass ought not to enjoy political rights; only the descendants of free men should be permitted to exercise them.

The State cannot be built upon a concept of humanity inherited from Christianity; the only possible basis is that of the double contract, which dominates history. Society therefore must be structured hierarchically, each class having its privileges which are granted to it in function of the role that it exercises in the State.

No doubt Möser was not entirely opposed to reform. In particular, he thought that the nobility should be reformed but in the sense of a return to the past, to tradition. The land-owning nobility must return to its role of protecting the peasants, whether subjects or serfs.

Thus Möser enters the lists as a foe, at once passionate and realistic, of the philosophy of the Enlightenment, which he sees as a philosophy of convenience that replaces the "perspicacity of the historian."

"The modern theories have undermined all established contracts, privileges and liberties, obligations and prescriptions in order to deduce, starting from a single formula, the set of rights which rules social life. . . . Speculative and reasoning philosophy has committed the fault of abstracting man from the society in which he lives to consider him in isolation." This reasoning has often found new exponents. Möser believes that in deducing the rules of right from pure reason, one opens up "the path to despotism, which is content with a few universal maxims and sacrifices the richness and diversity of particular rights."

Such were the essential ideas of these two precursors of the struggle against the Revolution in Germany. They probably would not have had the influence they did if their work had not been complemented by the influence of Burke's *Reflections*.

2 / Burke's Influence in Germany: Brandes and Rehberg

Burke's work, in fact, had a very great impact in Germany. After England, *Reflections on the Revolution in France* probably received its best reception in Germany. The translation in 1791 of the *Reflections* by Friedrich von Gentz, whose work we shall study later, greatly helped to spread Burke's influence. The important German periodicals—of which there were many—published exhaustive reviews of the work. Those of rationalist tendency were very reserved, particularly *Allgemeine deutsche Bibliothek*. Georges Forster, librarian to the bishop of Mayence and at that time a very well known figure in Germany, dealt severely with Burke's *Reflections*. A number of reviews, however, gave the English politician a cordial reception. In Hanover, particularly, the book was well received; this should occasion no surprise inasmuch as Hanover had as sovereign the king of England and was closely linked to Great Britain in the eighteenth century. The Hanoverian dynasty had been ruling over the two countries for almost a century. Hanover, bordering on the North Sea, was a maritime region which, by degrees, had merged its economic interests with those of England. The Hanoverian constitution had evolved since the departure of the sovereigns for London. Their absence had left a great margin of freedom to the provincial estates and, to a certain extent, the country's political organization approximated that of Great Britain. In fact, since the beginning of the eighteenth century it had been conceded that laws were valid in Hanover only after approbation by the provincial estates. These estates were dominated by the nobility and could be likened to the British Parliament in which the House of Lords still played an important role. As a result of the sovereign's absence, the nobility and the upper bourgeoisie had become very independent and dominated the country. Nobility and bourgeoisie alike were very hostile to despotism, even the enlightened despotism which reigned in most of the German states and particularly in neighboring Prussia.

The center of resistance to enlightened despotism, and even to the Enlightenment, was the University of Hanover located in Göttingen. This university had been founded by the English sovereigns in 1735. It differed from the older German universities because its paramount purpose was to study concrete facts, to develop practical research and to focus on the study of institutions, history and positive branches of learning, rather than on philosophy, metaphysics or theoretical law.

The students of the University of Göttingen were prepared in a practical manner for the functions they would have to exercise in the State of Hanover. At the end of the eighteenth century and at the time of the Revolution, remarkable professors lectured at Göttingen, such as August Ludwig von Schlözer, or L. T. Spittler, a specialist in the history of religions. These two men shared a common feature in their attitude of extreme reserve toward the French Revolution, in contrast to the professors at most of the German universities. Schlözer had already taken a position against the American Revolution. In the Staats-anzeigen in 1789, he extolled the ideas of Malouet, leader of the "monarchicals." Spittler in the *Göttingische Gelehrte Anzeigen* discussed in laudatory terms Necker's *Le Pouvoir exécutif* and, in particular, published an excellent review of Burke's *Reflections*.

The physics professor, Lichtenberg, violently attacked the work of the French Revolution. He treated the revolutionaries as vandals, and claimed that liberty and equality had been raised in France to the level of the eleventh commandment by people bent upon ridding themselves of the first ten. Men can feel a personal sense of attachment to their sovereign, but they are not capable of obeying the law, he stated. He was convinced that kings had been disposed of not because they were tyrants, but because people no longer wished to obey them, and he praised the British constitution.

Thus the great majority of the professors at Göttingen were favorably disposed to Burke's ideas and studied the works of Herder and Möser with sympathy. But among the Hanoverians who shared Burke's ideas two men in particular, through their works, contributed more than the others to spreading these ideas in Germany and thereby effectively fought against the Revolution. They were Ernst Brandes and August Wilhelm Rehberg.

Brandes was born in Hanover in 1758. His father was rector of the University of Göttingen, where Brandes later became a student and was to succeed his father. Accordingly, he is almost wholly identified with the university. He did however travel to England before the Revolution, and in 1785, in the course of a journey to London, he made the acquaintance of Burke. In 1791 Burke's son, in his turn, made a journey to Germany. Brandes was commissioned to receive him and to accompany him as far as Coblenz, where Richard Burke held talks with some French émigrés.

In 1786, upon his return from London, Brandes had published a laudatory article on the English constitution in the *Neue Deutsche Monatschrift*; in 1791, after Richard Burke's journey, he published *Politische Betrachtungen über die französische Revolution* (*Political Considerations on the French Revolution*), which betrays the influence of Burke's *Reflections*.

However, it should not be implied that the *Betrachtungen* was a mere copy of the *Reflections*. It was almost entirely written when the *Reflections* appeared on the German scene, and the publication of the translation of Burke's *Reflections* led Brandes to make only a few corrections in his *Betrachtungen*.

Brandes deals with the following three points in this work: First, was it necessary to go so far as to effect a sweeping change in the French constitution? Second, was this change necessarily to be accompanied by a revolution? And third, is the constitution of France properly modeled on the nature of the French State?

Brandes replies in the affirmative to the first two questions and thereby sets himself considerably apart from Burke. He feels that the outbreak of the Revolution in France was inevitable because in France, in contrast to what was happening in England, the people did not participate in the legislative power and the king alone legislated. The old constitution of France, therefore, was bad.

The Revolution was necessary, Brandes thinks, because the court had committed numerous mistakes. The dismissal of Necker, in particular, was the gravest of these and was bound to provoke an armed revolt. The nation believed its legitimate representatives, the deputies, threatened by the king; it was inevitable that it should revolt in order to give itself a new constitution.

But to the third question Brandes replies in the negative. He thinks that the Constitution of 1791 does not conform to the nature of the French nation, because the deputies were not ready to draw up a constitution. The French deputies to the Estates General, according to Brandes, did not sufficiently understand political science. They were for the most part judges or barristers, who were not in possession of sufficient culture; very few of these men knew anything about the English constitution which, in Brandes's view, should be taken as a model. Very few of them had traveled to England or read any works on the British constitution. Very few had read or understood Montesquieu; on the contrary, most of them were disciples of Rousseau. Says Brandes: "It is the Rousseau-American-economist clique which dominates the Constituent Assembly," meaning that the disciples of Rousseau and of the physiocrats dominated the Assembly and that this was not entirely wrong.

"The great mistake of the deputies," he writes, "was that of wanting to draw up a constitution based upon reason and not upon experience." Here we see Brandes join company with Herder, Möser and especially Burke. "They destroyed everything," he says, "before knowing what they would put in its place." There are some institutions that should have been suppressed, but others can be transformed. Abstraction is the great fault of the deputies to the Constituent Assembly, and especially of Mirabeau, to whom Brandes attributes an influence which in point of fact he did not have.

The great fault of the Constitution of 1791 is to have established the dictatorship of the Legislative Assembly—and here Brandes is very perceptive. He believes that the deputies overvalued the separation of powers extolled by Montesquieu. He also criticizes the suspensive veto, which greatly weakened the executive power, and the nomination of ministers obligatorily recruited outside the Assembly. In his view, this mode of nomination destroys the unity and harmony that ought to exist between the executive and the legislative power.

He criticizes the prohibition imposed on the king by the constitution to appoint most of the functionaries who, as we know, were elected under the regime of the Constitution of 1791. The election of judges in particular strikes Brandes as a great political heresy.

To be sure, Brandes opposes the system of a single chamber; he prefers the bi-cameral system. He thinks the creation of a House of Lords would have usefully compensated the nobles for the nullification of their privileges. He denounces the brevity of session of the legislatures, which ran for two years; and he criticizes the imperative mandate. But here he perpetuates an error (one also made by Rehberg, as we shall see) because the Constitution of 1791 was explicit on this point. In Section 3, Article 7, the constitution clearly states: "The liberty of the opinions of the representatives shall not be constricted by any mandate," which, by definition, excludes any imperative mandate. But Brandes had believed that the deputies would be furnished with imperative mandates which (unaware of his mistake) he denounces. His criticism of the brevity of the sessions is another mistake because the sessions were often protracted. More rightly, he criticizes the fact that it was impossible for the deputies to form genuine parties. In France in 1791, any grouping of deputies was considered a "faction" in the pejorative sense of the word. Until 18 Brumaire, although nonconstituted parties existed, public opinion was always hostile to them. Finally, he denounces the constant intervention of the public in the sessions of the assembly, and here he was again correct. As we know, the public applauded, at times even shouted, and thus influenced the voting.

In conclusion, Brandes says: "One cannot help regarding this new constitution as a metaphysical experiment, which looks very well in speculation; but we can hardly expect the experiment, as it has been made, to acquire a durable constancy in reality."

Thus he appears as a somewhat impartial observer. He is much less violently against the Revolution than Burke, or even Mallet du Pan. Above all, he does not condemn the Revolution; he considers it inevitable and even necessary, and condemns only the orientation it has taken. He approves the decrees of August 4 and the Declaration of the Rights of Man; he was even to approve the Civil Constitution of the Clergy of 1791. But he condemns the fundamental elements of the Constitution of 1791. In short, minus the violence, his position is close to that of Mallet du Pan and the "monarchicals."

Brandes, however, evolved in step as the Revolution progressed, and in the book which he published in 1792 under the title *Uber einige bisherige Folgen der franzosische Revolution in Rucksicht auf Deutschland* (*On Some Existing Consequences of the French Revolution in Relation to Germany*), he shows more hostility toward the Revolution.

This second work is much more deeply marked by Burke's influence than the first. Brandes asserts that the State must not take any measure that might weaken traditional beliefs, attachment to the existing order of things or respect for the past as such. Accordingly, he condemns the work of the Constituent Assembly in a more total and categorical way than he had done before.

But the Revolution is encroaching; there has been a considerable development of revolutionary propaganda in Germany and henceforth Brandes is more concerned about Germany than France. He recognizes that "enlightened" opinion in Germany is, for the most part, favorable to the revolutionary ideology. So he believes it urgent that Germans react against this tendency, failing which the Revolution will soon develop in their country. This is why his stricture of the Constitution of 1791 is more severe than in his first book: the constitution has taken no account of the national character of the people, it has respected neither the old customs nor the traditional relations with foreign countries.

In this work he denies the necessity and legitimacy of the Revolution, which he had conceded in the *Betrachtungen*. In conclusion, he thinks that the Revolution may have been useful for France, but that it is unquestionably dangerous for Germany.

Rehberg, a friend of Brandes, was to develop similar ideas. The son of a high functionary, he himself was to have a functionary's career in

Hanover. On the advice of Brandes, he had studied the British constitution as early as 1780; in 1783 he was appointed secretary to the bishop of Osnabrück and made the acquaintance of Möser.

In 1790 Rehberg was commissioned as literary critic of French books by an important German review, the *Allgemeine literatur-zeitung*. Thenceforth, he regularly reviewed books which were being published in France, especially those dealing with the Revolution.

He published a work in 1793, *Untersuchungen über die französische Revolution* (*Investigations Concerning the French Revolution*), which is a synthesis of all these critical reviews. It is Rehberg's principal work on the Revolution, and in it he studies three problems: first, the idea of natural law, the basis of the Revolution; second, the political legislation of the Constituent Assembly; and third, the social legislation of this Assembly.

In the first part, Rehberg applies himself at length to refuting the idea of natural right which presupposes that man lives independently of his past and his milieu; that man, at all points of the globe and whatever his color, his race, his past, is always equal. For Rehberg, men are different from one another, and bound to their past.

Man cannot be considered in isolation. He must be studied within the sequence of generations. Man is the sum of all his ancestors and of all his descendants. Consequently, he cannot commit himself by a contract because this commits his past, his ancestors, and even his children who, most probably, will not accept such a contract. Thus Rehberg is opposed to contracts, and therefore to constitutions, above all constitutions which have a simplistic appearance and are marked by a great clarity. The genuine constitutions are those that can be deduced from the past; they are necessarily complicated and particular to each people. A constitution that is valid for one people cannot be applied to another.

Rehberg concedes the equality of men, but an equality before God. On earth, men are unequal because it is absolutely impossible that all should accede to property. Proprietors are superior to those who possess nothing. Properties being transmissible, the same should apply to political rights: if it is conceded that only proprietors should have political rights, it logically follows that only their descendants will be endowed with them. Thus inequality must perpetuate itself.

The second point is a criticism of the political work of the Constituent Assembly very like that which had been formulated by Brandes. Nevertheless, it differs in several precisely defined developments.

Rehberg dwells on the will of the sovereign people. "The will of the sovereign people is not necessarily good," he states, "because the people is an uneducated and apathetic multitude; moreover, what is called 'the will of the people' is in reality only the will of some people; the mass follows." For Rehberg, liberty and equality signify only the coming to power of the lower classes and resultant anarchy. In France the bourgeoisie fancied that it could make the Revolution to its advantage; it was mistaken and the outcome was the advent of the popular masses, terror, pillage. Here Rehberg resumes all the criticism already formulated by Brandes against the work of the Constituent Assembly, the separation of powers which he deems excessive, the veto, the election of functionaries and magistrates, the selection of ministers from outside the Assembly, the overly large number of electors and the division between active and passive citizens, none of which satisfies him. He criticizes the permanence of the Assembly and the brevity of the sessions of the legislatures, and commits the same error as Brandes in believing that the deputies had received an imperative mandate. He concludes his criticism by a comparison of the English and French deputies, a comparison which is wholly to the advantage of the former.

The third part of the work is a criticism of the social work of the Constituent Assembly. First of all, its work in the field of religion. Rehberg condemns the Civil Constitution of the Clergy which Brandes had approved, because its only aim was "to extirpate the Christian religion in France." He condemns the sale of the properties of the clergy because the result will be a greater insecurity and instability of property.

As regards the nobility, Rehberg shared Brandes's view that it should be reformed, that it possesses a certain number of unjustified privileges that are outmoded and ought to be abolished. But it is not necessary to strip it of political power. The nobles should be gathered in a House of Lords. For Rehberg, the nobility remains the first class of the nation.

In conclusion, he does not censure the whole work of the Revolution. Some reforms were necessary, but they ought to have been effected by taking into account tradition and not by making a tabula rasa of the past. Rehberg, in short, is more hostile to the Revolution than Brandes, but less so than Burke. He could be placed alongside Mallet du Pan. Rehberg, perhaps, had a greater influence in Germany than Brandes because he contributed to the founding of the German school of historical law, which, with such men as Savigny and Stahl, achieved great fame in the nineteenth century. This was the school of historical right that formulated the doctrine of German conservatism during the second half of the nineteenth century and the first half of the twentieth. It engendered distrust toward intellectuals and rationalists, respect for the sovereign and the established authorities, defense of property in all its forms, the apologia of the role of the nobility and a growing contempt for liberty—even of the English variety—and for equality, which it viewed as absurd.

3 / Friedrich von Gentz

We shall now briefly discuss Friedrich von Gentz, Burke's translator, who has often been called the German Burke.

Gentz cannot be put in the same category as Brandes and Rehberg. He was not a Hanoverian, but a Prussian. He was born in Breslau in 1764. A remarkably intelligent man, of great lucidity of mind, he learned French, which he used perfectly, at a very young age. At the outset of his career he had been a faithful disciple of the *Aufklärung*, and in 1791 in the *Neue deutsche Monatsschrift* he published a violent criticism of Möser in the name of Kant, whom he had studied and revered.

But as early as the end of 1791 we see Gentz shifting his position. At that time he was a Prussian functionary and read Burke's *Reflections*, which he translated into German. The reasons for Gentz's change have been the object of much discussion: it has been said that he was paid by Austria, that his friends had exerted great influence on him. But the fact of the matter seems to be that the reading of Burke's *Reflections* alone converted him into a foe of the Revolution.

At all events, as early as April, 1791, he was writing his friend Garve: "As prejudiced as I am against its principles and conclusions, I am reading this book with infinitely more pleasure than one hundred insipid panegyrics of the Revolution. For I always prefer the voices of those of my adversaries who have real worth to the voices of those who share my views." Thus Gentz read Burke with prejudice but also with pleasure, and from then on we see him gradually draw closer to the latter's position.

Gentz published his translation in 1793. He wrote a preface for it which marks the evolution of his thought: "The abuse of knowledge," he says, "can be as disastrous for humanity as was ignorance. . . . There is no sword more formidable than a general principle in the hands of a man without instruction. The philosopher formulates systems, the populace forges weapons of death." This evolution is easy to understand. The

Revolution in France had developed toward a new stage since 1791. The fall of the throne, the September massacres, the Terror, all left their mark on Gentz's mind.

The translation of Burke is accompanied by four memoirs. The subject of one is political freedom and the comportment of governments; of the second, the Declaration of the Rights of Man. The third is a criticism of MacKintosh, who, as has been said, was one of Burke's first foes. The fourth treats of the national movement in France.

These four memoirs show that Gentz has already become a foe of the Revolution. But the shift is even more marked in the translation of Mallet du Pan's book, *Considérations sur la Révolution de France*, which he published in 1794. In his preface, Gentz claimed this work to be the most profound and powerful ever written. Earlier we said that it could be placed alongside Burke's *Reflections*.

In 1795 Gentz published a translation of a book by Mounier, *Les Recherches sur les causes qui ont empêché les Français de devinir libres, et sur les moyens qui leur restent pour acquérir cette liberté*; in the same year he also published in the German review *Minerva* two articles on the thought of Robespierre and Saint-Just, which he studied with great objectivity. Finally, in 1799, Gentz, in a journal founded by him, *Historisches Journal*, undertook a chronicle meant to be similar to the one which Mallet du Pan published in *Le Mercure de France* in 1789 and in *Le Mercure britannique* in 1798.

In 1801 Gentz wrote the *Essay on the Financial Policy and National Wealth of Great Britain*, which was followed by *Uber den Ursprung und Charakter des Krieges gegen die französische Revolution (Origin and Character of the War Against the French Revolution)*.

What are the ideas that Gentz develops in all these works? They are marked by the fundamental notion of balance of power. This was Gentz's great guiding idea, and he was to see its triumph when he became Metternich's most respected and consulted councillor, after 1814, in establishing the balance of Europe. To a great measure, "Metternich's system" is Gentz's system.

This equilibrium must be developed both inside and outside states.

In domestic policy, the balance must be found through wisdom, and Gentz sets wisdom over against law. Law can establish justice between individuals; wisdom, on the other hand, must effect the reign of well-being. In the name of wisdom Gentz criticizes the excessive separation of powers established in France, distinguishing between political liberty, which he would limit, and civil liberty, which in his view should be total. The notion of equality must be replaced by the notion of equilibrium, between classes and between individuals.

In foreign policy, Gentz considers that a stable peace can be established in Europe only within a system of checks and balances. Gentz, until 1800, was neither a nationalist nor a pacifist; he was still a cosmopolitan, a man of the eighteenth century. He reproves the patriots, saying: "No, Robespierre, love of country will not be awakened in this age of maturity, almost senility, in which humanity finds itself." He thinks patriotism and nationalism are outdated. He condemns the idea of nation and even more that of the "great nation." It is essential to establish a European balance of power through an agreement among the big powers or alliances of powers. This will have the double merit of maintaining peace and taking due account of the development that happens constantly within states.

But such a balance could not be realized at that time. From 1796 onwards, France became increasingly more powerful, increasingly more encroaching; and at that time Gentz felt that the first condition for the establishing of the balance he desired was the destruction of French power. But this could not be accomplished without the aid of England, true home of coalition. Hence Gentz was a passionate Anglophile. He extolled England, the British constitution and the strength of Great Britain in the works that appeared in 1801, and urged all the European powers to rally around England. Since Prussia at that period was practicing a neutralist policy, rather favorable to France and hostile to England, Gentz resigned from his post. Shortly afterwards he was to pass into the service of Austria, which was how he met Metternich.

Gentz appears to us above all as a realist. He had been a rationalist at the beginning of his career, but one can say that later he placed "reason in the service of tradition." He believed it impossible to base politics upon morality, and thought that no reliance should be placed, as Robespierre demanded, upon the virtue of citizens in order to create a State. Balance of power alone can realize the welfare of all and maintain general peace.

The work of Brandes, Rehberg and Gentz gave rise to a movement in Germany which was to be increasingly hostile to the Revolution and increasingly conservative; eventually, it was to join company with romanticism, which had already made its debut in literature with the works of the great writers Goethe and Schiller. From 1799 onwards, romanticism was to gain ground politically with the poet Novalis, who at that time published his book *Die Christenheit oder Europa* (*Christen-*

dom or Europe). Later, this work was regarded as the breviary of the counter-revolution and, at the same time, of political romanticism because of its extolling of the Middle Ages.

Moreover, in Germany the political opposition to the Revolution was strengthened by a Protestant religious movement, pietism, the German equivalent of the Wesleyan movement in England. Pietism devoted its efforts to the re-establishment of rigorism in religion and of traditions in politics. Under Stolberg's guidance it became increasingly conservative. United to romanticism, pietism acquired a very great strength in Germany. After 1806, these three trends—conservatism, romanticism and pietism— were to awaken German nationalism, whose first expression is formulated in *Reden an die Deutsche Nation* (*Addresses to the German Nation*) delivered by Fichte in Berlin during the winter of 1807–08.

Thus the doctrinal struggle against the Revolution in Germany was to bear its fruit later, especially under the Empire. Although it developed alongside the counter-revolutionary movement in Switzerland, England and France, the fountainhead of its inspiration lies in ancient German traditions.

CHAPTER VIII

The Political Ideas of Chateaubriand Prior to 1804

Chateaubriand's ideas underwent a great variation in the course of his long life. He appears as one of the theorists of the counter-revolution, and as one of the leaders of the Ultras between 1815 and 1830. But this had not always been the case. Admittedly, he was a counter-revolutionary at the time of the Revolution and of the Consulate, but one of the most liberal of counter-revolutionaries. Between 1815 and 1830, he was undoubtedly a leader of the Ultras, but even at that time he manifested ideas very different from those of Villèle, for example. After 1830 he joined the opposition to the July monarchy, and although a legitimist, cut a liberal figure. So Chateaubriand must not be presented as a monolithic figure, who remained totally inflexible.

In this work, we shall limit ourselves to an examination of Chateaubriand's political ideas during the time of the Revolution. These were expressed essentially in a book entitled *Essai historique, politique et moral sur les Révolutions anciennes et modernes considérées dans leur rapports avec la Révolution française, dédié à tous les partis*, published anonymously in London in 1797. The anonymity, however, was quickly exposed, particularly when the *Génie du christianisme* appeared in 1802. The latter perceptibly modified Chateaubriand's views on religious questions.

But before proceeding to an analysis of these works, we shall briefly review Chateaubriand's life up to the time of publication of these two books.

1 / Chateaubriand's Life up to 1804

François de Chateaubriand was born in Saint-Malo on September 4, 1768. He was the second son of an impoverished descendant of the old nobility. His father, Réne de Chateaubriand, had made a career in the merchant marine, where he occupied menial posts. He had been a cabin boy for a long time, then a novice, before rising to the rank of lieutenant, then that of captain, which he obtained only several years before his marriage in 1753 to the daughter of a Saint-Malo shipowner, Apolline de Bédée.

From the time of his marriage, René de Chateaubriand's sailing days were over; he seems to have utilized his wife's dowry to fit out vessels, with a view particularly to the slave trade. This enabled him to enrich himself considerably, and in 1761, eight years after his marriage, he purchased the château of Combourg (situated south of Saint-Malo, on the Brest to Paris highway) from a distant relative, maréchal de Duras, who belonged to the upper nobility of the court.

François was born in 1768, several years after the purchase of Combourg. But he was born in Saint-Malo. Indeed, for a long time his family did not live in the medieval château, flanked by four sturdy towers, which still exists almost unchanged.

François was put out to nurse, like many babies of that time, and spent his early youth in the tiny village of Plancoët. Thereafter he lived in Saint-Malo and, above all, at Combourg. He has left us an account of the life there that has become a classic, *Mémoires d'outre-tombe*.

His father would have liked him to enter the royal navy and make a career for himself that would be more gratifying than his own had been. At a very young age François was placed in the collège de Dol, in Brittany. He immediately ranked among the better pupils and at the end of four years was sent as a boarding student to the Jesuit school at Rennes, at that time an outstanding school. He remained at Rennes for two years, after which he was sent to Brest in the hope of obtaining a candidate's commission in the royal navy. There were no competitive examinations in those days: aspirant naval cadets were admitted by royal favor if they had the required descent from nobility, accompanied by a sufficient number of letters of recommendation.

During this period his father led an increasingly withdrawn existence at Combourg, concerned solely with the revenues from his lands, and demanding the feudal dues owed by his vassals with increased strictness. Thus René de Chateaubriand was one of the architects of the nobiliary reaction that emerged in France between 1750 and 1789. We see him asking the most extravagant honorific dues; for example, the pair of white gloves that the parishioners of Mont Dol had been under an obligation to send the lord of Combourg since the Middle Ages. This explains the hatred with which the peasants of the region pursued the Chateaubriand family during the time of the Revolution.

But what is curious is that René de Chateaubriand was not an enemy of the Enlightenment. On the contrary, he was a very assiduous reader of the *philosophes*. He was thoroughly acquainted with the works of Montesquieu and also with the *Histoire philosophique des deux Indes* by abbé Raynal, at that time the breviary of anti-colonialism. René de Chateaubriand does not seem to have been much of a believer. Although Catholic, he went to Mass only once a year, and in his general attitude he showed what could more properly be called a certain degree of anti-clericalism.

Such was the atmosphere in which François de Chateaubriand grew up. The result of his stay in Brest did not come up to his father's expectations. Lacking sufficient support, he did not obtain the naval cadet commission. Upon returning home he gave thought for a time to taking holy orders; but his older brother arranged for him to be granted a commission as a second lieutenant in the Navarre Regiment of the infantry, garrisoned at Cambrai. Accordingly, Chateaubriand left for Cambrai, passing through Paris, where he was received by his older brother, Jean-Baptiste. The latter had just married a young woman belonging to the uppermost nobility of the robe, who was held in very high esteem at the court. She was Mlle de Rosambo, daughter of the first president of the Paris Parlement and granddaughter of Malesherbes, the minister of Louis XVI, who was to assume the king's defense at the time of the trial of December, 1792.

Chateaubriand's father died in 1786. According to the laws and customs prevailing at that time among the nobility, the eldest son, Jean-Baptiste, inherited the title of lord of Combourg, as well as all the lands and the greater part of the family fortune. François, the younger son, received only the sum of 60,000 livres.

Chateaubriand spent a certain amount of time in the garrison at Cambrai but proved to be none too assiduous an officer; he was often seen in Paris at the Rosambo's or with his brother, Jean-Baptiste who, having already been introduced to the court, presented François to the king and queen in

1787. He also met the great thinkers of the age, the *philosophes*, and particularly Fontanes, still a very obscure figure at the time but who later, under the Consulate and the Empire, became very prominent and closely associated with Chateaubriand's success.

Chateaubriand was in touch with other men of letters, notably Ginguené. Above all, he had numerous conversations with Malesherbes who, although an old man at that time, was regarded as the Nestor among statesmen. Malesherbes represented what I have called the aristocratic current among the philosophico-political ideas of the eighteenth century. He was imbued with the theories of Fénelon and Montesquieu on the necessity of a dominant role for the nobility in the government. Moreover, not only had he read Rousseau, he had known him personally. Malesherbes admired Rousseau, but not without some reservations. For example, he enormously relished the feeling for nature that suffused Rousseau's works, but he criticized the notion of the social contract and, in general, Rousseau's democratic ideas. At all events, it was as a result of these conversations that Chateaubriand, like Robespierre, went off to Ermenonville, Rousseau's last home, on a pilgrimage.

It was also as a result of these conversations with Malesherbes that Chateaubriand for the first time thought of leaving for America. No doubt there was incessant talk of America in Saint-Malo, and in Brest where he had lived. The War of Independence of 1778–83 had placed large numbers of Frenchmen in contact with America. But with Chateaubriand the desire to know a new State, a free republic, was conjoined with the aspiration— borrowed from Rousseau—for contact with the man of nature, the "noble savage," eulogized by Rousseau. As early as 1788 Chateaubriand expressed to Malesherbes his desire to go to America, to become an explorer and discover the famous "Northwest Passage," for which intrepid explorers had been looking since the sixteenth century.

Chateaubriand was in Brittany when the Revolution broke out in 1789. He was linked closely to the new Breton nobility, which was in a state of extreme agitation, very rebellious and overtly very hostile to the court. Chateaubriand took part, to a slight but still discernible extent, in this phase of the Revolution, which is called the aristocratic revolution. In June of 1789 he returned to Paris just in time to witness the storming of the Bastille. This aroused great hopes in him, but also a violent repulsion. He believed that a new epoch was beginning and that great changes were in the offing, but he was horrified by the inhuman acts of cruelty. He witnessed the lynching of Bertier de Sauvigny, intendant of Paris, and declared: "I am searching again. There is nothing to be done here, the king is lost and you will not have a counter-revolution. I am doing as those puritans who, in the seventeenth century, emigrated to Virginia; I am going into the forests, that's better than going to Coblenz." Perhaps in order to avoid the obligation of taking sides for or against the Revolution and perhaps too because the ideas which he had discussed with Malesherbes in 1787 and 1788 still held him in their grip, he decided to set out for America.

He left Saint-Malo at the beginning of 1791, furnished with a letter of recommendation to George Washington written by the marquis de La Rouairie, a Breton noble who had participated in the American War of Independence and who was to play an important role in Brittany in the revolt of Vendée. Chateaubriand set sail for America on April 7, 1791, on the brigantine *Saint-Pierre*, which was transporting a group of French priests to the United States. After an uneventful crossing, he landed at Chesapeake Bay on July 11, 1791, and went to the capital, Philadelphia.

He was surprised by the extreme inequality of wealth, inasmuch as he had expected to find the greatest equality. He was also surprised by the immorality that prevailed, especially in the gaming houses that abounded in Philadelphia, since he had expected to see virtue triumphant. He was astonished by the noisiness of the theaters and by the royal airs of Washington, who went around in a carriage drawn by four prancing horses, instead of living like the rest of the citizenry. Chateaubriand obtained an interview with Washington and the President pointed out the utopian character of his plan: it was unthinkable that one man could discover the Northwest Passage; it would require the organization of a whole expedition, which was well nigh impossible. So Chateaubriand, very wisely, gave up the idea of becoming an explorer and contented himself with a modest tour of the United States.

In the various accounts he left of his travels in the United States, Chateaubriand greatly exaggerated the extent of the regions he visited. Now, thanks to a critical study of these accounts, we know exactly what he saw. He was at Niagara Falls and he visited a part of the Ohio Valley, after which he returned to Washington. It is very doubtful that he went as far as the Mississippi, which he nevertheless describes several times at great length. At all events, he was very disappointed by the savages, the Iroquois, whom he found vice-ridden, whereas he had expected to meet the "noble savages" extolled by the *philosophes*. But he was to base several stories on his contacts with the Indians, such as "Atala" and "Les

Natchez." Chateaubriand re-embarked after only five months; he sailed from America on December 10, 1791, and arrived in Le Havre on January 2 relatively swiftly, but not without experiencing a violent storm in which the tiny boat taking him home nearly sank.

He went immediately to Saint-Malo where he noted that the Revolution had made considerable progress and war threatened. It seemed to him then that further hesitation was pointless; he must emigrate. But emigration required money and during his journey he had spent the small capital inherited from his father. So he married in order to raise the money, taking as wife a very young girl, Céleste de Buisson de La Vigne, who was only seventeen. He left her almost immediately after the marriage, disappointed because the dowry was blocked and he could never touch a sou of it. The marriage gave rise to difficulties: it had taken place in secret before a refractory priest, but the Buisson de La Vigne family, which was revolutionary, had rebelled against this procedure and had the ceremony repeated before a priest who had sworn to the constitution.

Chateaubriand was forced to emigrate without money. He left with his older brother and reached Brussels, then Coblenz. There he enlisted in the army of the princes as a private and was assigned to the Brittany Company, where he re-encountered many comrades of his youth.

Chateaubriand was not too convinced an émigré because he did not believe in the counter-revolution. He dreaded a war between Frenchmen and participated without enthusiasm in the campaign of 1792, in which the army of the princes remained in the rearguard and limited itself to the siege of Thionville, without success. In the course of the campaign, Chateaubriand was wounded very seriously in the right thigh by a bursting shell, after which he contracted smallpox and almost died. Evacuated from hospital to hospital, from Luxembourg to Brussels and finally to Ostend, he reached the island of Jersey to which the Bédée family, and in particular his maternal uncle, had emigrated.

Upon learning of the draconian laws voted in France against the émigrés, Chateaubriand's brother, Jean-Baptiste, re-entered the country in order to prevent the confiscation of his château. As a result Jean-Baptiste, his wife and the whole Rosambo family were to be hauled before the revolutionary tribunal in 1794, condemned to death and executed.

Chateaubriand lived for some time in Jersey and later managed to make his way to London, with the help of a small sum of money his mother sent him from Saint-Malo, where she had remained. He fell sick in London and went to see a doctor who told him frankly that at best he had two

years to live. This prognosis led to a sudden change in his ideas: Chateaubriand, who had been an out-and-out unbeliever, began progressively to
turn once more toward religion.

What should be done with the two years that remained to him? He
thought of writing, first of all to earn a living, and translated French
works into English. Then he obtained a modest post as a French teacher
at a boarding school for young ladies in Suffolk and fell in love with the
daughter of a pastor. When the parents asked him to marry her, he was
forced to confess that he was married and that his wife lived in France.

But while he was teaching French at this boarding school, he received
a visit from a Parisian journalist, Jean-Gabriel Peltier, himself an émigré.
Chateaubriand confided to him his ideas and plans, particularly for a book
on revolutions which he was turning over in his mind. How would the
French Revolution end, everybody was asking. Chateaubriand thought
one might perhaps be able to come up with an answer if one studied all
the revolutions that had taken place in the world. He was thinking in
terms of a work that today we would class as political science or political
sociology, a comparative study of revolutions. Once it was understood
how all the various revolutions had evolved, by deduction it would be
possible to formulate conclusions on the ultimate outcome of the French
Revolution that would have some chance of being exact. Peltier was
enthused over this idea and found a printer called Baylis for Chateaubriand. Baylis not only agreed to print the book, but even to lodge the
author so that the printing of the work could proceed hand in hand with
its writing. Chateaubriand, however, asked for time because the work
required extensive documentation, which he gathered together in the
London libraries. Nevertheless, at the end of three years the work was
published. It was the *Essai historique, politique et moral sur les révolutions
considérées dan leur rapports avec la Révolution française* (London,
March, 1797).

2 / *The* Essai sur les révolutions

This is a very impotrant work from two points of view: first, because
it is Chateaubriand's first book, the work that made him known; second,
because it occupies an eminent place in the political literature of the time,
in the series of doctrinal works that we are reviewing here.

Later Chateaubriand was to say of his book: "It is a chaos in which
the Jacobins and the Spartiates, the 'Marseillaise' and the hymns of

Tyrtaeus come together," a definition that is not inexact. A logical plan can only be discerned with great difficulty; it is indeed a welter, a medley of confusion, but an extremely intelligent medley, replete with brilliant ideas and wholly new insights on the Revolution and its possible outcome.

If we wish to impose a modicum of order on the book, we can try to extract a certain number of questions for which Chateaubriand attempted to provide answers. First, what are the revolutions that have supervened in the government of men? Chateaubriand studies six revolutions in antiquity and seven in modern times. Second, among these revolutions are there any that can be compared to the actual Revolution in France? Chateaubriand tries to study these revolutions in relation to the French Revolution. Third, what are the causes of the French Revolution? Fourth, what is now the government of France—namely, the Directory—and is this government based on "true principles"? Fifth, if the Directory lasts, what will be the effect on the nations and other governments of Europe? Finally, if it is destroyed, what will be the consequences of its destruction for contemporary peoples and for posterity?

Thus Chateaubriand's work does not shape up as a systematic, dogmatic study like the books by Burke or de Bonald. Rather, it is a sociological study "avant la lettre," since the word "sociology" was not coined until the nineteenth century. Chateaubriand makes a great effort at impartiality. He writes:

> I know very well that there can exist very honest people with notions of things different from mine. . . . Each age is a river that sweeps us along according to the inclination of destinies when we surrender ourselves to them, but it seems to me that we are all outside its course. Some have traversed it impetuously and hurled themselves onto the opposite bank. Others have remained on this side without wishing to engage themselves. The two parties shout and insult each other, depending whether they are on one or the other bank of the river. Thus, the former transport us far from ourselves, into imaginary perfections, by making us go beyond our age, the latter keep us behind, refusing to be enlightened and wanting to remain men of the fourteenth century in 1797.

In these words Chateaubriand recognizes that the Revolution involves drafts on the future drawn on the epoch in which it has taken place and that reaction, in contrast, wants to transport the society of the end of the eighteenth century to a Middle Ages that has vanished forever.

It must also be noted that Chateaubriand gives an extremely broad meaning to the word "revolution." For him, the Revolution is not only a political change, as the majority of his contemporaries thought, but a total change of ideas and mores. He perceives revolutions as chain reactions, that kindle each other, particularly in this passage: "A spark of the conflagration lighted under Charles I falls on America in 1637, sets her ablaze in 1755 [the beginning of the Revolution in the United States], and crosses the ocean again in 1789 to ravage Europe once more. There is something incomprehensible in these generations of misfortunes." Incomprehensible in Chateaubriand's epoch, because no one at that time had sufficiently analyzed the causes of revolutions. But it is very interesting to note this conception of a chain reaction in revolutions, for which we can substitute the idea of a single Western revolution. In the presence of this chain reaction, which he finds incomprehensible, Chateaubriand has the same response as Mallet du Pan, whom he had read and whose acquaintance he was to make in London. Chateaubriand, too, believes in the "force of things," and he employs the expression "the course of events," against which, in his view, man can do nothing.

Chateaubriand asserts that the Enlightenment did not play an essential role among the causes of the French Revolution, but a trifling one. No doubt it contributed to the origin of the Revolution, but there were many other causes. And he analyzes these causes carefully. He thinks the government and the king have been very weak. At the time of his visit to Versailles, before the Revolution, the court produced an impression of mediocrity on him; it seemed to him that Louis XVI was surrounded by incompetents, was incapable of governing, that he was not the man who would be able to resist the Revolution. The ministers were weak or incompetent, the court corrupt and debauched, the nobles who peopled it degenerate or ignorant. The upper clergy, he writes, was "a disgrace to the order of the clergy"; most of its members resided at the court and not in the dioceses. Religion was undermined by the *philosophes*. France was prosperous, her population increasing; but morality was in constant decline.

It is curious that Chateaubriand, in contrast to most of his contemporaries, thought that the birth rate in France was declining in the eighteenth century. He attributed this to voluntary birth control and devotes the following paragraph to this problem:

Woe to the State in which the citizens seek their happiness outside morality and the sweetest sentiments of nature. If, on the one hand, the number of celibates has multiplied, on the other, married people have adopted ideas at least as destructive of society. The principle of a small number of children has been almost generally accepted in France; among some for reasons of poverty, among the majority for reasons of low morality.

Here then is expounded—perhaps for the first time at the end of the eighteenth century—the idea of a moral decline manifesting itself by way of a deliberate reduction of births.

Chateaubriand notes that the hatred of the poor for the rich is growing incessantly, especially in the cities, and says that this is the fundamental cause of the Revolution in France. The Enlightenment is but an additional factor: "Let it be clearly understood that the *philosophes* are not the only cause of the Revolution." At this time Chateaubriand most probably was abreast of the ideas of abbé Barruel and of other émigrés who pinned the chief responsibility for events on the *philosophes*. "The Revolution does not come from this or that man, from this or that book, it comes from conditions." Here Chateaubriand echoes Mallet du Pan.

It comes from the progress of society toward enlightenment and corruption at once. This is why we note in the French Revolution excellent principles and baleful consequences. The former derive from an enlightened theory, the latter from a corruption of morals. This is the real reason for this incomprehensible mixture of crime grafted onto a philosophical trunk.

For Chateaubriand, there is a kind of dualism in the Revolution. The Enlightenment produced everything that is good about the Revolution— he acknowledges that there is much good—but the corruption of morals, the moral decline, has led to all that is bad in the Revolution, to all its crimes.

Chateaubriand then studies the great periods of the French Revolution. For him, the heart of the Revolution is the Terror, the time of Robespierre, of the political domination by the Mountain. He does not condemn Robespierre; indeed, he pays homage to his idealism in words that the most noted Robespierrists would not have disavowed:

The Jacobins, to whom we cannot refuse the frightful praise of having been consistent in their principles, had perceived with genius that a radical vice existed in the mores and that in the state in which the French nation then found itself, the inequality of fortunes, the differences of opinion, the religious sentiments and a thousand others, it was absurd to think of a democracy without a complete revolution from the aspect of morality.

Thus Chateaubriand, like Robespierre, admits that democracy can be based only on virtue and that without this it cannot exist. He also admires the Montagnards for having known how to organize national defense and resist the coalition of all the European powers:

> Attacked by the whole of Europe, torn by civil wars, agitated by a thousand factions, the fortresses on her frontiers captured or under siege, without soldiers, without finances, a discredited paper currency that depreciated from day to day, discouragement at every level of society and famine practically assured, such was France, such the picture she presented at the very instant that plans were afoot to deliver her to a general revolution. It was necessary to remedy this compounding of evils. It was necessary simultaneously, by a miracle, to establish the republic of Lycurgus among an old people, nourished under a monarchy, immense in its population and corrupt in its mores, and to save a large country without an army, softened in peace and expiring amid political convulsions, from the invasion of 500,000 of the crack troops of Europe.
>
> Only these madmen [the Jacobins] could imagine the means for this and, what is more incredible, succeed in executing them. Execrable means, no doubt, but, it must be acknowledged, of a gigantic conception. These minds, refined in the fire of republican enthusiasm and, so to speak, reduced by their self-purging to the quintessence of crime, unleashed simultaneously an energy the like of which has never been experienced before and crimes which all those committed in history put together could scarcely equal.

In these phrases Chateaubriand pays homage to the heroism and courage of the Montagnards. But the Terror was a thing of the past as he wrote, and the Directory was in the seat of government.

Chateaubriand has no respect for the Directory. It is a weak form of government which, according to him, cannot endure and will end either in a restoration or dictatorship. Thus in his analysis of the Revolution, Chateaubriand voices extremely intelligent and discerning views. But does he propose a doctrine of government?

In its supposedly constructive part, the book exhibits much less clarity, much more hesitancy. Chateaubriand does not believe that the "social contract" is a good thing. The discussions he had with Malesherbes on Rousseau certainly left their mark on him: he rejects the idea of a social contract and of a constitution, but in an altogether explicit way.

Every State, he thinks, is composed of three elements: the king (K), the senate (S) and the people (P). The arrangement of these three elements gives to the different states their particular characteristics. Thus in England we have the arrangement KSP, the king, senate and people. But in Carthage (Chateaubriand often takes his examples from antiquity) we have PSK: here, the people commanded, the senate executed and the king was only an agent. Other combinations may exist. As a theory of government this is somewhat naïve. He does not condemn the republic out of hand. He saw it function in America, but he concedes that it is neither valid nor viable save for peoples of a very virtuous character. Virtue, he believes, is an indispensable quality for democracies.

As for France, Chateaubriand, although not very precise on this point, seems to envisage a constitutional monarchy and comes very close to the "monarchical" ideas expressed by Mallet du Pan.

> Individual independence, this is the cry from within that pursues us. Listen to the voice of conscience, what does it tell us? According to nature, "Be free"; according to society, "Rule." For if we deny it, we lie. Do not blush because with a bold hand I tear away the veil with which we try to cover from our own eyes the awareness that civil liberty is but a dream. . . . Let us laugh at the clamors of the crowd, content to know that as long as we do not return to the life of the savage, we shall always be dependent upon one man. Hence what does it matter whether we are devoured by a court, a directory, or an assembly of the people? . . . Any government is an evil, any government a yoke. . . . Since our fate is to be slaves, let us endure our chains without complaint, let us know how to compose its links of kings or tribunes, according to the times and above all according to the mores.

Then the book ends with the idea of relativity.

On the whole, this work is very hard to classify in terms of the theories of the counter-revolution and even those of the Revolution. There are few passages favorable to the clergy, and the book could be described as anti-clerical, for Chateaubriand often calls the clergy "fanatical." He is very hostile to the court and to the upper nobility, which has lived apart from the nation. But on the subject of the bourgeoisie, he is very discreet. Of the poor he remarks that above all they hate the rich. Thus the book is a condemnation of the Old Regime, but it is also a condemnation of the Revolution which has committed crimes, and of the Directory which, at that time, governed France.

Chateaubriand was much younger than Joseph de Maistre and Louis de Bonald; his knowledge of the society of the Old Regime was scanty and he had lived for a long time outside France, all of which explains the particular features of the book. As the American historian Paul Beik rightly asserts, Chateaubriand is a "traditionalist out of despair." He does not want to forswear either his ancestors or the nobility devoted to the king. "Persuaded that there is nothing new in history, he loses the taste for innovations." As has been pointed out, *Essai sur les révolutions* is more "the journal of a tormented soul than the learned treatise of a scholar" on political science.

This work, dedicated to all parties, was (as might have been expected) rejected by all of them. The revolutionaries viewed it as the work of an aristocrat; the émigrés, for the most part, were shocked. Chateaubriand's family, who lived in France and had suffered terrible losses, were overwhelmed by the *Essai*, which they found to be a scandalous work, rooted in wrong thinking, and something to be destroyed as quickly as possible. Only some "monarchicals," such as Mallet du Pan and Malouet, approved, but with many reservations.

3 / *The* Génie du Christianisme

In the *Essai sur les révolutions*, as we said, Chateaubriand takes an anti-clerical stand, even wondering whether Catholicism will endure. On this he professes the same ideas as the members of the French government under the Directory. What religion will supplant Christianity? In his view, all religions are caricatures of natural religion, that of Rousseau. "Religions," he says, "are born of our fears and our frailties, expand in the midst of fanaticism and die in indifference. The priests of Persia and of Egypt perfectly resembled ours, their minds were also compounded of fanaticism and intolerance." And again, "God, matter, fatality are but one and the same. This is my system, that is what I believe."

Alongside these words, however, which no French revolutionary would have disavowed, there is a certain emotional element when the Gospels are evoked. Chateaubriand believes in God; he affirms very loftily: "There is a God. The grasses of the valley and the cedars of Lebanon bless Him. . . . Man alone has said, 'There is no God.' Has he never, then, in his adversities raised his eyes toward heaven?"

But he was to abandon this somewhat agnostic position very rapidly. As early as the *coup d'état* of 18 Fructidor, which took place six months after the publication of his book, a new influx of émigré priests poured into England as the result of a renewed wave of anti-Catholic terror in France. Many priests were again forced to take the road to exile. The trials and tribulations suffered by these priests moved the English, even Protestants, and Chateaubriand himself underwent a change of heart. Moreover, Fontanes, who had known him in 1788, arrived among the émigrés of 18 Fructidor. Fontanes had been writing in French newspapers from 1795 to 1797, preaching tolerance, forgiveness for the past and religious rebirth. He explained to Chateaubriand that France was becoming Christian again and that the new anti-religious terror would be ephemeral.

Several months later, in 1798, Chateaubriand's mother died, news which had a shattering effect upon him. One of his sisters, Julie de Farcy, sent him a letter begging him to convert. At this point Chateaubriand wrote: "I did not yield, I must admit, to a great supernatural illumination. My conviction came from the heart; I wept and I believed." After his conversion, which occurred in 1799, he already was thinking of writing a work on the Christian religion in its relation to poetry. The work would be "analogous to the circumstancs," that is to say, it would coincide with the nascent religious revival in France and could even help it. At first, Chateaubriand had in mind a pamphlet of a few dozen pages, conceived, furthermore, in the form of a reply to a poem by Parny, a minor poet whom he had known in France and who had published an erotic and violently anti-religious book entitled *La Guerre des dieux*.

Julie de Farcy died in turn, and this strengthened Chateaubriand's convictions. When 18 Brumaire took place, Fontanes returned to France immediately and, noting that calm was being restored, advised Chateaubriand to return as quickly as possible. Chateaubriand came back to Paris in March, 1800, bringing with him the manuscript he had begun. Already, he was thinking of changing the title and calling it *Génie du Christianisme*. Fontanes, who at that time was very high up in literary and government circles since he had been commissioned by Bonaparte to deliver the eulogy on Washington (who had just died), set about finding a publisher for the *Génie*. At this time Chateaubriand learned that Bonaparte was about to enter into negotiations with Pope Pius VII for the signing of a Concordat. Clearly everything betokened a religious renewal and a revival of Christianity. Furthermore, Chateaubriand was under the influence of all kinds of men of extreme Catholic persuasion, such as de Bonald, whom he met; the philosopher Joubert; and, above all, his mistress, Mme de Beaumont, daughter of Montmorin, the former minister of Louis XVI. Under their influence, Chateaubriand transformed his modest pamphlet into a sizable book.

He thought to publish it in 1801, but the Concordat had just been signed and not yet ratified by the legislative body. Bonaparte, in fact, had not dared to submit it to that body's consideration, fearing a hostile reaction. Chateaubriand, under Fontanes's inspiration, decided to delay publication but in order to test public opinion, he published a chapter separately, the story of "Atala." It was a real trial balloon. "Atala" had a tremendous success, proving that henceforth nothing stood in the way of publishing the book. The legislative body ratified the Concordat on April 8, 1802. Several days later, on April 14, *Génie du Christianisme* appeared in the bookshops. Thus there is a distinct coincidence between the evolution of the religious policy of the Consulate and the publication of the *Génie*.

Génie du Christianisme was an instant and immense success, and made Chateaubriand a great and very celebrated writer. Although it expresses religious ideas, they are very vague, much less marked and infinitely less precise than those of de Maistre or de Bonald. Chateaubriand was not concerned with preaching in favor of the establishment of a kind of theocracy. De Bonald declared that Chateaubriand portrayed religion as a queen, whereas he had transformed himself into a knight to defend her, and he adds: "I administered my physic naturally, he administered his with sugar."

The book is divided into four parts: the first deals with dogmas and doctrine, the second the poetry of Christianity, the third the relationship between Christianity and poets and literature, and the fourth public worship and ceremonies.

Only in the first part can we find some developments relating to the influence of religion on politics, or of politics on religion. Chateaubriand's principal idea is that religion is the guarantee of freedom; the Catholic religion, which he calls the most poetic, most humane in the whole world, is also the religion most favorable to the development of culture and freedom. The world owes everything to it. This doctrine, then, is extremely vague, but it complements the ideas developed by Chateaubriand in the *Essai sur les révolutions*.

Whereas in the *Essai* he shows himself to be agnostic, relativistic as regards the value of governments and of religion, he takes an opposite view here and declares that no free government is possible without religion. Christianity is at the base of civil liberty.

A number of ideas can be extracted from these two works together. First, that of the relativity of institutions and governments, of the versatility of men. The second idea, and a most interesting one, is the first application of the sociological method to the study of societies, governments and revolutions. Third comes the attachment to freedom: Chateaubriand, for all his becoming an Ultra in later life, was to remain a passionate libertarian violently opposed to the famous law of "justice and love" which, under Charles X, aimed seriously to restrict freedom of the press. He was earnestly devoted to "honor," as conceived by Montesquieu, who defined it as "the prejudice of each person and of each condition."

It was respect for this concept of honor that induced Chateaubriand, after he had become secretary to the embassy in Rome in 1803, to resign his post upon learning of the execution of the duc d'Enghien. He believed in morality not toward people, because Chateaubriand's life is not an example of a moral life, but toward states. For him a state could not be built without morality and virtue; from this point of view, there is a certain kinship between Chateaubriand and Robespierre. For Chateaubriand the moral order is Christian morality. "Religion is the source of liberty"—a statement very far removed from the theocracy of de Maistre or de Bonald.

Nevertheless Chateaubriand did not believe that politics had to be based on religion; it was enough that it observed the great principles of the Christian religion.

In Chateaubriand's thought the counter-revolution seems to join company with the Revolution. The very difficulty that we encounter in classifying his work is one proof of this and Chateaubriand's own career is another. For after having emigrated and been a soldier in the army of the princes, upon returning to France he became a functionary of Bonaparte. Indeed, Chateaubriand can almost serve as a symbol of the conjunction between Revolution and counter-revolution, a conjunction that precisely characterizes Bonaparte's government under the Consulate since it united repentant former Jacobins and returned émigrés in the administration of public offices.

PART II:

ACTION

Having reviewed the typical theories of the counter-revolution, we turn now to study the action as such of the counter-revolutionaries.

In fact, we shall see that the connection between this action and the doctrine was often tenuous. The primary consideration was to stop the course of the Revolution; little concern was shown for the regime to be established afterwards. More exactly, lengthy discussions of this subject were avoided because they would quickly reveal the profound divisions that separated the various counter-revolutionary doctrines.

Counter-revolutionary activity took place amid great confusion, precisely because it was not guided by a single doctrine or a centralized general staff. It is therefore preferable not to adopt a chronological order for its study; a system like that followed by Emmanuel Vingtrinier, for example, engenders the greatest confusion. Actually the counter-revolutionary effort was directed from numerous centers. Sometimes it came from the émigrés, who themselves took their watchword from Turin, Coblenz, Verona, London; sometimes from the local leaders in France and poorly coordinated clandestine organizations. The action of the counter-revolution was marked by an extensive fragmentation and assumed extremely diverse forms, both inside and outside France. Consequently, it must be studied in a logical sequence if we are to shed some light on events.

We shall start with the activities directed by the émigrés, for among the counter-revolutionaries the most ardent, obviously, were those men who crossed the frontiers and cut themselves off totally, physically, from the Revolution, in order to have absolutely nothing to do with it.

Next, we shall examine the espionage network directed simultaneously in France and abroad by émigrés or the intelligence services of foreign powers. Since intelligence formed the very basis for action, such espionage was absolutely indispensable in order to guide it.

We shall then examine the development of counter-revolutionary resistance within France proper, a resistance which at first took the form of civil struggles, indeed of guerrilla warfare in the west. From 1794 onwards, this assumed a more political form, so we shall describe the political struggles conducted by the "Clichyans" against the Directory. Counter-revolutionary action took on a military dimension as well in that some French generals tried to defeat the Revolution from within, as our account of their intrigues will show.

We shall also study the counter-revolution in the countries occupied by the French armies, the Low Countries, Germany, Switzerland and Italy. And in conclusion we shall show the form taken by the counter-revolutionary movement at the time of the Consulate.

CHAPTER IX

The Emigration

In the first part of this chapter, we shall trace the broad outlines of the emigration. In the second, we shall study the counter-revolutionary action of the émigrés.

I / General Features of the Emigration

The first question to be resolved is, What was the importance of the emigration and how many émigrés were there? Different laws had decreed the establishment in each department of a list of émigrés, and of a general list for the whole of France. This list was closed by the first consul in 1800, at which time it included 145,000 names. But it is very inaccurate because in every department absent persons, who had not necessarily left France, were inscribed as émigrés; on the other hand, real émigrés could be omitted, deliberately or not.

Some authors have thought that the general list included far too many names: André Gain[1] has estimated the total number of émigrés at only 100,000. Taine, in contrast, thought that the list was deficient by default because the names of many persons who had left had not been inscribed; he estimated the total at 150,00 at least. Donald Greer, who applied himself to a more precise calculation by deducting all those who had been inscribed erroneously, arrives at the figure of 129,000. But he recognizes that this is certainly not correct because many of the émigrés were not inscribed, the bulk of those registered being proprietors inasmuch as their

1. André Gain, *La Restauration et les biens des émigrés* (2 vols., Nancy, 1929).

141

holdings were earmarked for sequestration. Greer concedes that perhaps 20,000 to 30,000 names were omitted, which brings us back to the figure of 150,000.

This total is approximately comparable to that of the émigrés who left France one hundred years before, in 1685, after the revocation of the Edict of Nantes. Two hundred thousand persons crossed the frontiers at that time, but in relation to the population this figure represents a much greater proportion because in 1685 the total population was 14 or 15 million, whereas in 1789 there were 26 million inhabitants. Consequently, the proportion of émigrés was lower during the Revolution than after the revocation.

The 150,000 émigrés did not leave France at the same time. Emigration took place in different waves. At first there were two great divisions: before the start of the war, that is, before April 20, 1792, when it was relatively easy to leave France; and after 1792, when it became very difficult to cross the frontier. We note that the great mass of émigrés left beginning in 1792, but in the different localities this was not always the case. There were departments in which the number of émigrés, in contrast, was greater after the declaration of war.

The emigration was contagious; people left because they saw their neighbors leave. There were waves of emigration as there were waves of fear, and the fear was contagious.[2] Emigration itself was a form of fear.

Three waves of emigration can be counted before 1792: the first in 1789, the second in 1790 and the third in 1791–92.

The wave of 1789 was heavy in July and August. The storming of the Bastille set off the "Great Fear" and the first émigré was Louis XVI's own brother, the comte d'Artois. He was accompanied by numerous princes, the prince de Condé, the duc de Bourbon, the duc d'Enghien, the Conti, to mention only the principal lords of the realm. These first émigrés did not leave secretly: they abandoned their homes conspicuously, indeed ostentatiously, in splendid liveried coaches, and often they brought with them all the money they could carry. The duc de Mirepoix, one of the great lords of Languedoc, arrived in Rome with the sum of 500,000 livres in gold and silver. These men, moreover, believed that their exile would be of brief duration, perhaps two months or at the most three. Their confidence was based upon what had transpired in Switzerland at the time of the Geneva revolution of 1782, as well as in Holland in 1787 or

2. In this connection, see the suggestive book by J. Palou, *La Peur dans l'histoire* (Paris, 1958).

still in Belgium in 1790; in these countries the counter-revolution had rapidly been victorious, owing to the intervention of foreign armies.

The "Great Fear" of July and the beginning of August, 1789, accelerated the departures; the march of the Parisians on Versailles of October 5 and 6, and the arrival of the royal family in Paris set off new emigrations. Already among these émigrés several officers of the royal army and several bishops appeared, among them Monseigneur de Grimaldi, bishop of Noyon. There were even several members of the Constituent Assembly, notably the "monarchical" deputies, who left France after the failure of their plan to draw up a constitution on the English model, with a lower and upper house.

The second wave, that of 1790, was set off by the decrees on the abolition of feudal dues. This had been decided in principle on the night of August 4, but the decrees of application were not promulgated until the following year. At that time the nobility was dispossessed of a part of its dues and revenues. But at approximately the same time the decrees on the reorganization of the administration of justice, which abolished the parlements, and the decrees placing the properties of the clergy at the nation's disposal were promulgated. This led to the departure of a great number of bishops, and several priests and magistrates. The first great military insurrections, in particular that in Nancy in the month of August, also took place in 1790. The mutinies accentuated the emigration of officers, who left their regiments since they no longer had any authority. These two first waves were, so to speak, spontaneous. Those who left did so because they were gripped by fear and because they thought it was better to spend a few months abroad than to run the risk of being killed in France.

But in 1791 the émigrés exerted a real pressure on their relatives and friends who remained in France. Those who had left wanted to drag the others along with them and there was a genuine propaganda campaign in favor of emigration. The flight of the king in June, 1791, and his arrest followed by suspension, set off a new wave of terror which, in its turn, sparked a massive emigration.

Infantry, cavalry and naval officers, in particular, left France: the emigration of naval officers was facilitated, indeed organized, by none other than the minister of the navy, Bertrand de Molleville.

In 1789 and during the greater part of 1790, the Constituent Assembly had adopted a passive attitude toward these departures. After all, those leaving were counter-revolutionaries; so much the better; they were easily expendable. But soon it appeared that the men who were gathering beyond the frontiers of France were becoming a threat and the first repressive measures ensued.

The first law against the émigrés dates from December 22, 1790. It decreed that any émigré occupying a governmental post in France was to forfeit it, and lose all his revenues and stipends if he did not return within a month. The law was very lenient; nevertheless, many of the émigrés who had been still receiving stipends and pensions thenceforth were deprived of them.

It was not until August 6, 1791, after the flight to Varennes, that a somewhat harsher law was voted. This prohibited Frenchmen from emigrating, prescribed that a passport was required for travel abroad and ordered emigrants to return on the promise that they would not be subject to any sanctions. But this law was suspended only one month later, on September 14, 1791, by the amnesty granted by Louis XVI immediately after he had accepted the constitution.

The amnesty, however, had an effect contrary to its underlying expectation. Departures resumed on a massive scale in September and October of 1791. The émigrés became increasingly violent against revolutionary France and appealed to their friends. Hence the law of November 9, 1791, which ordered them to return to France within a month, under penalty of death. The king refused to sanction this law which, consequently, was not applied; the exodus merely assumed even larger proportions.

On April 8, 1792, several days before the beginning of the war, the Legislative Assembly voted a major new law against the émigrés. This decreed the confiscation of the properties of all those "absent" from France since July 1, 1789—the word "émigrés" does not figure. There was no question yet of putting the émigrés' properties up for sale. Those who left France before July 1, 1789, were not alarmed, nor were those who left the country after that date, and with reason. Emigrés who had left France since July 1, 1789, but who had returned by February 9, 1792, or those who returned within a month from the date of the promulgation of the law, would be subject to a relatively light penalty: the doubling of their taxes for the current year and deprivation of their civil rights for two years. Those who returned after this reprieve, that is, after May 8, 1792, were to be deprived of their civil rights for ten years. This law was still relatively lenient, not as harsh as that which the Assembly had voted in November and which had not been sanctioned. Yet it did not achieve any of the anticipated results. On the contrary, the departures were further accelerated up to the end of April, when the beginning of the war seriously slowed down border crossings.

Alongside the emigration proper we must place the departure of refractory, or nonjuring, priests, which was not an emigration in the true sense of the word but a deportation. In fact, French priests had been divided into two categories since the voting of the Civil Constitution of the Clergy: priests who had sworn the oath required by the constitution and who showed themselves to be loyal *vis-à-vis* the Revolution, and refractory priests who had refused to take the loyalty oath. These refractory priests were often uneasy and restless. They fomented disturbances so that the authorities of the municipalities, the districts and the departments had repeatedly asked that measures be taken against them. On May 27, 1792, the Legislative Assembly decreed that refractory priests were to be deported outside France, if this measure was requested by twenty active citizens of the community in which they resided. But this law was not sanctioned by Louis XVI, and it was precisely this attitude on the king's part that provoked the revolutionary *journée* of June 20. Only after the fall of the throne, on August 26, 1792, did the Legislative Assembly vote a new law which was actually applied. This ordered the refractory priests to leave France within two weeks of their own free will, or face deportation. The departure of the priests, therefore, was an emigration ordered by the government, not a spontaneous one. Only priests over sixty, or those who were infirm, were authorized to remain in France, but they were to be confined within their administrative locales. As for the religious not subject to the oath, which only functionaries were obliged to take, they could be subject to deportation if they were denounced by six citizens of their commune. Many religious who were not under compulsion to leave France left the country of their own accord at that time.

At all events, the statistical curve of departures reached its peak in 1792. In some departments we even see that after 1792 there were no longer any émigrés to speak of. In the Indre there were 232 émigrés before the end of 1792 and only 16 after; in Creuse, 249 before and 31 after; in Hautes-Alpes, 95 before and 10 after; and in Haute-Garonne, 700 before and 457 after. In twenty-three departments on which we have very precise information, there were 12,753 émigrés before 1792 and 4,716 after, that is, 73 per cent against 27 per cent. Twenty-six other departments on which we possess less precise information, seem to have followed the same movement, but twenty-nine show a different trend: there is heavier emigration after 1792 than before. For example, Bas-Rhin had 811 émigrés before April 20, 1792, and 19,699 after; Bouches-du-Rhône 1,125 before, 4,000 after; and Var 545 before, 4,786 after.

The émigrés of the first period in the main were nobles, priests, members of the upper bourgeoisie; members of the Third Estate were very few. The situation was exactly reversed in the second period, which was marked by four waves distanced from one another and never lasting a long time.

The first wave was set off in June–July of 1793 after the *journées* of May 31–June 2. Those who left France at that time were Girondins, federalists, and in the main they belonged to the Third Estate, to the bourgeoisie, often to the peasantry. There was a new wave after 9 Thermidor in 1794. The prisons were opened upon the fall of Robespierre but a number of the released prisoners had no confidence in the government and hastened to leave France. Still another wave followed in October, 1795, after the fiasco of the royalist *journée* of 13 Vendémiaire. Finally, the last wave followed the *coup d'état* of 18 Fructidor, Year V (September 4, 1797). At that time it was the royalists who were once again being rounded up and left France, but for the most part they also belonged to the Third Estate.

Meanwhile legislation directed against the émigrés had been made considerably harsher. The law of March 8, 1793, had defined "émigrés" exactly; it declared them banished in perpetuity and their properties, including their eventual inheritances, confiscated for fifty years. However, this law had provided for a procedure of cancellation of charges against émigrés who had been wrongly inscribed. Such persons had to present a deposition by a great number of witnesses attesting to their presence in France. Emigrés who returned clandestinely, upon capture would be sentenced to death and executed on the simple verification of their identity. As for the priests, the law of March 23, 1793, aggravated their plight too and ordered the deportation of all religious, whether functionaries or no, who had refused to take an oath that was instituted after August 10, 1792. This oath was not the one provided by the Civil Constitution of the Clergy. It was prescribed on August 14 for all State pensioners, among whom were included many regular clergy, and merely expressed the recognition of "liberty and equality"; it was never condemned by the Pope and any priest faithful to the Roman Church could swear to it in good conscience. Many priests refused, however, and were deported. Deported priests who returned clandestinely were also liable to the death penalty upon capture. In the following year the law of March 20, 1794, placed all nonjuring priests in the category of émigrés.

The study of the geographic distribution of the emigration in France presents another problem. Emigration was not equally distributed; furthermore, it is very difficult to calculate the number of émigrés in each department precisely. However one can arrive at a certain approximation. Donald Greer has divided the French departments into four groups on the basis of the origins of the émigrés: (1) departments with a heavy emigration, that is, having more than 2,000 émigrés. This group is very neatly distributed on the map. It includes first of all the department of Paris, then the departments with continental or maritime frontiers: Nord and Pas-de-Calais, Moselle, Bas- and Haut-Rhin, Bouches-du-Rhône, Var and Alpes-Maritimes, Pyrénées-Orientales, Finistère, Côtes-du-Nord, Ille-et-Vilaine, Manche, Seine-Inférieure and, in addition, Mayenne, the only continental department close to the northwest frontier. A total of seventeen departments in all. Bas-Rhin furnished the greatest number of émigrés: 20,374. This was the result of specific circumstances: in 1793, Austrian troops penetrated into the department and even advanced to within a few miles of Strasbourg; upon retreating they took a great mass of peasants along with them.

(2) Departments that furnished less than 500 émigrés, that is, those with the lowest number of émigrés. They were essentially the departments of the Center, and of the high mountainous region, where travel was difficult and investigations and census takers could be escaped by hiding on the spot. These are the departments of Massif central, Hautes-Alpes, Hautes- and Basses-Pyrénées, Ariège, and Corsica. This also comes to a total of seventeen departments in all.

The two other groups fall between these extremes. One, consisting of an emigration averaging from 500 to 1,000, includes the departments located in the immediate vicinity of those just mentioned, that is, bordering on the mountainous regions; the other consisting of the departments that furnished between 1,000 and 2,000 émigrés. They form a belt between the departments of the previous group and those of maximum emigration, and there are twenty-seven of them.

The total number of émigrés by department, however, is an absolute figure which does not take full account of reality. Thus Greer calculated the proportion of émigrés to population as follows:

In 20 departments it varies from 0.03 to 0.02%
In 21 departments it varies from 0.2 to 0.3%

In 18 departments it varies from 0.3 to 0.4%

In 16 departments it varies from 0.4 to 0.6%

In 5 departments it varies from 0.6 to 1%. These five departments are: Meuse, Vaucluse, Vienne, Doubs and Haut-Rhin, in which the proportion of émigrés reached 1 per cent of the population.

Seven departments had from 1 to 4.5 per cent. These are: Mayenne, Moselle, Alpes-Maritimes, Bouches-du-Rhône, Var, Pyrénées-Orientales and Bas-Rhin, which leads both in the proportion and the absolute figures of émigrés, 4.56 per cent.

A number of anomalies should be noted. For example, the department of the Rhône, in which the Terror raged with extreme violence, had a total of only 332 émigrés, or 0.1 per cent, unless of course this figure was the result of error or omission; in contrast, the department of Côte d'Or, where there had been no serious disturbances and the Terror had hardly been felt, registered 1,781 émigrés, 0.5 per cent of the population. These anomalies can be explained only by the contagion of fear.

The distribution of émigrés in different social classes is another interesting criterion that merits study. It may be noted that around 24,000 émigrés belong to the clergy (25 per cent of the total) and 16,000 to the nobility (or 17 per cent). Thus, the two privileged classes do not constitute even half the total number of émigrés. The upper bourgeoisie furnished approximately 10,000 (or 11 per cent) and the petty bourgeois 6,000 (or 6 per cent). Unlikely as it may seem, the artisans are numerous—14 per cent. Lastly, the peasants form the great majority of émigrés, about 20,000, or 20 per cent. There remain a number of indeterminate émigrés, 7 per cent.

Taking one social class in detail, the clergy, we note that 11 per cent of the émigrés belong to the upper clergy and 89 per cent to the lower; and taking account of the division between secular and regular clergy, 90 per cent are secular and 10 per cent regular; in point of fact, many of the regular clergy had adhered to the Revolution. As regards the nobility, 5 per cent of the émigrés belong to the robe, 35 per cent to the army. Women constituted 15 per cent of the émigré exodus.

Finally, in which directions did the counter-revolutionaries emigrate? They set out for all the countries near France. The first rendezvous points were Brussels and Turin, then the Rhineland, with Coblenz as a center, and later England, where the émigrés hesitated to venture initially because of the traditional hostility between the two countries and the differences in religion. Switzerland was also a place of exile, but chiefly the Catholic and French-language cantons. It has also been pointed out that the fashionable elements of the emigration took up residence in London and Brussels, while the poorer elements went to Switzerland, where the cost of living was low, and the military elements to the Rhineland.

II / The Counter-Revolutionary Activities of the Emigrés

1 / The Beginnings of the Emigration (1789–91)

Why do the émigrés leave, what is their motivation? Fear is the first reason that impels them. They leave in order to escape prison, massacre, death. But they also leave because they do not yet possess the notion of "patrie," which did not develop in France until the nineteenth and twentieth centuries. For many of these émigrés, the notion of "patrie" is replaced by that of fidelity to the king. Now the king, a prisoner in Paris from October 6, 1789, onward, no longer has freedom of action. Fidelity to the king henceforth will be expressed by fidelity to his closest representatives, that is to say, to his brother, the comte d'Artois: "Where the fleurs de lis are, there is the *patrie*."

The comte d'Artois was the first French émigré, if we discount Calonne, the former controller-general of finance, who had left France in 1787. D'Artois left Versailles on the night of July 16/17, 1789, with a group of friends, and was followed by the Condés, the Contis, etc. These first great lords set out for Brussels, declaring, to those who cared to listen, that they would be back in three months. But the emperor Joseph II was beset by grave difficulties in the Low Countries, where the Revolution broke out in 1787. He feared the presence of these émigrés in his states and made this discreetly clear by requesting them to leave.

Where were they to go? The comte d'Artois was married to one of the daughters of the king of Sardinia, and his brother, the comte de Provence, who stayed behind in Paris, had married one of her sisters. So d'Artois decided to go to his father-in-law's court in Turin. This greatly embarrassed the king of Sardinia, Victor Amadeus III, because he too feared the presence of émigrés, which could provide France with a pretext to occupy Savoy and the county of Nice where there had been serious disturbances since June, 1792. Finally, after an agreement with Louis XVI, Victor Amadeus III granted the comte d'Artois permission to take up residence in Turin. D'Artois was soon joined by many other nobles.

As early as September, 1789, he had formed with them a committee of counter-revolution, which was to function throughout the prince's sojourn in Turin. The committee was composed of the comte d'Artois, the prince de Condé, his son, the duc de Bourbon, a certain number of nobles, de Sérent, d'Autichamp, abbé Marie, tutor to the princes and the marquis de la Rouzière, deputy to the National Assembly, secretary of the committee. Later, the bishop of Arras, Monseigneur Conzié, became a member.

It must not be thought that all these members of the committee of counter-revolution were in agreement with each other, nor that the émigrés were in agreement with the committee. On the contrary, serious disagreements appeared right from the start. Louis XVI took a very reticent stand. Officially, he disavowed the émigrés, first asking then ordering them to return to France. Secretly, he seemed to approve of them, but he often dictated a line of conduct quite different from the one they actually followed. There were émigrés who felt they must obey Louis XVI and others who felt they must be loyal to the comte d'Artois.

Soon the "monarchicals" were to join the emigration and some émigrés were to adopt their point of view. This led to the formation of a great number of cliques, but one man, Calonne, was to play a predominant role in the emigration. He had left for London in 1787, after his resignation had been forced upon him by the opposition of the notables, and settled there because he was married to a very rich Englishwoman. Upon his arrival in Turin, the comte d'Artois, who was closely allied with Calonne, immediately asked for his views, and soon Calonne was considered the oracle of the emigration. He advised the émigrés to address themselves to the European powers, to Emperor Joseph II or the king of Spain, Charles IV, urging them to put military pressure on France in order to liberate Louis XVI from Paris so that the monarch could then go where he pleased and rule without hindrance. The émigrés followed this advice, but Joseph II responded very vaguely. Shortly thereafter he died and was succeeded by his brother, Leopold II—formerly grand duke of Tuscany, where he had shown extremely liberal tendencies. Indeed, Leopold II was on the point of granting Tuscany a constitution that purportedly would have surpassed the French Constitution of 1791, but the Revolution and pressure from Austria had forced him to give up his plans. However, Leopold II showed himself as ill disposed toward the émigrés as Joseph II had been.

After this failure, Calonne advised the émigrés to form a military body by enlisting the services of the officers and soldiers who were leaving France. At the same time, he was secretly negotiating with Louis XVI and the duc d'Orléans. He still hoped that he would be able to return to France and play a great role there. But these negotiations were swamped by the swift flow of events that marked the year 1790, when the Revolution in France assumed ever more pronounced features. So Calonne broke off these negotiations completely and devoted all his energies to the émigrés. On November 10, 1790, he went to Turin and took up residence with the comte d'Artois; eventually he became the political soul of the emigration.

During the two years of its functioning, the Turin counter-revolutionary committee was to hatch conspiracies with aims that were very different and yet interconnected: first, to try to liberate the royal family and give the king the possibility of governing according to his will, either by kidnapping him or in some other manner; second, to foment an armed revolt in a number of French provinces.

As for the rescue of the king and the royal family, many plans were completed and set in motion, but all failed. The first—most probably the work of the comte de Provence, who remained in Paris, rather than of the comte d'Artois—provided for the rescue of the king at the Tuileries; the principal figure commissioned to carry out this rescue operation was the marquis de Favras. But Favras was betrayed by his accomplices, arrested, tried by the Parlement of Paris, sentenced to death and hanged on February 18, 1790. The trial bared the complicity of the comte d'Antraigues. Inasmuch as d'Antraigues had relations with the comte d'Artois, it is probable that the latter had known about the plan.

Despite this fiasco, the Turin committee hatched new plans in April and May of 1790. The king was to be removed from the Tuileries and brought to Spain or Piedmont, but this plan turned out to be a new failure.

In August, 1790, Marie-Antoinette sent an emissary to Turin, the marquis de Vioménil, in order to study with d'Artois the conditions that would make it possible for the royal family to flee from Paris. D'Artois set out a complete plan providing for the arrival of the royal family in Turin, but Marie-Antoinette rejected it because she detested her brother-in-law and did not want to fall into his power. This project, modified by degrees, ultimately led to the abortive flight to Varennes.

In short, all the plans for the king's rescue, escape and departure were fiascos. Nor was the one to foment insurrection to be any more successful, but it did bring in its wake a spirited counter-revolutionary agitation in France.

A number of French provinces seemed to be particularly responsive to the counter-revolution: they were Languedoc; the region of the southeast and the Rhône Valley; the region of the west; and Alsace and Franche-Comté. The plans to foment insurrection in these different regions were interrelated, but they are described here in turn for the sake of clarity.

In Languedoc one element particularly was exploitable by the counter-revolution: the opposition between Protestants and Catholics. The Protestants had passionately and enthusiastically supported the Revolution; many Catholics had declared themselves against the Revolution, more out of opposition to the Protestants than out of deep conviction. A lawyer from Nîmes, Froment, arrived in Turin in April of 1790 and demonstrated to the princes that the opposition between Protestants and Catholics could be exploited in order to foment an insurrection against the Revolution in Languedoc. The princes made him their plenipotentiary and he returned to Nîmes. Disturbances broke out just as he returned: the Catholics rose against the Protestants, but this insurrection was to end in utter confusion and even with the massacre of Catholics on June 13 and 14, 1790.

Similar disturbances were organized in Montauban where, on May 10, 1790, some Protestants were attacked by Catholics, but the toll of victims was not as high as in Nîmes.

There was even an attempt at revolt in Toulouse. On April 29, 1790, the legion of the National Guard of the Saint-Barthélemy quarter—where the parlement was located and which numbered a great many nobles and rich bourgeois in its ranks—made a public showing of unmistakably counter-revolutionary sympathies, but there were no further developments.

Despite the failures of the attempts to foment insurrections in Nîmes, Montauban and Toulouse, to which others of lesser importance may be added, the counter-revolutionaries tried to organize a federation like the revolutionary federations that had come into being since the end of 1789. This one was convoked at Jalès in the Ardèche. More than 20,000 men set out for Jalès and organized an encampment directed by a committee of nobles who drew up a manifesto. The work of Charles de Polignac and Laurent de Palarin (lord of Castelnau d'Estretefonds, near Toulouse), this declared: (1) that it held as null and void the entire work of the National Assembly, (2) that the members of this Assembly were criminals guilty of high treason and (3) that the constitution it was in the process of drawing up was monstrous. But this was a far as they got and the encampment was dispersed by the revolutionary national guards.

In the Rhône Valley, the principal instigator of the disturbances was Imbert-Colomès, the first magistrate of Lyons before 1789. He too went to Turin and assured the princes that it was possible to foment an insurrection in Lyons. He was supported by the chevalier des Pomelles. This insurrection led to the riots of July 25 and 26, 1790, which were quelled by the National Guard. However, the Lyons counter-revolutionary committee remained in office and functioned during the years 1790 and 1791.

Similar disorders broke out in other cities of the Rhône Valley, in particular Valence, where the military commander, the vicomte de Voisins, was assassinated. Instructions sent by the Turin committee were found on his body.

In Provence a nobleman, the comte de Vernègues, took orders from the princes in Turin. With the help of Pascalis, a lawyer in the parlement of Aix, he tried to foment uprisings in the large towns of Provence.

In the west it was once again a member of the nobility, the comte François d'Escars, who organized the coalition of Poitou directed by the baron de La Lézardière, whom we shall meet again as the instigator of the disturbances in the Vendée. The disturbances in Poitou, however, at that time were much less serious than those in Languedoc or the southeast.

In Alsace and Franche-Comté the Turin committee aimed to exploit the religious quarrels between Protestants, Catholics and Jews, as well as the problems posed by the German princes, who held seigniorial rights. Some German princes possessed fiefs in Alsace and had protested against the spoliation of which they were victims by virtue of the decrees of August 4. But in Alsace the intrigues of the Turin committee led only to some public demonstrations of no great importance.

These disturbances in the large towns of the four regions of France gave the Turin committee the impression that it was possible to foment a general insurrection. The moment this insurrection broke out, the princes would re-enter France through Chambéry, reach Lyons and arrange for the escape of Louis XVI, who would join up with them there, after which they would march on Paris. This plan was hastily put into execution in October, 1790. The date for what the comte d'Artois called the "general explosion" had been fixed for December 15, 1790.

At the beginning of December, 1790, the princes held themselves in readiness to leave Turin in order to assemble in Lyons. But then Louis XVI dispatched a messenger to Turin making known his formal opposition to this plan which, he asserted, would expose the royal family to the

gravest danger—which was true. After a lengthy discussion, the princes
finally decided to postpone their departure from Turin. Nevertheless,
they did not countermand the order for the insurrection and especially
that of Lyons. But several days earlier, on December 15, the plot to
instigate an insurrection in Lyons had been uncovered; in the papers of
arrested persons proof was found of the existence of a vast conspiracy,
which was to culminate in insurrections in all the cities of the southeast.
Numerous arrests were made and several royalists massacred, and the
princes were forced to accept the fact that their plan had failed even
before being set into motion.

It was precisely at this moment that the first measure was voted against
the émigrés: the mild decree of December 22, 1790. This caused consternation among the princes, who decided to give up their plans; as a result,
quarrels developed among them and aggravated the disagreements which
had broken out between the émigrés and the Turin court.

In fact the king of Sardinia had received a letter from Louis XVI asking
him to prevent the princes from carrying out their plan, by force if
necessary. So he intervened and the outcome was a very sharp falling out
between him and the princes. At the beginning of January, 1791, the
princes decided to leave Turin, where for several weeks they had met
with nothing but difficulties and hostility.

Most of the émigrés who were in Piedmont took the road to neighboring Switzerland, where Mirabeau-Tonneau had already established himself and organized a "Black Legion" which he assembled at Yverdon. The
princes joined Mirabeau-Tonneau; some enlisted in his legion, but the
cantons drove back these troublemakers, so they made their way towards
Basle. Shortly thereafter they crossed the Rhine to establish themselves in
the south of Germany.

The comte d'Artois wanted to have an audience with Emperor
Leopold II before making a decision, hoping that the emperor would
ultimately consent to mobilize his army against France. But Leopold II
was a peaceful soul, even a pacifist. For a long time he refused to receive
the comte d'Artois. Finally he yielded and granted an interview, which
was held at Mantua on May 17, 1791.

In the course of this interview, Leopold II explained why he had not
wished to do anything for Louis XVI, and why he could do nothing now:
any action on his part would only aggravate the dangers incurred by the
royal family. D'Artois did not share his view, so that after having
quarreled with the king of Sardinia, he was now on cool terms with the

emperor. Finally, d'Artois decided to leave Italy and take up residence in the Rhineland, on the lands of his uncle, the prince-bishop, elector of Trèves. What was more, he promised the emperor that he would not stir from there; the electorate of Trèves in fact formed part of the German Empire and the emperor had no desire to keep on his territory persons who threatened to promote a war between Austria and France. D'Artois, firmly resolved, it seems, not to keep his promises, arrived in Coblenz on June 15, 1791.

2 / *The Emigrés in the Rhineland*

The installation of the princes in the Rhineland led the mass of émigrés to go and join them there.

Mirabeau-Tonneau with his legion of volunteers, the Black Legion, left Swiss territory and established himself in the duchy of Baden, where Cardinal de Rohan, bishop of Strasbourg and himself an émigré, offered him hospitality.

Several days after d'Artois's arrival in Coblenz, the news of the flight to Varennes was received. At first it was believed that the flight had been successful and at the same time it was learned that Monsieur, the comte de Provence, another brother of the king, had also left Paris and was en route for Belgium. D'Artois immediately left for Brussels, where he hoped to join his two brothers. He thought that their arrival on Low Countries territory would coincide with a declaration of war by Emperor Leopold II against revolutionary France. But Leopold II, as peace-minded as ever, wanted to avoid war; Belgian territory, moreover, had itself been the theater of a revolution quelled with great difficulty by Austro-Prussian troops at the end of 1790, and the emperor wished to avoid a new revolt.

It seemed the hopes of the émigrés were not yet likely to be realized. Furthermore, they were soon to experience a crushing disappointment upon learning of the arrest of Louis XVI at Varennes. Admittedly not all the émigrés were grieved by this news; many had no confidence in Louis XVI, whom they accused of weakness. They set their hopes on the comte de Provence, who had been able to cross the frontier and who henceforth was to take the leadership of the emigration solidly in hand.

Nevertheless on July 10, 1791, Leopold II sent a first circular letter to the sovereign princes of Europe: the kings of England, Prussia, Spain and Sardinia and the empress of Russia. He asked them to come to an understanding with him for a common action against the French Revolution.

This action could take the form of a solemn declaration addressed to the National Assembly in Paris. The sovereigns would demand the liberation of the royal family—which had once more been forcibly confined in the Tuileries—its inviolability and freedom of movement within France. The declaration could conclude with threats against the Assembly in the event that the royal family was subjected to ill treatment.

By sending this circular letter Leopold II had yielded to the pressure from the émigrés and to the general indignation that had been manifested among the nobility and upper European bourgeoisie when news of the king's arrest and suspension after the flight to Varennes became known. But Leopold II still professed the same sentiments, he was still for peace and against the war, and wished to limit his action to intimidation of the French revolutionaries. Despite the urging of some émigrés, notably General de Bouillé, who had quelled the insurrection at Nancy and who had helped Louis XVI in his abortive flight, and despite Calonne, Leopold II refused to involve himself further.

Following the circular letter of July 10, a meeting between Leopold II and the king of Prussia, Friedrich Wilhelm, was agreed upon. This took place in Saxony, at Pillnitz. From the moment it was announced, d'Artois demanded an invitation. By his presence and action he hoped to put pressure on the king of Prussia and the emperor and induce them to declare war on France. After some initial tergiversations the emperor finally invited d'Artois, as well as Calonne.

But the emperor throughout the meeting showed great moderation; he thought that overexciting the revolutionaries should be avoided, and he discarded a plan outlined by Calonne which provided for immediate action against France. Finally, the emperor and the king of Prussia limited themselves to the promulgation of a vaguely worded declaration, the famous Declaration of Pillnitz. In this declaration, the rulers made it known that they regarded the situation in which Louis XVI found himself as "an object of common interest to all the sovereigns of Europe . . . and that they [with all the other sovereigns] will employ the most effective means to place the king of France in a position to affirm, in the most perfect freedom, the basis of a monarchist government. . . . " "While waiting," they added, they were "giving their troops the appropriate orders to put themselves in a state of readiness to move into action."

Fundamentally, then, the Declaration of Pillnitz was quite harmless; but it was susceptible to different interpretations. The émigrés, still confident in an imminent Restoration, deduced from it that war would soon be declared against France. In France, the revolutionaries were deeply affected by the declaration, viewing it as a threat. Enlistments in the battalions of national volunteers, created in June at the time of the flight to Varennes, rose considerably. France armed herself to resist the war believed imminent. Indeed, the Constituent Assembly took its first measures against the émigrés and against the refractory priests when the Declaration of Pillnitz became known.

D'Artois too believed that the war was imminent; no doubt the threats voiced by the émigrés and by the sovereigns of Europe against revolutionary France could lead to excesses, to ill treatment of the royal family, but the émigrés had arrived at the idea that the death of the king, perhaps, would not be too high a price to pay for a Restoration. Upon learning of such plans, Marie-Antoinette, speaking of the comte de Provence, screamed: "Cain!"

While waiting for war the émigrés began to organize their life in Coblenz. The comte de Provence wondered whether he should not immediately assume the title of regent, but refrained in view of the opposition he encountered in all the courts of Europe. He took up residence with d'Artois in one of the châteaux of the prince-bishop, elector of Trèves, sovereign of Coblenz. The princes gathered around themselves a council which continued the activity of the Turin committee. Calonne still exerted the major influence. Next to him, we find Monseigneur de Conzié, bishop of Arras; the duc de Broglie, who organized the army of the princes; and the marquis de Jaucourt, who was making his first appearance on the scene and who was to act as counselor to the comte de Provence for a very long time.

These councillors were in continuous contact with the two official ambassadors of France abroad: Cardinal de Bernis, archbishop of Albi, the French ambassador to Rome, who clearly betrayed the will of the National Assembly by serving the émigrés at the same time; and the duc de La Vauguyon, French ambassador to Madrid, who served the interests of the émigrés far more than those of his own government.

We must not give the impression, however, that this miniature court at Coblenz was united. As in Turin, it was split up into factions. The comte de Provence had his own party, and d'Artois his, which, from this time on, was always formed of the most extreme counter-revolutionaries, Ultras. However, there were also the more moderate émigrés and lastly some "monarchicals," who were unanimously detested by the majority of other émigrés.

The court of Coblenz maintained its own agents at the courts of foreign sovereigns. Thus Polignac represented it at the court of the emperor in Vienna, the comte Esterhazi at the court of Catherine II. And as we shall see in the next chapter, it was also in contact with a whole group of secret agents in France.

Calonne exercised the function of prime minister up to 1792; he assigned all tasks and missions, and maintained a voluminous correspondence with the émigrés, with their agents abroad and with foreign powers. This is preserved in the archives in London, publication of which has been begun by Christian de Parrel.[3] The only volume published so far concerns the finances of the emigration. It is very interesting because it shows the means employed by the princes to raise money. Since they were chronically short of money, they pawned their jewels and lived by begging subsidies from all the European powers. The sums were spent as soon as received and sometimes even before. During the entire winter of 1791, the princes tried to increase their army by hiring mercenaries in Germany; the army of the princes, in fact, was not composed exclusively of French émigrés, but of mercenaries as well.

Condé, established in the duchy of Baden, was not far from Coblenz. He had his own army and also his own party composed of Ultras, somewhat like that of the comte d'Artois. But Condé was more concerned with action than negotiation.

The émigrés also had their newspapers: Suleau, one of the most ardent counter-revolutionary journalists, emigrated and published a newspaper written in French, *Le Journal de M. Suleau*.

The favorites triumphed at Coblenz and in the duchy of Baden, as in Paris under Louis XV. Each of the major leaders of the emigration had his own: d'Artois took as his mistress Mme de Polastron, born de Lussan d'Esparbès; and the comte de Provence Mme de Balbi, wife of a rich Genovese banker who had gone mad. Mme de Balbi was inordinately fond of intrigue and very ambitious; she was the only one of the women in the little court at Coblenz who aspired to a political role and had real influence on the comte de Provence. Condé too had his mistress, Mme de Monaco, born Brignoles, whom he is said to have married secretly.

But the major business of the émigrés was the preparation for war, raising an army; in fact, they had not one but three armies. The smallest, but the first to be organized, was that of Mirabeau-Tonneau, the Black

3. Christian de Parrel, *Les Papiers de Calonne*, Vol. I—the only one published (Paris, 1932).

Legion, formed first at Yverdon. This later moved toward the north and took up quarters opposite Colmar, in the duchy of Baden. Condé's army established its headquarters slightly north of the Alsatian frontier. Lastly, the army of the princes had its headquarters in Coblenz. It had been mounted on a grand scale: the royal guard and the king's household with their dazzling uniforms had been reconstituted. The cost of this army was to weigh heavily on the finances of the princes because an ordinary soldier cost 45 livres a month in the infantry and 75 in the cavalry. Money to pay them had to be obtained somehow and during the years 1791–92 the princes lived on the subsidies granted them by the sovereigns of Europe. Emperor Leopold II gave them 1½ million, the king of Spain 1 million, the king of Prussia 2 million, the empress of Russia the same, and various German princes also made contributions; in all the princes raised 6½ million livres. On the other hand, they also borrowed from usurers on the money they expected to recover in France. They claimed to have more than 10 million livres hidden in France, which they promised to use to reimburse the lenders immediately France was "liberated."

To raise money, Calonne sold commissions in the army of the princes, which aroused a storm of protest. All émigrés fit to bear arms were forced to serve, to enlist in one of the three armies, under penalty of immediate expulsion. But all the émigrés who came from France and who, in the main, were nobles already holding commissions in the French army wanted to be officers. Thus there were more officers than soldiers in the émigré army. Companies of officers were formed, who naturally demanded officers' pay.

By the winter of 1791–92 all the subsidies received had been distributed and provisioning of the army ceased; it could not be entirely equipped and so it dispersed. Bands were formed whose members lived on the inhabitants by pillaging, which led to many complaints and to threats on the part of the German princes and the emperor. Some émigrés committed suicide for lack of food. Two hundred, most of them nobles, were expelled from the army for robbery or looting and, at the request of the princes, locked up in the prisons of Coblenz or elsewhere.

Nevertheless, the émigrés did not lose confidence. They were still convinced that the moment they set foot on French soil the revolutionary armies, which they held in contempt, would scatter. It would be a military parade for them as it had been when foreign troops intervened in Geneva in 1782, in Holland in 1787, and in Belgium in 1790.

In mid-January of 1792, Louis XVI, at the request of the Legislative

Assembly, sent the emperor and the German princes a comminatory note demanding the immediate dissolution of the émigré military units that had been formed in the Rhine region. Emperor Leopold, bent as ever upon avoiding war, told the émigrés that they would have to disperse. The German princes also made show of wanting to satisfy the French request. The émigrés did not budge, but they had to give up their uniforms, hide their weapons and show themselves to be less active. Nevertheless, the majority continued to consider war imminent. During the winter of 1791–92 Condé had also entertained the idea of moving into France with his army alone, by crossing the Rhine and launching a raid on an Alsatian town, Colmar, for example. But he was forced to give up this plan.

The émigrés also planned to foment a new uprising in the Midi. The encampment at Jalès was still in existence, and the princes designated two émigrés, the comte de Conway and the comte de Saillans, to go to France and take command of a royal Army of the Midi. De Saillans managed to reach the famous encampment, but he was attacked by the patriot national guards and massacred, along with several men who had accompanied him. One of his accomplices, Claude Allier, who tried to foment an uprising in the department of Aveyron, was also killed. Thus the émigrés lost all hope in terms of this approach; only a foreign war would enable them to re-enter France victoriously.

3 / The Campaign of 1792

Just such a war was to break out much earlier than might have been expected, in the wake of an unforeseen event: the sudden death of Emperor Leopold II, only forty-five years old, on March 1, 1792. The émigrés were accused of having poisoned him, but this is highly unlikely. Leopold was succeeded by his son Francis, who became king of Bohemia and Hungary while waiting to be crowned at Frankfurt under the name of Francis II. He was a very young man, only twenty-four, and little was known of his ideas. The émigrés, who had completely deceived themselves as to Leopold II's intentions, also deceived themselves, in the beginning, about those of Francis II. They had believed that Leopold II was disposed to wage war; now they thought that Francis II would be hostile to the idea. Exactly the opposite happened.

Leopold, until the day of his death, never ceased to resist the pressures exerted on him by the émigrés to declare war. Since 1792 the émigrés had also increased their missions to the courts of European sovereigns, importuning them to issue a declaration of war against France. The prince of Nassau, after having been sent to the court of Leopold II without success, was assigned a similar mission at the court of St. Petersburg. Calonne, for his part, had written several letters to the king of Spain asking him to start the war. A certain Christin had been delegated by Calonne to the court of the king of England in order to wrest a British declaration of war against France, but he had been checkmated by the counter-efforts of Talleyrand, the envoy of the French government.

The death of Leopold II and the advent of Francis II changed everything. Contrary to all expectations, Francis II showed himself to be a very bellicose monarch. As soon as he ascended the throne he resumed the negotiations between Austria and Prussia begun at Pillnitz. Francis II and the king of Prussia, Friedrich Wilhelm, decided that if war was waged against France, its aim would not merely be the integral restoration of the Old Regime in France, but would also include the payment of indemnities to the fief-holding princes of Alsace and the cession of territories to Austria and Prussia. Already it was a question of an annexation of Alsace and of the north of the province of Lorraine by Prussia and Austria.

A new event supervened several days after the death of Leopold II which upset the émigrés' plans. Gustav III, king of Sweden—one of the sovereigns most favorable to the counter-revolution—was assassinated on March 16, 1792, as he was leaving a masked ball. The crime was attributed to the Swedish monarch's ideas. He had modified the Swedish regime and tried to introduce equality of orders under an absolutist regime. The Swedish nobility, which up to then had been very powerful and very independent, decided to avenge itself and plotted the king's assassination. The disappearance of Gustav III removed an important figure from the counter-revolutionary coalition; his successor, Gustav-Adolph, was only thirteen years old. The royal power was exercised by the regent, the duke of Sudermanie, who was strongly opposed to any war.

Thus Austria and Prussia failed to obtain Sweden's support; nevertheless, the drive toward war was stepped up. Maréchal de Castries, who was an émigré, declared in March, 1792, that his hopes were high because they were "based on the insolences of the French National Assembly."

On April 5, 1792, the French ambassador to Vienna handed an ultimatum from the French government to the king of Bohemia and Hungary. The National Assembly and Louis XVI, who wanted a war for diametrically opposed reasons, asked the king of Bohemia and

Hungary to disperse the groups of émigrés who had remained in the Rhineland despite the note of January immediately, and to cease arming them. This ultimatum was rejected, and France declared war on the king of Bohemia and Hungary on April 20, 1792.

At this point the armies of the émigrés were in a state of disarray. They had not been paid, fed or clothed for three months. Many of the émigrés had been forced to go deeper into Germany in search of some means of subsistence; now they had to be rounded up.

As early as the end of April, the first war bulletins raised high hopes among the émigrés. At the beginning of May it was learned that the French forces which had penetrated the Low Countries were completely disbanded, and even dispersed in the region of Tournai. Maréchal de Castries was more optimistic than ever: "The declaration of war that the Assembly was foolish enough to promulgate," he said, "the setbacks experienced by the troops immediately thereafter, have all proved that it did not require great forces to defeat the sedition mongers who have seized the kingdom." So great was the optimism that any further discussion of the campaign or of the progress of operations ceased. Conversation centered primarily on the line of conduct to be followed after victory. Who would be minister? Would it be Calonne? What about maréchal de Castries, who was so confident and who himself had once been minister—but who had secretly been commissioned by Louis XVI to be his intermediary at the courts of the princes? Would it be necessary to oblige all the revolutionaries to make restitution? How many would be executed? Such were the topics discussed by the émigrés as they proceeded with the reorganization of their armies.

Mirabeau's legion melted away, and Mirabeau-Tonneau himself was to die of apoplexy shortly afterwards. So the armies were reduced to two: Condé's and the army of the princes. But since Prussia and Austria, by common agreement, had decided to appoint as generalissimo the duke of Brunswick, who seemed to be one of the most enlightened despots of Germany, an understanding with him about the use of the émigré forces was indispensable. Accordingly, it was necessary to negotiate with the duke. Maréchal de Bouillé, the comte de Caraman and the marquis de Lambert were sent to him to request that he place the army of the émigrés in the vanguard. It was to open up the way; the local populations would rally to them and the Austro-Prussian armies would merely have to follow. Bouillé declared that all the peasants would rise up to chase the Jacobins from the seat of power and whole regiments would come over to the allies; lengthy discussions ensued over what should be done with these regiments. Were they to be incorporated into the armies of the émigrés or into the armies of the Austro-Prussians? Finally it was decided that Prussia would take over their charge and pay them.

No agreement, however, was reached as to the place of the émigrés in the forces of the coalition. Brunswick had absolutely no confidence in them. He proposed that they should wait on the right bank of the Rhine until the Austro-Prussian armies rolled up some victories. Then the émigré armies could be called into France. The negotiations ended in total disagreement. Bouillé, as well as the princes, insisted that the émigrés be in the vanguard, whereas the duke of Brunswick wanted them to bring up the rear. The only agreement reached at the meeting was over the *principle* that the émigrés would participate in the campaign about to be initiated against France.

Upon his return, Bouillé had to confess the failure of his mission to the comte d'Artois. The latter went into a rage, denounced the king of Bohemia and Hungary as a "ruffian" and added that his conduct was due to the pernicious influence of his aunt, Marie-Antoinette, who headed the "Austrian Committee" in the Tuileries. D'Artois employed the same expressions about the queen as he had about the Jacobins. But it was useless to insist because the duke of Brunswick was the generalissimo of the coalition and it was necessary to bow to his will.

Another problem arose: at the point of launching the campaign was it not fitting that the commander-in-chief should issue a manifesto to the French people, calling upon them to rally around the coalition and the émigrés? Louis XVI and Marie-Antoinette had entertained the same idea. When Mallet du Pan left Paris for Switzerland, as described earlier, he had been charged with a mission to the princes, to the king's brothers and to the king of Prussia and the emperor. He was to request them to publish a decidedly moderate manifesto, to inform them that the lives of the royal family were in danger, and to tell them that if the manifesto was violent in character, the worst eventualities were to be feared. But Mallet du Pan was a "monarchical." When he presented himself at the Coblenz headquarters he was pointedly ill received by the émigrés; nevertheless, he talked about the king's intentions with maréchal de Castries, whom Louis XVI had secretly commissioned as his intermediary to the princes. Mallet thereupon went to Frankfurt, where he may have seen the king of Prussia but was not received by the emperor, there for his coronation. Finally, on July 12, de Castries handed the duke of Brunswick a note which had been drawn up subsequently to the instructions given by Louis XVI to Mallet, and which authorized the duke to compose a manifesto conforming to what "he believed was most in keeping with the evolution of the internal situation" in France.[4]

The duke of Brunswick had been thinking about a manifesto for a long time, so the émigrés decided to submit a draft of sorts to him. One of them, the marquis de Limon—who had been compromised in France in shady financial deals—assisted by Pellenc, a former secretary of Mirabeau, was given the task of drafting the major lines. The marquis de Limon's manifesto was then submitted to the duke of Brunswick, who accepted it, perhaps without having meditated at length upon its character or the influence it could have. So the famous "Brunswick Manifesto" was drawn up. By this manifesto, the powers declared that they had set themselves no other aim than the welfare of France, that they did not want to make conquests, that they wanted only to free the royal family and that they had no intention of meddling in matters relating to the internal government of France. Up to that point it was a very normal declaration and thus formulated the manifesto, no doubt, would have passed unobserved. But the duke of Brunswick had preserved in his text the final passage of the marquis de Limon's draft and it was precisely this passage that was to arouse the anger of the French. It read:

> The city of Paris and all its inhabitants without distinction are enjoined to submit, at once and without delay, to the king, to place this prince in full and entire liberty. . . . Moreover, their said majesties declare on their faith and word of emperor and king that if the palace of the Tuileries is forced or outraged, if the least violence, the least outrage is done to Their Majesties the King, the Queen and the royal family, if provision is not immediately made for their safety, their preservation, and their liberty, they will wreak an exemplary and never-to-be-forgotten vengeance by subjecting the city of Paris to military execution and total subversion.

This manifesto was to produce effects exactly opposed to those the émigrés had in view. It was to have those effects that Louis XVI and Marie-Antoinette might have dreaded, had they been really sincere in the mission entrusted to Mallet du Pan. We do know it was the Brunswick Manifesto which provoked the *journée* of June 10 and the overthrow of the throne.

4. Duc de Castries, *Le Testament de la monarchie*. Vol. II: *L'Agonie de la royauté* (Paris, 1959), pp. 343-345.

On the banks of the Rhine, however, none of the émigrés bothered themselves with considerations of this kind; they were wholly involved in a war which they hoped would be rapid and victorious. The coronation of Francis II took place in Frankfurt on July 19. All the French princes were present at the ceremony, surrounded by their *gards de corps*, by the royal household dressed in its new finery, thanks to a recent subsidy of 1 million livres sent by the czarina Catherine II. After the coronation, the émigré army passed in review. It was divided into three groups: the first, commanded by the prince de Condé, was to fight with the army corps of Wallis; it consisted of 5,000 men. The second group, commanded by the duc de Bourbon, was to form part of the corps of Clayrfait. The third group, and the most important was the 12,000-strong army of the princes; it was attached to the Prussian army and was to follow the duke of Brunswick in the rearguard. After the review, Bouillé declared: "I am responsible for the capture of the French fortresses because I have all their keys in my pocket." But Brunswick did not show the same confidence. He had a dread of this émigré army in which there were often two servants to one soldier. On August 7, Fersen, a friend of Marie-Antoinette, wrote to her from Brussels: "The armies of the émigrés are so wholly destitute that scarcely one-quarter of them will be able to keep up with the operations. The duke of Brunswick is already quite weary of them."

The campaign in France began. The corps of émigrés placed in the rearguard was assigned the siege of Thionville, a stronghold situated north of Metz. We possess a remarkable document on this siege, Chateaubriand's *Mémoires d'outre-tombe*. It was a complete fiasco, and the revolutionaries entrenched in Thionville foiled all attacks.

Elsewhere the Prussian army was advancing and approaching Longwy, the émigrés exulted. Calonne crossed into France behind the Prussian army in an attempt to raise money. He decreed that the taxes of the Old Regime were to be collected immediately, but contrary to his hopes, the collections were extremely meager, a pitiful failure. Calonne returned to Coblenz, from where he was soon to leave for England because his position had become untenable: he, the great minister of finance, had not been able to procure the indispensable funds.

In general, the campaign did not shape up as the émigrés had hoped. Most of the French fortresses encountered resisted. Thionville and Metz, in particular, seemed impregnable. It had, of course, been possible to capture Longwy, and owing to the intelligence agents the émigrés had within the fortress, they were also able to take Verdun, whose commander, Beaurepaire, conscious of having been betrayed, committed suicide. But the army could advance only with great caution because its rearguards were threatened by the strongholds that resisted. Moreover, the populace, which they expected to see run joyously ahead of the Prussian army, was very hostile; guerrillas began operations and the peasants attacked stragglers. Quarrels broke out between the Prussians, the Austrians and the émigrés; thus the duke of Brunswick placed the prince de Condé under a twenty-four-hour arrest for having replied in an impertinent manner to him. The comte d'Artois intervened to have the punishment lifted, but it was maintained. The émigrés had already spent all the money received before the entry into the campaign, and their situation became increasingly difficult.

It was under these conditions that news was learned of the *journée* of August 10 and, several days later, of the emigration of Lafayette. Lafayette, who commanded the Army of the Ardennes, had disapproved of the overthrow of the throne; he was a royalist and hostile to the republic. He crossed the frontier but was considered an enemy by the Austrians, who incarcerated him in a fortress in Bohemia. The émigrés viewed this as an excellent measure, because they thought Lafayette more to be feared than the Jacobins. Finally on September 20 the principal encounter of the campaign, the battle of Valmy, took place. The émigrés did not take part; they had several detachments at Verdun but none at Valmy. The battle of Valmy was a French victory, thanks above all to two factors: the considerable numerical superiority of the French troops following the junction of the two armies of Dumouriez and Kellermann, and the incontestable superiority of the French artillery, composed of new materiel perfected during the beginnings of the reign of Louis XVI by the engineer, Gribeauval.

After Valmy, the duke of Brunswick felt he could not continue his march forward, in the first place because of the French resistance and, aside from this, because he was cut off from his supplies, which had not kept pace with him, so that even the advanced depots were still in Luxembourg. Furthermore, the weather had been appalling since the beginning of the campaign; it rained without let-up, the roads were utterly washed out and transformed into bogs—one of the reasons why the supply wagons had not been able to follow the bulk of the army. Finally, with the bad weather, dysentery had set in with the Prussian army, more than half of whose effective forces were ill. The duke of Brunswick decided to retreat. Moreover, he negotiated this retreat with Dumouriez; the negotiation was secret and we are still poorly informed on it, but it is possible that the fact that the two commanders were Freemasons played a role.

At all events, Brunswick attributed his failure above all to the émigrés. He considered that he had been grossly misinformed by them and adopted a harsh attitude towards them as a result. There seemed no end to the bad news for the émigrés. It was at the time of the battle of Valmy that they learned of the September massacres, during which many of their relatives perished. Several days later they were informed of the triumphal entry of French troops into Savoy and the earldom of Nice and, finally, of the invasion of the Rhineland itself by the French troops of Alsace, who were marching towards the north.

The situation became grave and Emperor Francis II demanded the immediate dispersion of the émigré corps, held responsible for the Austro-Prussian defeat. The émigrés had no money. They sold their horses and equipment, and left for destinations judged more congenial. We know that Chateaubriand, wounded in the leg by a bursting shell, suffering from smallpox, left for Belgium and finally found refuge in England. Others reached Switzerland, northern Germany, Italy. It was an exodus.

Only the army of the prince de Condé remained intact. It had been massed in the duchy of Baden, where it remained with a view to effecting a Rhine crossing that never took place. Condé refused to discharge his army and in the face of his energetic attitude, the Austrian government decided to take the army under its charge. His troop thus remained a constituted unit until 1802, the only émigré army that existed for so long a period.

The comte de Provence went off to Coblenz, but he had hardly arrived when the French reached Mayence. Thereupon he left for Liège, where the comte d'Artois rejoined him. Their belongings were seized in Trèves by their creditors. Liège was not a wholly safe refuge because the victory of Jemappes took place shortly thereafter, followed by the entry of French troops into Belgium. The princes had to leave Liège and once more set out for Germany.

They petitioned the German sovereigns for refuge. Finally, the king of Prussia was willing to assign them a residence in the small town of Hamm, where they were kept under strict surveillance and could lead only a very modest existence.

4 / *Debut of Louis XVIII*

At Hamm the princes took up residence in a small wooden house, where they lived on the modest subsidies very stingily granted them by the king of Prussia. Here on January 28, 1793, they learned of the execution of their brother, Louis XVI. The comte de Provence was deeply grieved over his brother's death, but also rather happy to become regent. He issued a proclamation to the French people in which he recognized as king Louis XVII, son of Louis XVI, at that time imprisoned in the tower of the Temple, and declared himself regent. Through this proclamation, the comte de Provence also affirmed his wish to bring about the total restoration of the Old Regime. In the event he were to accede to power in France, declared the comte, he would set about to achieve the following points:

> First of all, the liberation of the king, Louis XVII, of his mother, of his sister and of his aunt, and, at the same time, the re-establishment of the monarchy on the unalterable basis of its constitution; the reformation of the abuses introduced into the regime of public administration; the re-establishment of the religion of our fathers in the purity of its cult and of canonic discipline; the reintegration of the magistrature for the maintenance of public order and the proper dispensation of justice; the reintegration of Frenchmen of all the orders in their legitimate rights and in the enjoyment of their invaded and usurped properties; the severe and exemplary punishment of crimes, the re-establishment of the authority of laws and of peace and, finally, the fulfillment of the solemn commitments that we have taken conjointly with our dearest brother, the comte d'Artois.

D'Artois was named lieutenant-general of the kingdom by the comte de Provence. This proclamation is very important because it fixes the attitude of the regent and later of Louis XVIII toward the Revolution. He was not to change it one iota until the famous declaration of Saint-Ouen in 1814. Only then was he to renounce a whole part of his program in order to adopt a more moderate attitude.

The first concern of the comte de Provence, now regent, was to have himself recognized as such by the foreign powers; but most of them refused. Only Catherine II recognized him. Despite this rebuff, the regent set up in the small town of Hamm his council, which included the same members as at Coblenz, minus Calonne, who had left for England.

Maréchal de Castries was added to it despite the failure of his predictions and soon his was the preponderant influence. The duc de La Vauguyon, who had left Madrid, was called to the council; the comte d'Artois set aside. The regent greatly feared being eclipsed by his brother. D'Artois was sent on a mission to Russia in order to persuade that country to wage war against France. He was very well received there but all he got for his pains was kind words. Catherine II was wholly ready to combat Jacobinism, but in Poland, not France.

D'Artois then asked England for permission to take up residence there. This was at the time when the news of the insurrection of the Vendée became known and d'Artois thought that in England he would be in a better position to aid the Vendéans. But the British government refused, stating that d'Artois's debts in London amounted to £2 million and that by order of his creditors he would be arrested the moment he set foot on British soil, an eventuality which the government would not be able to prevent. In fact, the British government at this time was not in favor of direct aid to the Vendéans and it wanted to prevent the comte d'Artois from establishing himself in England, where he would plot with the rebels of western France.

So d'Artois returned to Hamm, where he remained until July, 1794, the while continuing to negotiate with England. Only then did he obtain authorization to go to Great Britain, although he was asked not to disembark there without first having an interview with the duke of York, who was the commander of the British armies in the Low Countries. D'Artois left for Holland, arriving at the very moment when, after the victory of Fleurus, the French armies had penetrated into Belgium and begun to move toward the Rhine. He could not join the duke of York, who was falling back toward England. For several months he wandered about the United Provinces, often only just escaping the French troops, who during the winter of 1794–95 had crossed the frozen rivers and occupied Amsterdam. Finally he succeeded in rallying England to the émigré cause.

The regent for his part had remained in Hamm, but he was not happy there. During the summer of 1793 he learned of the revolt of the federalists of Provence and the occupation of the port of Toulon—at the request of the royalists of the city—by the Anglo-Spanish fleet. He thought that now he would be able to return to France by way of Toulon and act directly upon those faithful to his cause. But from Hamm, he had first to get nearer to Provence, so he decided to leave for Italy, which was closer to the theater of operations. He left Hamm on November 17, 1793, went to Verona and from there to Leghorn, where he planned to embark for Toulon on a Spanish boat. But at Leghorn he heard of the fall of Toulon which was attributed to the well-placed fire of the French artillery, commanded by an officer altogether obscure at that time, General Bonaparte. The regent made a half-turn and went back to Verona, which he reached only in June, 1794. He decided to take up residence there because in Verona he was close to the man who was the émigrés' and foreign powers' best source of information on events in France—the comte d'Antraigues. D'Antraigues, in fact, had taken up residence in Venice under the protection of the ambassadors of Russia and Spain.

At Verona, the regent continued the same policy as that pursued at Hamm. He showed a marked infatuation with his rights, a great hostility to the Revolution and little inclination to make the slightest concession to the revolutionaries. He maintained intact the terms of his Hamm proclamation. In Verona he learned of the death of Louis XVII, and immediately assumed the title of Louis XVIII, informing all the sovereigns of Europe and preparing a new proclamation to the French. He submitted this proclamation to d'Antraigues, an Ultra of the counter-revolution. "No accommodation," the latter counseled. The comte Ferrand, who was also consulted, was of the same opinion and demanded that the émigrés, upon their return to France, should order 44,000 executions, one per commune. The "monarchical" minority, under the ideological guidance of Mallet du Pan, protested against this intransigence and the threatened acts of force, but most of the émigrés wanted nothing whatsoever to do with the "monarchicals."

In his proclamation of Verona, Louis XVIII declared that he granted his pardon to those responsible for the errors of the people, but that he would make an exception in the matter of the regicides—which was tantamount to threatening half the members of the Convention with capital punishment. This was followed by the affirmation that France must without more ado return to her ancient constitution, that is, to the Old Regime, while reforming all its abuses. The Catholic religion must be reestablished as the State religion, the other religions to be merely tolerated. The royal power would once more be hereditary, with the three orders reconstituted; the Estates General could be convoked but only to vote new taxes or to increase the old ones. They would be granted the right to formulate demands, but could always be dissolved by the king. The parlements would be restored and would become the guardians of the laws. National properties were not on the agenda and from this it could be deduced that they would be returned to their former owners.

Louis XVIII reconstituted his council with almost the same people who had belonged to it at Hamm; he added to them the comte d'Avaray, who rapidly became his confidant and replaced the disgraced maréchal de Castries.

Louis XVIII was recognized as king first of all by Russia and Sweden. The other governments which were in the process of negotiating peace with France deemed that the moment for such recognition was not opportune. Finally Louis XVIII was recognized only by a handful of sovereigns.

In France he was totally ignored and, to the extent that he was known, appeared as a man who was either greatly to be feared because of his vengeful proclamations, in which he threatened all revolutionaries *en bloc*, or as a completely ridiculous figure because his proclamations were totally without effect.

Verona was not to shelter him for long. In April of 1796 the Army of Italy, commanded by Bonaparte, crossed the Alps and the Apennines. The intimidated senate of Venice, on April 14, ordered Louis XVIII to leave Verona forthwith. Grievously insulted, he replied by demanding that his signature be struck from the Republic's Golden Book. Thereupon he left in short stages for Switzerland and caught up again with the prince de Condé's army, which was still in the service of Austria. Austria, fearing that the presence of the claimant to the throne would provoke a French offensive, demanded that Louis XVIII quit the army. He then solicited Russia for a place of refuge. While awaiting the reply, he stayed for a spell in the small German village of Dillinge, where he was the victim of an assassination attempt: a bullet fired from a pistol missed his skull by inches. The would-be assassin has never been identified. Until the end of 1797 Louis XVIII remained at Blankenburg, where he lived in rather wretched conditions.

By that time peace had been signed between France and Austria at Campo-Formio. The emperor demanded that Louis XVIII leave the German states. Russia finally replied favorably to Louis's request for asylum and the czar, Paul I, who had succeeded Catherine II, assigned the small town of Mitau near Riga as a residence to him, while prohibiting him from leaving it without authorization.

Louis XVIII arrived at Mitau on March 13, 1798. He was to remain there until 1801, when he went to Warsaw where he lived until 1804. For the next three years he was to lead a life of turmoil, moving into

Sweden, returning to Germany, reaching Poland and finally staying in Mitau for another two years, until 1807. But after Tilsit, Czar Alexander no longer wished to tolerate his presence in his states. Thereupon Louis XVIII left Russia to rejoin his brother in England, where he was to remain until the Restoration of 1814.

As we have seen, the direct action of the émigrés against France was a complete fiasco. The armies of the émigrés played practically no role whatsoever in the operations conducted by the coalition against France. The proclamations of the comte de Provence, as regent and later as king, had no effect in France, or rather their effect was to harm the monarchist cause. On the other hand, the action of the émigrés was more effective in master-minding the conspiracies and insurrections which developed in France during the revolutionary period. This was the result of the excellent espionage and intelligence networks maintained in France by the counter-revolutionaries and we must analyze their operations before approaching the study of the great royalist insurrections.

CHAPTER X

The Intelligence Networks

After the failure of their attempts at armed intervention alongside the coalition forces in 1792, the émigrés clearly realized that they had failed because they had been poorly informed. At all events, if they did not realize this themselves, foreigners, and particularly the duke of Brunswick, did not fail to remind them of it. So the émigrés considerably improved their methods of gathering intelligence.

Little is known of these intelligence networks, however, for the obvious reason that they were secret, this being the very condition of their success. The members have left no memoirs: their history, the value of the information they furnished and the deductions one can draw from them in relation to the general history of the Revolution figure among the most obscure, most controversial, but also most exciting problems of revolutionary history.

1 / The Dropmore Bulletins

The *Dropmore Papers*, published from 1894 onwards, consist of numerous documents preserved at Dropmore Castle in England. These papers are extremely varied in character, but in the main they are letters addressed to the British government, or dispatched by it, during the revolutionary period.

The publication of 1894 contains twenty-eight bulletins sent by the British minister at Genoa, Francis Drake, between June and September 2, 1794. These bulletins—which, it seems, were drawn up by a royalist agent

—gave all sorts of details on the developments within France during the Revolution, details that appeared altogether extraordinary because, as we shall see, they were in frequent and often profound disagreement with the traditional history of the Revolution. Thus they portrayed Sieyès as the real organizer of the Terror, whereas Robespierre figured only on a secondary level.

When the bulletins appeared, Alphonse Aulard declared that they were "unworthy of the historian's attention," that they dealt with "grotesque trifles" and that the writer was "the most hoaxed of historians, unless he himself was a hoaxer." He categorically denied their authenticity. Similar observations were made by the English critic, Sir John Clapham, and the German critic, Hans Glagau, the former in the *English Historical Review* and the latter in the *Historische Zeitschrift*. Thus the bulletins were buried and no longer discussed. Nobody thought of comparing them to the extremely interesting information that Léonce Pingaud came up with in that same year concerning the organization of royalist espionage by the comte d'Antraigues.

It was not until 1914, twenty years later, that a historian of the stature of Albert Mathiez once more scrutinized the *Dropmore Papers*. In an article entitled "Histoire secrète du Comité de Salut public," published in the *Revue des Questions historiques* of January, 1914, and reprinted by him in Volume 2 of the *Etudes robespierristes*, Mathiez established that in the bulletins Sieyès appears as the secret leader of the Committee of Public Safety, and that most of his interventions were connected with efforts to organize the de-Christianization campaign, to bring about the fall of "factions," and to have former members of the parlements brought before the revolutionary tribunal. Now these observations were in absolute contradiction with those that Sieyès himself gives us in an anonymous account of his life. Here he declares that he had never addressed a word to Robespierre and that it was he, in speaking of the Terror, who pronounced the now celebrated phrase, "*J'ai vécu.*" Mathiez then established that the bulletins portray Saint-Just in a way that differs radically from the official documents. Not only was Saint-Just no friend of Robespierre, but he was in deep disagreement with him. Furthermore, Saint-Just supposedly had tried to save the detained Girondin deputies and committed a certain number of deputies at the Convention to protest against the law of 22 Prairial which organized the great Terror.

As for Robespierre, the bulletins affirm that the Incorruptible had made efforts to free the dauphin, the young Louis XVII. Robespierre himself, on the night of May 23/24, 1794, had supposedly gone to fetch the dauphin from the Temple and conduct him to Meudon. But for reasons that are not explained, the dauphin was said to have been brought back to the Temple. At the end of his study, Mathiez concluded:

> There is but one acceptable method to prove whether the bulletins of the royalist spy are worthy of credence, that is, to discover other authentic and incontestable documents which would confirm the data. Till then, historians can rightly hold them in legitimate suspicion since they are in manifest contradiction with all the known sources.

Mathiez began to dedicate himself to this extremely difficult detective work and he came up with some important findings. He verified, in particular, that an agent of the Committee of Public Safety, Eve Demaillot, arrested after 9 Thermidor, at that time drew up a memorandum that confirms the existence of political divergences between Saint-Just and Robespierre so that from this point of view, the *Dropmore Papers* are not absolutely false. Mathiez also established that the bulletins addressed to the British government were not sent to this government alone but were also communicated to other powers, and notably to the Spanish government via the Spanish ambassador to Venice, Las Casas. In fact, Mathiez discovered that the French chargé d'affaires at Constantinople, Félix Hénin, who remained in close touch with the Spanish ambassador, Las Casas, despite the war—a phenomenon that occurred rather frequently at that time—had passed on to the Committee of Public Safety a number of letters from Las Casas which alluded to events similar to those mentioned in the bulletins. For example, Hénin transmitted to the Committee of Public Safety a letter from Las Casas addressed to him, which began: "My dear enemy . . ." In this letter Las Casas said that at a meeting of the Committee of Public Safety, Hénin had been accused of not carrying out his duties faithfully. Hénin sent this letter in order to justify himself.

The Committee of Public Safety was shaken when it received news of Hénin's letter, which confirmed that its secrets had been "leaked," as we would say today. The meetings of the Committee of Public Safety in fact were secret, and it was true that Hénin had been accused in the course of them. How had it been possible for a royalist agent in the service of foreign powers to know this? Mathiez concluded that Las Casas had been informed by a royalist agent, who must have been with Louis XVIII at Verona.

On the other hand, the Committee of Public Safety was not satisfied with Hénin's explanations. It prolonged its inquiry and sought to determine who among its members was betraying it. In view of the fact that its meetings were secret, the leak could have come only from one of its twelve members. The committee's suspicions fell on an ex-noble, the former advocate-general of the Parlement of Paris, Hérault de Séchelles. At that time de Séchelles was on a mission in Alsace. Upon returning to Paris, he was not able to clear himself, and was promptly arrested, brought before the revolutionary tribunal and sentenced to death. But the "leaks" continued after the execution of Hérault de Séchelles, which proves that he was not the culprit.

In fact, Hénin subsequently received two further letters from Las Casas which contained extracts from espionage bulletins. In one of these letters, an allusion was made to a speech by Saint-Just delivered to the Committee of Public Safety on March 11, 1794; it was a very violent speech against Hénin and against Descorches, the French ambassador to Constantinople.

Mathiez studied Saint-Just's speech, referred to in his report, at great length. He established that it was well known and had been utilized formerly by the German historian, von Sybel, who had found a printed copy in Germany. The speech had held von Sybel's attention because it dealt with the enormous sums that the disseminators of French revolutionary propaganda supposedly had spent in neutral countries in order to foment revolutionary movements, notably in Turkey, Sweden, Germany, Switzerland, Genoa and Venice. Several hundred millions in the currencies of the time were involved.

Von Sybel believed the speech was authentic and from it he concluded that considerable importance had been assigned to the role of French revolutionary propaganda. But the French historian Albert Sorel, in his classic work *L'Europe et la Révolution française*, examining the considerable sums that France, according to Saint-Just, had spent for the dissemination of revolutionary propaganda abroad, believed that such a vast operation was technically impossible and therefore concluded that the speech was a forgery. Mathiez also views it as a forgery, at least in the form in which it had been printed. It may have had its basis in an original, but Mathiez conjectures that this printed speech had been fabricated by the royalist agent who wrote the bulletins for the foreign powers. Moreover, at this time the papers of a Milanese statesman, count Greppi, an acute observer of the revolutionary epoch, had just been published in Italy.

Greppi had been aware of Saint-Just's speech, which had been printed in some foreign countries to combat the revolutionary propaganda. According to Greppi, this speech was not only a forgery but a fabrication by the head of the most important intelligence network of the time, the comte d'Antraigues. Mathiez adopted this conclusion and from it deduced that the person who wrote the bulletins dispatched to London by way of Francis Drake, as well as those which were sent to Madrid by way of Las Casas and other bulletins found in the archives of other governments, could be none other than d'Antraigues.

In 1894 Léonce Pingaud published a book on the comte d'Antraigues which provided a great deal of information on the activity of this mysterious figure.

2 / D'Antraigues and His Intelligence Network

We mentioned earlier that the comte d'Antraigues was born in 1753, that through his mother he was the grandson of the intendant of Languedoc, Saint-Priest, and that he had published an important pamphlet on the Estates General, in 1788, on the eve of the Revolution. We also know that he was elected deputy of Vivarais to the Estates General and that he had emigrated as early as February 27, 1790, for two reasons: first for political motives, because he had passed very rapidly from hostility to the Old Regime to an intransigent royalism; but also because he wanted to marry his mistress, an actress, Saint-Huberty, despite his family's opposition.

D'Antraigues went off to Lausanne and married there on December 29, 1790; a son was born to him on June 26, 1792. D'Antraigues lived in Switzerland for a spell in the duchy of Vaud and in the Tessin. There he published many counter-revolutionary pamphlets, extremely violent and altogether intransigent in character. One of them bears the significant title *Point d'accommodement* (*No Compromise*); another deals with the French nobility. He made frequent trips between Switzerland and northern Italy, traveling under pseudonyms, chief of which was Marco Polo Philiberti. He tried to obtain the aid of Spain for Louis XVI and it was then that he made the acquaintance of Las Casas, the Spanish ambassador to Venice. D'Antraigues was supported in his efforts by the French ambassador at Rome, cardinal de Bernis, and by the comte de Vaudreuil.

The Spanish government, for that matter, was already well informed on events in France. Among the sovereigns of Europe, Charles IV of Spain

was the closest relative to Louis XVI. The latter had asked Charles IV
for assistance since 1789. Immediately after being brought by the people
of Paris from Versailles to the capital, Louis XVI had written a letter to
Charles IV in which he protested in advance against all the documents
that he might sign and declared that he would do so only under duress.
Indeed, as early as 1789 the Spanish government had organized in France
a *"correspondance"* as it was called, that is, an intelligence network, whose
principal members were Des Pomelles and Lemaître. It seems to have
been Las Casas who put d'Antraigues in touch with these men, the first
two agents of his network.

Thereafter d'Antraigues tried to obtain other intelligence data, and his
information increased in volume and importance from 1793 onwards, the
period when the pretender to the throne, Louis XVIII, left Germany to
take up residence in Verona.

D'Antraigues, who needed money—it seems that he took the job of
heading the intelligence network not only because of his royalist convictions, but also in order to earn a living—went to Verona to offer his
services to Louis XVIII and it was agreed that he would send his intelligence reports simultaneously to Louis XVIII and the Spanish government. The latter would remunerate the comte's services by paying him
50,000 reals a year and in addition, in 1793, awarded him the cross of
Charles III. He was also made a naturalized Spanish citizen so as to afford
him better protection against French counterespionage services. This,
however, did not prevent him from acting as the official representative
of Louis XVIII to the Republic of Venice.

Thenceforth d'Antraigues was the real head of a network whose two
principal agents in Paris were Des Pomelles and Lemaître. These agents
sent letters which apparently dealt with unimportant matters, commercial
questions; but between the lines, in sympathetic ink, they wrote political
intelligence reports on the situation in France. Soon d'Antraigues had
other intelligence agents in Paris: abbé Brottier, Sourdat, the former police
lieutenant at Troyes, La Villeurnois and Duverne de Presle.

D'Antraigues did not content himself with the transmission of these
intelligence reports to the Spanish government exclusively. Either because
he wanted better pay or because he was aiming for greater effectiveness,
he got in touch with the British representative in Venice, who sent him
to the English consul in Leghorn, Francis Drake. Drake had been posted
to Genoa and charged with the direction of the English espionage service
in the whole of northern Italy, and extending into the French Midi, so

that he could be closer to the theater of operations and perhaps even to d'Antraigues.

At the same time d'Antraigues made the acquaintance of the Russian representative in Naples, Golovkin. It appears that d'Antraigues also established contact with the representatives of Austria, of the Kingdom of Naples and of other countries.

Thus there are numerous copies of d'Antraigues's bulletins in existence today. In addition to the twenty-eight published in the *Dropmore Papers*, others are preserved in archives in London, Madrid, Naples and Vienna. In 1956 the English historian, H. Mitchell, published an article on the bulletins in the English archives in the *Bulletin of the British Institute of Historical Research*. He disclosed that there were also many unpublished bulletins in the Public Record Office, or in the British Museum: some precede the first bulletin published in the *Dropmore Papers*; ten are intercalated between the first and second bulletins of the *Dropmore Papers*. In all, Mitchell counted 131 bulletins sent by Drake and probably written by d'Antraigues.

Francis Drake had arrived in Genoa on August 15, 1793. His fundamental mission was to keep the British government and, in particular, Lord Grenville informed on happenings inside France. No doubt he met d'Antraigues through the English minister in Venice. At all events, for a very long time Drake concealed the name of the comte d'Antraigues from the English government. For many months he transmitted d'Antraigues's bulletins without identifying the author, no doubt because the latter did not want it known that he was the one who consolidated the intelligence received from Paris. It is also likely that d'Antraigues had no desire to advertise the fact that he was being paid simultaneously by the Spanish, English, Neapolitan and Russian governments. Francis Drake stated that these bulletins were transmitted to him by a royalist in whom complete confidence could be placed and that this royalist received them from a person "employed as secretary by the Committee of Public Safety." Drake first asked for £90 in order to pay d'Antraigues, then an additional £50 because the comte wished to be paid in advance. Later Drake regularly asked for money from the British government so that the bulletins could continue.

In examining the bulletins sent by Drake and drawn up by d'Antraigues, one notes that they have a political aim independent of the intelligence which they contain and which we shall study later. This aim is to show that an integral restoration is possible in France, providing the English

government will pay the price, give sufficient subsidies to the royalist
organizations, and effectively aid the revolt in Vendée. No doubt
d'Antraigues's intention, shared by Louis XVIII, was to dissuade the
English government from entering into a relationship with the "monarchicals." Both were anxious to persuade the British government that there
was only one possible solution to the Revolution; namely, the integral
restoration of the Old Regime. A more immediate aim of d'Antraigues's
was to obtain the British government's recognition of Louis XVIII as
regent, then, at the death of Louis XVII, as king of France. The English
government, in fact, had not recognized the comte de Provence either
as regent or king, and had not even replied to the request for recognition
he had addressed to it.

To the bulletins which d'Antraigues transmitted to the British government must be added the private letters written by d'Antraigues to Francis
Drake. These letters were not transmitted to the English government; they
remained among Drake's papers and were later deposited in the British
Museum. In them d'Antraigues dwells further on the necessity of
England's recognition of the comte de Provence as regent and elaborates
on how England's interest lies in supporting the intransigent royalists, not
the constitutionalists.

There is mention both in the bulletins sent to London and in the letters
to Drake of Saint-Just's famous speech; these documents show that the
speech had been printed and spread in Italy by the efforts of d'Antraigues.

The correspondence between Drake and the British government lasted
until the end of 1794. At this time Drake had to return to London and the
correspondence with him as intermediary ceased; but it was to resume
in another form.

This is what is currently known about the *Dropmore Papers* and the
bulletins by d'Antraigues. Mitchell is of the opinion that the bulletins sent
by Drake were all drawn up by d'Antraigues and that they constituted
the British government's principal source of secret intelligence on what
was transpiring in France from 1792 to 1794. Lord Grenville thought them
of such importance that he communicated them to the king. But what
was the value of the information given in these bulletins? Previously,
Léonce Pingaud considered that the reports received by d'Antraigues
consisted mainly of tittle-tattle, gossip of the "It is said" variety, stories
heard in the corridors of the Committee of Public Safety, newspaper
clippings more or less rewritten and pretentious considerations which were
the work of the intelligence agents themselves, and that amid all this

nonsense only a small number of intelligence items were worthy of credence. But the historians of the years 1894–1910 did not make any comparison between Léonce Pingaud's book and the *Dropmore Papers*, which explains why Aulard, who agreed with Pingaud's conclusions, condemned the papers.

In contrast, Mathiez, after his critical study of the *Dropmore Papers*, felt they had a certain worth but stated that it was necessary to identify the source of the intelligence data they contained. He found this source. In the archives of the Ministry of Foreign Affairs in Paris there exists a whole series of papers, deposited there by Louis XVIII in 1814, at the time of the Restoration. These constitute the Bourbon collection. Among them we find letters which include all kinds of inconsequential information, but between the lines we can dimly discern writing in sympathetic ink, developed and then almost blotted out again. There are many ways of writing with sympathetic ink: one method uses lemon juice; the paper is heated to make the writing appear but it disappears again very rapidly. Thus Mathiez was not able to read the additional lines clearly. With modern chemical processes the interlinear writing probably could be restored today but no attempt at such a restoration has been made to date.

What Mathiez was able to read has shown that the intelligence items sent from Paris were somewhat different from those found in d'Antraigues's bulletins. In other words, d'Antraigues centralized the letters sent to him by several agents and then composed a new letter while, at the same time, transforming the reports. Why? First, because he had his own ideas on the meaning of events, and second, because in communicating his bulletins he retained one fixed aim: to obtain the aid of foreign powers exclusively for the intransigent royalists, to prevent the "monarchicals" from receiving it, and to have the comte de Provence recognized as regent.

Despite Mathiez's observations, a certain number of historians have utilized the *Dropmore Papers* as though they were a source of uncontested authenticity. Guglielmo Ferrero, for example, in a posthumous book entitled *Les Deux Révolutions françaises*,[1] makes use of the intelligence provided by the *Dropmore Papers* on the subject of Robespierre's struggle against the factions, and on Sieyès. "For a long time," he writes,

we have believed that Robespierre was the inspirer of the grave decisions that were to be taken, that he conceived the idea of purging

1. (Neuchâtel and Paris, 1951).

the two parties of Left and Right, or, rather, of suppressing them by
the revolutionary tribunal and the guillotine. . . . Now some documents would lead us to believe that abbé Sieyès was the one who
probably conceived this purge and had Robespierre put it into
execution.

Ferrero in fact adopts the thesis of the *Papers*: he considers that Sieyès
did play a very great role, and that what the *Dropmore Papers* say of him
is correct: "Abbé Sieyès, the most wretched man who ever lived, is clearly
the cruelest man in France. . . . Abbé Sieyès is convinced beyond doubt
that the rule of kings is finished in Europe and that a century of anarchy
will exist in all states after which, he says, we shall see the rise of new
institutions." Ferrero, who considers this an accurate assessment, says:
"The role that he [Sieyès] supposedly played, likewise appears remarkable. But the great difficulty in believing that he played such a role arises
from the fact that nothing was known about it for a very long time and
from the fact that he himself publicly declared that he had never known
Robespierre."

Another author, Albert Ollivier, in his book *Saint-Just ou la force des
choses*,[2] also utilizes the intelligence information found in the *Dropmore
Papers*.

> In order to complete the facts that have been made public, we must
> have recourse to police memoranda, to the account of the secret
> intelligence networks established by the singular comte d'Antraigues.
> To be sure, intelligence of this order must be accepted cautiously
> and verified as much as possible, but it is very useful inasmuch as
> the official declarations themselves are not free of error or mendacities.

In fact, Ollivier uses most of the intelligence contained in the *Dropmore
Papers*, but he is familiar only with the twenty-eight published bulletins,
and ignores the existence of a hundred more such reports in the English
archives. In particular, he concedes the authenticity of Saint-Just's famous
speech.

We shall conclude our study on the historical value of these bulletins
with M. Reinhard's monitory reflection: "Let us not labor under any
misapprehension; the *Dropmore Papers* are not to be rejected out of hand.
And for many years now few historians have done so. But neither can

2. (Paris, 1954).

they be accepted uncritically. As with any document, each point advanced must be put to the proof and compared with other documents; only from this comparison can a useful conclusion emerge."[3]

3 / The "Factory"

We shall now try to reconstitute the intelligence network which sent d'Antraigues the material for his bulletins. The network was formed by a number of persons whose identities have been very gradually and painstakingly ascertained.

On the basis of d'Antraigues's papers, Pingaud already knew who the Parisian correspondents of the network were. But the thought never occurred to Mathiez that these could be the authors of the letters, written in invisible ink, which he had read at the Ministry of Foreign Affairs in Paris. The signatories of these letters were designated by pseudonyms or cryptograms and Mathiez was not able to identify all of them.

For example, Mathiez found a certain Le Tronne among the signatories; he then searched among the Le Tronnes known during the Revolution, those whose names were kept in the police files. His search yielded no such person. Later, Ollivier and also Bessand-Massenet reread these letters and established that Mathiez had read incorrectly. The signature is not Le Tronne, but Le Traime, an anagram of Lemaître, shown by Pingaud to be one of d'Antraigues's correspondents.

Again, a certain Thibault figures among the signatories: this was the pseudonym of Des Pomelles. There is also the question of a person designated by the figure 99, which Mathiez read as QQ. Now "99" was the identifying mark of abbé Brottier.

Thus the signatories have all been identified at last, and they are indeed those whom Léonce Pingaud, as early as 1893, indicated as the Parisian correspondents of the comte d'Antraigues. Who were these men who formed the "antennae" of the network by d'Antraigues from Verona and Venice?

Lemaître was a Parisian lawyer, born in Honfleur. He had been arrested in 1785 for printing pamphlets against Calonne, and imprisoned in the Bastille. On January 14, 1786, his sentence called for the confiscation of his printing equipment and the manuscripts found in his domicile, and for a reprimand. This Lemaître claimed descent from Antoine Lemaître, the

3. *Ann. hist. de la Rév. fr.*, 1958, no. 5, p. 18.

Jansenist, who had lived at Port-Royal. Before the Revolution, in fact, Lemaître seems to have been a "feuilliste," that is, a scrivener who furnished important personages with a newsletter which he wrote by hand or printed in a very small number of copies.

It is not surprising, therefore, that the Spanish government—or, more exactly, its representative in Paris in 1790, the comte de Fernan Nuñez—should turn to this Lemaître, whose business it was to provide information, when he wanted to obtain up-to-date intelligence on the situation in France. It was the Spanish government, through Las Casas, who gave Lemaître's name to d'Antraigues when the latter was looking for correspondents in Paris.

Lemaître was subsequently arrested, so we possess an impressionistic police description of him: "Old-fashioned wig, gloves, spectacles, glossy dress coat, back-biter, and sardonic smile." He lived on the rue Sainte-Croix-de-la-Bretonnerie, near the faubourg Saint-Antoine. Arrested after the *journée* of August 10, 1792, he was released thanks to the intercession of Tallien, his neighbor. Tallien certified that Lemaître was a gentleman, "who led a very secluded life and knew only good patriots." He was arrested again in Nivôse, Year II, for royalist opinions but was well treated in prison and again released, very probably because Tallien once more interceded for him. Lemaître will crop up again shortly.

The second agent, abbé Brottier, was born in the Nièvre, near Clemency. He had entered holy orders in emulation of his uncle, Brottier de Cuzy, who was a learned Hellenist. Brottier, who bears the number 99 in the correspondence, was also designated by the pseudonym Corbeau. He taught mathematics and Greek, and was also a numismatist: "Swarthy complexion verging on black, long and exposed ears, rotund face, crabbed, sullen character." He made the acquaintance of Mme de Rivière, whose cryptogram in the letters is RR. She was the wife of a naval officer who in Martinique in 1794 refused to hoist the tricolor flag over his ship and preferred to pass over to the Spaniards. Mme de Rivière was of great assistance to abbé Brottier. Brottier knew Lemaître from before the Revolution and was implicated in the latter's first arrest in 1785.

Des Pomelles, a former officer, lived near Paris close to Verrières Forest, in the house of a relative, Mme Bailly, who was also part of the network.

François Nicolas Sourdat, designated in the correspondence by the initials BB, was born in Troyes on July 14, 1745. A magistrate, father of seven children, he had been a police lieutenant before the Revolution. In

1790 his office was abolished and redeemed, as were so many similar offices. He subsequently attracted attention by his counter-revolutionary attitude, and his house was sacked during the disturbances at Troyes, after the events of August 10. At the time of the trial of Louis XVI, he volunteered to defend the king. Louis XVI rejected his offer, but Sourdat published his written defense. He took up residence in Paris in February, 1793, was arrested a year later and imprisoned from February 16 to August 28, 1794. After his release, he was able to resume his activity in the intelligence network.

These were the principal members of the network. How did they know what was going on inside the Committee of Public Safety? It does not appear that they were directly informed by the members of the committee, by Hérault de Séchelles, for example. But it is quite possible that Tallien, who was Lemaître's protector and who, moreover, was linked to certain members of the committee, had briefed Lemaître about the goings-on within it. It is difficult to substantiate this hypothesis, but the members of the network must have had their intelligence sources.

Now that we have reconstituted this network, we can understand how it functioned. Its Parisian members were rather inferior agents, obscure figures, but whose profession, particularly in the case of Lemaître, was to provide information to those desiring it. Probably they spoke among themselves, read the newspapers attentively and then, uncritically, drew up a synthesis of what they had learned. D'Antraigues improved upon these letters, rewrote them and issued his famous bulletins, which were spread throughout Europe, adding to them, on his own, the intelligence purveyed to him from Paris.

Thus the intelligence furnished by d'Antraigues had a certain value; some of it was true but no doubt a good deal was false. It is prudent therefore to heed Mathiez's advice: the *Dropmore Papers* should be used only after putting them through the crucible of meticulous criticism.

Let us now see what became of the members of this network. They hardly participated in the preparation of the royalist insurrection of 13 Vendémiaire, Year IV (October 5, 1795). This royalist insurrection was much more the work of the moderates, the constitutional royalists, than the absolutists. Most of the members of the network, and above all Brottier and Des Pomelles, were very much opposed to participation in the insurrection by absolute royalists. Only Lemaître played a role in the *journée* of 13 Vendémiaire, and had prepared for the day in a newspaper published by him, *Le Ventriloque*, whose motto was: "A hungry stomach has no ears." He had received at least 86,400 livres from d'Antraigues for his propaganda and had been in contact with a number of moderate deputies at the Convention, such as Cambacérès and Gamon, both natives of Languedoc and called to his attention by d'Antraigues.

After the failure of 13 Vendémiaire, Lemaître was arrested in a Paris café on October 12, 1795. His papers were seized and published by order of the Directory; among them were found many letters from d'Antraigues. These letters, little read by historians before the publication of Bessand-Massenet's book in 1956, tally with those that were found in London and Madrid. In the lists seized at Lemaître's home, the police found the name of Brottier, who was also arrested. Lemaître and Brottier were brought before a court-martial; Brottier loudly and convincingly denied that he knew Lemaître and won acquittal. But Lemaître was sentenced to death and executed. Thus one of the members of the network died.

The others continued their activity during the period of the Directory. They established a royalist organization, to which we shall turn later, the Philanthropic Institute. This organization was trying to foment an insurrection among the troops stationed in Paris, so its agents entered into relations with a colonel called Malo. Colonel Malo exposed the royalist organization to Carnot, a member of the Directory. On the day agreed upon for the insurrection, a trap was set and the royalist agents—Duverne de Presle, La Villeurnois, Brottier and Poli—were arrested. Des Pomelles, who had been forewarned, was the only one who managed to escape. A court-martial tried Brottier and his three accomplices, not under the charge of high treason but of soliciting soldiers to desert and join a royalist conspiracy.

The trial took place in March of 1797, that is, at the time of the elections, which were extremely favorable to the royalists, and the tribunal declared that the case was outside its jurisdiction. It was brought before the court of appeals, which demanded to see the "dossier," but the Directory refused to transmit it to that body and ordered the court-martial to try the case despite its first conclusions. The judges of the court-martial handed down a very lenient sentence, either because they were intimidated by the illegality of the procedure, or because they feared the vengeance of the royalists, who were thought to be on the verge of seizing power. Brottier was sentenced to ten years in prison, as was Duverne; Poli to five years, and La Villeurnois to only one year.

The Directory, furious with the light sentence, set it aside. It ordered that the accused be hauled before another court-martial, this time not for soliciting soldiers to desert but for plotting against the security of the State. This order, however, was never carried out and the accused remained in prison.

After the *coup d'état* of 18 Fructidor, the Directory published the lengthy confessions that Duverne de Presle supposedly had made in prison six months earlier, but since we do not possess an original of these confessions, their authenticity is suspect. Duverne went into great detail about the royalist agency, the intelligence network, which at times he cited as the "Factory" and at times as "The Royal Agency of Paris." He also gave precise information on the Philanthropic Institute and on the correspondence of the agents with d'Antraigues.[4]

The Directory seized the opportunity afforded it by the *coup d'état* of 18 Fructidor and of the full powers with which it had been invested to order the deportation to Guiana of Brottier and La Villeurnois. The latter died there in July, 1798, and Brottier followed him to the grave several weeks later. As for Duverne de Presle, he was simply banished from France, which lends a certain credibility to his "confessions"; a boat took him to the Canary Islands, but he immediately made his way back to Portugal where he lived until the Consulate. Then he returned to France. After 1814 he received a pension from Louis XVIII, with the cross of St. Louis. Thus it is debatable just whom he really betrayed, since he had been pardoned by the Directory and was also decorated by Louis XVIII. He died in 1844 at the age of eighty-two. Des Pomelles, who had managed to escape, disappeared leaving absolutely no trace.

That leaves Sourdat, who went over to the service of Bonaparte's police and became a double agent. So he was rewarded by the government of Bonaparte, who appointed him assistant judge in Pontoise; he died in Etampes. His son, Carlos Sourdat, who was also implicated in the trial of 1797 and had been acquitted, joined the *chouans*, fought with them at the end of the Directory and then rallied to the Empire. He ended his career as adjutant-general in 1815, and lived on until 1847, dying at the age of seventy-two.[5]

Such is the history of the first intelligence network masterminded by the comte d'Antraigues who, after its dissolution, created others.

4. On Duverne de Presle, see P. Tiersonnier, *Recherches sur l'affaire Duverne de Presle, 1797* (mimeo., Dornes, 1952).
5. On Carlos Sourdat, see Le Menuet de La Jugannière, *Le Chouan Carlos Sourdat et son père, l'agent royal* (Paris, 1932).

4 / *Reboul, Gamon and d'Antraigues*

Although we have been able to identify with near certainty some members of the "Factory" network, identification of most of the espionage agents whom d'Antraigues had as correspondents during the Thermidorian period and the Directory is much more difficult.

No doubt the "Factory" continued to correspond with d'Antraigues after 13 Vendémiaire, during the whole Thermidorian period, and up to 1797, that is, up to the time its members were arrested or dispersed. But as early as 1795 it appears that this network, all of whose members resided in Paris, did not suffice to give d'Antraigues the kind of intelligence, covering the whole of France, which the foreign powers were demanding of him.

In fact, peace was signed between France and Spain at Basle in 1795. At the same time the Spanish ambassador to Venice, Las Casas, was transferred to London. D'Antraigues was therefore led to approach the Russian embassy. Thenceforth he was in contact with the Russian minister to Venice, Mordvinov, as well as with the Russian ambassador to Naples, Golovkin. He continued to correspond with Francis Drake, who had returned to Italy and resided in Genoa, up to the invasion by the French army in 1796. Finally, d'Antraigues furnished intelligence reports to Louis XVIII. But during this period the particular powers with which he was in touch were Russia, Naples, England and Austria.

He also tried to obtain intelligence data on the Vendée. The Vendéan insurrection had assumed considerable scope in 1794, even after the defeat of the Vendéans, which we shall study in the following chapter. The insurrection had perpetuated itself in the form of the *chouannerie*, not only in the Vendée proper, but in Brittany particularly. Now the leaders of the *chouan* party began to have direct contacts with England, whereas d'Antraigues would have liked the negotiations of the Vendéan leaders with Great Britain to be conducted through his offices.

In 1795 d'Antraigues set the responsibility for the pacification of the west on England. In his opinion it had come about because the Vendéan leaders followed the advice of the English, so he made great efforts to enter into contact with the Vendéans. In May of 1795 he seems to have established a correspondence with a *chouan* leader, d'Andigné. On d'Antraigues's recommendation d'Andigné was able to leave for England, reach London and obtain very substantial aid from the British government. Indeed, he persuaded it to prepare an expedition, the outcome of which would be the disaster at Quiberon, as we shall see later. Thus the liaisons established by d'Antraigues with the Vendéans were neither very regular nor very auspicious.

D'Antraigues also turned elsewhere: he was in touch with a certain Reboul who, at his advice, from the end of November, 1794, onwards transmitted to Drake "observations on the current state of France." These observations are preserved in the Foreign Office in London.

Reboul was born at Pézenas in 1763.[6] It seems that he left Languedoc in 1785 for Paris. In Paris he made the acquaintance of Lavoisier and reputedly lived in the latter's house. Thanks to Lavoisier, he became a corresponding member of the Academy of Sciences. At the beginning of the Revolution, he returned to the Midi and became a functionary in the departmental administration of Hérault. In 1791 he was elected deputy to the Legislative Assembly, but he was not re-elected to the Convention. At the end of the Legislative Assembly, he seems to have returned to the Midi, perhaps even to Toulouse, and during the Terror he emigrated to Barcelona, from where he went to Genoa. It is impossible, however, to establish with certainty whether Reboul drew up his bulletins in Genoa itself. This at least would explain why he did not use a pseudonym, since he was in English-occupied territory. But it is possible that he returned to the Midi and that he made his observations himself.

At all events, Reboul furnished intelligence reports for seven months, from mid-November of 1794 up to the end of May, 1795. At that time the bulletins ceased and no more was heard of him. But it appears that I may have rediscovered his whereabouts. In May of 1796, that is, one year later, the commissaries with the Army of Italy denounced the embezzlements committed by an agent of the military administration named Reboul. I would be very surprised if this was not the same Reboul whose presence had been noted on the Riviera in 1795. It is quite possible that Reboul had found a way to get himself recruited into the military administration in 1796. Further, we find a Reboul—it must still be the same person—in the military agency that administered Lombardy during the summer of 1796. Finally, later in 1799, at the time of the creation of the Neapolitan Republic, we see the civil commission in the Army of Naples utilize as secretary an individual named Reboul who, in my opinion, is still the same person. Here, then, was a man with a very checkered career: functionary of the department of Hérault, deputy to the Legisla-

6. I am grateful to A. Birembaut for graciously communicating this information to me.

tive Assembly, émigré on the Ligurian coast during the Thermidorian Convention, then employed in the military administration, and finally member of a civil commission in the armies.[7] This career is very significant in that it shows that many agents of the French administration at that time could rightly be suspect to the republican government.

After the interruption of Reboul's correspondence, at the end of May, 1795, the English government set about looking for another correspondent. D'Antraigues proposed one of his friends, Gamon, to Francis Drake. Gamon was born in the village of Antraigues on April 6, 1767; consequently he was fourteen years younger than d'Antraigues. In fact, he was a son of d'Antraigues's steward. Gamon studied law at the faculty of Toulouse, so he belongs to the group of Toulousians and Montpellierians from which d'Antraigues recruited his agents in France. After obtaining his diploma in law, Gamon was received as a lawyer in the parlement of Toulouse, but it was in the department of Ardèche that he was elected assistant deputy to the Legislative Assembly in 1791. He did not take his seat in the Assembly until March 15, 1792. He was re-elected to the Convention and sat on the benches of the Right. He protested against the *coup d'état* of May 31–June 2, 1793, and left France for Switzerland the following October.

Soon after 9 Thermidor he returned to France and was reinstated in his deputy's seat at the Convention. He was in contact with the "Factory" agents: when Lemaître was arrested after 13 Vendémiaire, Gamon's name was found among his papers. Accused, he managed to clear himself and prove his innocence, falsely, as we now know. But his justification was accepted and on 20 Fructidor, Year V, that is, after the *coup d'état* of 18 Fructidor, in which he could have again been compromised, he was appointed judge to the court of appeals. Later, in 1804, he was to be one of the rare Frenchmen to vote against the Empire, but Napoleon was to bear him no grudge. In fact, he was to be appointed judge of the court in Nîmes and to crown his career as president of the court of appeals of that city.

Gamon was a prolific writer. If we could find his descendants or the owners of his papers, perhaps new light could be shed on d'Antraigues's espionage networks. In fact, in August, 1795, Gamon asked d'Antraigues to transmit the offer of his services to the British government. They were not to be free: Gamon demanded 500 gold *louis* on account before

7. Reboul was nominated corresponding member of the National Institute, as a geologist, on January 23, 1804. He died in Pézenas on February 18, 1839.

sending in his first intelligence bulletins. Furthermore, he demanded the promise, in the event that things turned out badly, of free access to the British Isles with a pension for himself and for the four correspondents whom he planned to set up in Lyons, Rennes, Ostend and Dôle in the Jura. He also hoped that in the event he was forced to leave France he could enter England with sundry merchandise to the amount of 300,000 francs in value or species currency.

Francis Drake showed some hostility toward an agent who made such extraordinary financial demands in advance, and did not report too favorably on him to his government. Nevertheless, Gamon insisted upon them as a precondition for establishing this correspondence. In the interval, he was elected deputy to the Council of Five Hundred, and he repeated his demands in his new situation.

The British government hesitated to pay sums which, in its view, were quite exorbitant, but Gamon was not discouraged. He wanted to give examples of what he could do, so he sent a series of letters to Francis Drake, at no charge, it seems. In these letters he declared that three-fourths of the French people were opposed to the restoration of the Old Regime and to any severance of national territory. But France, said Gamon, desired peace within the frontiers of 1792, and he made it understood that she could accommodate herself to a constitutional monarchy.

On receipt of these letters, Drake told the British government that the information contained in them appeared interesting to him and that perhaps Gamon could be subsidized, providing the exorbitant sums demanded could be lowered.

It seems that Gamon was connected with a struggle between the different intelligence networks at this time. Alongside reports that arrived from Italy, through d'Antraigues and Francis Drake, there were others that reached the British government through an English agent, Wickham, who had taken up residence in Switzerland since 1795. Now there was rivalry between the two networks, as often happens in the world of espionage, and each tried to injure the other. D'Antraigues and Drake wanted to oppose Gamon to Wickham, but finally Grenville preferred Wickham and plans to establish a correspondence with Gamon were not pursued further.

Nevertheless, Gamon did not change his attitude and another correspondent of d'Antraigues, Vannelet (whom we shall discuss later) wrote on May 15, 1798, that Gamon had just been re-elected deputy of Vivarais to the Council of Five Hundred, and that his election had been ratified.

Vannelet was very pleased with Gamon's election because Gamon, he said, would be able to continue his work and undertake a direct correspondence with England. Thus, in 1798, Gamon seemed once again disposed to correspond with the English government. Vannelet continued: "I have engaged Gamon to lend himself to what Lord Grenville desires of him and to correspond directly with him through the method indicated. He has written me that he consents." Actually, a short while later, in January, 1799, we learn, still from Vannelet, that Gamon has proposed to the English government that it send British agents to France. These agents were to arrive via Hamburg or Holland and could observe for themselves what was happening in France, so that the English government would be informed by agents in whom it had complete confidence. Vannelet declared that the two or three British agents who were to come to France would be received by Gamon, who would vouch for their safety with his life. He added that he himself would lodge one of them during his stay in Paris and that he would help him in his mission. We do not know whether this plan was ever carried out, but it probably was, because in the Foreign Office archives in London there are numerous intelligence reports sent from France in 1799. The British government at this time maintained a whole swarm of agents on the continent.

As for Gamon himself, it does not appear that the government of the Directory, nor that of the Consulate or the Empire, ever suspected his secret activity inasmuch as they showered him with honors.

5 / Counter-Revolutionary Espionage in the Army of Italy

In April, 1796, the entry of the French army of Bonaparte into Italy provoked a recrudescence of espionage activity. Francis Drake, who was forced to leave Genoa before the advancing French, installed himself in Venice, and he and d'Antraigues tried to establish contact with some officers of the French army.

In the archives of the Foreign Office in London[8] there are many unpublished letters in which either Drake or d'Antraigues boasts of maintaining relations with extremely important members of the Army of Italy. It has been said the d'Antraigues had been in contact with Bonaparte himself but, as we shall see later, the documents which would have been able to furnish proof of these contacts have been destroyed. However, a letter dated June 23, 1796, from Venice sent by Drake to Lord Grenville shows

8. Public Record Office, F.O. 28/15.

that the English agent was in touch with the "commissary general" of the French army.

The expression "commissary general" corresponds to a rank that did not exist at that time in France. But in the French army the head of the military administration bore the title of "commissaire ordonnateur en chef" (chief pay commissioner) and we presume that the letter concerns the person whom Drake calls the "commissary general." But which "commissaire ordonnateur en chef" is in question here? In fact, in June of 1796 three chief pay commissioners succeeded each other in rapid succession. First Denniée, chief pay commissioner at the beginning of June of 1796, who was almost immediately replaced by the commissary Lambert. Given the date of Drake's letter, June 23, it seems hardly likely that Denniée is the person involved. It could have been Lambert, about whose ideas we have some indications. General Clarke, who inspected the Army of Italy in November of 1796, said of Lambert in his report: "He has talents, but no probity." This absence of probity renders Lambert suspect. It is possible that he had transmitted information to d'Antraigues. But Denniée was recalled not only because of his poor health, but also because of his "lack of energy." Thus Denniée also could appear suspect.

Lambert was very quickly replaced by Villemanzy. Now General Clarke in the same report notes that Villemanzy is "cold about the Revolution." Here are three men who inspire little confidence. It is possible, therefore, that one or the other provided intelligence information to d'Antraigues and to Drake.

At all events, it was one of this trio who communicated to them a letter addressed to "a French general" in Verona that Bonaparte had written from Bologna. This letter is unpublished; it is not in the *Correspondance générale de Napoléon*.

We know from Bonaparte's itinerary that he stayed in Bologna from June 20 to 23. Since Drake redispatched the letter from Venice on July 3, it can concern only this stay of Bonaparte's at Bologna and not his stay of July 2 in this city. The problem is to determine its authenticity, which is difficult to decide with authority. There is mention in the letter of taxes. In fact, Bonaparte did impose taxes on Bologna; there is also talk of a tax on the Jews of Bologna; now Bonaparte emancipated the Jews of Bologna and did not levy any tax on them. The letter therefore is suspect and could have been a fabrication.

The "commissary general" placed d'Antraigues and Drake in contact with a general of Bonaparte's army named Boulard. D'Antraigues claims to know this General Boulard very well because Boulard had been a lawyer in the Vivarais before the Revolution. Now we have a list of all the generals of the Army of Italy in 1796. We also have exact knowledge of the composition of Bonaparte's general staff, and there is no General Boulard on the list. If a General Boulard existed, it is a pseudonym.

General Boulard sends extremely important intelligence on the decisions taken by Bonaparte's general staff. On July 14, 1796, Boulard addresses Drake in a letter, the essential passage of which reads: "I shall not be able to make use of the cipher that you have managed to forward to me because I cannot comprehend it; perhaps it's very easy, but I do not understand it." This is why General Boulard writes in clear: "You are mistaken on my account. I do not have the influence that you believe, at least I do not have it personally. Through my friends it is different. I am very well informed when I am at the general staff, because as a general officer I have entry to all. In [my] absence, the 'tall I' keeps me abreast of things." Is not this "immense I" Villemanzy? Boulard adds that an important council of war was held on the night before, July 13, and he gives details on this war council that we find nowhere else:

> These councils of war always begin with the reading of all the letters from the Directory and from the ministers, then with the reading of the letters from the officers commanding the detached corps, then the letters from spies. After that, a chief engineer demonstrates with diagrams the position of the army, and it is then that the general-in-chief makes his report. This report is divided into matters that are to be deliberated as regards substance and as regards mode . . .

Boulard goes on to speak of the capture of Mantua, decided by the Directory, and provides a great deal of information on the operations prepared in this connection.

We possess a whole series of letters sent by General Boulard during the month of July, 1796, after which the correspondence ceases. But we come upon this General Boulard again in 1798. Vannelet, who has already been discussed and whom we shall meet again, writes on March 15, 1798, that General Boulard has just arrived in Paris and that he has been appointed division general and is to be sent to Le Havre. Several months later, Vannelet informs us that Boulard must leave for the expedition that Bonaparte is preparing, and is embarking on the vessel *L'Orient* with General Casabianca, a general whose existence is well known.

Who then is Boulard? D'Antraigues tells us that Boulard was a native of the Ardèche. Now, among the generals who were natives of the Ardèche, there was only one in the Army of Italy, Baillard de Beaurevoir. He had been posted to Italy on April 14, 1796, and remained there until 1799; thus he did not leave with the Army of the Orient. "Beaurevoir," writes General Clarke in his report, "is patriotic and honest." There is truly no reason to suspect him. Moreover, Beaurevoir had not been a lawyer as was the case with Boulard, according to d'Antraigues.

General Serviez, although he was not born in the Ardèche, came from the province of Gard close by. Is he perhaps the person in question? In his report, General Clarke notes him as "maintaining correspondence with some journalists in Paris opposed to the Revolution in their opinions," which warrants suspicions. But Serviez was put on half-pay on March 18, 1797, and no longer served subsequently. Thus his biography does not correspond to that of General Boulard.

If we set aside the generals born in the Vivarais or the Cévennes, and if we investigate those who were lawyers without taking account of their place of birth, we find one general, a certain Cervoni, who was a lawyer in Corsica before 1789. It is possible that General Cervoni came to the Ardèche as a lawyer before the Revolution and that there he made the acquaintance of d'Antraigues, but of this we know absolutely nothing. General Cervoni served in the Army of Italy and in approximately the same localities as Boulard in 1796. He was attached to the army's general staff in June and July. However, he is noted as a great patriot. He was appointed to the Army of England in 1798 and promoted to division general on February 15, 1798, that is, at approximately the time when Vannelet reports that Boulard had just received this rank.

Are Cervoni and Boulard perhaps the same man? Any deductions that we might make are subject to great caution and would require more serious proof to be considered valid.

One fact remains clear. There were highly placed officers living in Bonaparte's entourage, even at general staff level, who kept d'Antraigues and Drake and, through them, the British and Austrian governments informed on Bonaparte's plans. We must note, however, that this betrayal did not prevent Bonaparte from winning sensational victories.

6 / The Arrest of d'Antraigues

For that matter the far-reaching activities of the comte d'Antraigues were well known to Bonaparte. In the spring of 1797 when he suddenly declared war on the Republic of Venice after a massacre of French soldiers in Verona, Bonaparte showed his resolve to get his hands on the comte. For a long time the French minister to Venice, Villetard, had been demanding that the French troops, upon occupying Venice, were to begin with the seizure of d'Antraigues who, in his opinion, was the most dangerous of the espionage agents at that time swarming all over Italy.

As relations between the French Army of Italy and the Republic of Venice grew more tense, d'Antraigues placed the greater part of his papers in safety with the Austrian legation in Venice. These papers were subsequently burned. However, d'Antraigues kept three portfolios with him and found refuge at the Russian legation. On May 15, as the French were approaching Venice, the Russian representative Mordvinov requested his passports from the Venetian government and a safe-conduct from the minister of France. The legation of France granted a safe-conduct to Mordvinov but on condition that d'Antraigues, who had meanwhile acquired Russian citizenship, was not to figure among the embassy personnel. Mordvinov promised to exclude him. Nevertheless, Villetard, mistrustful, alerted the French generals whose armies occupied the territories adjoining Venice and asked them to search the coaches carrying diplomatic personnel and to arrest the comte d'Antraigues if he were found in one of them.

On May 16, d'Antraigues with his wife and son left Venice in the convoy which was taking away the Russian functionaries. He passed through the first French lines which surrounded the city but at Trieste, on May 21, he was recognized by the military gendarmerie and immediately arrested. During the procedure to establish his identification, his wife found time to burn two of his three portfolios. Thus the gendarmerie could seize only one portfolio, but it contained extremely important papers.[9]

Immediately upon his arrest, d'Antraigues was sent to Milan under heavy guard, his wife and son authorized to follow him. At Milan he was imprisoned in the dungeon of a castle.

Bonaparte, after signing the preliminaries of the Peace of Leoben with Austria, asked for a report of what had been found in d'Antraigues's portfolio. He was extremely interested in perusing these papers and, above all, the report of a lengthy conversation which d'Antraigues had had with another royalist agent, Montgaillard. In this conversation Montgaillard

9. On the arrest of d'Antraigues, see Albert Ollivier, *Le Dixhuit Brumaire* (Paris, 1959), pp. 44–62 and 76–91.

had apprized d'Antraigues of all that he knew about the royalist organization in France. It appears that d'Antraigues had also revealed to Montgaillard the contacts he had with various republican generals. At the end of this reading Bonaparte, on June 1, 1797, at nightfall, went to the prison where d'Antraigues was being kept. He had a long talk with him, without witnesses, and asked d'Antraigues to recopy the "conversation with Montgaillard." Today we no longer possess the original of this "conversation." We have only the copy of it executed in Bonaparte's presence, and an account of it which was made later, on September 14, 1797, by d'Antraigues for Mordvinov. In this account d'Antraigues explains that Montgaillard's conversation as he had transcribed it covered thirty-three pages in its original form, whereas the text that we have contains only sixteen.

So it seems probable that important passages of the original manuscript were suppressed. Historians have wondered whether Bonaparte did not force d'Antraigues to recopy the conversation, eliminating passages in which he himself, or at least his officers, were compromised. For in the conversation between d'Antraigues and Montgaillard as it was transmitted by Bonaparte to the Directory, there is mention only of Pichegru's betrayal. This is the document on which the Directory was to base its reasoning in order to justify, three months later, the *coup d'état* of 18 Fructidor and to arrest General Pichegru as a traitor to the republic. From it, scholars have deduced that Bonaparte promised d'Antraigues his freedom if he would modify the original document. In fact, immediately after the nocturnal interview and the copy of the conversation with Montgaillard, the treatment of d'Antraigues changed totally. He was transferred from his dungeon to a very beautiful apartment in the castle of Milan, where his wife and son were permitted to join him. Several days later, on June 7, he obtained authorization to lodge with the marquise Andreoli where he was guarded by a squad of twelve soldiers commanded by an officer, but enjoyed great freedom of movement. At all events, a short time later, on August 29, d'Antraigues escaped without difficulty, after having sent his wife and child off by a different route.

But d'Antraigues underwent extreme vexation as a result of the incident. In fact, as far as the royalists were concerned he had "blown his cover," as we would say today. They wondered what had been found in his papers, and rightly feared that the whole counter-revolutionary organization in France would be exposed.

From the very first moment of his stay with the marquise Andreoli, d'Antraigues had written lengthy memoranda in an attempt to demonstrate that the conversation with Montgaillard, transmitted by Bonaparte to the French government, was entirely false and had been written under the general's dictation. This seems to be incorrect, since its content is confirmed by other documents.

Louis XVIII was extremely displeased by this adventure, and withdrew his confidence from d'Antraigues, but the latter tried to maintain his relations with foreign governments. Although he gave up his correspondence with Louis XVIII and with England, he continued it with the Neapolitan and Austrian governments. At the end of 1797 and the beginning of 1798, he tried to establish a new intelligence on behalf of the Austrian government in particular, and for this purpose he found a correspondent in France.

7 / *Vannelet*

He calls this correspondent "Vannelet." It is evident that Vannelet is only a pseudonym as has been proved by all the research up to the present time. It seems that on January 2, 1798, a person about whom we know nothing contacted Vannelet on behalf of the comte d'Antraigues. The letter which reports this fact has recently been published.[10] D'Antraigues's anonymous correspondent wrote to him: "I have seen M. Vannelet." No doubt, d'Antraigues had known him previously, but it was in January of 1798 that the intermediary persuaded Vannelet to begin a correspondence with d'Antraigues. This letter also informs us that Vannelet was no longer with the diplomat Bonnier; he had left him in October and was now employed at the treasury.

A very regular correspondence was established between Vannelet and d'Antraigues. The latter recopied Vannelet's letters and transmitted them to the ministers of foreign affairs of Austria and Naples. They give all sorts of information on the plans and intentions of the Directory in 1798 and 1799. These intelligence items seem very important. Unfortunately, when one tries to verify them, it proves almost impossible.[11]

In Vannelet's letters we find, for example, the copy of instructions issued by the French government to its ambassador in Naples, Lacombe-Saint-

10. A. Rufer, "En Complément des 'Dropmore Papers,'" *Ann. hist. de la Rév. fr.* (1958), no. 4, pp. 14–43.
11. A copy of Vannelet's correspondence is preserved in the *Österreichisches Staatsarchiv*, in Vienna, Friedensacten, c. 147.

Michel. Since it is a copy and all the instructions given to the ambassadors of France are preserved in the Ministry of Foreign Affairs, we should be able to find the original of these instructions there, but it is not to be found. Raymond Guyot, in his book, *Le Directoire et la paix de l'Europe*, already knew of this copy of the instructions transmitted to Lacombe-Saint-Michel. After verification he concluded that it was a forgery. I can only formulate the same conclusion and deduce that Vannelet gave false intelligence.

In other letters Vannelet says that in August, 1798, he had been sent on a mission to Alsace and Switzerland in order to attend both to the taxes levied by the French army in Alsace and to the financial organization of the Helvetic Republic. Attempts to verify Vannelet's journeys to Switzerland and Alsace have proved fruitless.

Vannelet gives intelligence of a more credible nature on the preparations for the expedition that was to lead Bonaparte to Egypt, on the financial policy of the Directory and even on its foreign policy.

Who then is Vannelet? Certainly he gives us prodigious intelligence about himself. In one of his letters he says that he was born in 1753 and explains that he is a commissioner at the National Treasury; on the other hand, he informs us, in 1799, that he is also a member of the Council of Administration of the Caisse de Comptes courants, which was the biggest bank in Paris and was to become the Bank of France.

Thus verification appears easy. All we have to do in order to identify Vannelet is to find a person who was both a commissioner at the treasury and an administrator of the Caisse de Comptes courants in 1799. These were two very important institutions, and the names of their functionaries were printed in the *Almanach national*. If we take the *Almanach national* for Year VII, we find among the commissioners of the treasury a certain Desrez and in the list of the administrators of the Caisse des Comptes courants a certain Desprez. They are the only names that are similar, but they differ by a letter. We could be tempted to think that it is the one and same person whose name has been incorrectly spelled in one case. It is nothing of the sort. Desrez, the commissioner at the treasury, is a functionary of the financial administration whose career has remained obscure.[12] Médard Desprez, in contrast, became regent of the Bank of France, then an associate of Ouvrard at the head of a firm of suppliers, the "Négociants réunis," commissioned to provision the French armies in

---

12. I thank J. J. Hémardinquer, who kindly assisted me in these difficult identifications.

1806. He became immensely rich but later went resoundingly bankrupt, which earned him a twelve-month prison sentence. The wealth of Médard Desprez is a feature which approximates him to Vannelet, who tells us in 1799, in fact, that he possesses 2 million in gold. But they differ in many other respects. Identification, once seemingly resolved, is not possible. We are compelled to conclude that no real personage corresponds to Vannelet. Not only is the name a pseudonym, but the person, like that of General Boulard, seems to be a complete invention. It is probable that a good part of the intelligence given by Vannelet in his correspondence was false. D'Antraigues's intelligence networks had never been very reliable; under the Directory they were more suspect than ever. The French royalists no longer used them and it does not appear that the foreign powers lent them great credence.

CHAPTER XI

The Counter-Revolutionary Insurrections in Western France, 1792 to 1795

The peasant insurrections in western France were the first of this type among the counter-revolutionary insurrections. But in the course of the period that interests us there were many other peasant risings directed against either the men or the institutions of the Revolution: the insurrection of the Vendée broke out after 1795; it was resumed in 1799 and once more in 1830. The peasants of Normandy, Brittany, and the western borders of the Parisian basin took up arms against the Revolution from 1793 to 1799; this was the *chouannerie*. In 1799 the peasants of southwestern France rose in the name of the king. In Italy one can count several peasant insurrections from 1796 to 1799, notably in Calabria, the Papal States and Tuscany. In Belgium in 1798 there was a "Peasants' War" which was a counter-revolutionary insurrection. The peasants of Germany and Switzerland took up arms against the Revolution on several occasions between 1796 and 1799. After 1800 numerous peasant risings of a counter-revolutionary nature broke out in different regions of Europe. The most famous, and the most important because of their consequences, were the peasant insurrections of Spain, known under the name of the War of Spanish Independence. The German wars of "liberation" in 1813 and 1814 were also in part peasant insurrections.

All these insurrections belong to the same genre and it is legitimate to ask whether they obey similar causes. Historians are deeply divided as to the causes of the insurrections in the west. Numerous books have been published on the insurrections in western France, but most of them are apologetic or hagiographic works written by royalists who extolled the Vendéans or *chouans.*

In their studies of the causes of the insurrections in the west, historians are divided into two schools, according to their political sympathies. Those who are hostile to the Revolution sustain the thesis of a spontaneous uprising: that the constitution and revolutionary institutions were in contradiction with the natural order of things, and that the peasants, struck by this anomaly, spontaneously rose in revolt against them. They also rose against atheism, all religious innovations and unjustified reforms. On the other hand, historians favorable to the Revolution sustain the thesis of an insurrection provoked either by the action of the clergy and the nobility, or by the agents of the émigrés or of the foreign powers at war with France.

Owing to the dearth of adequate studies, however, we are ignorant of the economic and social structure of the insurgent regions, whether western France or the other regions in which peasant risings occurred. In two works only have the authors sketched the social structure of the insurgent regions: for France, the book by Léon Dubreuil, *Histoire des insurrections de l'Ouest;*[1] for Italy, the book by Gaetano Cingari.[2] Other works tend toward the anecdotal; they recount the history of events without truly analyzing their causes. Moreover, the study of the social structure of the insurgent regions in Dubreuil's book is very summary; but there are works in progress which are trying to dig deeper into this question.

1 / General Features of the Counter-Revolutionary Peasant Insurrections

Scholars have wondered whether the peasant insurrections were provoked by a geographical determinism. When we analyze the insurrections in the west, we note that they developed in woodland districts, subdivided regions in which the fields under cultivation were encircled by hedgerows crossed by winding paths, where concealment was easy. The fields under cultivation were scattered, the peasants isolated. But if one examines the other peasant insurrections, it is evident that they took place in regions of a different character. Calabria, in south Italy, is a region of scrubs where the peasants are grouped in very large villages, real rural towns which at times number more than 20,000 inhabitants. But communications are as

1. See the bibliographical notes to this chapter.
2. *Giacobini e sanfedisti in Calabria Nel 1799* (Messina, 1957).

difficult as in the districts of western France. In Spain the insurrection in 1809 took place on the plateau of Castille as well as in the "huerta" of Valencia or on the plains of the province of Aragon. But communications were also difficult in Spain under the Old Regime. Thus we can hardly distinguish a geographic determinism operating as a causal factor in the peasant revolts. Can we then speak of a social determinism, a social structure predisposed to insurrection?

We must note that in all the insurgent countries during the revolutionary period—France, Italy, Spain, and elsewhere—the insurrections took place particularly in the regions where the peasants were greatly subjected to the seigneur, the proprietor. To this day in the Vendée the peasants still refer to the proprietor only as "Not' maître." Perhaps this is a last vestige of the former submission. In these countries the peasants either respect the proprietor and master and are submissive to him, or they are very hostile to him. The proprietor exercises his authority in the material domain to collect the rents that are due him, and in the spiritual domain as well. He can force his tenants to attend Mass, to receive the sacraments and to send their children to the Catholic school.

It has also been noted that in these countries the authority of the clergy and especially that of the parish priests is very great. In the Vendée as well as in Calabria, when the priest adhered to a new regime, the populace followed him; when the opposite was the case, the populace also took the same attitude. The influence of the clergy seems preponderant in all the regions where peasant insurrections have been signalized, whether in western France, southern or eastern Italy, Spain, Belgium or Switzerland.

Is it a question of faith or practice? It is hard to answer this because in these countries with difficult communications, education is rare and little developed, superstition rampant. It seems that the clergy incited the peasants against innovations in the external form of worship rather than for profound reasons of faith. Thus we can also wonder about the role played by a secret religious association of which we still know very little, the Aa, in the preparation and development of insurrections. This association, sprung from the Congregation of the Blessed Sacrament, and linked to the Jesuit order, brought together the refractory priests, especially in southwestern France. It is also possible that it was the driving force behind the rebellion.[3]

3. On the Aa, see B. Fay, *La Grande Révolution* (Paris, 1959); P. Droulers, *Action pastorale et problèmes sociaux sous la monarchie de Juillet chez Mgr. d'Astros, archevêque de Toulouse* (Paris, 1954); also the *Dictionnaire de spiritualité*, article Aa. More thorough studies of the Aa are in progress.

As regards Calabria, Cingari has established that believers and unbelievers were to be found both in the revolutionary and in the opposite
camps.

It appears that the peasant insurrections to a certain extent were provoked by a geographic determinism, the difficulty of communications,
which prevented the spread of new ideas. But they were also the result
of the social structure. Insurrection spread in regions where peasants,
sharecroppers or tenant farmers were strictly obedient to the proprietor,
but often also in regions where the peasant was hostile to the bourgeois,
whom he knew primarily in the form of tax collector (either on behalf of
the State or the lord), or as a merchant exploiting the district and lending
money, often at a usurious rate of interest. The influence of religion and
religious practice is also undeniable, and that of the clergy certain.

Turning more specifically to the conditions that prevailed in western
France, we must first of all determine the attitude of the peasants *vis-à-vis*
the Revolution. At the beginning of the Revolution, the regions which
were to become so violently and profoundly insurgent were not hostile to
the reforms. On the contrary, the peasants favored them. In 1789 they
had enthusiastically hailed the abolition of tithes and feudal dues, against
which they protested in their lists of grievances (*cahiers de doléances*).
Under the Old Regime, the peasants were discontented with the salt tax
and happy over its abolition. They were also hostile to drawing lots for
the militia which, in actual fact, did not burden them over much.

There were, however, peasants whose claims were not satisfied by the
reforms of the revolutionary epoch. Western France had tenants of a
particular category, namely, tenants of *domaines congéables** and *colons
partiares***—both specific forms of tenure that one finds only in this
region. The peasants who were not delivered from these particularly
burdensome forms of tenure were in general faithful to the Revolution
from which they expected, in spite of everything, the transformation of
their special problems.

The peasant therefore was not a priori hostile to the revolutionary
regime; on the other hand, he was often displeased with the bourgeois,
which he knew only in the form of the lord's employee, the noble's
auxiliary. The bourgeois collected the feudal dues for the lord and sold
the peasants the objects which were indispensable to him. So the peasant
felt that he was being exploited. In the peasant milieu the bourgeois had

* Revocable tenancies held at will—trans.
** Tenant farmers who paid part of the produce as rent—trans.

the reputation of being miserly, hard, selfish; the peasant generally was therefore against him. We find the same attitude in Italy, Belgium and Spain. The alliance of bourgeoisie and peasants enabled the Revolution to triumph in France as in other regions; in the countries where this alliance was not effected, the Revolution failed.

The attitude of the peasant in the west toward religion has not yet been studied by the methods of sociological analysis recently perfected. In general, the peasant in western France was very attached to religious practice, if not to religion itself, and very faithful to the formulas, rites and ceremonies, to which he tended to attach a magical virtue. The closing of the churches and interruption of the cult no doubt were a source of discontent to him. These innovations struck him as intolerable. The situation was the same in Calabria and in Spain.

In western France the peasant submitted to the directives of the clergy. Before the Revolution, the clergy was divided into two categories: the lower clergy, which was not very educated but was very close to the people, obliging, charitable and loved by its flocks; and the higher clergy, which, with rare exceptions, was arrogant, recruited among the nobility, and often belonged to the lodges of Freemasonry; it was richly endowed and contrasted sharply with the poor parish priests. The richest of the bishops was the bishop of Bayeux, endowed with 90,000 livres in revenues; the poorest, the bishop of Saint-Brieuc, had 12,000 in revenues. The lower clergy of western France welcomed the convocation of the Estates General. At the time of the elections very few bishops were elected; in the archdiocese of Rouen, only two bishops out of seven; in that of Tours, two out of twelve; and in that of Bordeaux, seven out of ten. But the archdiocese of Bordeaux was the one least troubled by insurrections. In Brittany, no bishop was sent to the Estates General.

Thus the clergy had warmly welcomed the Revolution. But after the first measures were adopted the clergy showed its displeasure. Although it was happy over the abolition of the Old Regime salary scale of the parish priests (*portion congrue*), it displayed hostility to the abolition of tithes decreed on the night of August 4, and even greater hostility to the nationalization of Church property, voted on November 2, 1789. The freedom of worship formulated in the Declaration of the Rights of Man and spelled out more clearly later in a series of laws also irritated this almost exclusively Catholic district (it contained only a small number of Protestants). The clergy was particularly displeased because the revolutionary reform placed religion and its ministers in a subordinate rank instead of maintaining them in the first as before 1789. As early as September 12, 1789, the bishop Le Mintier of Tréguier, in Brittany, published a mandamus that was very hostile to the Revolution. He attacked the philosophical spirit, condemned liberty of the press and put his faithful on guard against dangerous innovations, which place "the nerve of royal authority in the hands of the multitude." He deplored "the enervated military discipline, citizen armed against citizen . . ." "The Church," he says, "is falling into abasement and servitude, her ministers are threatened with reduction to the situation of appointed clerks. The supreme tribunals are disregarded, humiliated." Le Mintier then protested against the substitution of welfare for charity and against the abandonment of a number of old laws which were pre-eminently sensible. Finally he put the peasants on guard against the acquisition of national properties which, at that time, had not even been put up for sale. Le Mintier's mandamus had enormous repercussions and won the approval of all the nobles of the region. It marks the beginning of the rupture between the populace of western France and the Revolution.

The publication of the Civil Constitution of the Clergy increased the irritation of the clergy particularly because of the reduction of the number of dioceses. Seven dioceses had been abolished in the western districts and in these regions where communications were difficult this could give rise to enormous disadvantages. Many priests, incited by the Aa, refused to take the loyalty oath prescribed by the Civil Constitution. In the diocese of Angers, more than 50 per cent of the priests were refractories or non-jurors; in the Vendée and in Brittany, more than 80 per cent. However, this was not the major cause that sparked the insurrection, because we find an equal number of refractories, at times even larger, in other regions of France where there were no uprisings. Of the priests around the Massif central, 80 per cent were refractories; in the departments of Moselle and Bas-Rhin, 92 per cent.

The replacement of refractory priests by priests who accepted the constitution, depicted as bad priests, began to provoke a certain amount of agitation; arrests of refractory priests aggravated matters. Refractory priests celebrated Mass secretly, religious processions took place at night and these nocturnal ceremonies awakened the mystical spirit that characterizes the populaces of western France. The fears and superstitions of the Bretons, who were deeply attached to their legends and lore and who believed in goblins that roamed the dunes at night, were aroused to fever pitch, creating a state of mind hostile to the Revolution. Hatreds were exacerbated.

On the other hand, the bourgeoisie took a favorable attitude to the Revolution. The bourgeoisie in western France, as everywhere else in the country for that matter, was a composite class. We find in it merchants, men of law, minor functionaries; on the whole, however, the bourgeoisie was less numerous in the western regions than elsewhere. In 1789 it was not a numerically significant social grouping, save in Nantes.

From the beginning of 1789, the bourgeoisie gained access to the municipal councils of the large cities. When the national properties were put up for sale, the bourgeois constituted the mass of buyers. However, it must not be thought that the bourgeois all shared the same attitude. Although many favored the Revolution, others were very much against it. A whole category of bourgeois was tied to the nobility by family bonds and aspired to the status of nobles. Nobles and bourgeois mixed socially in the "sociétés de pensée" and in the Masonic lodges. In the lodges of Le Mans, for example, one finds nobles, merchants and functionaries.[4]

Despite all this, the bourgeois followed the revolutionary movement for the most part. But the majority of peasants in the west showed an increasing hostility to reform.

2 / The Origins of the Insurrections

The general conditions just analyzed undoubtedly played a very great part in originating the insurrections in the west, but they required a driving force. We cannot entirely discard the thesis of the republican historians, according to which the insurrection originated in conspiracies organized either by refractory priests or the nobility. It is certain that the influence of the nobility and clergy was a determining factor in the preparation of the insurrection. Here it seems that a conspiracy organized by a nobleman, the marquis de La Rouairie, did play an important role.[5]

The marquis de La Rouairie was born in Fougères in 1750. He had a very checkered career as a young man, fighting many duels and engaging

4. A. Bouton, *Les Francs-Maçons manceaux et la Révolution française* (Le Mans, 1958).
5. See in this connection A. Goodwin, "Counter-Revolution in Brittany: The Royalist Conspiracy of the Marquis de la Rouërie, 1791–1793," *Bulletin of the John Rylands Library*, 1957, pp. 326–355. The marquis's name is indiscriminately spelled La Rouairie or La Rouërie.

in extraordinary love affairs; he distinguished himself by an attempt at suicide and participated in the War of American Independence at the head of a partisan unit, under the name of Colonel Armand, which made him famous. He returned from America an enthusiastic lover of liberty, but he had neither the intelligence nor the social rank of Lafayette and, upon his return, was very coldly received in France. It appears that the comparison between the glacial reception accorded to him and the effusive one reserved for Lafayette displeased and embittered him.

In 1788, at the time of the agitation that preceded the convocation of the Estates General, he was a strong partisan of the parlement of Brittany and was commissioned to bring to Paris the list of grievances of the Breton nobility, which was hostile to the measures recently taken by the king. La Rouairie was arrested and locked up in the Bastille. Freed upon the fall of the Brienne ministry, he returned in triumph to Fougères, his native town. He protested against the ordinance which regulated the system of election to the Estates General because it disregarded the laws and customs of Brittany, and was especially opposed to the doubling of the Third Estate. After the formation of the Constituent Assembly, he emerged as a foe of the first reforms. It appears that he had planned to organize a counter-revolutionary movement as early as the beginning of 1790. He assembled a number of friends belonging to the nobility at his château near Saint-Brieuc; even at that time some of those present at the gathering proposed that an appeal should be addressed to England to aid a counter-revolutionary movement.

La Rouairie left France in May of 1791. Provided with a regular passport, he reached Coblenz, where he claimed to represent a "Breton Association" composed of Breton émigrés. The aim of this association was the restoration of a monarchy "tempered" by the old constitution of France, respectful of the ancient Breton freedoms and of "the religion of our fathers." La Rouairie, as a means of action, wanted to provide the association with bands of partisan fighters, similar to those he had commanded in the United States. The Breton Association soon had branches in all the western provinces, Brittany, Normandy, Anjou and Poitou. It was based upon a whole series of committees organized in each city in which there had been a bishopric before the Revolution. These committees were composed of six members and a secretary; there were less important committees in other large towns. They received orders from the leader, the marquis de La Rouairie himself. Article 6 of the manifesto that was sent to these committees declared that the aim of the association was to contribute "by the most gentle means" to the return of the absolute monarchy, and to the recognition "of the rights of the province, to those of the proprietors, and of Breton honor." It stipulated that members of the association were to exert every possible effort to attract the national guards to their program. Article 11 declared: "The military organization shall be set up at the proper time." Thus the association was preparing to establish a genuine counter-revolutionary militia.

In June of 1791 La Rouairie obtained from the comte d'Artois his recognition as leader of the Breton Association. He went to see Calonne in order to obtain money, but all the latter would give him was a pathetic subsidy in the form of devalued promissory notes issued by the Caisse d'Escompte, and counterfeit "assignats." Later, the comte de Provence confirmed La Rouairie's authority. La Rouairie had many accomplices in Brittany: his mistress, Thérèse de Moëlien; his brother, Gervais de la Rouairie; other nobles, Boisguy and Picot de Limoëlan, who was to achieve a certain notoriety; as well as a dismissed former naval officer, the chevalier de Tinténiac. On the membership lists of the Breton Association we also find the name of Jean Cottereau, who was soon to adopt the pseudonym of Jean Chouan, from which the word "*chouannerie*" apparently derived.

The troops were formed by former salt smugglers who were without a job now that the "gabelle" or salt tax had been abolished, by émigré Bretons living in England, Jersey and Germany, by persons who had lost their posts in consequence of the reforms, and by some members of the general staff of the National Guard.

The large towns, Nantes and Brest, for example, were rather unresponsive to the association, but it was very successful in the smaller towns. It imposed on the conspirators dues equal to a year's income, but many of the members did not pay and the finances were never flourishing. However, at the beginning of 1792 the association possessed more than 6,000 muskets, gunpowder and four cannon.

The conspirators had planned to take over Rennes, synchronizing their action with a planned landing in Brittany of a group of émigrés and the beginning of counter-revolutionary action in the departments of Cévennes, Lozère and Ardèche (which will be discussed later). But the synchronization of all these movements could not be properly assured; moreover, the victory of revolutionary armies at Valmy intervened to disconcert the conspirators. They had planned to launch the insurrection at the very moment the Austrian and Prussian armies would be approaching Paris. The defeat completely upset their plans. The revolutionary authorities knew all about the conspiracy as early as May, 1792. On the night of May 31–June 1, 1792, a secretary of La Rouairie was arrested along with other conspirators, and their papers seized. Others betrayed the cause, notably a certain Chévetel. However, the authorities did not dare to proceed against the conspirators until the overthrow of the throne. Only after August 10, 1792, did the new minister of justice, Danton, order the investigations of the conspiracy to be hurried up. The warrant to arrest the principal members of the conspiracy was issued: La Rouairie managed to escape the gendarmes, but he fell seriously ill and died on January 30, 1793, in a château in the department of Côtes-du-Nord.

A number of conspirators were arrested and twelve of them were placed on trial, sentenced to death and guillotined on June 18, 1793. Thus the conspiracy ended in fiasco. Nevertheless, it seems to have played a great role in preparing for the insurrections in the west. It formed cadres, organized committees of counter-revolution, established contacts with those who could be, or could become, the principal leaders of the counter-revolutionary movement.

It appears that the Breton Association had aimed not only at an insurrection in Brittany, as its name indicates, but in all the western regions between the estuaries of the Gironde and the Seine. The conversations of the Vendéan leader, d'Elbée with General Turreau on the isle of Noirmoutier, several days before d'Elbée's execution, seem to indicate the aims of the Breton Association. D'Elbée, in effect, told Turreau that the insurrection in the Vendée had taken place before the time determined for the general explosion, and that he had done everything in his power to restrain it and prevent any premature action because all the means of action were not properly coordinated and he immediately sensed the danger of a partial movement.

On the other hand, in the archives of the Ministry of Foreign Affairs in Paris a paper has been found among the documents relating to the emigration which contains the following question posed by an agent of the comte de Provence: "What determined the moment at which the Vendéans went into action?" And the answer: "The coalition, having been compromised by the death of M. de la Rouairie and the removal of his papers, was forced to manifest itself, and its first act, with 150 men, was to disarm the National Guard of a tiny village." These documents prove that there were definite links between La Rouairie's conspiracy and the insurrection in the Vendée which marks the beginning of the insurrections in the west. It seems, in fact, that it was the seizure of the papers of the

Breton Association at the time of the arrest of its leaders that set off the Vendéan insurrection. The compromised Vendéan leaders of the Breton Association feared arrest and in order to forestall such an eventuality decided to launch their rising at the beginning of March, 1793.

So this was the immediate cause of the insurrection in the Vendée; however, it took advantage of a whole series of recourses to arms. Minor riots and uprisings had already taken place in the region. As early as September, 1790, in the tiny village of La Croix de la Viollière, in the department of the Vendée, the peasants took up arms during a village fête but this riot was easily put down. In October of 1790 an administrator writes: "The aristocrats have exerted all their efforts . . . to bring on a civil war and to have some persons in their pay take up arms against the friends of the people." In February of 1791 a peasant riot broke out near Sables-d'Olonne, and acts of violence were committed against functionaries. On March 1, 1791, at Saint-Christophe-de-Ligneron, the gendarmes were attacked by armed peasants. Dumouriez, who commanded the military division of this region, was charged with restoring order. Again in 1791, another seigneur, the marquis de La Lézardière, organized a conspiracy with the notables among his neighbors but was denounced to the authorities and arrested before the rising could break out. The conspirators assembled in Lézardière's château were jailed and the peasants, who were marching to gather around the château, dispersed. Thirty-six persons were brought before the tribunal of Sables-d'Olonne and sentenced. But shortly thereafter the amnesty promulgated on September 15, 1791, following the king's acceptance of the new constitution supervened and La Lézardière's conspiracy was not checked as severely as that master-minded by the marquis de La Rouairie. Yet the conspiracy of the marquis de La Lézardière played a role in sparking the Vendéan insurrection.

In 1792 arms were again taken up in the Vendée on August 20, several days after the fall of the throne. The former mayor of Bressuire, named Delouche, grouped some peasants in a military formation and occupied the tiny village of Châtillon. The peasants assembled by Delouche came from eighty villages; they were led by nobles whom we shall find again at the head of the Vendéans, for example, La Béraudière and de Béjarry. The National Guard of Bressuire arrested the armed peasants and their leaders. If the capture of Bressuire had taken place then, the Vendéan insurrection might have begun in August, 1792, instead of March, 1793. After the march on Bressuire, most of the nobles and peasants arrested were released. No punishments were meted out.

Such were the conspiracies and riots that preceded the Vendéan revolt. They seem to have been facilitated by the social structure of the district, the poorness of the means of communication, the influence of the proprietors, the nobility and the clergy, the discontent caused by the Civil Constitution and the influence of the refractory priests. But another element was to play a decisive role. At the end of February, 1793, the Convention, in order to resist a coalition that included almost all the countries of Europe, decreed the levy of an army of 300,000 men. Now the peasants of western France had always been very hostile to military service. Under the Old Regime the regular army was recruited from volunteers, but it was complemented by a militia composed of peasants drawn by lot. The militia did not impose a heavy burden on the peasants because the lottery was restricted only to a very small number among them, and those whose names were drawn had to undergo only several periods of military training each year. Nevertheless, the militia was unpopular in all France and particularly in the west. The peasants had always tried to evade the drawing by lot for the militia.

The volunteers raised in 1791 and 1792 by the Constituent and Legislative Assemblies had rallied to the colors with a genuine spontaneity, but in 1793 the capacity to draw on the volunteer spirit of the French was exhausted. The Convention was forced to decree that in the event that there were not enough volunteers to furnish the contingent of 300,000 men, the soldiers would be designated by a municipality or by any other practicable means. In practice the municipalities were able either to designate those whom they wanted by authority of the law, or by drawing lots. Thus the militia was re-established under another form. There is no doubt whatsoever that the levy of 300,000 men considerably aggravated the discontent prevailing throughout the western district.

The chronology of the insurrection is very clear. The decree which ordered the levy of 300,000 men was dated February 24, 1793. It was made known in Angers on March 2 and published in the various communes of the western regions on March 10. On March 11 the insurrection broke out on the entire left bank of the Loire to the cries: "No drawing lots! Down with the militia!"

On March 12 the peasants who had shouted "Down with the militia! No drawing lots!" seized a particularly important locality, Saint-Florent-le-Vieil on the left bank of the Loire, a point enabling passage from the Vendée to Normandy and Brittany.

However, what tends to prove that the insurrection was not spontaneous or caused exclusively by the recruiting law is that, from the outset, we see nobles placing themselves at the head of the peasants, whom they organized into military formations. Thus d'Elbée commanded a band of peasants that occupied Beaupréau, and Lescure and La Rochejacquelein placed themselves at the head of peasant bands. But peasant leaders also appeared who were to distinguish themselves during the war of the Vendée: Cathelineau, Stofflet. Initially, however, on March 12, 13 and 14, it was the nobles who acted with the greatest effectiveness.

From the outset, in fact, the war of the Vendée took on a dual aspect: on the one hand, it was a peasant insurrection—the peasants, exceedingly indifferent to the form of government, wanted their religion, "good priests," and above all, no militia, no drawing lots. On the other hand, it was a counter-revolutionary movement: the nobles wanted to take advantage of the peasant revolt in order "to restore the throne and the altar," according to the formula which they employed at that time.

The war of the Vendée began on March 12. This war, like all the insurrections in the west, showed predominantly the characteristics of a guerrilla war. It was a war of "maquis," to use a modern expression, a war of ambush. When the insurgents, bands of armed peasants, hurled themselves against regular troops, they were generally beaten. But not always. For initially the peasants clashed with the National Guard, composed of other peasants who were no better armed or trained than themselves. But the insurgent bands were rapidly outclassed in the battles in open country by the regular army. In contrast, they were to maintain their superiority in the war of ambush, in the defense of small hamlets, in attacks along pit-strewn paths. The war of the Vendée was marked by another characteristic of guerrilla action, ferocity. It was difficult to recognize an insurgent peasant, because he fired from the corner of a wood or from a pit-strewn path, after which he immediately hid his musket and resumed his plowing. There was nothing to prove that he had fired the shot. The republican troops were to take terrible reprisals against the civil population: villages destroyed, burnings, summary executions were the current coin of this war. In their turn the insurgent bands were to distinguish themselves by the cruelties inflicted on isolated soldiers, captured patriots, prisoners.

The war of the Vendée has a very particular character in the history of the Revolution and this character was to give birth to types exploited by the writers: the Vendéan and the *chouan*. Balzac, Victor Hugo, Alexandre Dumas and Michelet all devoted books or short stories to the wars of the Vendée and to the *chouannerie*.

The wars of the Vendée are very hard to study because they are made up of a whole series of episodes that have hardly any connection with each other. We shall not examine these insurrections in complete detail as that would not be of great interest. They are marked by several major periods. The first covers the first three months: March, April and May of 1793. It comes to a stop on May 31. The Vendéan insurrection would probably have terminated then and there if it had not been given a new lease on life by the Parisian *coup d'état* of May 31–June 2. At that time the Girondins were eliminated from the Convention and the upshot was a general insurrection in France, the "federalist" insurrection, which was particularly developed in the west. The Vendéan insurrection, which had suffered a devastating blow by the end of May, 1793, was reborn thanks to federalism, and extended to all the districts of the west.

A second period begins on May 31–June 2 and lasts until the pacifications of 1795, nearly two years. It is the longest, most important period, and is itself subdivided into several phases, the *grande guerre* and the *chouannerie*. The pacification of 1795 seemed to put an end to these insurrections when an action belatedly taken by the émigrés aided by the English called everything into question again, with the landing at Quiberon in the summer of 1795. This landing constitutes the third period of the war of the Vendée.

3 / The First Period of the War of the Vendée (March 10 to May 31, 1793)

At the beginning of the insurrection, the peasant bands were little organized; they were led by nobles, by some bourgeois, by a surgeon named Joly, at times by other peasants. They captured a certain number of localities, the most important of which were La Roche-sur-Yon, Saint-Gilles-sur-Vie and the isles of Noirmoutier and Yeu. But from the outset they failed before Les Sables-d'Olonne, which immediately appeared as a center of republican resistance. The insurgents also captured the small market town of Machecoul on March 11. A former finance officer named Souchu organized a "royal committee" there, proclaimed Louis XVII king and declared that the Convention would no longer be obeyed. Then Souchu decided to wipe out the patriots of the district; those arrested in Machecoul and its environs were executed during Easter week, strung together and dragged before firing squads.

There has been much controversial discussion on the executions at Machecoul: estimates of the number of victims vary accordingly as they come from the "Blues" or the "Whites." The Whites set the figure at 100 persons, the republicans raised it to 1,000. The excesses committed by Souchu at Machecoul inaugurated the cruelties of the war of the Vendée by provoking reprisals. The belligerents were to be permanently caught up in the vicious circle of civil war, cruelties leading to reprisals and reprisals to new atrocities.

The insurrection also spread to the region of the Marches, situated slightly east of the maritime Vendée. Montaigu was taken on March 13, Clisson on March 15. On April 6 the leaders of the bands that had become masters of the towns in the region of the Marches decided to send an emissary to ask for assistance from England and Spain. These were the first attempts by the insurgents to enter into contact with foreign powers, but they were fruitless at a moment when they could have been very dangerous for the Revolution. The insurrection then spread to the region of Les Mauges, situated even further east.

Saint-Florent-le-Vieil was occupied by the nobles under d'Elbée and Bonchamps, and also by bands commanded by the gamekeeper Stofflet, the coachman Cathelineau and by a certain Forest, a valet recently returned from the emigration with his master. On March 15 the leaders who had captured these small towns joined forces and decided to attack larger towns. They marched on Cholet, which was occupied on March 14; then on Saumur which, however, they failed to take at that time.

On March 20 these united bands for the first time assumed the title of "Roman Catholic Army," soon altered to that of the "Catholic and Royal Army." But Easter week arrived and the peasants declared that they wanted to go home for the holidays. So they dispersed. This is a characteristic feature of the wars of the Vendée; immediately an objective was attained, the peasants left the army. The Vendéan armies dissolved as swiftly as they were assembled.

The insurrection stirred the Convention deeply. On March 17 it took stern measures, declaring that all the leaders of the insurrectionary movement, nobles, priests, their agents, Old Regime functionaries of the insurgent region, as well as the rebels captured bearing arms, would be declared outlaws, sentenced to death and executed upon simple verification of identity. This was to decree the death sentence against a great

number of persons. Captured rebels found without weapons on their
persons were to be imprisoned. The Convention organized three armies to
fight against the insurrection. One, under the command of General
Berruyer, in the Angers region, another under the command of General
Boulard,[6] which was to operate from Sables-d'Olonne, and a third under
the orders of General Beysser at Nantes.

Boulard took the offensive with some battalions of volunteers. On
April 8 he marched westward and won victories over the band commanded by Joly, who was killed, then retook Saint-Gilles-sur-Vie.
Beysser began his movement around April 20. He retook Machecoul, and
ordered the execution of Souchu and a large number of insurgents. And
he re-established communications between Nantes and the Vendéan coast.
In contrast, Berruyer failed in his action and the offensive that he launched
from Angers set off a general uprising in Les Mauges. A new Vendéan
army of 20,000 men was formed under the command of Henri de La
Rochejacquelein. Berruyer was forced to beat a retreat, while one of his
subordinates, Colonel Quetineau, was taken prisoner with 3,000 men at
Thouars. La Rochejacquelein and d'Elbée organized a "Catholic and Royal
Army" of 40,000 men, which captured Fontenay-le-Comte on May 25.

Nevertheless, the successes of Boulard and Beysser considerably improved the situation. No doubt the Vendéan insurgents were still strong in
the south of Les Mauges, in the region of Fontenay, but the revolutionary
generals could hope to isolate and defeat them. And this might have
happened had not the *coup d'état* of May 31–June 2 called everything into
question again by setting off a general insurrection in Normandy and
Brittany, not to mention the risings in the southwest and southeast, at
Lyons, and in the region of the Cévennes, Marseilles and Toulon. A new
period begins in the first days of June, 1793.

4 / Federalism in the West and the Failure
of the Vendéan Revolt

During May 31 and June 2, 1793, the "sans-culottes" of Paris, directed
by the Commune, went to demand from the Convention that it arrest
the leaders of the Girondin "party." When this news reached the
provinces, a large number of administrations of departments and of districts, as well as certain municipal administrations, refused to recognize

---

6. This is General Henri Boulard, who died in 1793, not to be confused with the
General Boulard mentioned on pp. 193–195.

the fait accompli in Paris, declared that the Convention was no longer free and decided to obey it no further—a resistance movement known as "federalism," because each department tended to take decisions on its own and obey only its own authorities. France seemed to be splitting up into innumerable tiny republics. The country was tending towards the federalism which, moreover, the Girondins had been proposing for six or eight months in opposition to centralization, under the direction of Paris, which had been the objective of the Montagnards.

The great majority of the federalists were revolutionary, indeed republican. But this majority was very quickly swamped by counter-revolutionists and by royalists who perceived how the resistance could turn to their advantage.[7]

How did the federalist opposition, in general, manifest itself? In every administrative center of a department the general council met in session, once news of the events transpiring in Paris became known. Often the council declared itself in permanent session and convoked a meeting of all the authorities of the administrative centers. At Toulouse, the primary assemblies, that is, the assemblies including all the citizens, were called together and asked for their opinion on the events in Paris. Primary assemblies were convoked not only in the Haute-Garonne, but in the Hautes- and Basses-Alpes, Cantal, Isère, Jura, etc.

Once in session, these primary assemblies sometimes instituted commissions of public safety or departmental committees of public safety whose purpose was to prepare for action against Paris. At times, the federalists passed to a second and much more serious stage: the preparation of a military expedition against the capital, that is, open revolt. This happened only in some twenty departments. But the departmental committees of public safety which decided to move on to the stage of military action against Paris were, in general, composed only of a minority of republicans and dominated by royalists.

To fight against Paris was to unleash civil war. A number of committees of public safety took the leap. In France five regions passed to the stage of armed revolt against Paris; elsewhere the disturbances were rapidly calmed down.

These five regions were first the west and northwest, along with Normandy, Brittany and the Vendée; then the southwest, with Bordeaux

---

7. On the federalist revolt see in particular the articles by P. Nicolle, "Le Mouvement fédéraliste dans l'Orne en 1793," *Ann. hist. de la Rév. fr.*, 1936, pp. 481–512; 1937, pp. 215–233; 1938, pp. 12–53; 289–313; 385–410.

and the Gironde. The danger would have been all the greater if the whole of western France had united against Paris, but in the southwest there was also a center of resistance, Montauban, a city that was rabidly Montagnard. Montauban, which prevented the junction between the federalists of Bordeaux and those of Toulouse, defended the general loyalty of the southwest to the Convention and thus reduced the danger presented by Bordelais federalism. The third insurgent region was that of the southeast, including Marseilles and Toulon. The federalists of this area attempted to extend their influence to a fourth region including the Cévennes and the Vivarais so as to effect a junction with the royalists on the rim of the Massif central. It failed above all because of the solid resistance of the department of Aude and of the attitude of the Protestants of the Cévennes, who displayed a staunch republicanism. Finally, the fifth region was that of Lyons and the Franche-Comté. The federalists of the latter regions planned to march on Paris; in Franche-Comté, federalism rapidly simmered down, but in Lyons the revolt assumed extremely serious dimensions.

The Convention tried to combat this federalism in two ways. First of all, by reassuring the departments that had simply registered protests. It demonstrated to them that the majority of the Convention was still there and explained that disunity before the enemy was to be avoided because France was at war, attacked on all her frontiers by the whole of Europe. The Convention also buttressed this reassurance by rapidly voting the Constitution of 1793.

The second method was the struggle against the departments which had raised troops and were marching on Paris, a struggle that ended more or less swiftly in victory. As for the insurgents of the west, victory was achieved very quickly. The insurgents of Normandy had sent toward Paris a small army commanded by Puisaye, which we shall re-encounter in the Vendéan insurrections. This army was defeated on July 13, 1793, at Pacy-sur-Eure.

In the southwest, the Bordelais directed a detachment of 400 men toward Paris. These federalists were to effect a junction with Normand troops, but when they learned about the defeat at Pacy-sur-Eure they hastily fell back on Bordeaux. Thus the Bordelais insurrection was reduced to a hostile attitude toward the Convention and its representatives, and this opposition was rapidly overcome without great bloodshed.

In the west, therefore, the two most serious insurrections were checked a month and a half after their beginning and the Vendée once more isolated. Two serious dangers obviously remained: the Provençal insurrection and the Lyonnais insurrection, which we shall study in the following chapter.

Nevertheless, the six weeks of the federalist insurrection in the west, enabled the Vendéans to organize themselves by deflecting from their destination those columns intended to march against them. This respite enabled them to structure a new organization, not only military but also civil, the principal founder of which was abbé Bernier, curate of the church of Saint-Laud d'Angers. He was aided by the marquis de Lescure, a former captain and returned émigré, young, educated and very devout, dubbed the "saint of Poitou."

Abbé Bernier and the marquis de Lescure decided to give a generalissimo to the Catholic and Royal Army, and they chose a poor weaver, Cathelineau, thirty-four, very pious, soon called the "saint of Anjou."

As for the civil organization, it was dominated by three superior councils created at Châtillon-sur-Sèvre: an ecclesiastic council, a civil council and a military council. These three councils began by decreeing the re-establishment of the tithes in what they called the "conquered districts," the part of the Vendée occupied by the insurgents. Admittedly this move was not very popular with the peasants, even causing some of them to turn aside from the insurrection.

The councils also decreed nullification of the sale of national properties, and the purchasers of national properties had to return lands they had bought to the former proprietors. The royal courts were re-established. But, in fact, this civil organization functioned very poorly because the district was not really dominated by the Vendéan leaders. The Vendéans administered certain localities when they were there but as soon as they disappeared, the republicans took over their functions again.

As for the Catholic and Royal Army, it too was very poorly organized and undisciplined. The soldiers imposed their will on the leaders. To be sure, there was no uniform. The peasants had muskets or sometimes only pikes or scythes. They recognized each other often by a badge, a Sacred Heart cut out of red wool, which they wore on their chests or clothing; or by a white cockade stuck in their hats, or ribbons on their short tunics. These peasants were impatient of any military discipline. They were not formed into regiments but into bands; they assembled in order to march into combat, then, once the republicans seemed to gain the upper hand, someone would shout "Scatter, lads!" and everybody swiftly disappeared and hid their weapons; soon the only persons to be seen in the area were peaceful tillers of the soil. Nevertheless, these peasants, who were excellent hunters and often former smugglers, were also good shots and their deadly accuracy took its toll among the republican troops.

The major problem of the command of the Catholic and Royal Army was to keep it together. As long as the fighting was in the Vendée, the peasants consented to come to the assembly areas for a few days, but then they cited untilled fields, family matters that had to be regulated or holidays as pretexts to return to their parishes.

After their victory over the federalists, three republican armies faced the Catholic and Royal Army. At their head was General Biron, appointed on April 30. He commanded not only the ensemble of the three armies but in particular the army of the coast of La Rochelle, nearest to the main theater of operations. The two other armies were that of the Brest coast, commanded by General Canclaux, with its headquarters in Nantes, and that of the Cherbourg coast, commanded by General Wimpffen, who was quickly compromised by his association with federalism.

The republican armies were not much better than the Catholic and Royal Army since in all they included only a regiment of dragoons provenient from the old regular army. The rest was composed mainly of battalions of national volunteers, called up hastily and at the same time as the Catholic and Royal Army, and of free corps formed of revolutionary Parisians, notably the corps commanded by Rossignol, Westermann, Augereau and Marceau, whose reputation dates from this time. We also find in the republican armies the German Legion, composed of German and Alsatian volunteers whose leader was an authentic prince of the Holy Empire, the prince of Hesse, who had become a republican and had himself called General Marat.

These republican troops were just as insubordinate as the Vendéan troops. They were great pillagers, prone to all kinds of atrocities in reprisal for Vendéan atrocities. The republican troops were accompanied by a swarm of representatives on mission and of commissaries of the executive power. Among the latter we note in particular Ronsin, a Parisian Hebertist who in four days had been promoted from the rank of captain to that of general, so that he had been advanced more rapidly than Bonaparte himself, but failed pitifully in his command.[8] These representatives and commissaries made their headquarters at Saumur, around the chief of the general staff of the armies of the west, General Berthier, Bonaparte's future general staff chief.

8. General Herlaut, *Le Général rouge, Ronsin* (Paris, 1957) and *Deux Témoins de la Terreur, Dubuisson et Haindel* (Paris, 1958).

An extraordinary disorder prevailed in the republican armies and the Vendéans took advantage of it to march on Saumur, which they captured on June 9. After the fall of this city, the so-called court of Saumur retreated in disorder with their wives and mistresses, a lamentable spectacle.

Once in Saumur, the Vendéans could have easily marched on Paris; nothing stood in their way. The Revolution unquestionably would have taken on a different aspect had they done so; later, the insurgent Calabrians, in the course of a similar insurrection, marched directly on Naples and restored the Old Regime. But the capture of Paris appeared a very difficult operation and the Vendéan combatants were loath to go so far away from their homes.

So, after the capture of Saumur—as the result of which 50 cannon, 1,500 muskets and considerable provisions fell to the Vendéans—their leaders decided to march on Nantes along the right bank of the Loire. They captured Angers on June 18. Angers incidentally was not defended by republican troops. The Vendéans then approached Nantes at the same time that another band, commanded by Charette, attacked the city from the left bank. But at Nantes General Canclaux and Beysser had actively prepared the defense. In the course of the attack, the generalissimo of the Catholic and Royal Army, Cathelineau, was mortally wounded on June 29 and after his death the army dispersed.

Replacing Cathelineau turned out to be a difficult problem and gave rise to all sorts of disputes. There were at least four candidates for the command of the Vendéan army: d'Elbée, Charette, Bonchamps and Stofflet. Finally d'Elbée was named general-in-chief, with Stofflet as second-in-command. But the two other candidates, Charette and Bonchamps, were very displeased and thus the seeds of discord were sowed in the Vendéan armies.

On the republican side, the general-in-chief, Biron, held responsible for the loss of Saumur and Angers, was recalled to Paris, brought before the revolutionary tribunal, sentenced to death and executed on December 30, 1793, although his responsibility in the defeat had not been proved. He was replaced at the head of the armies of the west by the Hebertist, Rossignol, who proved to be an inferior general. Thus towards the end of July, there was a brief lull in operations on both sides.

After their failure before Nantes, the Vendéans were not clearly decided on what their next step should be. Finally they set out for Sables-d'Olonne, but failed in their attempt. They then made contact with

England through the intermediation of the chevalier de Tinténiac, who informed them that England was disposed to assist them, but on condition that they first capture an important port. Once installed in a port, the English would be able to recruit an army of émigrés in their country to whom they would add British contingents and then effect a landing with these troops.

The Vendéan leaders were forced to recognize that to mount an important operation against a port was no easy task. One of them wrote: "It is impossible to propose a fixed plan to oneself as one would like, not having disciplined troops. After combat, every peasant goes home to rest, he cannot be kept in the army, serving without pay." Thus the Vendéans were at an utter loss, and their hesitation enabled the defense to get hold of itself again.

In fact the Convention on August 1 decreed "total" war against the Vendée. The decree was particularly harsh: "Forests are to be felled, the hideouts of the bandits destroyed, crops cut down and carried away on the backs of the army, livestock seized. Men, women and children shall be conducted to the interior, their subsistence and security being provided for with all the respect due to humanity." This is what was later to be called the "scorched earth" policy. In order to carry it out, the Convention decided to reinforce its army in the west. At that very point the French garrison at Mayence, in Germany, after being under siege since March, surrendered; and a condition of the surrender was that this army could no longer serve against the coalition, but would be repatriated with its arms and baggage to the interior. This clause did not prohibit the use of the army of Mayence against the French insurgents, so it was directed towards the Vendée.

The Mayence army was an excellent force, commanded by leaders like Kléber and Aubert-Dubayet. No doubt initially the Vendéans made fun of the "army of fayence," which was defeated at Torfou on September 19. But it was not long before the Mayençais was victorious when the army of Ronsin and Santerre was defeated near Saumur, at Coron on September 18. The noose around the Vendée was drawn tighter and the Convention decided that the war should be brought to an end by October 20. Thereupon four important columns were organized: one commanded by Westermann, which was to operate from Saumur and which set out for Thouars and Châtillon, south of Cholet; a second coming from Sables-d'Olonne and pointing toward Luçon; a third commanded by Kléber, starting out from Nantes, which would march toward Clisson; and a fourth column debouching from Fontenay to the south, which would make its way toward the north, Bressuire and Châtillon-sur-Sèvres.

These four columns met and combined on October 17 and defeated all the Vendéan leaders at Cholet. D'Elbée, Bonchamps and Lescure were killed or wounded in the course of this battle. Among the important leaders, only Charette escaped by reaching the isle of Noirmoutier. The rest of the Vendéans, now become a kind of mob of 40,000 persons, of whom 10,000 were combatants, fell back in disorder toward the Loire, with the republican troops in hot pursuit.

After d'Elbée's death, Henri de La Rochejacquelein and Stofflet took over the command. At the Loire, they hesitated between two courses: whether to return toward the west to join Charette and establish a line of defense on the coast; or to cross the Loire, march toward the north and bring the war to Brittany or its borders and so try to reach a port, Granville, for example, where they could receive assistance from England and the émigrés.

They adopted the latter solution, and so began the great march of the Vendéans, who crossed the Loire at Saint-Florent-le-Vieil, on October 20, after which, by way of Laval taken on October 23, they reached Granville on November 14. In the course of this march, the Vendéans seized and shot all republicans in their path and committed all kinds of atrocities; the republicans soon took to their heels at the approach of this mass and when the disorderly mob arrived before Granville with the hope of seeing the locality fall rapidly into its hands, it realized on the contrary that the resistance had been seriously organized and that no English sail was in sight. On the assurances of the chevalier de Tinténiac, the Vendéans had been led to believe that the English would land at Granville and that they would find considerable aid there. They were extremely disappointed.

The Vendéans were not properly equipped to lay a siege; after a few hours they decided to fall back. In the second phase of the campaign, the disorderly throng which still included many women and children fell back toward the Loire and reached Angers on December 4. Then the Vendéans, unable to recross the river, set out towards Le Mans, where they were defeated on December 12 and 13 by Marceau, Kléber and Westermann, losing more than 3,000 men. A lamentable retreat ensued from Le Mans toward Nantes, during which the Vendéans lost more than 9,000 men among the combatants and the families accompanying them. Finally, on

December 23, the remnant of the Vendéan army was defeated, captured and massacred or shot at Savenay by the republican armies under Kléber's command.

Thus the Vendée affair was brought to a close, at least in its first phase, the "grande guerre" phase of the war waged by the Catholic and Royal Army. Henceforth in the Vendée, as in Normandy and Brittany, another type of war was to succeed this "grande guerre," the guerrilla war that has come to be known as the "*chouannerie*." The defeat of the Vendéans, however, was followed by terrible repression throughout the region. Numerous military commissions were created. They traveled throughout the Vendée and, without any form of trial, shot anyone found bearing arms, judging and sentencing accomplices of the insurgents to diverse penalties. At Nantes the revolutionary tribunal functioned without let-up and in order to speed the executions of the Nantais, Carrier, or rather the Nantais in his entourage, suggested drowning the prisoners in the Loire. Boats in which scuttle holes had been bored were readied and as they crossed the Loire they sank with all their passengers. We do not know the exact number of victims; estimates vary between 2,800 and 4,600. But we possess the list of those ordered shot by the revolutionary commissions: there were 1,896 victims between January 12 and February 10, 1794, and 292 from February 10 to the end of April. These persons were executed by firing squads near Ancenis at a site thereafter called "the field of the martyrs." Finally, General Turreau traversed the Vendée at the head of "infernal columns" that pillaged and massacred so wantonly that the repression, rather than leading to the pacification of the Vendée, produced the opposite effect. After the insurrection the peasants, no doubt, would have yielded, but upon seeing this savage repression, they thought they had no other alternative but self-defense in order not to be killed. Thus the few surviving Vendéan leaders, Charette on the littoral, Stofflet in the interior, saw new partisans come over to them, while their bands grew ever larger and were reorganized. But there was no longer to be a "Grand Army," only bands of *chouans*.

5 / The Chouannerie

The name "*chouannerie*" was given to the Breton and Normand insurrections from 1793 onwards. Nevertheless, the *chouannerie* has origins going further back into the past. It was not a result of the Vendée, having existed beforehand. It did stem from the same state of mind and the same geographical and sociological causes, but there is an essential difference between the Normand and Breton *chouannerie* and the Vendéan insurrection. In Normandy and Brittany the insurgents, the *chouans*, were never more than a minority; the mass of the population remained faithful to Paris and the republic, whereas in the Vendée, the "Blues" were always in the minority. The difference between the *chouannerie* and the Vendéan insurrection lies also in the form assumed by the insurrection. As we have seen, the Vendéan insurrection was based upon the formation of a large army. In contrast, the *chouannerie* bore a far closer resemblance to the "maquis" underground fighters of the last war. The *chouans* gathered in small bands commanded by leaders who were for the most part obscure; these bands operated at night by surprise attacks and ambushes, after which they melted away in the darkness. Their cadres were composed above all of ex-salt contrabandists, one of whom, Jean Cottereau, took the pseudonym of Jean Chouan and very probably gave his name to the insurrection.

Whereas the Vendéans had the complicity of the population, the *chouans* were in general hated by the populations on which they lived. The following letter from the representative on mission, Bourbotte, to the Committee of Public Safety, is altogether characteristic in this respect. It is dated September 10, 1793:

> In all the communes through which the brigands have passed, we have consulted with the people on the impression that this horde had made upon them. Everywhere they are execrated as thieves, held in horror as fanatics and royalists, and this army composed of refractory priests, ex-salt-tax-collectors, bankrupts, excise men, solicitors' clerks, valets of émigrés, male and female religious, marquises, comtesses and former nobles, leaves such a moral and physical stench behind it that in all the districts it traverses it is called the army of the "puants"* [instead of *chouans*].

What were the intentions of the *chouannerie?* They are much less clear than those of the Vendée. The Vendée wanted to re-establish the absolute regime, whereas the aspirations of the *chouannerie* were very vague; it was more democratic than the Vendéan insurrection and would accept a constitutional monarchy. Thanks to their mobility and small number, the *chouans* were able to hold out for a long time. The Vendée lasted barely nine months, the *chouannerie* ten years. It was able to keep going

* Stinkers—Trans.

because of the terror with which it bore down upon the population, forcing the peasants to provision its bands. At times it also obtained the complicity of some administrators and indeed, until 1795, of some purchasers of national property, who paid off the *chouans* in order to be left in peace. Finally, the *chouannerie* had obtained the aid of refractory priests, of whom there were many. Nevertheless, although it had been a source of great concern to the French government until 1804, the *chouannerie*, was never really dangerous; it never required forces comparable to those which had to be mobilized to put down the Vendéan insurrection.

Wherein, then, do the origins of the *chouannerie* lie? Apparently, like the Vendéan insurrection, it derived from the Breton conspiracy of the marquis de La Rouairie. After La Rouairie's death, the marquis de Dresnay, then Puisaye—the leader of the Normand federalists—took command over all the *chouans*, insofar as it was possible to command them.

But the *chouannerie* goes far back in the history of the Revolution. As early as 1791 the commune of Saint-Julien (Côtes-du-Nord) suffered an uprising that has the character of a *chouan* insurrection. And in June of 1792 in the region of Guérande, near Saint-Nazaire, there was another peasant insurrection also of a *chouan* nature. In September of 1792—a long time before the Vendéans had crossed the Loire—nuclei of *chouans* formed all over Brittany, particularly on the Côtes-du-Nord and in the Finistère, in the region of Morlaix.

In March, 1793, at the time of the levy of 300,000 men, bands of *chouans* gathered in Brittany and disturbances broke out nearly everywhere. Thus the Vendée cannot be held responsible, and it would be erroneous to think that the passage of the Vendéans to the north of the Loire left the *chouannerie* in its wake. The *chouannerie* was born simultaneously, perhaps even before the Vendéan insurrection; but one result of the passage of the Vendéans north of the Loire was the great strengthening of the *chouannerie*. The Vendéans who were not killed at Le Mans or Savenay did not all return to their native towns; some of them remained on the Breton and Normand borders to form the nucleus of the *chouan* bands. These bands also kept themselves going by infusions of refractories (that is, young men who were affected by the military draft and who refused to leave), by deserters—soldiers who had left their regiments—and, of course, by counter-revolutionists and royalists.

Given these characteristics, one can understand why the *chouannerie* could not strike heavy blows. Expeditions analogous to those of the

Catholic and Royal Army were simply out of the question. The *chouannerie* proceeded by surprise attacks, which it would be tedious to describe in detail.

To give just one example, in Brittany it organized an attack on Vannes in March, 1794 which was abortive; the following May 10 the *chouans* took the little town of Brignac in the Morbihan. At the same time they took possession of the forest of Rennes under the command of Puisaye. But above all the *chouans* organized assaults against patriot purchasers of national properties, mayors of little towns, constitutional curates, and even against stage coaches in order to seize the money being transported, as well as any republicans among the passengers.

6 / The Pacifications of 1795

Accordingly, the *chouannerie* took the place of the Vendée and kept the agitation alive during the whole of the year 1794. After the fall of Robespierre, however, on 9 Thermidor, it appeared to the Convention that perhaps it had been mistaken in its organization of the repression. Since appeasement was the main order of the day, it tried to seek ways to achieve the pacification of the Vendée. What is more, even without waiting for Robespierre's fall, as early as May, 1794, the Committee of Public Safety, informed of the atrocities that were being committed throughout the west, at Robespierre's instigation had recalled Carrier from Nantes and revoked General Turreau's command. It abolished the "infernal columns." Indeed, the committee itself admitted that Turreau's columns had provided Stofflet with 25,000 recruits.

After 9 Thermidor, the *chouannerie* experienced a revival, thanks to this appeasement policy, but attempts at negotiations continued. They were facilitated by the fact that the *chouannerie* seemed to be clearly subordinated to one leader, Puisaye. Puisaye had formed a royalist central committee, which included notably the comte de La Bourdonnaye, the comte de Boulainvilliers, and other nobles, such as Boisguy. Puisaye went to England in an attempt to obtain not only money but men: a person of great ability, he quickly won Pitt's favor and had been imposed as the leader of the insurgents of the west. But upon leaving for England, he had entrusted the command to a certain Dezoteux, who had himself called baron de Cormatin, after a property owned by his wife in Saône-et-Loire. Now, while Puisaye was proposing to Pitt the organization of an army of émigrés supported by English troops, which was to attempt a landing in Brittany and an action against Paris, Cormatin was entering into relations with the representatives on mission. Negotiations spread little by little between the representatives on mission and the *chouan* leaders north of the Loire, and the Vendéan leaders in the south.

As early as August 16, 1794, at the instigation of Carnot, the Committee of Public Safety had given very strict orders to the troops in the west to cease from making further exactions on the local populations. Looting was to be ruthlessly checked, troops henceforth to be quartered in camps and no longer in the villages. When insurgents were caught, only the leaders were to be sentenced to death, the others merely imprisoned until the pacification. Lastly, General Hoche was appointed commander-in-chief of the armies of Brittany, the Brest coast and the coast of Cherbourg, and General Canclaux commander of the Army of the Vendée. Now, Hoche and Canclaux had both been imprisoned by the Montagnards several weeks before the fall of Robespierre. They were inclined to indulgence toward the rebels and were bent upon fostering the pacification.

These two generals, as well as representatives on mission and Boursault, in particular, while pursuing secret negotiations with the leaders of the *chouans* and the Vendéans, promised an amnesty and 20 livres in silver to all the insurgents who would hand over their muskets. A considerable number of insurgents began to surrender their muskets. At this point news arrived that the trial of Carrier had begun in Paris and that the Convention was preparing harsh punishment for all those who allowed the reign of terror in Brittany. This created a favorable atmosphere. Finally, Hoche and Canclaux organized anti-*chouan* companies, bands composed of republicans who used the same methods as the *chouans* and thus fought more effectively against them than the regular troops.

On December 1, 1794, Carnot had the Convention vote a decree published the following day. It granted full and complete amnesty to all rebels who surrendered within the period of one month from that date; many rebels laid down their arms.

Nevertheless, the negotiations continued because the government wanted to sign a formal treaty with the leaders of the insurgents. On January 12, 1795, the Committee of Public Safety authorized Carnot to grant the rebels a cease fire. The republicans were to withdraw to their positions and the rebels, *chouans* and Vendéans, to cease their attacks. At the same time, a reinforcement of 12,000 men was sent to the west to show that the republicans would have a great number of troops at their disposal in the event of a renewal of the struggle. All these decrees and actions favored pacification.

A first pacification was signed on the outskirts of Nantes, at the château of La Jaunaie. It was concluded with Charette between February 12 and 15, 1795. It was a true peace treaty between two enemies: the rebels in the future would be protected from any investigation of their past; the republic would grant assistance and indemnities to all victims of the war, whether they were former Vendéan insurgents or former republicans, and would participate in the reconstruction of destroyed villages. All their properties would be returned to the Vendéans, even to the émigrés and the heirs of those who had been sentenced to death and whose properties had been confiscated. In future, the young men of the Vendée would be exempt from military service, a regulation that was to remain in effect up to the Consulate. The government did not lay claim to any of the weapons held by the insurgents. This was very risky, and was doubtless a mistake on the part of the representatives of the people. The Vendéans were organized into "territorial companies" serving on the spot, and their only mission was to maintain the security of their district; in fact, these companies prolonged the organization of the Vendéan bands and made them official. Freedom of worship was granted in the Vendée even to refractory priests. The Vendéans had issued paper currency during the insurrection: the sum of 2 million of this paper was exchanged for the "assignats" of the republic. Finally, the leaders were given a special indemnity in reward for the pacification; Charette himself received a gratuity of 200,000 livres. The next day, in celebration of the peace, a great fête took place in Nantes.

The pacification of La Jaunaie seemed to put an absolute end to the war of the Vendée. Similar pacifications took place a little later at La Prévalaye and at La Mabilais, near Rennes; treaties were signed with the leaders of the *chouans* and the conditions were the same as for those of the treaty of La Jaunaie. Stofflet was the last to give in on May 2, 1795; he too finally signed a treaty which stipulated analogous conditions.

There has been and continues to be much discussion of these events in the attempt to determine which was the duped party in this pacification. Did the Vendéan and *chouan* leaders negotiate simply to obtain a respite, while awaiting the landing of the army of émigrés and the English army for which Puisaye was negotiating? Did they knowingly want to deceive the republicans by laying down arms which, for that matter, they did not turn in? Or did the *chouan* and Vendéan leaders, ignorant of what was transpiring in London, sincerely stop the war in the hope that the republican government would not last much longer, that it would be overthrown from within and followed by the installation of a monarchist government in keeping with their wishes? These are questions that have not yet been resolved. But one fact is certain: the pacifications in the west were ephemeral. Only a few months after they had been signed, the war was resumed in the entire region, and in the summer of 1795 it was followd by the émigrés' attempt to effect a landing at Quiberon, supported by the British. Thus the question of the sincerity of the pacifications remains.

CHAPTER XII

The Counter-Revolutionary Insurrections in Southeastern France, 1792 to 1795

The insurrections in southeastern France took place in the region of the Vivarais—these were the earliest—the region of Lyons, and in Provence.

1 / The Disturbances in the Vivarais

Local sociological causes lay at the base of the disturbances in the Vivarais: the ancient animosity between Catholics and Protestants, and the struggles between some inhabitants of the Comtat Venaissin, who would have preferred to remain papal subjects, and the majority, favorable to union with France. These existing divisions were exploited by royalist agents and, above all, by the Turin counter-revolutionary committee from the moment of its establishment at the beginning of the Revolution. The proximity of the Vivarais facilitated this action.

Other causes were geographical. In the Vivarais we find the same features already described in the Vendée and in Brittany: isolated farms and hamlets, scattered dwellings, difficult communications, the great authority preserved in many villages by noble or priest over a peasant populace which, especially in the Catholic areas, was illiterate, wretchedly poor and very ignorant. Finally, there was the hostility, frequently marked, between rustics and town dwellers.

The disturbances in the Vivarais might have become extremely serious, but they never attained the importance of the revolt of the Vendée. This was due essentially to the fact that the Vivarais and the adjoining regions had always been greatly divided between Catholics, only a portion of whom were hostile to the Revolution, and Protestants, who were almost unanimously in favor of it. The Vivarais disturbances were essentially marked by the formation of royalist "encampments" at Jalès.

The first of these encampments, which was at the root of the insurrectional movement of the Vivarais, took place on August 18, 1790. It met at the instigation of the Turin counter-revolutionary committee, with the aid of a number of members of the local nobility: the Du Roures, proprietors of the château de la Banne, near Berrias, a small village situated in the south of the department of the Ardèche; the mayor of Berrias, de Malbosc, a lawyer in the parlement of Toulouse; the parish priest of Chambonas, Claude Allier; and his brothers, abbé de Siran, vicar-general of Mende, and the bishop of Uzès, de Béthizy, as well as a number of other figures.

It was at the gathering of 1790 of the federations of the national guards that the counter-revolutionaries of the Cévennes got the idea of convoking a federation of the national guards of the departments of Ardèche, Lozère and Gard, 25,000 men in all. But they were careful to choose national guardsmen among those most hostile to the Revolution. The first encampment at Jalès was perfectly legal: the sponsors of the gathering had obtained all the requisite authorizations from the Directory of the department, the district, etc.

On the morning of August 18, 1790, 25,000 men gathered on the plain that surrounds the château of Jalès, near Berrias; the general staff of the different battalions of the National Guard met at the château. The members of the general staffs rehashed the incidents that had taken place since the beginning of the year, the fights between Protestants and Catholics at Montauban, at Nîmes and all over the Midi. Feeling ran high, and some demanded that they fall upon the Protestants and kill them then and there. Finally, a series of motions clearly hostile to the Revolution was voted. A demand was made for the release of Catholics imprisoned at Nîmes after the June days during which Catholics and Protestants were engaged in violent rows. There was also a demand for the reorganization of the municipalities of the departments of Gard and Ardèche, so as to eliminate the Protestants. Finally, before the gathering broke up, a permanent committee was formed consisting of members elected by the legions of the national guards; all were royalists and hostile to the Revolution.

These events did not go unnoticed in the National Assembly. In Paris the Committee of Investigations of the Assembly was informed of the goings-on; it charged the Directory of the department of Ardèche to open an investigation on the formation of the encampment at Jalès, and it ordered the tribunals to prosecute the authors of the counter-revolutionary motions.

The tribunals acted slowly; soon a pamphlet appeared entitled: *Manifeste et protestation de 50,000 Français fidèles, armés dans le Vivarais pour la cause de la religion et de la monarchie contre les usurpateurs de L'Assemblée soi-distant nationale (Manifesto and Protest of 50,000 faithful Frenchmen, armed in the Vivarais region for the cause of religion and the monarchy against the usurpers of the so-called National Assembly).* This had been printed clandestinely through the good offices of Malbosc and it was supposed to have been drawn up by the comte d'Antraigues himself. The manifesto protested against the whole work of the National Assembly; it declared the members of the Assembly criminal offenders against "divine and human lèse-majesty," and proclaimed that the federalists of Jalès would prosecute the instigators of the *journées* of October 5 and 6, 1789. Finally, it exhorted every province in France to follow the example of the Vivarais and destroy a constitution that was shaping up as a monstrous creation.

Throughout the year 1790 more or less significant incidents continued to take place in the Vivarais. At the beginning of December, 1791, the committee of Jalès met once more in the residence of Malbosc. It decided to convoke a second encampment for February 20. This time the national guards were asked to come with arms and munitions; the château of La Banne was stocked with provisions sufficient for 35,000 men for three days, and wages of 10 sous a day were provided as compensation for needy federalists.

But the committee made one serious error: the convocations were sent by post and thus the authorities were rapidly apprized and took instant action. They dissuaded many of the national guards from going to Jalès. Despite their efforts, some Catholic national guards responded to the convocation on February 20; they placed themselves in position around the château and on the plain and designated as camp commander a naval officer who commanded the National Guard of Largentière, Chastanier de Burac. De Burac, moreover, was a moderate, a constitutionalist, but the extremists intended to take advantage of the situation and march on Nîmes and Uzès. Chastanier prevented them from doing so. Finally, most of the national guards dispersed.

In the meantime, the Protestant national guards had been alerted. They had converged on Jalès, but did not arrive until February 22, after the departure of the federalists. Nevertheless, some quarrels flared up, leaving seven dead. Malbosc was arrested, along with a few of the members of the committee of Jalès. Several days later Malbosc was found dead on the bank of the Rhône, near Pont-Saint-Esprit. Had he drowned, been murdered, or was his death accidental? Mystery still shrouds his death, but the second encampment at Jalès was a complete fiasco.

These two encampments at Jalès, however, had restored hope to the Turin committee, which had counted upon making the Vivarais the center of the counter-revolution. An émigré officer, the comte de Saillans, counseled the princes to help along the outbreak of a new revolt both politically and financially. They decided to convoke a third encampment for July of 1792.

The general circumstances were favorable, very different from the previous ones. War had broken out between France, Austria and Prussia, the throne was threatened, disturbances were developing everywhere.

As commander of what they already called "The Catholic Army of the Midi," the princes appointed Thomas de Convay, a noble of "monarchical" sentiments, and gave him the comte de Saillans as an adjutant. Claude Allier was commissioned to assure liaison between leaders and troops.

This encampment at Jalès, prematurely convoked and arranged, also became known to the authorities. As early as February they arrested a great many royalist leaders of the departments of Ardèche, Gard and Lozère. Thus by May, 1792, the royalists of the region were deprived of their leaders and their number had been reduced. The comte de Saillans was nevertheless confident. He assumed the title of "General of the Christian and Royal Army of the Orient," in contrast to that of "the Occident," which it was hoped to raise in the west. An enormous quantity of food supplies and munitions was stored at the château of La Banne and the date of the encampment and the start of the rising fixed for July 8. The royalist troops were to gather at Jalès, from there march on Le Puy-en-Velay and spread the insurrection along the entire eastern border of the Massif central. But this plan too was communicated to the authorities, and the Directory of the department of Ardèche took measures to nip the insurrection in the bud. It directed all the available battalions of national volunteers to the château of La Banne: to give one example, the first battalion of volunteers from the department of Haute-Garonne, re-cruited in Toulouse and Rieux and commanded by Viçose and Dupuy upon its transit through Nîmes, was requisitioned by the department of Gard and sent to Jalès. An attack was launched against the château of La Banne. The battalion of Haute-Garonne captured it, and the neighboring villages were set to the torch, including Berrias. Discouraged, the comte de Saillans issued a proclamation to his partisans, calling upon them to disperse and return to their homes. He himself tried to escape, but was caught and murdered in the village of Vans, killed, supposedly, by the famous terrorist Jourdan, nicknamed the "Headcutter," who had already exercised his special talents in Avignon.

Numerous royalists were massacred in the environs of Jalès on July 12 and 13; around 200, according to estimates by the deputy Boissy d'Anglas. At all events, the fiasco was complete. This third encampment at Jalès put an end to the attempts at insurrection in the Vivarais. Not completely, however. Despite their repeated failures, the royalists believed they could still create a center of insurrection in this region.

At the beginning of 1793, at the very moment when the Vendée was in a state of rebellion, the royalists commissioned one Charrier to organize a rising in the Lozère. Charrier marched on Marvejols and captured the town, thus cutting communications between Saint-Flour and Millau, after which he directed his troops on Mende, assisted by Dominique Allier, brother of Claude Allier.

But the republicans organized a defense and retaliated energetically. As early as the first engagements, most of the royalists who accompanied Charrier dispersed and deserted. Charrier was arrested on June 24, 1793, and quickly brought before the criminal court of Rodez, which sentenced him to death; he was executed on July 17. Claude Allier escaped despite continuing searches and tried to join the royalists of Lyons, whose insurrection began at this time. But he too was finally captured by the gendarmerie. Like Charrier, he was sentenced to death, and executed on September 5, 1793.

The arrest and execution of Charrier and Allier put an end to the attempts at insurrection in the Vivarais. Had they succeeded, they might have created a situation altogether analogous to that of the Vendée, but they failed, chiefly because of the political divisions of the populace. The Protestants, in fact, almost unanimously had sided with the Revolution and only a minority of Catholics had declared themselves hostile to it.

2 / The Insurrection at Lyons

The insurrection at Lyons was of more account and its causes were rather different. Here it involved a city, not the countryside. On the eve of the Revolution, Lyons was overpopulated. The economic crisis which had been going on since 1774 had caused the excess population of the neighboring rural.areas and of the very poor mountainous regions—the Alpes, the Jura and the Massif central—to pour into Lyons. There were also foreigners in Lyons—Swiss, Sardinians and Savoyards.

The gulf between the enlightened faction and the bourgeoisie and the enormous mass of beggars and unemployed became increasingly marked among the Lyonese populace. The beginning of the Revolution aggravated the economic crisis. Lyons, in fact, was the center of a luxury industry—silk goods, and as early as 1790 the fabrication of silk declined. Unemployment increased, and the abolition of the corporations, decreed at the beginning of the Revolution, combined with the prohibition of journeymanship, aggravated the malaise; the fate of the workers, isolated in the face of the owners, became very precarious.

Moreover, mysticism spread among the Lyonese intellectual élite, which had been influenced by the Enlightenment; indeed, Lyons was the center of mysticism in France at the end of the eighteenth century, a city in which romanticism appeared very early. In Lyons, a certain form of Freemasonry, Martinism, sprang to life under the influence of Willermoz, disciple of Claude Saint-Martin, the "unknown philosopher." As we have seen, Joseph de Maistre went several times to Chambéry in Lyons and affiliated himself with Martinism. Thus social malaise doubly intensified the economic crisis and affected the bourgeoisie and a part of the nobility in this city.

On the other hand, communications between Lyons and Turin, where the Committee of Counter-Revolution had established itself as early as 1790, were good. Lyons was also very near Switzerland which, like Piedmont, rapidly became a gathering place for émigrés and a center of counter-revolutionary propaganda. Finally, in Lyons itself there existed within the industrial upper bourgeoisie a group of people very hostile to the Revolution. This group was directed by the former mayor, Imbert-Colomès, who was not long in going to Turin for his orders.

Imbert-Colomès was removed on February 27, 1790. From then until the end of 1792, the Girondins were the masters of the mayoralty of Lyons. Among them, the friends of Roland and his wife had a preponderant influence. But despite the presence of this "Rolandiste" municipality, the agitation remained strong, still directed by the royalists, and in particular by Imbert-Colomès.

After the *journée* of August 10 and the fall of the throne, Roland, who had become minister, suspended from their functions the public prosecutor and the Directory of the department of Rhône-et-Loire—at this time, Rhône and Loire formed a single department. In fact, this administration appeared to him as too royalist under the circumstances. After the suspension of the Directory the Jacobin agitation directed by Chalier, increased.

Chalier was the son of a notary of Briançon. He had been a teacher, a tutor and then a merchant. Since 1792 he had converted to Jacobin extremism. A violent orator, he made staunchly republican speeches which at times even had a pronounced social character and were very hostile to the bourgeoisie. He soon became the *bête noire* of the Lyonese bourgeoisie, but the idol of a segment of the unemployed and wretched who had poured into Lyons during the past few years. Nevertheless, Chalier's partisans, the extremist Montagnards, formed only a small minority of the population. At the municipal elections of February, 1793, the Montagnards received only 2,000 votes out of 10,000. The electoral districts of the city of Lyons were dominated by the moderates and violently opposed to Chalier and his friends.

From September, 1792, onwards the tension in Lyons increased without let-up. During May of 1793 a struggle began between the Montagnard minority, directed by Chalier, which had taken over the municipality, and the Rolandiste majority in control of the directories of the department and of the district. The Rolandistes were supported covertly by the moderates and the royalists.

The betrayal of Dumouriez and the preparations for the defense on the Savoyard frontier only a few miles from Lyons aggravated the struggle between the moderates and the Montagnards. On May 29, 1793, elections were to be held for the members of the Watch Committee, created by the law of March 21 preceding. The purpose of the Watch Committee was to keep an eye on foreigners, but it had also been designed to play an important political role. In order to avoid the choice of a Jacobin Watch Committee, the electoral districts of Lyons demanded the removal of the municipality and the arrest of Chalier. The demonstration developed into a riot, the Hôtel de Ville of Lyons was seized by the moderates and soon events took a tragic turn. On May 30 Chalier was arrested, along with a number of Montagnards.

No doubt this episode would not have had any very serious consequences if it had not coincided with the *coup d'état* of May 31 and June 2,
1793, which in Paris led to the elimination of the Girondins from the
Convention. This made the difference in attitude between Paris and Lyons
appear even more striking: whereas the Mountain had triumphed in Paris,
the moderates had carried the day in Lyons. Nevertheless, the Convention
did not want to push things to the worst. It sent some representatives on
mission to Lyons in an attempt to calm the populace and to re-establish
an agreement with Paris. They were Dubois-Crancé, Albitte and Robert
Lindet—all Montagnards but not terrorists.

These representatives were badly received by the departmental administration of Lyons, and vehemently reproached for the arrest of the
Girondist deputies. After June 7, 1793, the Lyonese administrations acted
as if they were autonomous, taking no notice of the laws, circular letters
or orders of the Convention. This amounted to an insurrection, and Albitte
and Dubois de Crancé wrote the Convention: "Lyons must be declared
in a state of revolt." On June 27 a Jacobin was arrested in Lyons, murdered
soon after and his body thrown into the Saône. This crime marked the
onset of the bloody revolt of Lyons against the Convention. A battalion
of volunteers was raised to march on Paris, but it was soon realized that
a battalion was not enough. The battalion was then assigned to the defense
of Lyons because an attack by the Parisians was feared. On June 29 a
grand fête was celebrated in Lyons: speeches were delivered demanding
the "deliverance of the Convention," now under the domination of several
Parisian extremists. A people's commission was formed on July 5. It was
composed of the departmental administration of Rhône-et-Loire, the
administrations of the districts and of the municipality of Lyons, and a
number of delegates from nearby towns and departments. This commission began by ordering the arrest of a representative on mission, Noël
Pointe, one of the two workers who sat at the Convention and a deputy
from Saint-Etienne. He was quickly freed. But what was important was
that the commission decided it would no longer carry out the decrees of
the Convention promulgated after May 31, and sent a copy of this decision
to all the municipal administrations of the department.

The commission then took upon itself the task of organizing the city's
defense, and looked around for a general. To find one, it turned naturally
to the royalists; several candidates to whom feelers were extended refused,
but finally the comte de Précy, a colonel before 1789 and former member

of the royal guard, accepted. He decided to form an army of 10,000 volunteers, which would be supported by the National Guard.

The revolt of Lyons might have been extremely dangerous if, as Précy and the popular commission had hoped, the Lyonese had been supported by the inhabitants of the neighboring departments—Franche-Comté and the Midi. These regions, in fact, had adhered to federalism, but the revolt there had not been very profound nor very extensive. Lyons was rapidly isolated. After several days of hesitation, Franche-Comté yielded to the Convention. The southeast of the Massif central could not revolt because all the royalist leaders there had been arrested or murdered. As for the Provence region, it never succeeded in joining with Lyons. Thus Lyons was isolated as early as the beginning of July, 1793.

The situation worsened; no attention was paid to the decrees of the Convention which had declared Lyons in a state of rebellion. Chalier's trial took place on July 15: he was condemned to death and executed the following day. The Jacobins were to make him a martyr of the Montagnard cause. The execution of Chalier completed the total rupture between Lyons and the Convention; moreover, it pushed the Lyonese Girondins and moderates toward the right. Thenceforth the revolt was increasingly to assume the character of a royalist insurrection.

During the siege of Lyons, which lasted from August 8 to October 9, 1793, the city passed progressively under the authority of the royalists. The problem of the development of the Lyonese revolt from federalism toward royalism has been studied principally by Riffaterre,[1] who set himself the task of determining whether Précy had received, as he was accused of having done, 4 million in gold from the British government. It has not been possible to resolve this, but there is no doubt that Précy was a royalist. It is certain that he was in constant contact with the émigrés and foreign powers. In later writings, many royalists claimed that "If the cry 'Long Live the Republic' was on the lips of all Lyons, in reality the cry 'Long Live the King' was in their hearts."

It has also been asserted that the Lyonese had sent memoranda to the Spanish Admiral Don Juan Langara, commander of the Mediterranean fleet, asking him to send relief troops to Lyons. Were these drawn up by Lyonese royalists in their own names or by the authorities who directed the revolt? This is a further point that has not been clarified. The duc de

1. C. Riffaterre, "Le Mouvement antijacobin et antiparisien à Lyon et dans le Rhône-et-Loire en 1793," *Ann. de la Fac. des Lettres de Lyon*, Vol. I, 1912; Vol. II, 1928.

Bourbon, who was one of the leaders of the emigration, declared later: "I was not in any direct correspondence with Lyons." Thus the problem of the royalist character of the revolt remains entirely open. Edouard Herriot concludes that the revolt in Lyons was a revolt of moderates, Girondin rather than royalist. But it is beyond doubt that during the siege the royalists organized the resistance to the Convention and the struggle against the Montagnards.

This siege began on August 8; it was directed by General Kellermann, commander of the Army of the Alps. But at this very moment the hostilities which had started with the Kingdom of Sardinia took on a very serious character. There was fear of a counterattack by the Sardinians on the French slope of the Alps, and Kellermann needed all his forces to resist the columns which tried to make their way through the Alpine passes. Thus he could assign only very few forces—some 10,000 men— to the siege of Lyons; for that matter, Précy did not have many troops either. At the most he could assemble only 10,000 men, and undoubtedly he was never able to have more than 5,000 at his disposal at one time.

The members of the Convention, even after the beginning of the siege, tried to achieve an amicable solution: numerous offers of negotiations were sent to the Lyonese, but Précy, supported and spurred on by the royalists, still refused to negotiate.

Then the siege assumed an increasingly more savage character, and the representatives on mission who were directing the struggle tried to isolate the city even more. They decided to divide the department of Rhône-et-Loire in two: a department of the Rhône, reduced to Lyons and its suburbs, and a department of the Loire, which was to have Saint-Etienne as its administrative center. This division still exists. The department of the Loire recognized the authority of the Convention.

Now began the bombardment of Lyons, creating great havoc. The blockade was drawn tighter. Soon Lyons was at the end of its resources, without food supplies, and the city was forced to cease its resistance. Précy evacuated Lyons with his last troops on October 9. He tried to fall back to Switzerland, but the republicans caught up with his soldiers, who were captured or murdered. He himself managed to cross the frontier and we shall find him later in the ranks of the émigrés as one of the leaders of the counter-revolution.

The suppression of the Lyons revolt was particularly terrible and fierce. In a famous decree issued by the Convention on October 12, 1793, the National Assembly declared: "Lyons waged war on liberty, Lyons is no more." The name of Lyons was stricken from the lists of the cities of France and thereafter Lyons was called Ville-affranchie (freed city). The inhabitants were to be disarmed, the houses of the rich demolished. In point of fact, only some houses on the Place Bellecour were torn down. But a military commission, later a commission of popular justice, held a mass trial of the rebels and sentenced them. The executions had a particularly atrocious character: whole batches of condemned rebels were felled by cannon on the plain of Brotteaux. Fouché and Collot d'Herbois were accused of being the initiators of these massacres, but it has not been possible to prove their responsibility any more than that of Carrier in the mass drownings at Nantes. In all, 1,940 executions have been authenticated, but numerous individuals and anonymous massacres certainly raised the number of dead to a much higher figure.

At all events, the revolt at Lyons was crushed and this center of insurrection, which might have been infinitely more dangerous than the Vendée because of its proximity to the front, disappeared.

The Lyonese revolt might also have been exceedingly perilous for the republic had the Lyonese managed to effect their junction with the insurgents of Provence. In fact, the federalist insurrection in Provence was assuming its most acute form at the very moment when Lyons rose in revolt.

3 / Provence: Marseilles and Toulon

In Provence, the insurrection was the consequence of deep division between revolutionaries and counter-revolutionaries. From the beginning of the Revolution, there had been a violent struggle between the Jacobins of Marseilles and the moderates of Aix-en-Provence, the Jacobins of Tarascon and the moderates of Beaucaire, and the "chiffonistes," that is, the royalists of Arles and the revolutionaries of the same town. At the very moment when these struggles were unfolding in Provence, local authorities showed a marked tendency to act autonomously. It has been observed that there had been a Jacobin federalism in Provence before the movement of moderate federalism came into being. But up to May 31 nothing had come of it. In fact, it was the Parisian *coup d'état* of May 31– June 2 which unleashed the insurrection in Marseilles, as in many other cities in France.

Furthermore, the situation was very tense at that moment. For some time, Marseilles had sent thirty-two commissaries and a number of extraordinary deputies to Paris to outline to the Convention the events which had troubled the city and which had resulted in the removal of the Jacobin mayor, Mourraille, and the replacement of the Jacobin municipality by one composed of moderates. Thus the situation was very similar to that obtaining in Lyons. On the other hand, Barbaroux, one of the most ardent Girondists, was among the deputies of Marseilles to the Convention; he had been included in the proscription of June 2.

When the events of June 2 became known in Marseilles, the sections demanded that the imprisoned Jacobins be tried by a popular tribunal. Barbaroux incited the Marseilles moderates, writing: "It is impossible, magistrates of the people, that the *Attentat* committed against the national representation should not bring about a great movement in France." On June 6 the administrations of the department, of the district and of the commune gathered and decided to install a popular tribunal, or rather re-install it, one having already existed several months earlier and been suppressed. They also ordered the levy of an armed force, symbolic more than anything else because it never numbered more than 500 men. This troop was ordered to march on Paris and deliver the Convention. It did not march off but formed the kernel of the "Marseillais Departmental Army." On June 12 a general committee of the sections composed of the delegates of the different sections of Marseilles declared itself "in a state of legal resistance to oppression." On June 22 it resolved no longer to obey the orders of the Convention: an attitude similar to that of Lyons.

Had Marseilles raised a much stronger army at this point and had this army been able to effect a junction with the Lyonnaise, an extremely grave situation would have been created and it is probable that the course of the Revolution would have been altered. But the Marseillais departmental army was too small. It took the offensive and entered Avignon, but went no further. In fact, Dubois-Crancé, the representative on mission, had concentrated a small force of 2,000 men at Valence. This was more soldiers than the Marseillais had at their disposal. Moreover, these 2,000 men were excellent soldiers who had been hand-picked from the ranks of the legion of Allobroges, composed of Swiss and Savoyard volunteers, commanded by the Jacobin doctor, Doppet. Soon Dubois-Crancé's troops increased and the general command was turned over to Carteaux, a former painter, promoted general-in-chief of the troops of Provence.

Despite the presence of Carteaux's army, the Marseillais tried to continue their offensive. They managed to occupy Orange and Pont-Saint-

Esprit, but on July 14, 1793, Carteaux himself started his own push forward. He retook Pont-Saint-Esprit, then Orange. On July 25, he was in control of Avignon.

Upon hearing this news the Jacobins of Arles, who had remained calm until this moment, rose in revolt against the "chiffonistes." The Jacobin sections of Marseilles were in ferment and the unity of the Provençal revolt threatened. No doubt it would have dissolved then and there if an insurrection had not broken out in the port of Toulon at that very moment.

In fact on July 18 the Toulonnais celebrated their union with the federalists of Marseilles with a grand fête. On this occasion they too formed a central committee of sections, which decided to arrest the representatives on mission in Toulon—Pierre Baille, Beauvais, Barras and Fréron—a very serious step. Barras and Fréron managed to escape in short order.

The revolt at Toulon was particularly disturbing. From the outset of the Revolution, incidents had erupted incessantly between the workers at the arsenal, the sailors and the naval officers. Many of the naval officers had emigrated, but those who remained were still animated by a distinctly royalist mentality, so that the Toulonnais federalist movement soon was being directed by naval officers and took on an increasingly marked royalist aspect. The Toulonnais federalists, guided by the royalists, suddenly decided to negotiate with the English admiral, Hood, commander of the Mediterranean fleet which had just arrived in sight of cap Sicié. The negotiations did not get very far at first, because the moderate federalists and the Girondists viewed them as treason. They managed to prevent the conclusion of an agreement with Hood, but these initial negotiations were to leave their mark.

After the fallback of the Marseillais departmental army, which had evacuated Avignon, the Marseillais federalists were seized with great dread. They too were approached by the royalists, who believed that the only way to save the situation was to turn abroad for help. Soon the Marseillais federalists were headed by a distinguished royalist named Villeneuve-Tourette, who managed to inject a certain vigor into the defense. He organized a forward march and reoccupied Salon-de-Provence. But the Marseillais departmental army was of inferior fighting ability. Bonaparte, who was in the region at that time, has described it in his famous *Souper de Beaucaire*. According to him, the Marseillais federalist army was composed of aristocrats, returned émigrés, several large merchants and above all, of mercenaries paid 300 sous a day. This army failed to impose discipline on itself and, after the capture of Salon, once more became a disorderly rabble which retreated in disorder to the city. The central committee of the sections formed a Committee of Public Safety of five members, which decreed exceptional measures: closing of cafés and gambling houses, public processions in order to petition the "Bonne Mère" to deliver the city and, above all, the dispatch of emissaries to the commanders of the British and Spanish fleets in the Mediterranean to obtain their aid against the troops of the Convention.

On August 22 under the pretext of an exchange of prisoners an English frigate docked at Marseilles. Negotiations were begun, but Admiral Hood made known his conditions: he would aid Marseilles only on condition that the Marseillais federalists committed themselves to proclaim the kingship of Louis XVII. Nevertheless the arrival of this British vessel and the rumors of negotiations with the English sowed panic among the populace. The Jacobin leaders of Marseilles swung into action while Carteaux's army increased its pressure on the city. On August 19, the Marseillais departmental army was again beaten near Salon. On August 22, Carteaux entered Aix-en-Provence. In Marseilles the White Terror was intensified and eleven Jacobin prisoners executed on August 20. But the Jacobin sections kept a tight hold on a few quarters in the city. Street fighting broke out in Marseilles on August 23 and 24, Jacobins against federalists and royalists. Finally, on August 25 Carteaux entered the port. The leaders of the federalist movement boarded the ships which were in the harbor and went off to Toulon. Carteaux reinstalled the Jacobin authorities. Marseilles, like Lyons, was debaptized and renamed "Ville-sans-nom" (city without name). Many federalists were arrested and a revolutionary tribunal set up, and repression ensued, but it was an infinitely less bloody affair than in Lyons.

In Toulon, the revolt continued, reinforced by the arrival of the federalists and royalist leaders of Marseilles, who evidently were increasingly hostile not only to the Convention but to the republican regime. Only one hope of saving their skins was left—to obtain aid from foreign powers, England and Spain. The negotiations that had been started with Hood and Don Juan Langara were resumed and pursued at a great rate.

On August 23 the Toulonnais requested the English and Spanish fleets to occupy the city and the port until peace was restored. Admiral Trogoff, commander-in-chief of the French maritime forces at Toulon, who had not yet taken sides in these quarrels but who at heart was a royalist, adhered to the convention signed with the English admiral. His subordinate, Admiral de Saint-Julien, who was a republican, tried to organize resistance but was deserted by a part of his troops and forced to flee. The English and Spanish fleets occupied the port. They landed English, Spanish, Sardinian and Neapolitan troops, although in small numbers, and Louis XVII was proclaimed king.

The Spaniards would have liked to establish the capital of royalist France at Toulon and it was at this point that the comte de Provence was asked to come to Toulon. But it was the English who in fact preserved higher authority throughout the duration of the occupation, and they did not permit the royalist administrations to set themselves up in that city.

After the capture of Marseilles, the army of the Convention marched on Toulon. Its general, Carteaux, had been replaced by Dugommier, and the lieutenant Bonaparte, promoted captain, had been appointed commander of the artillery. Since no French fleet was available, Toulon could not be attacked by sea, but soon it was tightly blockaded by land. Bonaparte indicated to Dugommier what positions he would have to seize in order to render the roadstead untenable to the English and the Spanish, and Dugommier followed suit. On December 17 the forts which commanded the roadstead at Toulon were occupied by republican forces, who greatly outnumbered the foreign troops and the royalists. The English and Spanish ships were forced to evacuate the roadstead swiftly. While retreating, the British burned the French vessels they could not take along with them. The next day, December 18, Toulon was reconquered by the troops of the Convention. The name of Toulon was also stricken from the list of the cities of the republic and changed to Port-la-Montagne.

The history of the insurrections in the southeast of France comes to a close with the capture of Toulon. They could have had infinitely more dangerous consequences for the republic than the insurrection of the Vendée in view of the proximity of the insurgents and enemy forces, separated only by tens of leagues. But they failed because they had not broken out simultaneously, because there was no liaison between the insurgents of the various provinces, because the insurgents themselves remained very divided and also because the Convention swiftly took energetic countermeasures. As a result the counter-revolution in southeastern France, after having dangerously agitated the country, ended in total failure.

CHAPTER XIII

The White Terror and the Royalist
Failures of the Summer of 1795

1 / The White Terror

The fall of Robespierre on 9 Thermidor provoked a spontaneous and deep movement of reaction which had not been foreseen by all those who had contributed to it. There were, in fact, Thermidorians of the Left and the extreme Left who reproached Robespierre for wanting to stop the Revolution and slow down the Terror. This was the case, for example, with Billaud-Varenne, Collot d'Herbois and Vadier. But the Thermidorians of the Left were very quickly swamped by the former Dantonists, the Girondins and even the Feuillants. A great wave of leniency swept over France, and prisons were opened and emptied.

At first the demands were limited to the liberation of prisoners, suspects. But when these suspects were liberated, they sought revenge for their detention and revenge for their relatives who had been sentenced and executed. Matters moved to a new stage, that of reprisals. This phase constitutes the White Terror.

The White Terror began very slowly, as early as 10 Thermidor; it was intensified in the course of 1795 and came to a close in the summer of 1795, after the royalist fiasco of 13 Vendémiaire (September 4).

What are the characteristics of the White Terror? Louis Blanc, a republican who wrote *The History of the Revolution* during his exile in London, after 1848, declared that "the White Terror outstripped in horror even the September massacres, even the executions by cannon at Lyons, even the mass drownings ordered by Carrier." This seems an exaggerated assessment, but there is no doubt that the White Terror had a particularly heinous character. Although it registered fewer victims than the Red Terror, the latter at least had a justification, to save France and the republic, threatened on all frontiers and beset from within by dangerous revolts. In contrast, personal vengeance was the only aim of the White Terror. But the massacres of the White Terror do not share the same characteristics as those of the Red Terror. In the Red Terror the massacres were dreadful, yet legitimate. Those who had been found guilty of intelligence with the enemy or of engaging in a conspiracy were sentenced to death and executed. In the White Terror, those individuals who had suffered wrongs as a result of the Red Terror—whether to property, person or family—avenged themselves on those they accused, often wrongly, of having been the authors of these ills.

In most cases, the White Terror took the form of assassinations, massacres; the Red Terror, except in the case of the massacres at Nantes and the executions by shooting at Lyons, respected formalities which no doubt were very harsh but still legal.

The White Terror established itself by stages: it was barely perceptible from 10 Thermidor, Year II (July 28, 1794), the date of Robespierre's execution, up to the beginning of January, 1795. During this period there was a massive liberation of prisoners. From January, 1795, onwards, the White Terror took on a more marked character. Above all it was the consequence of the law of 20 Nivôse, Year III (January 10, 1795), which authorized the return of émigrés who worked with their hands and who had left France after May 31, 1793. In other words, this law authorized the re-entry into France, on the one hand, of Alsatian peasants who had fled during the retreat of the Austrian army; and on the other, of Lyonese workers who had emigrated or simply gone into hiding at the time of the repression. It also authorized the return of Marsellais and Toulonnais émigrés, as well as refugees from the west. The émigrés of the Midi in particular took advantage of this law, which is why the White Terror was particularly marked in the southeast of France.

Another law promulgated somewhat later, 3 Ventôse, Year III (February 21, 1795) at the proposal of Boissy d'Anglas, decreed the reopening of the churches, although proscribing the outward symbols of worship. Priests, even refractories, were authorized subsequently to re-enter the country if they took the oath of loyalty to Liberty and Equality, instituted after August 10, 1792, and which had never been prohibited by the Pope. They could freely celebrate Mass. Many returned, of course, or emerged from their hiding places. But a number of refractory priests, émigrés or deportees also came back, did not take the "Liberty and Equality" oath and swelled the membership of the royalist party.

On 5 Ventôse (February 23, 1795) another law was proposed, this time by Merlin de Doual. It ordered that all members of district or department administrations, of municipalities and of watch committees who had been removed or suspended since 10 Thermidor should be placed under surveillance in their native communes, under penalty of six months' imprisonment. This law is very important for the history of the White Terror. In effect, it led to the grouping in their communes of all those who were considered terrorists and, consequently, made them individual targets for reprisals by the suspects who had been liberated from the prisons.

The White Terror again intensified after the failure of the Jacobin riots of Germinal. On 12 Germinal, Year III (April 1, 1795) a very serious riot took place in Paris and the Convention was threatened by the inhabitants of the faubourgs. After this riot, two laws were voted, on 21 and 22 Germinal (April 10 and 11): the first ordered the disarmament of terrorists. Thus terrorists were not only concentrated in their communes, marked targets for the vengeance of the aristocrats or moderates, but also placed in a position where they could not defend themselves. The second law, voted on 22 Germinal, authorized the return of all émigrés who had left after May 31, that is, not only those who worked with their hands, but also the bourgeois and aristocrats, their leaders. Durand de Maillane, who had proposed this law, declared that he approved the return of people like Précy and those who, at Toulon, had proclaimed Louis XVII or who had solicited the English and the Spanish presence in that city. The returned émigrés obtained the restitution of their properties even when these had been sold. After the promulgation of these laws, the White Terror entered its third and most distinct stage, which lasted until 13 Vendémiaire.

The White Terror, however, did not spread to all France. To be sure, the reaction was evident to some extent everywhere, in a variety of forms, but it did not really rage except in the region delimited by the Saône, the Rhône, the Mediterranean coast and the frontiers of the Alps and the Jura. It assumed a particularly violent form in the Lyonese region, in the valley of the Rhône and in Provence.

The representatives on mission who were in the departments on 9 Thermidor, in the main, were recalled; some of them were even accused of terrorism. They were replaced by moderates. These moderate representatives on mission opened the prisons and, sometimes, filled them up again with former terrorists. Thus at Bourges, for example, the representative Laurenceot drew up a list of thirty-three terrorists. When this list was published in the rural districts, Liberty trees were chopped down amid cries of "Long live the king! Long live religion!" In the Marne, a representative on mission had two terrorists brought before the criminal tribunal, which sentenced them to death; one of them was the maternal grandfather of Hippolyte Taine who, as we know, was to profess opinions of a very different kind.

We could give many more examples of this kind, but they were totally sporadic and the condemnations of the terrorists were carried out in perfectly legal forms.

After the law of 21 Nivôse (January 10, 1795) things changed and from April on the White Terror intensified. Without going into details, we shall limit ourselves to a study of its manifestations in Lyons, in the Jura, and in the lower valley of the Rhône, in Provence.

The White Terror was particularly violent in Lyons. This is explained by the very violence of the Red Terror. The Montagnard repression had left behind searing memories that still seethed in the mind of the Lyonese: death sentences, executions by the guillotine and firing squads, the demolition of the most beautiful section of Lyons. Finally, after the repression, the atrophy of business, the disappearance of the luxury industries. Thousands of persons were thrown on the street. At the same time the Lyonese bourgeoisie experienced enormous difficulties. Poverty was general for everybody in Lyons, as in the rest of France, and it was aggravated by the devaluation of the "assignats."

The émigrés, nevertheless, returned in great numbers as early as the day after 9 Thermidor, even before the voting of the laws which legally authorized their stay in the city. The refractory priests arrived in bands; the swiftness of these returns is explained by the proximity of Lyons to the Swiss and Italian frontiers. To these returned émigrés and refractory priests, we must add the numerous deserters from the armies of the Rhine and of Italy who streamed toward Lyons.

In Lyonese circles people were already thinking not only of avenging the terrible repression of which Lyons had been the victim in 1793, but of going further and preparing a royal Restoration in favor of Louis XVII, still imprisoned in the Temple and believed to be in good health.

The person who took in hand the direction of these operations was an

English agent sent to Switzerland at the end of 1794, who we shall be mentioning a good deal, Wickham. In France Wickham directed all the royalist plots whose aim was the restoration of a constitutional monarchy. It was thought, moreover, that the advent of Louis XVII, within a constitution like that of 1791, would not create difficulties. Wickham was the major distributor of funds furnished by England and provided the royalist organizations of France with these monies. He established an agency in Lyons and later was to organize another in Swabia under the direction of none other than the former leader of the Lyonese insurrection, General Précy.

We find Imbert-Colomès, the former mayor of the city, at the head of the Lyons agency. At his side was an aide-de-camp of Précy, Bayard, the marquis de Bésignan, and other aristocrats. It is certain that the majority of the Lyonese population was altogether won over by the idea of a royalist Restoration; Wickham's reports agree with those of the representatives on mission in Lyons and with the correspondence of Mallet du Pan on this. Thus on May 12, Wickham wrote to the British minister, Lord Grenville: "All the young people, without exception, desire the return of royalty. . . . At the beginning of the disturbances in 1793, there were hardly a hundred genuine royalists in the place. Now the decided and pronounced opinion of the very great majority is in favor of the monarchy."

When Lyons learned of the news of the death of young Louis XVII, a great number of Lyonese went into mourning and walked the streets openly wearing mourning bands on their sleeves. Theaters were closed and there were all kinds of manifestations of public grief. Wickham would have liked to see General Précy, at that time a refugee in Turin, head a new movement of insurrection, but the memory of the ferocious repression of 1793 was still painfully alive: although Lyons was royalist, it did not want to take the initiative in an insurrection.

On the other hand, acts of private vengeance multiplied. These were carried out by a group of royalists known by the name of the "Company of Jesus." The expression "Compagnie de Jéhu," which crops up from time to time, has no historical basis. The "Company of Jesus" at Lyons joined the *muscadins*, the young people who were preparing the Restoration, as well as those who were seeking personal vengeance.

The first disturbances were not too serious. They began with the destruction of the bust of Chalier, the Jacobin who had been sentenced to death and executed at the very outset of the Lyons revolt. Next came *muscadins*, *merveilleux* and "black collars," who fought in the street with the "drinkers of blood," the *mathevons*. Later the situation worsened. On February 14, a former member of the revolutionary commission of Lyons who had pronounced numerous death sentences was assassinated. On March 11 and 12 a former commissioner of the terrorist municipality of Lyons was killed and two of his colleagues seriously wounded. Assassinations multiplied, hardly a day going by without bodies of *mathevons* who had been murdered in the streets of Lyons being found in the Rhône or Saône.

On May 15 a letter from the representatives on mission in Lyons informed the Convention of the activity of the "Company of Jesus." According to this letter, the company was formed of *muscadins*, returned émigrés, deserters and foreigners introduced by refractory priests. The deputy Marie-Joseph Chénier, brother of the guillotined poet, took the floor at the Convention on June 24 and denounced the White Terror that was raging in Lyons. He declared that the "Company of Jesus" had connections with other similar groups that existed in Provence, known as the "Companies of the Sun." The "Company of Jesus" had sponsored the printing in Lausanne of a "General List of Accusers and Accused." This "List" included, in alphabetical order, the names of persons accused of having denounced others during the Terror, giving their addresses and the list of denounced persons. It was an open invitation to the members of the "Company of Jesus" to go straight to these persons' homes—had they been so imprudent as to remain there—and to murder them.

Nevertheless, Mlle Fuoc feels that the actual existence of the "Company of Jesus" has not been proved.* There were groups of *muscadins* and terrorists who organized the White Terror. But was there really an organization called the "Company of Jesus" or was this the name given to the reactionaries by the republicans? The problem has not been clarified.

The assassinations became increasingly more numerous, when the decree of 22 Germinal ordered the disarming of terrorists. As soon as this was known in Lyons, the moderate municipality ordered a vast operation of domiciliary visits. All apartments, all houses, especially those where former terrorists lived, were visited. There was a sweeping roundup of terrorists, who were carried off to prison and subsequently tried. During the trial of a former member of the revolutionary committee of Vaise, the mob

* See Bibliographical Notes to this chapter—Trans.

invaded the courtroom and manifested its hostility. The court session was dissolved because the judges were loath to pronounce a death sentence under pressure of the demonstration. Thereupon the mob invaded the prisons and massacred the prisoners. A first massacre took place on May 4. It was followed by new invasions of other prisons. In all there were more than 120 killed. It was a repetition of the September massacres, but this time the terrorists were the victims. No doubt there were fewer victims than in Paris, but in proportion to the number of the imprisoned, and to the number of inhabitants in Lyons, the figure nevertheless was high. Moreover, once the prisons had been opened, the prisoners who were not massacred escaped, which enabled a great number of terrorists (as well as common criminals) to make a break for freedom and go into hiding.

The representatives on mission on the spot and the Lyonese authorities do not seem to have taken great pains to stop the massacres, so that the *muscadins* felt tacitly encouraged. The assassinations became extremely frequent up to June 24, the date when Marie-Joseph Chénier presented his report on the situation in Lyons to the Convention.

After hearing this report, the Convention voted a decree suspending the powers of all the administrative bodies of Lyons. It transferred them to other representatives on mission, ordered the disarming of the Lyonese National Guard and commissioned the new representatives on mission sent to Lyons to restore order in the city. In other circumstances this decree could have provoked an uprising. Nothing of the sort happened because the painful memory of what had happened two years earlier persisted; Lyons yielded. The suspension of powers and of the National Guard could be effected without difficulty. The new representatives on mission easily restored order. The White Terror came to an end at Lyons in July of 1795.

In Franche-Comté and particularly in the Jura, the White Terror raged with less violence. Nevertheless, the terrorists of the department of Ain, arrested on order of the representative on mission Boisset, were massacred outside the town of Bourg-en-Bresse on April 19. Massacres also took place in the prisons of Lons-le-Saunier on May 25 and 26. On June 1 a convoy of prisoners, composed almost exclusively of terrorists, was massacred by a band of masked men, *muscadins* or members of the "Company of Jesus." These incidents marked the White Terror in Franche-Comté; they were less grave than those which broke out in the south of the valley of the Rhône and in Provence.

In these regions the White Terror resulted from the action of the representatives on mission. From February of 1795 representatives Girod-Pouzol, Cadroy, Mariette and Chambon made decisions which facilitated reprisals by the returned émigrés or by the suspects who had been liberated. For example, they ordered the transfer of the seat of the criminal tribunal of Bouches-du-Rhône to Aix-en-Provence, a staunchly royalist town. This tribunal had been victoriously led to Marseilles by the Jacobins after August 10, 1792. The same representatives prescribed the disarming of the terrorists of the district of Arles. They closed down the popular societies, dismissed the Jacobin National Guard and reorganized it with moderates who were soon dominated by the royalists.

The representative Chambon is accused of having himself formed the "Company of the Sun." Did this "Company of the Sun" really exist? In any event, it is referred to by the republicans. The same charge was leveled against the representative on mission, Isnard. In point of fact he organized at Brignoles a "Free Company of the National Guard" to which the Jacobins gave the name "Company of the Sun." The result of all these measures was the concentration of terrorists in certain localities, their disarmament and the arming of their former foes, which facilitated acts of private vengeance.

On February 23, in Nîmes, four prisoners being transferred from one prison of the town to another were massacred, although they were being escorted by 300 soldiers! In Toulon on March 10 the Jacobins took action; seven returned émigrés were killed but after this massacre, the representative Cadroy ordered the arrest of the principal Jacobins and decreed a general disarming. On May 10 the *muscadins*, grouped in "Companies of the Sun," marched on Aix-en-Provence where the arrested terrorists were concentrated, forced open the prisons and massacred the prisoners as in Lyons; the death toll numbered sixty. Thirteen prisoners who had escaped the massacre and were being transferred to the prisons of Orange were killed en route.

On May 17 in Toulon there was a new revolt of the Jacobins, who arrested returned émigrés, some of whom flaunted on their hats the words "Long live Louis XVII!" The Jacobins had control of the city for four days; representative on mission Brunel, unable to restore order, committed suicide in desperation. The Jacobins decided to march on Marseilles in order to deliver their fellows imprisoned there, but the representatives on mission in Marseilles rallied the "Companies of the Sun," the National Guard and the royalists, and dispersed the Toulonnais. The day's toll was 40 dead and 300 prisoners, 47 of whom eventually were executed.

The march of these Jacobins on Marseilles produced a kind of "Great Fear" in all Provence: it was thought that there would be a repetition of the events that marked the end of 1793. The offensive of the Toulon Jacobins aggravated the struggle between royalists and terrorists; in Aix-en-Provence the representative Isnard harangued the mob: "If you don't have any weapons, if you don't have any muskets then just dig up the bones of your fathers and use them to exterminate these brigands." After such exhortations it is not surprising that massacres took place on a grand scale.

In Tarascon on May 25 *muscadins* invaded the prisons and massacred twenty-four inmates. In Marseilles on June 5 other *muscadins*, firing cannon, smashed the gates of the fort of Saint-Jean where numerous terrorists were packed in and more than 100 of them were murdered. Representative Cadroy prevented the National Guard from intervening to halt the massacre.

On June 28, in Tarascon, there was a new invasion of the prisons, with the massacre of twenty-three prisoners. It is impossible to count the isolated assassinations. At this time terrorists were killed in every commune of the department of Bouches-du-Rhône.

2 / Quiberon

The royalist movement in Provence assumed the character of a genuine *chouannerie*. But it was not marked by any overall action, being composed of individual acts of vengeance which could not have an important political effect. However, it gave royalists and émigrés the impression that the situation was developing favorably for them, and that soon it would be "ripe," as they said, for a Restoration. This impression was strengthened by the attitude of the Convention at the time of the days of 1, 2 and 3 Prairial (May 20, 21 and 22, 1795).

As had already happened in Germinal, the Convention was invaded by the "sans-culottes" during these three days. But for the first time the Convention called in the Army of Paris, commanded by General Menou. General Menou dispersed the Jacobins, and the Convention, in contrast to what had occurred on May 31 and June 2, 1793, remained master of its deliberations. The faubourgs were definitely defeated and the inevitable reaction developed. The Convention decreed the arrest of a great many terrorists and even of simple republicans who had been more or less active. According to Mathiez, more than 30,000 patriots were arrested during the month of June, 1795. Recent historians have not come up with a figure valid for the whole of France, but Tønnesson points out that in Paris alone there were about 1,200 arrests an 1,700 citizens were disarmed.[1] Thus the royalists regained hope.

The death of Louis XVII, however, occurred at precisely this moment, on June 8. If Louis XVII had lived, it seems probable that the Restoration would have taken place in the following months. The tender age of Louis XVII would have required the nomination of a regent, and France would have been provided with a constitution similar to that of 1791. Louis XVII's death completely changed the nature of the problem. Thenceforth the normal heir to the throne was the comte de Provence, who took the name of Louis XVIII. We know his feelings and ideas through his proclamations, delivered at Hamm and at Verona, the latter following upon the death of Louis XVII. They show that Louis XVIII wanted to restore the absolute monarchy "minus the abuses," but also without any concession to the new institutions. Thus precisely at the point when it appeared that the royalists would be able to restore the throne, the death of Louis XVII supervened to complicate the situation by creating deep divisions among them: on the one side the absolutists, who formed only a small minority inside France but who were a majority in the emigration; on the other, the constitutionalists, the Feuillants, the "monarchicals" who, although they constituted the great majority in France, hardly counted abroad. Thus the royalists were to lead their action without unity. During the summer of 1795 two royalist offensives, nearly concomitant, were to be led by different men with different aims.

In Paris a great effort was made to overthrow the republican regime and establish a constitutional monarchy in its place. But in favor of whom? There was considerable uncertainty on this score. Some thought of the duc d'Orléans, the future Louis-Philippe; but others considered that Louis XVIII, faced with the possibility of immediately ascending his throne, would perhaps make some concessions.

In Brittany another action, completely different and with no significant connections to the one mentioned above, aimed at the restoration of the absolute monarchy.

The situation of the royalists was further complicated because peace abroad, devoutly wished by the majority of Frenchmen, seemed to be in

1. Kåre D. Tønnesson, *La Défaite des sans-culottes* (Paris and Oslo, 1959), p. 339. See also R. Cobb and G. Rudé, "Les Journées de germinal et de prairial an III," *Rev. hist.*, 1955, pp. 250–281.

the offing right at that point. France had just signed the peace with Tuscany, the United Provinces, Spain and Prussia. A number of moderates who desired the monarchy because they believed that only the monarchy could restore peace rallied to the republic which had just concluded it.

Thus the situation was extremely complex. Nevertheless, royalist propaganda continued full speed, encouraged by the White Terror and by the measures taken against the terrorists. This propaganda was carried on through the press, via many newspapers which without proclaiming royalism covertly propagandized in favor of the Restoration. This was true of the *Journal de Perlet* and of the *Gazette française*; Lacretelle the younger stands out among the most active counter-revolutionary journalists. The royalist newspapers mocked republican institutions and the men who served the republic. Royalist propaganda was spread by all kinds of badges, insignia and prints representing the royal family. One of these prints, which is still available today, was extremely popular: it shows a weeping willow, but when examined from a certain angle, the branches sketch the silhouette of the heads of Louis XVI, Marie-Antoinette, the dauphin and his sister. This was pulled in an edition of more than 50,000 copies. Songs served the propaganda of the moderates, notably "*Le Réveil du peuple*," which is not particularly royalist, but which was their rallying hymn.[2] Among the *chansonniers* the famous Ange Pitou figured, who received subventions from Louis XVIII and also trafficked in arms, passing muskets to the Vendéans.

In these circumstances the absolutists abroad, and especially the entourage of the comte d'Artois in England, thought that the war in the west could be resumed. Had the pacifications concluded at the beginning of 1795 in Brittany and the Vendée been sincere on either side? As we have said, it is very difficult to answer this question. Did the Vendéans and *chouans* lay down their arms simply to gain a respite, or had they been sincere and taken up arms again only as a result of new persecutions on the part of the republicans? Or, further, did the war start again at the order of the émigrés? It is practically impossible to resolve these problems. We must, nevertheless, recognize that after the pacifications of February, 1795, the *chouannerie* had not entirely disappeared. Throughout the spring of that year, authorities denounced the attacks carried out by the *chouans* against persons or property. In his reports, General Hoche signalized that

2. The text can be found in the collection edited by P. Barbier and F. Varnillat, *L'Histoire de France par les chansons* (Paris, 1958).

Cormatin dominated an entire part of Brittany and that he went so far as to distribute passports in the name of Louis XVII.

Cormatin and several of his companions were arrested by Hoche's troops on May 25 and these arrests served as a pretext for the resumption of the revolt. Were they justified? It seems clear that the proofs of Cormatin's disloyalty cannot be contested. But the real leader of the *chouannerie*, Puisaye, had left for England before the signing of the pacification. He had negotiated with the English government which, yielding to the instances of Burke and of the minister Windham, had decided to equip a corps of French émigrés, who would land in Brittany and be followed by an English corps. The negotiations had been conducted by Puisaye in person, without the comte d'Artois having been informed. It seems, in fact, that Puisaye had thought of restoring a constitutional monarchy but without combining his efforts with those of the Parisian royalists. Nevertheless, he was forced to keep the comte d'Artois abreast of the results of his negotiations. D'Artois could not but approve them; he even gave Puisaye, whom the English had appointed lieutenant-general in their army, the same rank in the service of the king of France. Despite Puisaye, d'Artois's ideas ultimately prevailed and the landing in Brittany took the course of an attempt to restore the absolute monarchy in France.

After the signing of the treaty, it was decided that the landing would take place between the mouth of the Vilaine and Loire rivers. On landing, the émigrés were to receive the aid of all the *chouans* of Brittany, as well as that of a corps of Vendéans raised by Charette and Stofflet. These troops would march on Nantes. Having taken Nantes, they would set out for Rennes, Laval and Paris. At the same time the army of Condé, which was still stationed opposite Alsace on the right bank of the Rhine, would cross the river with the assent of General Pichegru (whose betrayal we shall discuss in the next chapter). A great royalist uprising would take place in the Jura, in conjunction with the White Terror. Finally, another landing would be attempted on the Mediterranean coast at Aigues-Mortes; the English and the émigrés would meet with the royalists of the Vivarais, who would take up arms again in the region of Jalès.

All these decisions were taken in April of 1795 and communicated to the *chouan* leaders, and particularly to Cadoudal, leader of the *chouans* of Morbihan.

The landing was scheduled for the end of June. On June 25 the British fleet came within sight of the coast of Brittany, while the Vendéans and the *chouans* again took up arms, attacked the republican posts close to the coast and massacred their soldiers. Charette issued a proclamation: he called the Vendéans to the struggle by declaring that the republicans had poisoned the dauphin, news of whose death had just been learned. He declared that this murder constituted a breach of the pacifications that had been signed.

The English fleet was to transport a corps of émigrés consisting of 12,000 men; in point of fact, England did not honor the commitments to which she had put her signature. There were only 4,500 men in the corps of émigrés. It was also supposed to have been supported in a second echelon by an English corps which never set out. Thus only 4,500 men were landed on the French coast, not all of whom furthermore were émigrés. There were only about 1,000 genuine émigrés; the rest of the landing corps had been completed by French prisoners who had been forcibly enrolled.

The landing took place without any difficulty at Carnac near Quiberon, under the protection of 15,000 *chouans* who had been assembled in the region. Emigrés and *chouans* marched on Auray, the nearest town, which was captured. At the same time they seized Fort Penthièvre, which defended the Quiberon peninsula from the land side.

General Hoche had his headquarters at Vannes. On learning of the arrival of the British fleet he rallied his troops immediately. When they were concentrated, he set out for the Auray, which he recaptured very easily, and the *chouans* and émigrés were thrown back to the Quiberon peninsula. Hoche then organized a methodical siege of the peninsula. Penned in on this strip of land, without resources, food supplies or water, the *chouans* and émigrés could hope to save themselves only by sea, reaching the British fleet by boats.

On July 15, a second batch of émigrés—around 2,000 strong, and commanded by Sombreuil—landed and the next day attempted an offensive which ended in total failure. General Hoche had positioned his batteries on the cliffs dominating the peninsula: when the émigrés tried to break out, they were riddled with grapeshot and forced to fall back. Their leader, Hervilly, was mortally wounded and 3,000 émigrés taken prisoner.

On July 21, the republican army took the offensive in its turn and easily captured Fort Penthièvre, then forced back the émigrés by degrees towards the extremity of the peninsula. There were not enough English boats to transport all the émigrés and the *chouans* who had joined them to the English vessels. Finally, 8,000 men were captured. All the provisions landed by the English were seized—enough to equip 40,000 persons. Hoche seized 20,000 muskets, 150,000 pairs of shoes and 10 million in counterfeit "assignats." The repression was dreadful. The law was categorical: any returned émigré bearing arms was to be summarily executed on simple verification of his identity. The representatives on mission in Brittany, Tallien and Blad, decreed that military commissions were to be formed to ascertain the identity of the émigrés. A distinction was made, however, between those who had voluntarily left France and enrolled on the lists and the French who had been forcibly enrolled in the enemy army. In fact, out of 8,000 prisoners, only 751 real émigrés were found who fell under the penalty of the law. Nevertheless, this figure was very high, and the republican officers hesitated to proceed to the massive execution of these prisoners. Representative Tallien, although he was a moderate Thermidorian at that time, decided to forego these qualms and ordered the execution. There were 748 victims, among them many former officers of the royal navy who had made their way to England. The other prisoners were acquitted, including the *chouans*, even those who had been captured bearing arms. In reprisal, Charette ordered the execution of all the republicans whom he had captured.

It was a disaster for the royalists. Nevertheless, little by little, taking their time, the English had been preparing a third echelon composed of British troops. This had already left England when news arrived of the disaster at Quiberon. The comte d'Artois was on board one of the English vessels which was transporting the troops. He decided not to turn around but to try another landing, more to the south, in the proximity of the Vendée. This landing took place on the isle of Yeu, on September 30. D'Artois established himself on the island: on October 10 he received reinforcements in troops and arms but this corps nevertheless found itself in an extremely perilous situation. At the end of October the storms made it difficult to provision it. The English government felt responsible for the comte d'Artois; what would happen if he were captured by the republicans? On October 25 the English minister, Windham, ordered the evacuation of Yeu and the repatriation of the troops.

Thus this adventure ended lamentably. The Vendéan and *chouan* leaders who had taken up arms in response to Puisaye's appeal were abandoned to their fate with all their men. Thenceforth they were to be constantly harassed by the republican troops. Charette and Stofflet were hunted. Abbé Bernier intervened to negotiate a pacification between them and the government, but Hoche, once duped, refused to negotiate and demanded an unconditional surrender. The ring around Charette and Stofflet grew tighter and tighter; finally Stofflet was captured, sentenced to death at Angers and executed on February 25, 1796. Charette, wounded in an engagement on March 22, was also captured and executed at Nantes on March 29, 1796.

3 / The 13 Vendémiaire

The execution of Charette and Stofflet marks the definitive end of the adventure of Quiberon and also of what is called the second war of the Vendée. While the absolutists failed in their poorly prepared attempt to organize an insurrection in Brittany and the Vendée, the constitutionalists were attempting a *coup d'état* in Paris.

The Quiberon disaster seemed to have consolidated the republic by terminating the war of the Vendée and the movement of the *chouannerie*. But it also demonstrated the imprudence of the absolutists and appeared to consolidate the constitutionalists.

The "monarchicals" and the constitutionalists hoped to seize power legally. The Convention during the summer of 1795 was discussing the new Constitution of Year III, the text of which was very close to that of the Constitution of 1791. It organized a qualified, nonparlementary, constitutional regime. All that would be required to establish a constitutional monarchy would be to replace the executive power, entrusted to a Directory of five members, by a king. The moderates hoped that this could be effected peacefully because they thought they would obtain the majority in the two councils created by the new constitution, the Council of Five Hundred and the Council of Elders.

But in the face of the royalist peril made manifest by the landing at Quiberon, it was precisely the majority of the Convention which regained control. This wanted to maintain the republic, chiefly because it considered that in the event of a Restoration those of its members who had voted the death of Louis XVI would certainly be arrested and condemned. Thus, seeing the evolution of public opinion and fearing elections that would give the royalists the majority for which they were hoping, the Convention sought for a way to maintain itself in power. It was under these circumstances that it voted the decree of the two-thirds, on 4 Fructidor, Year III (August 21, 1795). By this decree, the Convention ordained that two-thirds of the future deputies were to be chosen from its own members. The decree of the two-thirds was to be submitted to a referendum at the same time as the constitution.

The "monarchicals" were furious with this decision, because they saw that the accession to power was escaping them, at least in the immediate future. At the time of the referendum they asked the electors to vote for the Constitution of Year III with which they were satisfied, but against the decree of the two-thirds.

The vote took place in September, 1795. In Paris, the sections followed the order of the constitutional royalists, who accepted the constitution but rejected the decree. The result of the referendum was officially known on September 23. The constitution was accepted by 914,853 "yeas" to 41,892 "nays." It was a solid majority, but only a minority of electors had voted. The Constitution of Year III obtained less votes than that of 1793. As for the decree of the two-thirds, it was accepted by 167,758 "yeas" against 95,373 "nays." This decree therefore was accepted only by a very slim majority.

To the "monarchicals" it seemed that the referendum on the decree of the two-thirds had been faked. So they decided on an act of force to oblige the Convention to nullify the decree. The sections of Paris, notably, that of Le Peletier, the most royalist, decided to act against the Assembly.

On 11 Vendémiaire (October 3, 1795) the Le Peletier section convoked a general meeting of the sections of Paris at the Odéon Theater. This meeting took place, but many were absent: from the outset it could be seen that there was scant enthusiasm for a march against the Convention. On the other hand, the Convention, which knew that an act of force was being prepared against it, decided to organize resistance. It created an extraordinary commission of five members, among whom was Barras, who displayed remarkable energy. The Convention proclaimed itself in permanent session; and it called upon officers who had been dismissed as republicans or even as terrorists, and who were without employment in Paris, to defend it.

On the following day, 12 Vendémiaire (October 4), General Menou, who had already defended the Assembly in Prairial against the terrorists, received the order to march against the sections and above all Le Peletier. But Menou, who in Prairial had acted in agreement with the moderates against the terrorists, hesitated to turn against his former friends. He feared the terrorists more than the moderates, and acted with laxity. The Commission of Five, in contrast, was determined. It immediately pronounced Menou's dismissal and appealed to another general currently on the inactive list in Paris, Bonaparte, with whom Barras had become acquainted during a mission in Provence.

Because his career was at stake, Bonaparte did not hesitate to save the Convention. The sections of Paris armed themselves on the night of 12/13 Vendémiaire; it was decided to carry out the *coup d'état* on the morrow. But Bonaparte did not lose a moment. He appointed one of his former companions of the Army of Italy, General Murat, as aide-de-camp, and commissioned him to go to the Sablons camp to fetch the cannon kept there. These cannon were placed at the heads of all the streets leading to the Convention. During this time the Central Committee of the Sections had fallen little by little under the influence of the royalists, who were the least constitutional-minded and the most absolutist. It was thus that Richer-Serizy became president of this committee. Apparently it was no longer a question of a coup attempted by the constitutionalists, because it was becoming increasingly evident that the royalists would profit from the situation. Richer-Serizy appointed as general-in-chief of the army of the sections Danican, a former Herbertist who had gone over to the royalists. The latter assembled 25,000 men, but no cannon.

Bonaparte had only 5,000–6,000 men under his orders, but a good artillery. At three o'clock in the afternoon the Convention was surrounded. The sections tried to fraternize with the soldiers who were defending the Assembly and persuaded them to come over to their side. Barras gave the order to open fire and Bonaparte commanded the cannoneers to shoot. The sections immediately dispersed. There were about 300 dead among the aggressors.

Thus 13 Vendémiaire came to a close with the victory of the Convention and the republic. These events dashed the hopes of the moderate royalists and of the constitutionalists, almost as Quiberon had destroyed the hopes of the absolutists. Nevertheless, it must be noted that no violent repression ensued after 13 Vendémiaire. The barriers of Paris remained opened so as to enable the insurgents to leave the capital. In the days that followed only some ten death sentences were pronounced, among them that of a royalist agent, Lemaître, already mentioned.

Although the republic triumphed, the counter-revolution did not renounce its action but lived on. It still had men, means of propaganda and money, furnished largely by England. But it would have to change its tactics. It could try legal methods and await the elections of Year V, in order to conquer in the legislative councils the majority that it could not obtain in September, 1795; or it could count upon the betrayal of republican generals. Failing this, the Restoration risked being postponed to an indeterminate and doubtless very distant future.

CHAPTER XIV

The Counter-Revolution Under the Directory

After the dual failure that marked the summer of 1795—the landing at Quiberon on the one hand and 13 Vendémiaire on the other—the royalists were forced to admit that a restoration of the monarchy by force was becoming increasingly improbable. And at the end of three years of warfare, they had to admit that a decisive success of the coalition against the French armies was also very doubtful, the coalition having fallen apart in the spring of 1795 after the peace treaties signed by France with Spain, Tuscany, Prussia and Holland.

Apparently there was only one way out: to follow the example of the English after the death of Cromwell, and appeal to a republican general who would "pronounce" himself and his army in favor of a monarchic Restoration.

But to which general should such an appeal be made? The royalists thought of Pichegru.

1 / The Treason of Pichegru

In the spring of 1795 Pichegru was incontestably the republican general who had rolled up the most brilliant successes on the battlefield. During the winter of 1794–95, at the head of the Army of the North, he had successfully carried out an operation that had seemed extremely difficult, indeed almost impossible, the crossing of the rivers that separate Belgium from Holland—the Meuse and the Rhine. True, this operation had been much eased by a premature and exceptional freezing over. Pichegru had also successfully carried out another exploit which, although it had been greatly exaggerated, remained no less praiseworthy, the capture of the Dutch fleet blocked by the icy waters of the Texel. In reality, this fleet had surrendered at the approach of a small French cavalry detachment. But this event, embellished and exaggerated, appeared altogether extraordinary.

In the wake of these successes, General Pichegru had been appointed commander of the Army of the Rhine-and-Moselle, which was fighting on the frontier of the Rhine, from Basle up to Mayence. Jean Charles Pichegru was still very young to be the commander-in-chief of an army. Born in 1761, near Arbois in the Jura, he was only thirty-four.

The command he assumed on March 3, 1795, was a difficult one. In fact, his front, at least its northern sector (the northern frontier of Alsace and Mayence), was hard to hold because the fortresses of Mayence and Luxembourg, solidly defended by the Austrians, constituted two gaping holes in the line. True, Luxembourg was totally blockaded by the French armies and its fall, caused by the famine, was only a matter of days away. In contrast, Mayence was connected by bridges to the right bank of the Rhine and therefore could be continually supplied with men, munitions and foodstuffs, so that it could hold out for a long time. These two gaps in the French front made it difficult to hold in its northern sector. Moreover, the troops were in a pitiable state. In the spring of 1795 desertions had substantially reduced the numbers of the Army of the Rhine-and-Moselle; the army had also lost the greater part of its horses as the result of a particularly harsh winter. The soldiers who still remained under the colors lacked clothing, arms and munitions, and the number of those who were fit for combat had dropped to a very low point.

Nevertheless the Convention, through the intermediary of the representatives on mission to the army, authorized a hurried offensive of the Army of the Rhine-and-Moselle, commanded by Pichegru, and of the Army of the Sambre-and-Meuse, commanded by General Jourdan. The latter was holding the north of the Rhineland region up to the "line of neutrality" established by the Treaty of Basle signed between France and Prussia.

The capture of Luxembourg took place on May 7, 1795. This event should have made it possible for the two French armies along the right bank of the Rhine to launch an offensive in order to force the capitulation of Mayence. But Pichegru stubbornly refused to undertake this offensive despite the comments, indeed the upbraidings, of Jourdan and the representatives on mission. He cited paucity of effectives and of supplies, and even showed great hostility in answering the letters dispatched to him by the Committee of Public Safety and the representatives on mission. He replied to these letters only after an extraordinary delay, which showed that he was in no great hurry to execute the orders being transmitted to him.

What was the reason for this attitude? Pichegru was dissatisfied. Dissatisfied with the government and the Committee of Public Safety. He reproached it for letting the army suffer all sorts of shortages, for continuing to pay the soldiers in worthless "assignats" which were contemptuously refused everywhere in Germany. He reproached it for not paying his officers, his generals, and his own general staff in hard cash: Pichegru's general staff lived exclusively on requisitions. On September 14, 1795, the Convention belatedly decreed that henceforth the soldiers and officers would receive their pay in actual currency, 2 sous a month and 8 livres a month respectively, to complement their pay in "assignats." It was a trifling sum.

In July of 1795 Pichegru had written to General Moreau, who had succeeded him in command of the Army of the North and with whom he was bound in friendship, to thank him for a loan of 50 *louis*. "I am here like a beggar with a stuffed purse, the troops complain loudly because there's nothing to be found in Alsace with 'assignats'." Pichegru compared his present situation with that which had obtained earlier in Holland, where the troops had been paid in currency.

Pichegru, in fact, was a man of pleasure. He was very fond of eating well and equally fond of drinking, and he found the privations imposed on him very painful. He was reduced to selling the wagons and horses that he had brought in from Holland to raise money. Moreover, as soon as he arrived in Alsace he became a boon companion of General Lajolais, a debauchee, up to his ears in debt, living on expedients. Mme Lajolais, who had been the mistress of the vicomte d'Osmond, became Pichegru's mistress. This woman had an insatiable need for money and Pichegru could not give her all she demanded; it is certain that his connection with the Lajolais *ménage* had a baneful influence on the general's political behavior.

Pichegru, dissatisfied, embittered, did not believe that a republic which paid its soldiers so little and was so niggardly in recognizing the services rendered by its generals could last for long. He thought that the republic was bound to end up in a military dictatorship and, as early as the spring of 1795, envisaged himself called upon to exercise this dictatorship and, perhaps, to restore the monarchy.

Condé's army was among the troops facing Pichegru on the other side of the Rhine. This army, organized in 1792, had not participated in the campaign of France, but it had entered Alsace in 1793 when Wurmser had penetrated to the north of the province. At the time of its retreat, Condé's army had taken along with it more than 20,000 peasants who formed the bulk of the Alsatian émigrés. Since this retreat, Condé's army had been camped, immobile, on the right bank of the Rhine, a little to the south of Strasbourg. Condé was not on very good terms with the Austrians. He reproached them for leaving his troops without sufficient money and provisions; moreover, he suspected their political intentions. He feared that in the event of victory, they might wish to annex Alsace. Hence Condé's idea to restore the monarchy with the aid of Frenchmen exclusively and, if possible, with a republican general, who would come over to the royalist side with his army.

In the spring of 1795, when Condé learned that Pichegru, most prestigious of the French generals, had been made commander of the army facing his, he naturally got the idea of entering into contact with him. On May 1, 1795, Condé wrote the regent: "There is no salvation save from within the country." At that time a combined operation was being prepared in England, which culminated in the landing at Quiberon in the spring. The English thought that this action would be more effective if it sparked an uprising in eastern France, supported if possible by French troops and by Condé's army. This uprising, in the view of the British government, could take place in Franche-Comté, in the Jura and in the region of Lyons.

Wickham, in charge of the English espionage services in Switzerland, approved the idea. Thereupon the English government assigned Colonel Craufurd to work with Wickham and help him in this enterprise. Wickham and Craufurd were to be closely linked with the plot hatched between Condé, dissatisfied with the Austrians, and Pichegru, dissatisfied with the French government.

Circumstances seemed favorable for contacts between the two men. Pichegru's army lacked everything, and a number of officers did not hide their pro-royalist sympathies. During the Terror, in 1793, many royalists had enrolled in the armies in order to avoid prison. In 1795 they made manifest their feelings. Now, many of the officers of the Army of the Rhine-and-Moselle were royalists.

An event was to give further substance to these plans for negotiations. Pichegru happened to be in Paris when the faubourgs rose against the Convention on 12 Germinal, Year III (April 1, 1795). The Convention was looking around for a general willing and able to take command of the troops to be used against the rebels. Pichegru, with the prestige of his victories, was in the city on leave. The Convention turned to him and he energetically suppressed the revolt. Thus he had won a victory over the terrorists and returned to the Army of the Rhine-and-Moselle crowned with this new success over the "drinkers of blood."

On May 17, 1795, the comte Ferrand, whose counter-revolutionary ideas we have already examined, wrote to Condé to persuade him to reach an understanding with Pichegru by hook or by crook: "If I am not mistaken, Pichegru has a great desire for it, he will serve the genuine royalty, if only not to imitate Dumouriez." Thus Condé had already been prepared not only by circumstances but also by counsels received to make contact with Pichegru. But the person who was really at the heart of these negotiations was an adventurer, the comte de Montgaillard.

The comte de Montgaillard was born in the environs of Toulouse, near Villefranche-de-Lauraguais. He had two brothers, the abbé, a witty hunchback, renowned for his sallies, and the marquis. Montgaillard had studied at the college of Sorèze, after which he became an officer and a secret diplomatic agent in the first years of the Revolution. A born intriguer, he seems to have played the role of a double agent from then on. He probably received subsidies both from the coalition and the French government. His *Mémoires secrets* enjoyed a great success, although replete with lies and errors.

Montgaillard had gone to London in 1794, but he had been quickly expelled because his intrigues there looked particularly shady to the authorities. Thereupon he made his way to Switzerland. During his journey, he met one of his former schoolmates from Sorèze, the vicomte de MacCarthy-Lévignac, an officer of Condé's army, in Germany. Mac-Carthy offered to introduce Montgaillard to Condé. The meeting took place on May 22, 1795, and Montgaillard suggested to Condé that he enter into relations with Pichegru. After this interview, Montgaillard addressed lengthy memoranda to the prince, which have been preserved to this day in the archives of the Condé family in the château of Chantilly.

Montgaillard expounded all the reasons that were to persuade Condé to negotiate with Pichegru and detailed what, in his opinion, should be promised to Pichegru in order to obtain his adherence to the royalist cause. Montgaillard counseled Condé to guarantee that Pichegru would receive a marshal's baton, the red ribbon, that is, the commander's cross in the order of St. Louis; the château of Chambord; 1 to 2 million paid in currency and an annuity of 100,000 livres revertible by half to his wife and by one-quarter to his children; and, finally, four pieces of cannon.

Condé did not reply to Montgaillard until June 29, 1795. The situation had changed. Louis XVII had died in the Temple and the comte de Provence became king. Now Condé had greater freedom of action. Before, he had not known whether Louis XVII, a prisoner, would approve his negotiations with Pichegru; from now on, he could ask Louis XVIII to sanction his actions. So he replied to Montgaillard that he agreed with him as regards the promises it was expedient to make to Pichegru but that he, too, had some particular demands to make of the republican general.

Pichegru, he thought, must recognize Louis XVIII and make his troops take an oath of loyalty to the king; he must surrender Huningue, as a pledge of his goodwill, to Condé, who would occupy it; and, finally, he must immediately conclude an armistice with the Austrians. At the same time Condé wrote Louis XVIII, advising him to leave Verona and move closer to his army because, as he said, "Great events are being prepared in the interior. It is necessary to draw nearer in order to profit from them."

Upon being consulted Wickham fully approved the plan and at his advice, Condé decided to send an emissary to Pichegru to proposition him according to the plan worked out with Montgaillard. The emissary was a Swiss, Fauche-Borel, a Neuchâtel bookseller who had been recommended to Condé by Montgaillard. Since 1792 Fauche-Borel had published numerous royalist pamphlets in Neuchâtel, some of which had been written by Montgaillard.

Another agent, Courant, was attached to Fauche-Borel. He too was from Neuchâtel and had formerly been employed in secret diplomacy by the king of Prussia, Frederick II. He was bold, discreet and able. Wickham placed £6,000 at Condé's disposal in order to get the negotiations going. On July 19, Louis XVIII sent his approval from Verona.

The negotiations between Condé and Pichegru dragged on over a very long period of time. They can be divided into two phases: the first beginning on August 16, 1795, lasted until the end of the year; the second took up the whole of 1796.

The first phase of these negotiations was itself divided into two distinct parts by the *journée* of 13 Vendémiaire, which modified both Condé's and Pichegru's attitude.

The initial interview between Pichegru and Condé's agents took place in August, 1795. Fauche-Borel and Courant crossed the Rhine without difficulty and saw first of all the adjutant-general Badonville. They gave him 10 *louis* for him to put them in contact with Pichegru: the receipt is in the archives of the château of Chantilly. Badonville obtained from Pichegru assurances that he would meet with Fauche-Borel and Courant on August 16, 1795, in the tiny village of Blotzheim in southern Alsace. But Pichegru did not trust the verbal promises of Condé's two emissaries, and he demanded proposals in writing. Fauche-Borel returned to Basle and entreated Montgaillard to draw them up. These proposals of Montgaillard's were to be seized later by the Directory from the portfolio of the comte d'Antraigues in Trieste in 1797.

Fauche-Borel took the proposals to Alsace. He could not hand them over personally to Pichegru, but he had them delivered to the general. At the same time Condé wrote a signed letter to Pichegru requesting him to send a confidential agent.

A new interview took place between Pichegru, Fauche-Borel and Courant in another little Alsatian village, Illkirch, on August 20. Pichegru told Fauche-Borel that the plan seemed to him likely to succeed, but only after his entire army had crossed over to the right bank of the Rhine, that is, after a victorious offensive. He requested that his army be allowed to pass over to the right bank of the Rhine unopposed by Condé's troops. Pichegru's reply could appear to be taken as suspect and a maneuver. Nevertheless, he accepted the 100 *louis* which Fauche-Borel offered him, although he refused to write a signed letter to Condé or to send him a confidential agent.

Fauche-Borel and Courant returned to Basle and reported on their interview to Montgaillard who, in turn, reported it to Condé, exaggerating, as was his habit, Pichegru's favorable disposition. In fact, the interview in Illkirch was not conclusive. From it one could easily deduce that Pichegru was playing a double game and, indeed, Condé's reaction to the report was very negative.

Nevertheless, Montgaillard did not acknowledge defeat and together with Condé he hatched and perfected another plan. Pichegru was to have all the representatives on mission arrested during the night. He was to order his army to replace the tricolor cockade by the white cockade, hoist the white flag over the stronghold of Huningue and surrender the representatives as hostages to the prince de Condé.

Fauche-Borel returned to Alsace on August 25 and handed Pichegru the signed letter that Condé had written on the twenty-second. At the sight of this letter Pichegru supposedly promised to send a confidential agent immediately to Basle, who would carry a letter signed by him, but he asked for time. Nevertheless, he immediately wrote the following note, which is still preserved in the archives at Chantilly: "Z [the letter which was thenceforth to designate Pichegru] has received the proposals of X and will examine them in order to make use of them under suitable circumstances; he will take care to apprize X." This is an important document because it provides crushing evidence against Pichegru, demonstrating his guilt and proving that he was in collusion with the enemy.

This note from Pichegru was enthusiastically received by Montgaillard and Condé. Montgaillard, ever prone to exaggerate, thought that Pichegru was disposed to make a "pronunciamento" within forty-eight hours and Condé's army was alerted. Lookouts kept the other side of the Rhine under constant observation so as to catch sight of the white flag being hoisted, but a week went by without sight of anything.

Thereupon Montgaillard again sent Courant into France as his delegate. Courant asked Pichegru what was happening. The general replied: "We must wait, nothing must be left to chance"; the different parts of the plan "must be subject to due deliberation, which alone can assure success." To Courant's request that Huningue be surrendered to Condé, Pichegru replied that such a maneuver would be meaningless. What was necessary, he said, was to strike a major blow and not to proceed by minor actions: "In the name of God, let us not do anything that is unmethodical, half-hearted, or all will be lost." His army must first be won over entirely to royalism, before it could "declare itself." He counseled Condé to spread royalist propaganda in the Army of the Rhine-and-Moselle, and declared that he himself needed money, 100,000–200,000 livres in cash, to be precise.

Condé was profoundly disappointed with this reply. It was then that news arrived of the royalist failure of 13 Vendémiaire and of the disaster at Quiberon. This marked the end of the "great plan," which combined a landing in the west, an insurrection in the east and an act of force in Paris to restore the monarchy. From now on the idea of a "pronunciamento" to Pichegru's army seemed very difficult to bring about. Moreover, relations between Condé and Pichegru became strained. Courant, who had left for Switzerland in order to bring Pichegru a new sum of 1,000 *louis* in gold, was arrested by the French customs guards. He managed to swallow Condé's signed letters for Pichegru before being searched, but the money was seized. When asked what he had planned to do with it he gave some very tortuous explanations; nevertheless, he was not arrested, only the *louis* were confiscated.

The new situation involved the resumption of negotiations on other levels. Wickham felt that the "pronunciamento" of the Army of the Rhine-and-Moselle was still possible: "If this army decides for the monarchy, the Restoration would be possible, despite everything." Wickham and the British government believed it was only a question of money and that Pichegru could be won over if his price were met. Thus Fauche-Borel received a draft of 7,000 *louis*, drawn on the bankers of Lausanne, and a new sum of 1,000 *louis* in gold for Pichegru. The receipts for these amounts are preserved in the London archives.

On September 20 Fauche-Borel has an interview with Condé. The latter still insisted on the surrender of the stronghold of Huningue as a pledge of Pichegru's goodwill; moreover, he asked Fauche-Borel to inform Pichegru of the new intentions of Louis XVIII, who was ready to show a certain goodwill toward the revolutionaries. Louis XVIII, said Condé, intended to grant not a general amnesty but a pardon to those who would render him service at the time of the Restoration. On the other hand, the king had taken no decision in the matter of national properties nor regarding the form of the future government. Condé limited himself to specifying that the main issue was the restoration of the Old Regime "minus the abuses." It was not until October 13 that Fauche-Borel was able to meet with Pichegru, who this time was on the right bank of the Rhine, in Mannheim. Pichegru told Fauche-Borel that the situation was "not ripe" so it was necessary to wait and that he had not yet decided on surrendering Huningue, much less Strasbourg. He insisted once more on the necessity of winning over his whole army to the monarchy through propaganda before he was asked to "declare himself," and he counseled Fauche-Borel to distribute tracts to the soldiers and officers. Fauche-Borel remained three weeks in Mannheim and, according to his own statements, saw Pichegru five times. But he also met often with Badonville, who is called "Coco" in the royalist correspondence.

In the course of these numerous conversations Fauche-Borel could not obtain any definite commitment either from Pichegru or from Badonville. Pichegru was as vague as ever. However, he did demand a general amnesty and made known his preference for a "limited monarchy" with national representation. He also demanded assurances for the purchasers of national properties.

The correspondence between Pichegru and Condé continued. Pichegru returned to Alsace in November and a certain Demougé served as intermediary between Pichegru and Condé. Demougé wrote that "Pichegru no longer talked of delivering Huningue or any position whatsoever, but of winning over his army to the royalist cause." He thought that royalist propaganda would have an easier time of it after his army was defeated because, "It was first necessary to make it feel disgusted" with the republic. At this time (November 20, 1795) a royalist agent, the marquis de Bésignan, was arrested in France by the Directory police. On his person was found a complete documentation of plans for revolt in eastern France and notably in the Franche-Comté. By chance, the name of Pichegru did not appear in uncoded form in these documents and the Directory failed to identify the people cited by pseudonym. But the arrest of the marquis de Bésignan made Condé more prudent. The émigrés did not know exactly what documents the Directory had seized. Negotiations consequently were broken off for three weeks and not resumed until December 17, 1795. At that time Demougé had another interview with Pichegru, who talked with him at length. He declared that he did not think the government of the Directory was viable. He believed the French had been worn down by the Jacobins, a great number of whom had been recalled to public offices. And he thought that the defeats suffered recently by the armies of the Sambre-and-Meuse and Rhine-and-Moselle would have an influence on French opinion and dispose it to accept a royalist Restoration. In conclusion, Pichegru counseled the royalists to continue their propaganda and to leave the rest to time.

The problem posed here is not that of determining whether or not Pichegru was in collusion with the enemy. This has been proved. Rather, we have to establish whether subsequent to this collusion, he willingly allowed himself to be defeated and deliberately committed military blunders that could imperil France and the republic.

We must now, therefore, examine whether or not Pichegru was guilty of military treason during 1795. Without studying his military operations in detail, we can point to some notable and incontestable facts about them. During the fine weather in the spring and summer of 1795, it is noteworthy that the Army of the Rhine-and-Moselle never budged and undertook no operation whatsoever, despite the upbraiding of the Committee of Public Safety and of the representatives on mission, and despite the urgings of General Jourdan, commander-in-chief of the Army of Sambre-and-Meuse. Only in the autumn of 1795, when the weather was bad, did General Pichegru decide to cross over to the right bank of the Rhine and thus force the surrender of Mannheim. But he did not take advantage of this capitulation. The forces with which he crossed over to the right bank of the Rhine were entirely insufficient and were defeated by the Austrian troops at Heidelberg. The conclusion to be drawn is that Pichegru was certainly guilty of a serious military blunder. He acted belatedly and with too few troops; hence he must have courted defeat or he would have conducted himself differently.

After the defeat, Pichegru had a conference with General Jourdan and with the representatives on mission attached to the two armies in the village of Ober-Ingelheim. The representatives on mission gave Pichegru in the name of the Convention the formal order to strengthen his army on the right bank of the Rhine. Pichegru flatly refused, declaring that this would force him to withdraw troops from Alsace and endanger his right flank.

After this conference the representative on mission to the Army of Sambre-and-Meuse, Joubert, wrote to the Committee of Public Safety that Pichegru's conduct appeared confused to him. And he advised that the general be recalled as quickly as possible. Yet Joubert had no inkling whatsoever of the negotiations which Pichegru had been conducting with the royalists for six months.

Since Pichegru had refused to reinforce the part of his army which was positioned on the right bank of the Rhine, the Austrians had an easy time besieging Mannheim and retaking the city on November 23, 1795. This setback served Pichegru as a pretext to beat a retreat to the northern frontier of Alsace, a retreat which swiftly changed into a rout. The soldiers, worked up by the royalist propaganda organized by Pichegru or by Fauche-Borel, evinced an increasingly greater hostility to the republic. The retreat came to a halt on what at that time was called the lines of the Queich, the walls of the fortress of Landau, a few miles from the French frontier.

An armistice was then concluded with the Austrians by General Jourdan and Pichegru. This should not strike us as strange. In eighteenth-century wars, battles were not fought in winter and the troops took up their quarters in this season; nevertheless, this practice had not been observed during the winters of 1793 and 1794. Thus, to the Directory which had just taken office, the return to this former custom appeared abnormal, and the Directory annulled the convention of the armistice immediately it was apprized of it. The commissaries of the armies who had succeeded the representatives on mission, however, described the Army of the Rhine-and-Moselle as worked up by royalism. Rivaud warned the Directory that if the armistice was broken, the soldiers, disgusted and lacking in all manner of provisions, might revolt. So the armistice was annulled only *pro forma*. The Directory requested the generals to insert some new articles bearing on points of detail in a second convention. Hostilities between the French and the Austrians ceased. The armistice was to be in effect until one of the parties denounced it, and operations were not to be resumed until ten days after such a denunciation.

But Pichegru can certainly be accused of having deliberately provided very poor quarters for his troops. In fact, the ten-day clause had been set forth in such a way as to enable the generals commanding the opposing armies to transport their troops to a spot ten days march from the front, that is, to a region that had not been ravaged by the war. Ten days march equals 125 miles. Thus Pichegru could have sent his troops to spend the winter in Lorraine, in the vicinity of Nancy or Metz, that is, in a well-stocked province where they would have found good cantonments. But he did nothing of the sort. He kept his troops massed towards the front line in a zone where pre-provisioning was extremely difficult, indeed impossible. Only the division commanded by General Gouvion-Saint-Cyr left the front, but on the initiative of its chief, who did not apprize Pichegru of his move. At least this is what Gouvion-Saint-Cyr affirms in his memoirs, where he also makes the grave charge against Pichegru that he had deliberately quartered his troops for the winter in a devastated region and thereby aggravated their discontent.

Thus Pichegru can be accused of having curbed military operations in such a way as to facilitate the success of the enemy and of having accentuated the stripping of his army in order to further royalist propaganda. The testimony of émigrés, moreover, was precise. They always believed that Pichegru had deliberately let himself be defeated at Heidelberg. Pichegru knew that a victory for his army was equivalent to a new defeat for the royalists inside France. On the other hand, the Austrians, who up to then had remained completely aloof from the negotiations between Condé and Pichegru, began to grow suspicious. Pichegru's conduct struck them as passing strange, and the Austrian general-in-chief also persuaded himself that it was possible to win over Pichegru to the cause of the coalition. Pichegru's treason seemed crystal clear to them. Colonel Craufurd, the English delegate in Germany, also noted Pichegru's bizarre behavior. However, he declared that this was not "a positive proof of his good intentions," and added, "I would not be inclined to place too much confidence in him. We should suspend judgment until we have the facts to resolve it."

The armistice concluded between the French and Austrian troops served Pichegru's purposes more than the prolongation of the campaign. In fact, during the truce royalist propaganda was conducted on a grand scale. Fauche-Borel circulated freely in the French cantonments, distributing money, watches and horses to the officers, and to the soldiers shoes, boots and, above all, royalist tracts written by Montgaillard or others, for example, *La Tragédie de Louis XVI, La Relation du siège de Lyons, La Grande Maladie*, etc. Other tracts were simple leaflets calling upon the soldiers to desert, to commit treason. Fauche-Borel was aided by a group of Frenchmen and foreigners who had penetrated inside the lines. Demougé and a certain Mandel, whose pseudonym in the royalist correspondence was Le Retour, and many others. Fauche-Borel worked like a beaver. He ended up by being denounced to the Directory of the department of Bas-Rhin and was arrested, but he had time to destroy all compromising papers. In the absence of proofs he was released a week later, so that he was able to continue his underhand dealings unmolested throughout the winter of 1796.

2 / The Recall of Pichegru

Pichegru's intrigues could not pass unobserved. The commissary Joubert and then the commissary Rivaud had pointed out his strange conduct and the development of royalist propaganda in the Army of the Rhine-and-Moselle.

On January 19, 1796, Pichegru solicited a leave in order to come to Paris. He asked to be replaced "provisionally" during his absence. The Directory granted the leave on February 6, and appointed General Desaix as provisional commander. Why did Pichegru ask for leave? We do not know the exact reasons, but several appear probable. On January 5 and 11, 1796, the Directory had ordered Pichegru to receive in Strasbourg the French garrison of Mannheim, which had been captured by the Austrians and then released in an exchange for prisoners in French hands. This garrison was to be dispatched in part toward the north, in part toward Franche-Comté. It is possible that Pichegru found it repugnant to receive troops he had deliberately delivered to the enemy. On the other hand, the order to send these troops to Franche-Comté must have appeared very disagreeable to him because in the plans which he had elaborated with Condé, the insurrection was to break out in Franche-Comté at the moment that the Army of the Rhine-and-Moselle "declared" itself for the king. This insurrection could take place only if there were few troops in that region.

An operation of the armies known as "*embrigadement*"—that is, the formation of demi-brigades composed of former battalions of the regular army plus battalions of volunteers—was scheduled for the winter of 1795–96. A result of the *embrigadement* was the discharge of numerous surplus commissioned and noncommissioned officers. It is possible that Pichegru did not want to effect this operation because he did not wish to displease officers and noncommissioned officers who might make charges against him later.

Moreover, an attempt at insurrection was made at Besançon, organized by General Ferrand with the aid of the 8th Hussars. This attempt failed completely, but Pichegru feared that his name might figure among the papers seized at Besançon. Finally, one must not exclude Pichegru's desire to get away from camp life. He was a man of pleasure and he must have looked forward to return to the capital where the *merveilleuses* and the *incroyables* were flourishing in all their brilliance.

Nevertheless, Pichegru was quite taken aback when he learned that his demand for a temporary leave had suddenly been transformed into a permanent recall by the Directory. On March 13, 1796, the Directory decided in fact to relieve Pichegru of his command and to replace him at the head of his army by General Moreau, who had already succeeded him in the Army of the North.

Did the Directory at that time have precise suspicions as to Pichegru's conduct? No doubt the failure of Ferrand's insurrection in Besançon had occasioned some misgivings in the Directory about Pichegru's conduct; but the government had no positive proof. On the other hand, the Directory had received some rather characteristic letters from Switzerland. On February 13, 1796, its minister Bacher in Basle had written: "I must confide to you something that is weighing heavily on my heart and which truly torments me; it is Pichegru. Is he a man of integrity or is he not? I do not know and this doubt afflicts me. I must tell you that this man is the hope of our enemies." Almost simultaneously, on March 17, Mallet du Pan informed the court of Vienna that Pichegru was "the object of distrust." Finally, the commissioners with the armies, particularly Rivaud, constantly complained of the increase in royalist propaganda in the Army of the Rhine-and-Moselle.

Immediately upon his recall, Pichegru had an interview with Demougé. He exuded optimism, declaring that he was going to Paris where he would extirpate the evil "by the root." He thought that in Paris he would be able to provoke a royalist movement or a *coup d'état*. Pichegru also had talks with his successor, Moreau, who perhaps had been appointed at his suggestion. It appears that Pichegru had informed Moreau vaguely of the intrigue he was in the process of working out with the émigrés. For, as we shall see, Moreau likewise acted in a way that warrants suspicion.

After his recall, Pichegru went to Paris, where he visited the Directory and complained bitterly about having been replaced permanently and not provisionally. The Directors, however, showed no animosity towards him; indeed, they treated him cordially. The reason was that at this precise moment the conspiracy of Babeuf, communistic in tendency, had just been discovered. The Directors had become alarmed and were beginning to draw closer to men of the Right.

But the Directors' attitude to Pichegru changed again in April. At this time news was first learned of Bonaparte's great victories in Italy. Pichegru was no longer the only victorious general. The memory of his victories in Holland, now one and a half years old, was beginning to fade; at all events they were being eclipsed by those of Bonaparte. So the Directors, after having treated Pichegru royally, now began to give him the cold shoulder. Nevertheless, he was appointed ambassador to Sweden on April 3, 1796, but affected to send the Directors neither a word of thanks nor a letter accepting or refusing his appointment. Two weeks went by before he requested the Directory for authorization to take a prolonged leave before giving his answer. The Directory granted this and, strangely enough, Pichegru used it to make an immediate return to Strasbourg, where his status was only that of potential ambassador. There he saw Moreau and it is probable that in their conversations he apprized his friend in greater detail of the intrigues in which he was involved. He also saw the agents of the prince de Condé again. Pichegru explained to Demougé that the Austrians should immediately break the truce and attack before Moreau had a chance to restore discipline and order in the Army of the Rhine-and-Moselle, adding cryptically: "A sensational event could happen." But Pichegru, who had been in contact with the "monarch-icals" in Paris, also said that Louis XVIII "must not go against opinions" when he was restored to his throne. Pichegru seems to have had in mind a constitutional monarchy.

Demougé informed Condé and Wickham of these conversations. The remarks disappointed Condé, who feared that Pichegru had abandoned the cause of restoration of the absolute monarchy. The correspondences continued, nevertheless. On May 17, Condé had another 300 *louis* handed over to Pichegru. Next day Pichegru left Strasbourg to retire to his native village in Arbois. Three days later, on May 21, the truce was denounced by the Austrians, and operations were resumed on June 1, after the agreed-upon ten days delay.

But these did not turn out as Pichegru had anticipated. First of all, they ended in a resounding Austrian defeat. Jourdan crossed the Rhine in the north and penetrated very deeply on the right bank, as far as Bavaria. Moreau crossed the Rhine in the south, at a much slower pace and more cautiously, but he advanced as far as the outskirts of Munich. At the same time, Bonaparte was scoring brilliant victories in Italy.

All these victories consolidated the position of the republic and the Directory, and made the realization of the plan drawn up by Condé and Pichegru a risky venture. Negotiations between Pichegru and the émigrés slackened.

Pichegru had purchased a national property, an abbey in which he took up residence during the summer of 1796. It was there that he received Major Rusillion, and then Fauche-Borel. He told them that further attempts at restoration were no longer possible in view of the military victories won by the French. Nevertheless, he pocketed the *louis* in gold which had been sent to him. Upon learning of this conversation Louis XVIII and Condé were plunged into despair. Furthermore, Louis XVIII was forced to leave Verona before the approaching French armies, so he went to Germany. But the operations forced him to leave Condé's army.

The situation shifted once more in the autumn of 1796 when the armies of Jourdan and Moreau were defeated in Bavaria. Moreau's conduct in this affair is not absolutely clear; it is possible that he deliberately let himself be beaten. It also seems that during his retreat across the Black Forest he had had contacts with agents of Condé's army which was facing him. At all events, these defeats rekindled the hopes of the émigrés and in turn of Pichegru. The latter came to Strasbourg at the end of September and met with Moreau on October 14. It would be extremely interesting to know what these two generals said to each other. Pichegru, at all events, must have declared that either Archduke Charles should penetrate into Alsace to inflict a total defeat on Moreau, after which Pichegru would take it upon himself to attempt "le grand coup"; or, the archduke Charles would not be able to cross the Rhine, in which case Pichegru would give up the attempt at a military *coup d'état* and transfer the royalist conspiracy to the political level. Elections were to take place in six months, the famous elections of Year V. Pichegru would be a candidate. Once elected, he would take upon himself the task of organizing the Restoration of the monarchy no longer through a "pronunciamento" but by acting through legislation.

Pichegru left Strasbourg on November 5, 1796, and reached Besançon, where he carried on his correspondence with the agents of the émigrés, England and Austria. He continued to receive large sums of money, but seems to have totally given up his plan to make a "pronunciamento." He planned another form of counter-revolutionary activity, which he was energetically to try to realize in 1797. Events, in fact, made it increasingly difficult to put into execution his original plan. Meanwhile, Bonaparte continued to roll up victories: in 1797, his offensive, combined with an action of the armies of the Sambre-and-Meuse and the Rhine-and-Moselle, forced Austria to sign the preliminaries to the Peace of Leoben on April 18. Thenceforth, the war was over on the continent, and it was therefore necessary for the royalists to act on the electoral and parlementary level.

3 / The Royalist Efforts on the Electoral and Parlementary Level

The elections of Year IV had not been as unfavorable to the royalists as they might rightly have feared after the vote of the two-thirds decree.

Following the adoption of this decree, the 750 members of the two councils of the Directory, the Council of Elders and the Council of Five Hundred, included 507 former members of the Convention, elected on the basis of the decree of the two-thirds, and 234 new deputies. There were only four members of the Convention among these 234 deputies, which proved that in the free sector the members of the Convention had suffered a very heavy defeat. There were also 34 former members of the Constituent Assembly and 25 of the Legislative among these 234 new deputies. But among the 507 members of the Convention, according to

Suratteau, there were 44 confirmed royalists and 139 moderates. Of the new 234 deputies of the new third, 117 were royalists. Thus in all, there were 300 royalist deputies or moderate republicans whose republicanism was very moderate indeed. Out of a total of 750 deputies, nearly half were royalist or moderate.

So, despite the failure of the *journée* of 13 Vendémiaire and the adoption of the two-thirds decree, the councils numbered a very high proportion of moderates. According to Suratteau we must also add 84 undecided and 52 indeterminate to the 300 royalists and moderates, meaning that 436 deputies might vote for royalist or anti-republican motions. This majority of 436 deputies, however, was not only lacking in cohesion but anomalous in composition.

Moreover, the royalist attempt of 13 Vendémiaire had led the Directory to take all kinds of measures favorable to Jacobins. The old Convention members of the Left who had been persecuted after the *journées* of Germinal and Prairial, or who had been imprisoned, were freed and amnestied. For six months the Directory practiced a policy favorable to the Jacobins.

As of March, 1796, the exposure of Babeuf's conspiracy—the aim of which was to replace the bourgeois republican government of the Directory with a dictatorship of Jacobin inspiration, with a social revolution, a new division of land and the organization of a regime approximating communism—alarmed the members of the Directory and the deputies of the Center Left. They drew closer to the Right. From March, 1796, onward, the government and the councils pursued a policy increasingly hostile to the Jacobins and increasingly favorable to the moderates and royalists, a policy which Albert Mathiez has very accurately called one of "rallying to the Right."

The attitude of one of the directors, Carnot, was of vital importance in the evolution of the Directory. Of the five members of the Directory, in fact, two—Reubell and Larevellière-Lépeaux—favored a fairly democratic republic. Two others were partisans of the moderates: Carnot and Le Tourneur. As for the fifth member, Barras, cynical, ambitious and greedy for money, he was ever ready to rally to the strongest or the highest bidder. In the field of domestic policy, Carnot was the man whose influence could be decisive. Carnot was not averse to the republic and he was to prove it; he was, above all, a man of order. He had helped make the Revolution and affixed his signature to some extremely violent measures, as has been shown in Reinhard's excellent biography. Nevertheless, he believed that the first requisite for the restoration of prosperity to France was the re-establishment of order. He had no objection to the Constitution of Year III, but it had to be made to function properly if order was to prevail. Thus Carnot went into a fury upon learning of the papers found on Babeuf and his accomplices at the time of their arrest, and he moved closer to the Right immediately thereafter. Further, he had numerous Jacobins, who had been called to power after 13 Vendé-miaire, removed from office. Even Jacobin generals were replaced; for example, in Marseilles, Puget-Barbentane, who had begun to fight the "Company of the Sun," was replaced by General Willot, who was to become its protector. Many Jacobins, members of municipal councils, were recalled and commissaries of the Directory in the departments were dismissed and replaced by moderates.

But one measure led to the formation in the councils of a majority of the Right; among the accomplices of Babeuf figured Drouet, the former member of the Convention famous for having ordered the arrest of Louis XVI after his flight to Varennes. A deputy to the Convention, he had been taken prisoner by the Austrians in the course of a mission to the armies, freed through a prisoner exchange at the end of the Convention and elected to the councils. Drouet, a Jacobin, had drawn close to Babeuf, and at the beginning of the Directory he figured among the members of his insurrection committee. According to the constitution, deputies were inviolable; they could not be arrested without a vote of the Council of Five Hundred. The Directory asked for the vote and obtained Drouet's arrest. This vote clearly delineated the Rightist majority in the Council of Five Hundred.

Another event known as the "Grenelle camp affair" further con-solidated this majority. On the night of 23/24 Fructidor, Year IV (September 9–10, 1796), several Jacobins, very probably stirred up by *agents provocateurs*, appeared at the camp of Grenelle in Paris and tried to incite the troops against the Directory. The government linked this attempt to Babeuf's conspiracy, which was not at all surprising inasmuch as the Grenelle affair, no doubt, had been got up entirely by the police.[1]

The Grenelle camp affair enabled the Directory, henceforth an ally of the Right, to liquidate the last followers of Babeuf—the "anarchists," as they were called in Paris. The deputies knew nothing about the secret side of the affair; they thought that Babeuf's arrest had not necessarily

1. J. Javogues, "L'Attaque de Grenelle," *Ann. hist. de la Rév. fr.*, 1925; P. Bessand-Massenet, *L'attaque de Grenelle: les communistes en 1796* (Paris, 1926).

put an end to the intrigues of the "anarchists," in consequence of which the majority of the Right was consolidated. Thenceforth, all kinds of measures demanded by the Right were voted by the councils with the approval of the Directory. The comte de Vaublanc, one of the leaders of the insurrection of 13 Vendémiaire, who had been sentenced to death after this day but had not been executed, was amnestied and reintegrated into the Council of Five Hundred. The two younger sons of Philippe-Egalité who were in France were freed and placed on board a ship bound for America after being completely outfitted and given 4,000 livres in cash.

Other reactionary measures of a social character were taken. The revocable tenancy (*domaine congéable*) in Brittany, which had been considered a feudal tenure by the law of August 27, 1792, was again subsumed under the category of rented landed property and, as a result, the rents owed by the tenants were maintained rather than annulled. The terrorists who had been amnestied after 13 Vendémiaire and who, according to Albert Mathiez, numbered 30,000 (an exaggerated figure, no doubt) were once more dismissed from the public offices to which they had been appointed. The refractory priests who had voluntarily left France were authorized to return and their property restored to them.

The majority of the Right saw in these measures only a beginning. They hoped that after the next elections, those of Year V, which were to replace a third of the members of the councils, the royalists would have an absolute majority and would therefore be able to restore the monarchy. But which monarchy? It was here that difficulties set in.

The Rightist majority was, in fact, heterogeneous; it included royalists and moderate republicans. The moderate republicans were satisfied with the bourgeois republic of Year III and were not wedded to the idea of the restoration of the monarchy. The royalists themselves were divided, inasmuch as a gulf existed between the constitutionalist royalists and the "absolutists," which Louis XVIII made no attempt to bridge. The Declaration of Hamm of January 28, 1793, and, later, the Verona Declaration of June 21, 1795, on the occasion of the death of Louis XVII, show that Louis XVIII wished to restore the Old Regime in its quasi-totality, minus the abuses. Since that time, he had given no indication that he was disposed to make any concessions whatsoever. The constitutional monarchists, therefore, were led to orientate themselves toward other candidates to the throne. As we have seen, for their principal theoreticians they had Mallet du Pan, then Chateaubriand in his *Essai* and Lacretelle the younger, and they were more or less agreed on a program. What did they want? The return to the Constitution of 1791, with a hereditary king and qualified suffrage. They would be satisfied with maintaining the Constitution of Year III with the substitution of a king for the Directory. The constitutionalist monarchists were hostile to the "absolutists" and to the émigrés, to the prolongation of the war, and to the conquests, but in favor of preserving the sale of national properties. Abroad, they were supported by England and by her agent in Switzerland, Wickham, who believed that the advent of a constitutional monarchy in France was the only solution for ending the Revolution. But the important question of who would ascend the throne was not resolved. It is probable that the Orléanists were numerous, more numerous than is generally believed, even by historians like Mathiez and Aulard. To be sure, Louis-Philippe had been living in the United States since the beginning of 1796; he had refused to join Condé's army because it had been placed under Austrian command. Louis-Philippe stated his candidacy without, perhaps, being too overt about it and without, at that time, having given his consent to those who wanted to seat him on the throne. On August 30, 1796, a deputy of the Council of Five Hundred, Dumolard, said: "One constantly talks of royalists to the people; well, a party which really wants the throne does exist, it is the party of Orléans." Two days later, the same deputy declared: "Let surveillance be directed towards Blankenburg [the residence of Louis XVIII], but also against Orléans." Finally, the aforementioned English agent, Colonel Craufurd, wrote on May 20, 1796: "There is again much talk about the young duc d'Orléans, and there will be a return to a constitutional king, I am sure of it."

It was said that Carnot had been secretly won over to the Orléanist party. It was also said that Sieyès was an Orléanist and that one of the principal generals of the Directory, General Clarke—who was Carnot's military advisor, director of the topographical bureau where the maps used to lay out campaigns were kept and former secretary of the duc d'Orléans—was his representative in France. On December 15, 1796, a French agent wrote to the minister Drake, at that time in Venice, that "the Orléanist faction is stronger than is believed."

Two deputies, Morisson and Rouzet, were openly favorable to Louis-Philippe. At that time Rouzet was the lover of the duke's mother; after 18 Fructidor, he was to take the duchesse d'Orléans to Spain and marry her, which explains why he was later buried in the chapel of the family of Orléans in Dreux.[2] At all events, the law voted the day after the *coup d'état* of 18 Fructidor was to strike at all those "who want the return of the king, anarchy or d'Orléans," and in the wake of the coup the restoration of Louis-Philippe was considered as likely as that of Louis XVIII.

The royalist party did not include only Orléanists. There were also those who thought that Louis XVIII would rally to the constitutional monarchy at the last minute, once he had been told: "Everything is ready on condition that you accept the Constitution of 1791 or another similar to it." This is what actually took place in 1814. True, by then he was to have the experience acquired by a seven-year stay in England. In 1797, perhaps, he might have acted along these lines. Many "monarchicals" also remained attached to Louis XVIII despite the Hamm and Verona declarations. But there were monarchists who had another candidate in mind: they had advanced the name of the archduke Charles, the Austrian general who had put up a brilliant resistance to generals Moreau and Jourdan on the Rhine and even to Bonaparte in Italy. According to the arrangements worked out, Archduke Charles would marry Mme Royale, the daughter of Louis XVI, and thus would enter the Bourbon family. But this does not appear to have been a serious plan. There was talk of a Spanish prince and there was also mention of the brother of Frederick II, Henry of Prussia. But the fact that he was a Protestant constituted an additional obstacle to his accession to the throne of France.

Thus the constitutional monarchists, who formed a large portion, perhaps even the majority of the royalists, were deeply divided among themselves. They decided to meet in a building placed at their disposal by Bertin, a former intendant of commerce. This house was situated on the rue de Clichy, for which reason those who frequented it were dubbed "Clichyans." Among the first "Clichyans" we find deputies such as Durand-Maillane and Dupont de Nemours, the physiocrat Boissy d'Anglas and bankers such as Defermon. The "Clichyans" established contact with the royalists' Parisian agency, the "Factory," discussed in a previous chapter.[3]

Through the intermediary of royalist agents, the "Clichyans" were in contact with the comte d'Antraigues, who was at the center of all the royalist conspiracies and who was himself in direct contact with Louis

2. On the role of Rouzet, deputy of Toulouse, see P. H. Thore, "Fédérations et projets de fédérations dans la région de Toulouse," *Ann. hist. de la Rév. fr.*, 1949.
3. See Chapter X, pp. 183–187.

XVIII. He was commissioned to sound out Louis XVIII in order to find out whether he would accept a constitution upon his restoration. He was also to ask him to promise a general amnesty to all those who had been involved in the Revolution, if he were to ascend the throne. Louis XVIII refused to commit himself.

Alongside the constitutionalist monarchists were the absolutists. "L'Ami des lois," in 1796, declared that the royalists were recruited from among the elderly, the devout, courtesans, nonjuring priests, the relatives of émigrés, peasants "led astray by fanaticism" and, above all, "papists." This article is obviously a caricature, but it is certain that absolutists were numerous, in particular among those who had been the losers as a result of the change of regime, the former "officers" of the epoch prior to 1789. The absolutists wanted an integral restoration of the Old Regime —minus the abuses—with Louis XVIII as king. It was the absolutists, as we have seen, who organized the landing at Quiberon, whereas it was the constitutionalists who had attempted the *coup d'état* of 13 Vendémiaire in Paris.

When Louis XVIII rejected the proposals set forth by the constitutionalists, Wickham felt that this decision "was the *coup de grâce* for the royal family." The tergiversations of Moreau and Pichegru during the summer of 1796, and the hesitant attitude of another general, Marceau, who was contacted by the royalists and had seemingly been won over to their plans when he was killed at Altenkirchen on September 21, 1796, no doubt ensued from the position taken by Louis XVIII. Marceau's death was an unfortunate blow to the royalists. It is possible that Bernadotte had also been in contact with them. Louis XVIII's attitude and his refusal to consent to rule with a constitution were the major reasons for the timidity exhibited by the royalists during 1796 and at the beginning of 1797.

The policy of "rallying" did not however last very long. Begun in March, 1796, it hardly survived the end of the same year. In fact, the divergences between the majority of the Right, which we can call "Clichyan," and the Directory were accentuated. The Clichyan majority demanded peace, even peace at any price, peace without annexations. At most it allowed the annexation of Belgium, although Carnot was not ardently in favor of this. But the Clichyans were opposed to any annexation of the Rhineland, to any annexations in Italy and even to the constitution of an independent republic in this country. Now, Bonaparte himself essentially was bent on the establishment of a republic in Italy, in which he could exercise a great influence and acquire the apprenticeship to power he hoped to obtain in France in the still vague future.

The French Army of Italy shared Bonaparte's ideas completely. Moreover, from an economic point of view, renunciation of the conquests was extremely dangerous for the Directory. The seizures carried out by Bonaparte in Italy, the heavy war taxes that he had levied there and the requisitions he had established had substantially contributed to making up the Directory's budgetary deficit. Renunciation of these conquests would place France once more in a difficult economic situation. After lengthy deliberation, the Directory decided that it could not conclude a peace based on the abandonment of Italy, the Rhineland and, perhaps, Belgium; so it chose to continue the war until a victory enabled France to retain the major part of the occupied territories.

This decision led to a rupture with the Clichyans who, nevertheless, were not unduly grieved; they thought it would not last long because the elections of Year V were in the immediate offing and they hoped that the new third which was to be elected to the councils would be composed of their supporters. In fact, the Clichyans had prepared for these elections very actively: they had sent emissaries to Switzerland to obtain money from Wickham. A certain Duplantier had been to see Wickham and had obtained large sums of money. He had also entered into relations with the "monarchicals," who had taken refuge in Switzerland, as well as with the former member of the Constituent Assembly, Adrien Duport.

The Clichyans had also induced one of their number, the duc de La Vauguyon, to approach Louis XVIII once more and to take up again the steps initiated by Dandré, aiming at obtaining from the pretender to the throne some new concessions which could strengthen the royalist bloc and heal the breach between the constitutionalists and the absolutists. La Vauguyon asked Louis XVIII to recognize the division of France into departments, the suppression of the parlements and the preservation of the new judicial organization. He also proposed that the municipal officers be appointed by the king and not elected, the ban on religious orders remain in force except for those dedicated to charitable and teaching activities, the new taxes be preserved, the three orders not be re-established and finally that a constitutional regime be introduced into France with three chambers, one of peers and two others which would include the members of the clergy and lay persons, nobles and commoners, mixed.

Once more Louis XVIII refused and the duc de La Vauguyon fell out of favor. The joining of the two royalist groups was not realized, so they worked separately in preparation for the elections: on one side the absolutists, on the other, the constitutionalists.

The absolutists still pinned their hopes on an act of force or a conspiracy. An absolutist, the comte de Rochecotte, a former *chouan*, had drawn up a plan to go to Paris with a group of *chouans* in order to provoke an uprising there, while a republican general whose troops were stationed in the west, General Beauregard, would go over to the *chouans* with 15,000 men. Louis XVIII would be proclaimed king simultaneously in Brittany and in Paris. The conspiracy was exposed to the Directory by the duc de Carency, La Vauguyon's own son. On the other hand, Colonel Malo, one of the Camp Grenelle leaders who had helped to foil the attempt of the "anarchists" the year before, was contacted by the members of the "Factory," as we have seen.[4] But, while pretending to side with them, he exposed the conspiracy to the Directory. The members of the "Factory" were arrested, which was a grave blow to the activity of the absolutists.

Thus the constitutionalists had a free path before them. They prepared for the elections of Year V by setting up a solidly structured organization, the so-called Philanthropic Institutes. An "Institute" was created in each department, ostensibly to engage in charitable and philanthropic activities. The organizations were established on the same basis as the Masonic lodges or the Babeuf conspiracy, and may even have had the Aa as a model. The secret aim of the Philanthropic Institutes, however, was the destruction of the republic and the restoration of the monarchy. Institutes apparently were established in seventy departments, that is, in the vast majority of departments. Each institute was headed by a president, who corresponded with the royal agency in Paris, and also included a secret agent in each canton. This agent kept the president informed on public opinion, contacted persons favorable to the royalist movement and to the Restoration, recruited new members and above all concerned himself with the elections, the essential aim. The agent's job—with his friends and accomplices—was to try to keep republicans and Jacobins away from the polls, by whatever means, at election time and to guide "decent people," that is, royalists or moderates, toward the polls.

The membership of the Philanthropic Institutes was divided into two groups. One, the most secret and the most restricted, was composed of

4. Cf. Chapter X, p. 186.

"legitimate sons"—royalist militants, including a large number of absolutists; the second, more numerous group brought together the "friends of order"—those with the limited pledge to vote "the right way" at election time. Essentially, they were constitutionalist royalists and moderates, in general those labeled "Clichyans." The "friends of order" were unaware of the existence of the "legitimate sons."

The "legitimate sons" were not only to prepare for elections but, in the event of failure, to organize a general insurrection in all France. With this in view, France had been divided into military districts, the command of which was attributed to the princes or to the king himself. Thus the command of the military districts of Normandy, Brittany and the Vendée belonged to the comte d'Artois; those of Alsace, Franche-Comté and the Lyonnais region were headed by the prince de Condé. The others were answerable directly to Louis XVIII. Under these princes a military commandant, appointed by them, was assisted by a council of six members. At the apex, finally, was a royal council which, however, was not formed until 1798. The arrest of the royalist agents in Paris, Brottier and his friends, for a time threw the Philanthropic Institutes into disarray.

Thanks to M. Caudillier, we are particularly well informed about the operation of the Philanthropic Institute at Bordeaux. It was founded by an agent of the king, in Languedoc, Dubourg de Pourquerie. As deputies he had Caire, whose pseudonym was "Jardin"—he was Dandré's representative—and Dupont-Constant, a former colonist in the Antilles. The Bordeaux institute grouped malcontents, those who had been disappointed by the revolt of the blacks in the colonies and by the breaking off of trade relations with the Antilles; it also rallied the *muscadins*, the so-called gilded youth, *la jeunesse dorée*. The Bordeaux institute acted through public demonstrations. At the theater they sang *"Le Réveil du peuple,"* hooted at patriotic songs and plays and loudly applauded any illusions to the counter-revolution: matters reached such a point that a railing had to be installed to separate the stage from the audience because at times the demonstrations grew so stormy that the stage was invaded and the actors themselves became the victims of the struggles between Jacobins and *muscadins*. The situation grew worse. The former Jacobin mayor of Toulouse, Groussac, was assassinated 5 miles from Bordeaux by members of the Philanthropic Institute. The Jacobin circle of Bordeaux was attacked by members of the institute and if there were no victims it was only thanks to the intervention of the National Guard, which arrived in the nick of time. The royal council of the region of Bordeaux was made up of Dupont-Constant; Duchesne de Beaumanoir, a former subdelegate; the lawyer Brochon; Caire, an officer of the engineers corps; and a merchant.

In Lyons the famous General Précy became the head of the Philanthropic Institute. The institutes of other departments have not yet been studied; we know nothing of their composition.

The institutes prepared for the elections of Year V, which took place beginning on 1 Germinal (March 21, 1797). The Directory had also made a great effort to obtain the election of republicans, to the exclusion of "anarchists." But the influence of the Philanthropic Institutes was more effective. Several weeks before the election Louis XVIII had published a manifesto to the French people somewhat less intransigent than his previous declaration. He disavowed despotism "as odious as anarchy" and, in the event that he should reascend the throne, he pledged himself to improve the old constitution. But he did not promise any amnesty and affirmed his desire to re-establish the "religion of our fathers."

The newspapers conducted an extremely violent campaign for the elections. The royalist and moderate newspapers were the most numerous, and "Peace" was their watchword. At this time, in March, 1797, the victory over Austria had not yet been won and peace signified the abandonment of annexations in the Rhineland, in Italy and, perhaps, in Belgium.

The results of the elections were very favorable to the Clichyans. Of 216 outgoing members of the Convention, only 13 were re-elected, which constituted a new and striking defeat for the members of the Convention. Out of the 13 re-elected, moreover, 5 were Clichyans. Consequently, only 8 republican Convention members were returned to their seats in the council. Among the re-elected Jacobins, we find Barère, the deputy from Tarbes, General Jourdan, and Joseph Bonaparte, Napoleon's brother.

The absolutist royalists formed a rather large contingency among the 200 Clichyans elected: Fleurieu, former minister of Louis XVI; Murinais, former brigadier-general; Quatremère de Quincy; General Willot; and many others.

The elections of Year V disconcerted the Directory. Reubell immediately proposed that they be annulled by the councils still in office, which were charged by the constitution with the validation of elections of new deputies. But Carnot was against any act of force. He wanted to allow the Constitution of Year III to function normally, and believed it was possible to come to an agreement with the new royalist majority, which he thought would not be able to re-establish the monarchy. Further, he considered that it was necessary to allow the moderate, bourgeois republic to function as provided by the constitution.

4 / The Activities of the Clichyans and 18 Fructidor

From the elections of Year V, that is, from March, 1797, up to the *coup d'état* of 18 Fructidor, a genuine crisis existed as a result of the divergence between the Directory, which was distinctly republican, and the majority of the councils, unquestionably moderate and even royalist. The crisis did not immediately erupt into violence because the royalists were split into absolutists and constitutionalists. Only one point united them: the immediate conclusion of peace without annexations, without the creation of a republic in Italy. They were in hopeless disagreement on all other problems.

To begin with, the new majority elected General Pichegru to the presidency of the Council of Five Hundred. No doubt, Pichegru's treason was not known at that time, but it was suspected. Yet this election proves that the Clichyans had confidence in Pichegru. Under his presidency, a series of revolutionary measures was voted by the council; abrogation of the law on refractory priests, removal of the Jacobins and partisans from the Directory, reorganization of the guard of the councils by the recruitment of "safe" soldiers in the armies. Pichegru and Mathieu Dumas themselves hand-picked men upon whom they could depend from the different armies. In this connection Mathieu Dumas wrote to General Reynier, an intimate friend of Moreau: "We desire men who have distinguished themselves by their attachment to order. It is also important to give some consideration to their political opinions. I think that you will understand me clearly enough."[5] The councils, as one may see, wanted a devoted and faithful guard.

The Clichyans wondered whether it was necessary to wait in order to bring about the Restoration. But Dandré, whose opinions carried the greatest weight among them, felt that it was better to postpone the operation until the royalist majority was more homogeneous, that is, until the elections of Year VI. Once the "third section" was replaced and the vast majority of the Convention members eliminated, the councils, in Dandré's view, would present a majority to whose will the Directory

5. This letter was published by J. Godechot in the *Ann. hist. de la Rév. fr.*, 1932, p. 168.

would have to bow. In one year, public opinion would be further won over to the idea of restoration by the royalists. Finally, the National Guard would be reorganized in all France by this time, and would be headed by dependable officers, nearly all of whom would have been won over to the royalist cause.

Dandré's assessment of the situation was accepted and the Clichyans did not bring their immediate action to bear except on detailed measures, for example, decrees in favor of émigrés; the émigré peasants of Alsace were authorized to return. Measures were also taken regarding the property of these émigrés. The surveillance over suppliers of the armies, who were enriching themselves by taking advantage of the republican regime, was also strengthened. And persecution of royalists ceased, which led to a resumption of the White Terror. In Lyons the "Company of Jesus" reappeared on the scene, assassinations were resumed, a cavalry sergeant-major was killed. In Provence, numerous murders took place—six in one week in the department of Basses-Alpes.

These reactionary measures alarmed the republicans, who began to wonder just where the Clichyans wanted to lead them. Even more alarmed were the soldiers and generals who were outside France, in the occupied countries. The Army of Italy and, in Germany, the Army of the Sambre-and-Meuse, both staunchly republican, were disturbed, whereas the Army of the Rhine-and-Moselle, swamped with royalists ever since it had been under the command of Pichegru and Moreau, remained passive. In the Army of Italy there was much discontent over the events in France and even more over those that were being prepared. Bonaparte deplored the laws that had been voted and the plans which he attributed to the royalists. His position now was increasingly strong because he had just signed the preliminaries of a peace with Austria in the wake of his victories. No other general could match him.

Bonaparte seized the occasion of the festival of July 14, 1797, to have the various corps of the Army of Italy vote to send to the Directory addresses that severely threatened the royalists. That of the general staff of the Army of Italy read as follows: "Soldiers, mountains separate us from France; you will cross them with the swiftness of an eagle, if necessary, in order to preserve the constitution." The Army of the Sambre-and-Meuse forwarded a similar address, whereas the Army of the Rhine-and-Moselle abstained.

When these addresses arrived in France and the royalists ascertained that the armies were beginning to stir, it appears that they planned to accelerate their attempt to seize the government. In July, at the time of the addresses, Wickham sent Dandré £10,000 a month, plus a credit of 50,000 livres, and Dandré placed this credit at Pichegru's disposal. This money was intended to facilitate a *coup d'état*.

At the Directory the members were worried. Reubell and Larevellière were resolved to swing into action by dispensing with Carnot. The director, Le Tourneur, had been replaced by Barthélemy, the negotiator of the treaties of Basle, who had been won over by the royalists. Barras, irresolute as usual, wondered which party would get the upper hand. It seems that he tried to come to an agreement with the royalists. It has been said that he had asked 12 million in gold from Louis XVIII in order to throw in his lot with Carnot and Barthélemy. The royalists did not possess 12 million and Louis XVIII appealed to Pitt, who found the sum too high. It is possible that this refusal led Barras to join forces with Reubell and Larevellière.

On the other hand, it was at this point that Bonaparte dispatched to Paris the papers found on the comte d'Antraigues at the time of his arrest in Trieste, and particularly the famous conversation with Montgaillard which unquestionably established Pichegru's treason.[6] From now on the Directory had in its hands stunning evidence against Pichegru and his followers. These papers were not published but held in reserve; they were not shown even to Carnot. Only Barras, Reubell and Larevellière had read them and waited for the propitious moment to make use of them.

Now the majority of the Directory was resolved to eliminate the royalists. Its members decided that the coup would take place in the month of July. Specifically, the Clichyans were demanding a modification of the ministry, which they no longer found in harmony with the majority of the chambers. The regime of the Constitution of Year III was not parlementary; the ministers did not have to be chosen from the majority. But Barras, Reubell and Larevellière accepted the demand of the Clichyans and decided to transform the ministry. However, they modified it in a completely different way from what had been hoped for by the royalists. They eliminated the Clichyans and their friends: Bénézech, minister of the interior; Cochon, minister of police; and Petiet, minister of war. In their place they put genuine Jacobins: Lenoir-Laroche; then Sotin to the Ministry of Police, François de Neufchâteau to the Ministry of the

6. See above, Chapter X, pp. 196–198.

Interior, and Hoche to the Ministry of War. Hoche, commander-in-chief of the Army of the Sambre-and-Meuse, was the key man in this arrangement. We must add also that Talleyrand was appointed minister of foreign affairs, in place of Delacroix, and that Truguet, minister of the navy, was replaced by Pléville Le Peley.

Immediately Hoche became minister of war, the decision to act was made. He ordered some of his soldiers to the region of Paris under the pretext of reinforcing the Army of the West, with a view to a landing in England. Now, the Constitution of Year III forbade troops to approach within 60 kilometers of Paris without authorization of the councils. The troops, of course, in this case by definition would have to go beyond the "constitutional limits." The Directory awaited their arrival so that it could then proceed to order the arrest of the Clichyan leaders.

The Clichyans had been deeply stirred by this *journée des dupes*, the "day of dupes," as the day of the nomination of new ministers was called. Soon, they learned that Hoche's troops had crossed beyond the "constitutional limits." The violent interpellations in the councils bore on the illegal crossing of limits and on the nomination of Hoche to the ministry, since he was not of the age required by the constitution. The Directory's plans were thus exposed and it yielded, revoking Hoche's nomination and declaring that the troops had gone beyond the constitutional limits in error. The *coup d'état* was postponed to a later day.

The timing apparently would have been favorable for the royalists. They themselves should have attempted a *coup d'état* after this capitulation by the Directory; but Pichegru was afraid. It has been said that a deputy, Fabre, from the Aude—a friend of Barras who had been apprized of the contents of the papers found on the comte d'Antraigues—probably alerted Pichegru who, aware that he was compromised, may have hesitated to take the initiative in an act of force. On the other hand, Pichegru wanted to act only if he could base himself on a loyal National Guard, and the reorganization in progress had not yet been completed. Hopes had also been placed on Moreau, commander of the Army of the Rhine-and-Moselle, but he too showed a very hesitant attitude.

At the time of his offensive, in April of 1797, Moreau had seized the papers of an Austrian general, Klinglin, which contained an important part of the correspondence in code between the Austrians and Pichegru. This correspondence proved the general's treason. But Moreau, instead of doing his duty and notifying the Directory of his discovery and Pichegru's treason, did nothing at all for the time being. It was only when he learned by telegraph of the coup of 18 Fructidor that he informed the Directory —in a letter antedated by two days—of the content of Klinglin's papers which he had seized six months earlier. This conduct shows that Moreau had been won over by the royalists. But his evasions prevented the royalists from making a *coup d'état* to their advantage in August.

Meanwhile the Directory did not remain inactive. When the attempt arranged with Hoche had failed, it turned to Bonaparte. He delegated General Augereau to Paris, and the latter, in order to avoid violation of the constitutional limits by his troops, gave out a great number of leaves to his soldiers and officers who thus came to Paris according to regulations. The capital was flooded with soldiers on leave, notably Hussars of ardent Jacobin persuasion who engaged in violent street fights with the *muscadins* and the "black collars" (loyalists who wore such collars as a sign of mutual recognition).

On 6 Fructidor, Year V (August 23), the presidency of the Directory fell to Larevellière. Four days later, he delivered a very violent speech against the Clichyans, who were disoriented by these attacks. They wondered whether they should act, but Pichegru still counseled temporizing. His advice turned out to be wrong because on the night of 17/18 Fructidor (September 3/4) the leaders of the Clichyans were arrested, the barriers of Paris closed and the mails interrupted. The Directory issued an appeal to Hoche's troops, who were stationed not far from the constitutional limits, and to the soldiers of the Army of Italy on leave. It removed General Moreau and arrested a great number of Clichyans. It decided to deport to Guiana forty deputies of the Council of Five Hundred, thirteen deputies of the Council of Elders and two directors, Carnot and Barthélemy. Carnot escaped with the help of Barras; only Barthélemy was arrested and deported. The Directory also ordered the deportation of the royalists arrested earlier and of the former minister of police, Cochon. It arrested forty-two newspaper printers, eighteen of whom were deported, and in a fortnight it banished all returned émigrés. Finally, it re-established all kinds of revolutionary measures.

For a time the *coup d'état* of 18 Fructidor crushed the hopes of the Clichyans and foiled their attempt to seize power by legal means. Through this *coup d'état*, the Directory once more became master of the situation, but it could not remain so except by depending on the Jacobins and even on the anarchists, a position that was to prove very difficult. The *coup d'état* provoked a blaze of anti-royalism but it did not last long: the royalists were to continue their underground action in the interior of the country. Nevertheless, it gave the Directory a respite. The counter-revolutionary movements ceased for a spell within France, but abroad, in the countries occupied by the French armies, counter-revolutionary activity begun in 1796 persisted and even grew more pronounced. We shall examine this next.

CHAPTER XV

The Counter-Revolutionary Movements in Italy and the Mediterranean Countries, 1790 to 1798

1 / The Conditions of Counter-Revolutionary Action in Italy (1789-96)

In order properly to understand the characteristics of the counter-revolutionary movements in Italy, we must go back a little in time to see how the struggle against the Revolution had been conducted in Italy, long before the arrival of French troops.

From 1789 to 1796 Italian newspapers, very few in number and all subject to strict censorship, had constantly published articles which were hostile—indeed, often virulent—to the Revolution. Among these papers, those published in the Papal States, *Il Giornale Ecclesiastico di Roma* and *La Gazzetta di Bologna*, had distinguished themselves. Alongside these periodicals, a large number of pamphlets hostile to the Revolution, which often deliberately distorted events, had been published in the different cities of Italy, especially in the Papal States and in the Kingdom of Naples. These articles and pamphlets attacked the makers of the French Revolution, who were identified with the Freemasons, with the "Jansenists," who were numerous and influential in Italy, and with the *philosophes* in general. The destruction wrought in France by the Revolution was exaggerated at will and the Revolution, with the disasters that accompanied it, presented as divine punishment. Accordingly, this propaganda fastened onto and fostered the thesis of a number of authors hostile to the Revolution, notably Joseph de Maistre and Edmund Burke.

In Italy, however, doctrinal propaganda did not have so great an influence as it did in other countries, such as England, Spain or Germany. Burke's *Reflections on the Revolution in France* had been translated into Italian, but by a mediocre and obscure writer named Scrofani, and had created very little stir. Mallet du Pan's *Considérations sur la Révolution française* was also translated into Italian but this too found only few readers. And although Joseph de Maistre was the subject of an Italian sovereign, the king of Sardinia, his *Considérations* likewise failed to achieve any great success in Italy. Consequently, the counter-revolutionary propaganda in the peninsula consisted above all of newspaper articles and virulent anonymous pamphlets, which preached struggle against the Revolution without expounding on the regime or doctrine by which the revolutionary regime and ideology were to be supplanted.

Nevertheless, a number of famous Italians had written against the French Revolution. Most of them were poets and for a time their works enjoyed some success; but their influence was ephemeral. The poems reached only the cultivated public, a weak minority. Vincenzo Monti wrote the *Bassvilliana* on the occasion of the assassination of Bassville, a French diplomatic agent in Rome, in 1793. The *Bassvilliana* was not hostile to France, for Monti was a great admirer of France, but it was clearly directed against the ideas of the French Revolution. However, nothing resembling political doctrine can be extracted from the piece. The poet Vittorio Alfieri also composed verses hostile to the Revolution, although in earlier years he had published tragedies inspired by the philosophical ideas that had paved the way for it. In one of his poems, the *Misogallo*, he ridicules France and the French Revolution.

These poems, as well as the translations of the great doctrinaires of the counter-revolution, affected only a tiny segment of the Italian population, the "literati," who in the main were imbued with the ideas of the Enlightenment and very favorable to the Revolution to the extent that they knew anything of it. What is important to understand, however, is the state of mind of the rural populations because, in Italy, the counter-revolutionary insurrections were above all peasant movements. And this state of mind varied greatly according to region because the social structures prevailing in Italy at that time also varied greatly.

In northern and central Italy the peasant was in actual fact a free man. He was a husbandman, a small proprietor, a small farmer or sharecropper. Feudal rights had practically disappeared; only a few vestiges remained. On the other hand, in southern Italy and in the southern part of central Italy, as well as in the islands, it was the large landed property, the *latifundium*, that predominated. The peasant did not own lands in his own right or only a tiny holding, for in most cases the *latifundium* was associated with the *microfundium*, insufficient to keep the peasant alive. The feudal regime was still in effect in the Kingdom of Naples, where the peasants were subject to numerous seigniorial dues, to payments in kind and to forced labor comparable to that which existed in France. But this description must not be oversimplified. In the regions of the north there were localities where the peasant was still subject to a quasi-feudal regime, whereas in some regions of the south such as, for example, the Compagna or the plain that borders Mount Etna in Sicily, he was practically emancipated.

In general, however, the peasant remained very much subject to the Church, to the parish priests. The Church was very powerful in Italy and the peasant extremely docile to the directives of her ministers. He was also subject to the lords in the regions where they still resided in the countryside, that is, in central and southern Italy. In northern Italy and in the northern part of central Italy there was no nobility in the sense that it existed in France. To be sure, there were nobiliary titles but they had been given to enriched bourgeois, to patricians. Such was the case, for instance, with the Venetian and the Florentine nobility. In southern Italy, on the other hand, there existed a true nobility in the same sense as in France. Nevertheless, this nobility, in the years that preceded the Revolution, increasingly left the land to take up residence in Naples and other cities where its members occupied high State offices or remained idle while trying to cultivate their minds.

The nobles who remained on their estates were still known by the local inhabitants. But when they left the land they levied feudal dues by way of intendants and bourgeois farmers. For the peasants, the collector of taxes, or "*gabelloto*," was the living translation of the seigniorial regime and as such was generally detested. By extension, the peasant population was ready to carry over its hatred of the "*gabelloto*" to the entire bourgeoisie and, consequently, to the ideas it professed. Since the bourgeoisie was at the head of the philosophical movement, the movement of the Enlightenment, the peasants, in general, were therefore very hostile to revolutionary ideas.

The Revolution had been able to succeed in France in 1789 because the bourgeoisie had allied itself with the peasants. We do not find this alliance in Italy. On the contrary, there was a profound divorce between the peasants and the bourgeoisie—at times veritable hostility between the two classes. This was due to the fact that in his day-to-day relations the bourgeois seemed to be the peasant's enemy. In the eyes of the peasant, the bourgeois was the lord's intendant, the "*gabelloto*," the one who collected the manorial dues and sometimes the tithes. The bourgeois was also the city merchant to whom he had to have recourse from time to time in order to purchase certain indispensable items. The bourgeois, also, was often the lender, who quickly transformed himself into a usurer. So the bourgeoisie was not loved by the peasants who, by an obvious association of ideas, rejected the bourgeois' ways of thinking.

There were still other reasons why the rural population was hostile to the new ideas. Among these ideas those relating to economic transformations were widespread in Italy. There were not, of course, any economic theoreticians comparable to those living in France at the time, but the works of the physiocrats were widely circulated. Many Italian thinkers concerned themselves with them, not only translating them but very often transforming them and adapting them to their own country.

We must not forget that the first chair in political economy in Europe was established in Naples by Genovesi in 1755. Now, the principal economic theories concerned the free circulation of grains, a measure very advantageous to proprietors and above all to those whose lands yielded big harvests. This was viewed with hostility by the peasant because he thought that its first result would be the exportation of grain reserves, which would result in famine in the event of a poor harvest.

The economists also insisted on the necessity of putting an end to common rights and usages. In Italy, as in France, and above all in southern Italy, communal properties were vast; and although the peasants of Italy possessed only a very tiny property, not enough for them to make a living, they enjoyed very extensive rights on these communal lands. Thus each peasant could possess a small flock which he could pasture on the enormous stretches of communal lands which covered the mountains. Now Italian, French and English economists and physiocrats considered the flocks of goats and sheep grazing in the communal lands harmful: the animals ate the young shoots and so prevented the reforestation of the mountains, which brought in its wake excessive soil erosion, arrest of agriculture, accumulation of alluvions in the plains, formation of bogs, development of marsh lands, and outbreaks of malaria. From the technical point of view, the economists and physiocrats were right. But for the peasants, the division and closure of the communal lands were an evil because, in the last analysis, they forced the peasants to sell their flocks. Most of the time in fact the parcel of communal land allotted to the peasant in the case of division was not enough to keep even a small flock alive. At the time of the division of these lands, moreover, the lord was greatly benefited inasmuch as he received a considerable portion—in France, a third of the communal lands; this was the right of selection. Altogether the division of communal lands and the installation of enclosures around the properties of each peasant translated into a lower standard of living for the peasants. It should occasion no surprise, therefore, that they were against new ideas and those who propagated them.

They were also wronged by the suppression of the rights of usage. As in France, the right of *vaine pâture* existed in Italy. After the gathering of the harvest, the peasants could lead their flocks onto lands belonging to others; these flocks grazed what still remained to be grazed, preventing a second harvest and reducing the proprietor's profit. The peasants were as opposed to the suppression of common pasture as they were to the partition of communal lands.

And they were equally hostile to new ideas in matters of religion. These ideas are difficult to expound simply because they are highly nuanced. In a general way, they were grouped at that time in Italy under the term "Jansenism." But Italian Jansenism was very far from the doctrine of Jensenius. It was an extremely confused movement of ideas, whose aim was to reduce the authority of the Pope over the bishops and to remove from the bishops the supremacy they exercised over parish priests. Accordingly, it was a movement of egalitarian tendency. It also aimed at a return by the Church to a more austere life, that of primitive Christianity. Jansenism was hostile to the religious orders. It had been associated with the expulsion of the Jesuits and the suppression of this order by Pope Clement XIV in 1773. At the end of the eighteenth century, the Jansenists also demanded the suppression of other religious orders. Many monasteries with only a small number of monks or nuns were closed.

In many regions of Italy the peasants looked very disapprovingly on these measures, which they considered anti-Catholic, Scipion de Ricci, bishop of Pistoia, headed the movement in Italy before the Revolution. When this prelate tried to bring about the triumph of Jansenist ideas in all Tuscany, he provoked a riot directed against him personally in Prato, near Florence, on May 18, 1787. This incident underscores the hostility of the peasant masses to religious reform.

2 / Italy at War Against the Revolution

The counter-revolutionary tendencies which had appeared in Italy since 1789 were intensified further when most of the Italian states were in a state of war with France. The Kingdom of Piedmont-Sardinia was swept into the struggle in September, 1792; in the following year, 1793, the Kingdom of Naples, the grand duchy of Tuscany, the duchy of Modena and the Pope joined the first coalition. In 1794 the only states of Italy which remained neutral were the two republics of Venice and Genoa, as well as the duchy of Parma. Moreover, the neutrality of Venice, Genoa and Parma was somewhat relative. Despite their neutrality, the two republics and the duchy had been compelled to authorize the passage of Austrian and Sardinian troops on their territory. The recruitment of soldiers was conducted without distinction on the territories of the states at war as well as in the neutral countries.

From 1793 onwards, practically all Italy was at war with France. But it was the Papal States above all that displayed a great hostility. This is understandable. The Pope reproached France for the secular and religious measures taken since 1791, the annexation of Avignon and of the county of Venaissin, as well as for voting the Civil Constitution of the Clergy. Most of the French diplomatic agents had left Italian cities even before the Pope's declaration of war against the French republic. In 1792, the only Frenchmen who remained in Rome were the consul Digne, the commercial agent Moutte, the director of the Académie de France, and the secretary of the minister of France to Naples, Hugo de Bassville.

Hugo de Bassville had left Naples when the kingdom declared war against France and had taken refuge in Rome with the intention of continuing his journey toward France. Upon arriving in Rome, he noticed that the French consulate was still adorned with the royal coat of arms. Bassville asked Digne to replace the royal coat of arms with the republican coat of arms. After being consulted, the pontifical government allowed the removal of the royal coat of arms, but opposed the installation of the blazon of the republic. In Paris the Convention, in fact, had ordered the removal of the pontifical coat of arms on the nunciature. Consul Digne then reported the matter to the French ambassador in Naples, Mackau, and the latter ordered the consul to have the republican coat of arms placed on his door despite the prohibition of the pontifical government.

The discussions eventually became known to the people of Rome. The

Roman Jacobins prepared a demonstration in sympathy on the very day on which the republican coats of arms were to be installed on the door of the French consulate. The counter-revolutionaries in Rome, of whom there were many, organized a counter-demonstration. Both demonstrations took place on January 13, 1793. The counter-revolutionaries shouted anti-French slogans in front of buildings occupied by Frenchmen, particularly the Académie de France and the consulate. They shouted: "Long live St. Peter! Down with the French!" The mob invaded Villa Medicis, seat of the Académie de France, and then the residence of Hugo de Bassville, fatally wounding him. He died two days later. The demonstration fanned out as far as the ghetto because the Jews were accused, not incorrectly, of being very favorable to the revolutionary ideas. The looting of the ghetto lasted two days; it was halted only by the intervention of pontifical troops and was resumed the following month, on February 11 and 12, when news reached Rome of the execution of Louis XVI.

The assassination of Bassville constitutes an important episode in the history of the counter-revolution in Italy. This was the first time that a violent counter-revolutionary movement surfaced in the country. Its significance did not escape the counter-revolutionaries, since Monti immediately thereafter wrote his *Bassvilliana*, the anti-revolutionary epic destined to celebrate what he hails as a glorious act, the assassination of a representative of the Revolution.

The assassination also provoked counter-revolutionary movements in other cities of the Papal States, notably Bologna, but the Jacobins to some extent answered these demonstrations.

The most direct consequence of Bassville's assassination was the rupture between France and Rome, and the Pope's entry into the war. From January, 1793, up to the entry of the French into Italy in 1796, any demonstration favorable to the Revolution was brutally repressed. Counter-revolutionaries took over the leadership of governments. Censorship became extremely severe, publications arriving from France or Switzerland were confiscated and could barely make their way inside more or less neutral countries such as Genoa and Venice despite their proximity to the Swiss border. Opponents of the Revolution had a free hand to wage a vigorous propaganda campaign for three years. Hence it is not surprising that upon the arrival of French troops counter-revolutionary movements broke out almost everywhere in the different regions of Italy.

3 / The Counter-Revolutionary Insurrections in Northern Italy, 1796–97

In April of 1796 General Bonaparte's army penetrated into Piedmont, and then Lombardy. On May 16, 1796, Bonaparte entered Milan and continued his march toward Mantua, the great strongpoint where the bulk of the Austrian army had been concentrated. A warrantable supposition would have been that the country would remain calm after the sensational victories scored by the French troops since the beginning of the offensive. However, peasant counter-revolutionary insurrections broke out from the outset in the rearguards of the army. These insurrections were particularly dangerous. Had they been more widespread the French Army of Italy would have risked being cut off from its rear bases, situated on French territory.

The principal counter-revolutionary insurrections in 1796 took place in the region of Pavia, in May, and then in Lugo, in the province of Emilia, the following month. On May 23 and 24, when the French army was in the environs of Mantua and facing the Austrians, an extremely violent insurrection broke out in Pavia and in the neighboring village of Binasco, as well as in Arquata Scrivia, situated where the road which crosses the Apennines linking Genoa to Milan by way of the Giovi pass debouches.

Why the insurrection? A rumor suddenly made the rounds that the French army was in flight, that the Austrians were coming back. It was a false rumor and it is not exactly known how it started. Had it been deliberately spread or risen spontaneously? At all events, the fact is that it was obligingly echoed by the municipality in Pavia, which had not been replaced after the arrival of the French troops; its composition was the same as under the Austrian regime.

The rumor of the victorious return of the Austrians spread in Pavia and reached the surrounding countryside, particularly the village of Binasco. In that region of Lombardy, on the borders of Piedmont, the aristocracy was very powerful and the clergy there very hostile to the Revolution. Nobles and priests incited the peasants and demanded that they take up arms in order to join forces with the approaching Austrian army.

A counter-revolutionary troop was formed in Pavia itself, and its command was taken over by a mason, Barbieri. The troop was composed primarily of peasants of the region and of Pavian artisans. It blocked up the small French garrison of Pavia in the fortress; after two days the garrison, which had run out of food, surrendered and was held by the insurgents, but not one French soldier was killed. The insurgents controlled the city, and the houses of patriots were pointed out to them. One was massacred, others wounded. Pavia lay in the hands of the counter-revolution.

Bonaparte was quickly informed of what was happening. As early as May 25 he dispatched a large detachment to the spot with orders to put down the insurrection: he could not risk such a revolt in the rear of his army. This detachment seized Pavia. Many insurgents were killed, the city looted and a high tax levied on the inhabitants. The village of Binasco was burned, the chief instigators of the insurrection arrested. Responsibility for the insurrection clearly lay with members of the former municipality of Pavia. They were arrested and sentenced, but acquitted. Nevertheless, they were held for a long time as hostages in the fort of Antibes. On the other hand, many of the leaders of the insurrection who had been captured bearing arms were shot.

In Arquata Scrivia the lord of the village, Agostino Spinola, had provoked the revolt. He was of Genoese origin and married to a French-woman who, it seems, professed counter-revolutionary ideas. The village was occupied on June 9; the revolt came to an end after Spinola's arrest, and his château and most of the houses of the locality were set to the torch.

This first Italian revolt was only a flash in the pan, a sudden jolt, born of a false rumor. It was arrested by the brutal intervention of French troops. But it was significant and a presage of others to come. In fact, the revolt that broke out in Lugo a month later shows similar features.

Lugo is a small town situated south of the Po. French troops had not occupied the region of Emilia. They had only traversed certain regions after their victories in Piedmont and Lombardy. Thus the Italians had seen them pass on to Bologna where, on June 23, 1796, an armistice had been signed between France and the Pope. The inhabitants of that region might have had the impression that their country had been surrendered without a fight to the French and that the French were extremely weak, for no garrison had been stationed in most of the localities. On the other hand, peasants and townsfolk were dissatisfied with the armistice, which had stipulated the levy of requisitions and high taxes. Moreover, the municipal pawnshops had been seized by the French troops. These pawnshops played an important role in Italy's social and economic life, being the equivalent of real banks. Established in the Middle Ages, they were of considerable economic importance, especially in Milan and Bologna. Now, the French since their entry into Italy had decreed the confiscation of everything found in the pawnshops save objects of little value which were restored to their owners without charge. This was a demagogic measure directed against the rich and designed to favor the poor. Nevertheless, the confiscation of the pawnshop depositories set off a wave of indignation. Disturbances broke out in one of the towns in the east of Emilia, Cesena, on June 22. At this time this tiny town enjoyed great notoriety as the birthplace of Pope Pius VI, one of the Braschi family. It was also the birthplace of the future Pope Pius VII, Chiaramonti, who at that time was cardinal and bishop of the neighboring town of Imola.

On June 27, the rumbling of revolt was heard in another town, Faenza. Then an uprising of a much more serious nature broke out in Imola and Lugo, in the same region.

In Imola on July 4 two French officers who were passing through the town were attacked. They were about to be killed and were only saved at the last moment by the intervention of Bishop Chiaramonti. But things took a tragic turn in Lugo. In order to understand the events clearly we must follow Canon Leflon, who has brought to light the underlying causes of the insurrection there. Lugo had a long history of independence; it was a small city but it had always considered itself the equal of Ferrara and even its rival. But the French had established a financial administration in Ferrara and not in Lugo, and the administration of Ferrara had assessed the taxes imposed by the French among the whole region. Thus, for the first time in its existence, Lugo was subject to Ferrara. The inhabitants of Lugo were greatly vexed over this subjection. So the Lugo revolt is explained not only in terms of hostility to the French alongside the spread of revolutionary ideas but also by a particular circumstance, the subordination to Ferrara.

On June 26, two commissaries from Ferrara arrived in Lugo to levy the war tax established by Bonaparte and to take away the silver plate in the churches. There was a third reason for discontent: the levy of the war tax, its collection by the Ferraresi and the fear that while taking the silver plate from the churches, the commissaries would also remove the silver bust of St. Hilary, the city's venerated patron. The latent unrest rose to the surface and increased. The commissaries from Ferrara were insulted and the statue of St. Hilary borne in procession to the Carmelite convent where it was thought it would be better protected; the citadel, defended only by a few soldiers of the militia, was seized. The inhabitants of Lugo took the muskets stored there.

Now armed, the Lugosians proclaimed the insurrection against the French. They organized militarily and issued an appeal to the inhabitants of the region to join forces with them in order to expel the French.

It seems quite clear that the Lugo insurrection, like that of Pavia, was instigated by artisans and peasants supported by some nobles of the environs, and perhaps also by some parish priests, all of whom were ignorant of the real situation of the French army. The Lugosians entertained the illusion that they would be strong enough to drive out the French. No doubt, if all the inhabitants of the Romagna had joined the uprising at that moment the situation of the French army might have become critical; accordingly, Bonaparte was vitally concerned to put down the insurrection in Lugo. He had no doubt that the army would easily gain the upper hand, but its victory would be marked by looting and very probably by the execution of many of the insurgents. This was why the bishop of Imola made every possible effort to arrest the insurrection and, at all events, to prevent its spread to the whole of the Romagna.

The moment he learned of the revolt, Cardinal Chiaramonti decided to go to Lugo in person in order to urge the populace to remain calm. But the overexcited inhabitants of Imola prevented him from leaving the city. Then the cardinal sent two priests to Lugo as bearers of a proclamation signed by him, requesting the inhabitants to lay down their arms. "Let the Lugosians," he said, "renounce their animosity in order to restore to their country that tranquility which is, incontestably, the first and most precious of possessions." The cardinal also asked the clergy of his whole bishopric to preach sermons urging calm and obedience.

However, in Lugo even the clergy, which had decided to obey these orders, was outstripped by events. The proletariat, the artisans and peasants of the vicinity rose in insurrection. As leader they chose among the small craftsmen a certain Mongardini, nicknamed "Buonapace," in derision of Bonaparte. When the cardinal's proclamation was read to the inhabitants of Lugo, the prelate was denounced as a Jacobin. The priests who had brought this proclamation were ill treated and forced to leave the city precipitately to take refuge in Imola.

The situation became very tense. The cardinal, unable to restore order, wrote to General Robert, who was in command at Ferrara, informing him that he had done everything possible to prevent the insurrection from spreading. He acknowledged his failure but declared that he would renew his efforts and begged General Robert to postpone any military operation until his efforts were crowned with success.

After this letter to General Robert, the cardinal in fact made another written appeal to the inhabitants of Lugo: "I am deeply grieved by the futility of my exhortations, which purposed to prevent the massacre of this beloved populace. A massacre will result because you are dealing with a powerful, seasoned army." This second appeal was as useless as the first. The inhabitants turned a deaf ear. They believed that with the help of the peasants in the vicinity, they could inflict a defeat on the French army.

The situation was becoming difficult for the French army. Bonaparte was apprized of the fact that General Wurmser, who had withdrawn into the Alps, had assembled a new army and was drawing nearer. Bonaparte reckoned it indispensable to have order in the rear of his armies in order to fight the Austrians. Accordingly, he ordered General Robert to resume operations against the insurgents of the Romagna.

On July 4, General Pourailly, subordinate to General Robert, ordered a patrol to enter Lugo and arrest a printer who had published seditious proclamations against the French. To send a small patrol into Lugo, where the whole population had taken up arms, was an act of great impudence. The patrol was attacked, suffering one dead and one wounded. Upon hearing of the incident, General Augereau, General Robert's superior, decided to send a greater number of troops to put down the revolt. An entire brigade, under the command of General Beyrand, received the mission to capture Lugo, while General Pourailly, with a sizable troop, was to attack the inhabitants from the rear.

Nevertheless, at the request of the bishop of Imola the negotiations continued. The cardinal made fresh efforts to prevent the revolt from ending in a blood bath. General Beyrand installed his headquarters in Imola: at the cardinal's urging, he granted the insurgents a twenty-four-hour truce to lay down their arms and submit to his authority. If the conditions of the truce were not fulfilled, they would be attacked by substantial forces. General Augereau accepted the truce, preferring a submission obtained through negotiation to repression with all its consequences.

When news of this decision and of the arrival of larger contingents of troops was learned in Lugo, the moderates, the bourgeois, wanted to accept General Beyrand's conditions. But the extremists and above all "General" Buonapace rejected any surrender.

The fight therefore continued. The French columns set out on July 6 but before reaching Lugo were halted in their tracks by armed peasants who had been hiding on each side of the road. These peasants, says a report, "show themselves to be as fierce as the fanatics of the Vendée." The comparison is significant. At all events, the resistance of the peasants was effective because General Pourailly, himself wounded, suffered enormous casualties—200 soldiers killed and many wounded.

Despite this setback, General Beyrand gave the insurgents three more hours during which to surrender, in default of which the city was to be set "to fire and sword." He was again rejected.

The attack was launched, this time without great losses; Beyrand's columns captured Lugo. Buonapace fled and took refuge in Ravenna but a French bearer of a flag of truce who had tried to conduct last-minute negotiations with the insurgents was assassinated by fanatics. Sixty insurgents were killed in the course of the city's capture. On July 8 the city was looted, like Pavia, but the massacre feared by the cardinal did not take place. Apart from the insurgents killed during the fighting, there were no other victims. As for the looting, all the houses were equally affected, those of insurgents as well as patriots. And when it was over, the peasants who had previously risen up against the French entered the city and continued the looting begun by the soldiers.

After the repression of the revolt, General Augereau assumed braggadocio airs in an effort to create the impression that he had repressed this insurrection against the French with great savagery. In a letter to Bonaparte, he declared: "The apostolic army and its general headquarters no longer exist; the *chouans* of Romagna have been driven out, defeated, scattered in all directions"—an exaggeration inasmuch as the repression had been strictly limited to Lugo and the nearby villages.

In an unpublished letter cited by Canon Leflon, Pope Pius VI, who had been informed of the revolt, categorically disapproved of the insurrection and called upon the people of Lugo to submit in observance of the armistice his envoys had concluded with the French republic at Bologna. Contrary to what, at times, has been affirmed, the Pope had not been the instigator of the insurrection. At the origin of the revolt, we find ordinary folk supported covertly by a few nobles and, perhaps, a few parish priests.

In order to prevent a new revolt, Augereau tried to frighten the populace, which had remained calm, by a proclamation published the morning after the repression:

You have just witnessed a terrible lesson, blood still steams in Lugo.
A calm, tranquil Lugo would have been respected. Like yourselves,
it would have enjoyed repose, mothers would have had no occasion
to weep for their children, widows for their husbands, orphans for
the authors of their days. May this shattering lesson, therefore, be
instructive to you and make you appreciate the friendship of the
French.

At the end of his proclamation, Augereau threatened to shoot any individual bearing arms and to set any locality to the torch if one Frenchman were killed. After the revolt, eighteen accused were arrested and
brought before a court-martial, but only two of them were sentenced
to death.

I have dwelt at length on this revolt, first, because it has been studied
in great detail by Canon Leflon, who set the action of Pius VI and of
Cardinal Chiaramonti, bishop of Imola, in a proper light; secondly, because
it shows the character of insurrections of peasant origin, fomented by
humble folk, supported by some nobles and several members of the clergy
who do not follow the directives handed down by the episcopate.

The suppression of the Lugo revolt gave a year of calm to the French
army. A new insurrection did not break out until the following year, this
time in Verona.

This insurrection took place on Easter Sunday, for which reason it
has been called the "Veronese Easter," in an allusion to the Sicilian Vespers
which also took place on Easter Sunday of the year 1282 against the
French in Sicily.

Verona had been occupied by French troops since 1796. Probably no
insurrection would have broken out if secret agents of the French army
had not deliberately provoked it.

At this point Bonaparte was very far advanced in the Alps and on the
point of concluding the armistice of Leoben (April 18, 1797) with the
Austrian armies. Through this armistice he had planned to cede to Austria
a part of the Republic of Venice in exchange for recognition of the
Cisalpine republic which he was in the process of creating. But Bonaparte
could not cede what did not belong to him. Venice was an independent
and neutral Republic, therefore he required a pretext to intervene in
Venetian affairs.

Now, Verona was situated on the territory of the Republic of Venice.
If an insurrection developed in the region of Verona, the French army

would have a valid reason for acting against the government of *La Serenissima.*

We know from his memoirs that it was the chief of the secret service in Bonaparte's army, the adjutant-general Landrieux, who was charged with the organization of disturbances against French troops.[1] The scope of the revolt, however, came as a surprise. It was much more serious than had been planned: obviously, it is possible to foment a revolt but difficult to fix its limit afterwards.

The peasants of the region of Verona rose in revolt on Easter Monday, April 17, and the revolt quickly spread throughout the city. The French garrison stationed there was very small because the bulk of the troops was in the Alps. Soldiers, sick and wounded, were massacred in hospitals, isolated soldiers assassinated on the streets. Patriots, those who had collaborated with the French army, were arrested or killed. The Jews, as in Lugo and Pavia, saw their homes pillaged, and some among them were also murdered.

The bulk of the French garrison of Verona, however, was able to re-group in the fortress, which had been well stocked with provisions. It held out for seven days against the siege under which it was placed by the insurgents. Bonaparte meanwhile dispatched troops who immediately on arrival in the region of Verona again took the situation in hand, put down the insurrection, entered the city and forced the insurgents to surrender. There was no looting, but the leaders of the insurrection, who were easily identifiable because the secret service had been in contact with them, were arrested, tried, sentenced to death and executed. A heavy war tax in money and works of art was imposed on the city.

The Verona insurrection served Bonaparte's plans. Immediately after the Veronese Easter he sent an ultimatum to the senate of Venice and his troops marched on the city. They entered it on May 12 and proclaimed a democratic republic which, however, was to last only six months because Venice was ceded to Austria by the Treaty of Campo-Formio, in accordance with the promises made at Leoben.

There is one feature about the Verona insurrection, however, that is markedly different from that of Lugo. Its spontaneity is not certain; it seems to have been provoked by secret agents of the French army.

---

1. Albert Ollivier, in his recent work on *Le 18 brumaire*, disputes (p. 48) this inter-pretation traditionally approved by historians, but his supporting arguments carry no conviction.

Several months later, in September of 1797, an insurrection of unmistakably counter-revolutionary character broke out in the Ligurian republic. Admittedly it was not directed against the French, but against the constitution of the new republic inspired by the French constitution. This constitution contained two articles in particular that had greatly vexed the parish priests of Liguria. One declared that the property of the Ligurian clergy was placed at the disposition of the nation, which was to employ it to defray Church expenses but, in case of need, for other purposes as well. The other article stipulated that conferment of benefices and ecclesiastical employments in the Ligurian republic was independent of the Roman Curia and to be made exclusively to favor Ligurian citizens. The Ligurian clergy exhibited violent hostility to the constitution, so the government decided to delay the referendum which was to approve or reject the constitutional text, and announced that the constitution was to be revised and "purged of what could be contrary to religion." Unrest mounted nevertheless. On September 4, 5 and 6, 1797, the peasants armed themselves and marched on Genoa to the battlecry of "Viva Maria!" singing hymns. They captured the fort of Eperon, one of the most important forts defending the port. A deputation, including the archbishop of Genoa, Lercari, and two patricians, went to parley with the rebels. The archbishop published a pacifying pastoral letter, assuring the faithful that "the Catholic religion would remain intact," that national properties would be respected, the insurgents pardoned, and those among them who had been imprisoned freed. Most of the insurgents returned to their homes but the most fanatical among them continued to keep the field. The Ligurian government asked the French general Duphot to launch a military action against them. He attacked them on the morning of September 6, retook the fort of Eperon and captured 500 insurgents. Order was rapidly restored.

Such were the principal insurrections which developed in northern Italy during the presence of Bonaparte. They were very limited in time, lasting about twelve days at the maximum. They were also limited geographically. Only four centers of insurrection are identifiable: one in the region of Pavia, another in the region of Lugo-Imola, a third in the region of Verona and a fourth in Liguria. Finally, these four insurrections were very easily crushed. We find approximately the same characteristics in the insurrections that took place in 1798.

4 / The Counter-Revolutionary Insurrections of 1798 in Italy and the Other Mediterranean Countries

In 1798 the French troops stationed on the plain of the Po were ordered to march toward central Italy and this movement unleashed new insurrections. A counter-revolutionary assassination in Rome, very similar to the assassination of Bassville, provoked the new advance of French troops.

Ever since the installation of the democratic republics in Milan and Genoa, the Jacobins of Rome had acquired the habit of massing in front of the palace of the ambassador of France, Joseph Bonaparte, brother of Napoleon. At those demonstrations they hailed France and called for the creation of a Roman republic. The French embassy in no way discouraged these demonstrations; indeed, there is reason to believe that it itself encouraged them.

A new demonstration of this sort took place on December 28, 1797. But the partisans of the Pope, the counter-revolutionaries, organized a counter-demonstration, as they often did. They pursued the Jacobins and a clash took place between the two columns not far from the French embassy. At the sound of the uproar, the members of the embassy left the palace, among them General Duphot, who had arrived only a few days before from Rome. He had not come on a mission, but in order to marry Joseph Bonaparte's sister-in-law, Désirée Clary. Duphot left the embassy with members of the embassy staff and tried to separate the demonstrators. A shot was fired; he crumpled to the ground, dead.

The assassination of General Duphot created a huge stir because this was the second time in four years that a French diplomatic agent had been killed in Rome. Both Joseph Bonaparte and the Directory decided that this second assassination must be revenged in a striking way. Indeed, the vengeance was to be all the more striking because France was now all-powerful in Italy and could dictate orders.

General Berthier, who replaced Bonaparte at the head of the French troops in northern Italy, received the order to march on Rome, expel the Pope from the city and establish a republic with the aid of the Jacobins.

Berthier's march began on April 20 but did not proceed without difficulty. After starting out from the littoral of the Adriatic in the region of Ancona, he crossed the Apennines by going around Tuscany and set out toward Rome through the valley of the Tiber. In the course of the march he did not run into resistance from the pontifical troops, but rather was forced to cope with a number of peasant insurrections. The most important took place in Masaccio. This city was taken by assault, a heavy war tax imposed and captured insurgents bearing arms shot. Certain villages, whose inhabitants had revolted, were set afire.

Finally the French troops arrived in Rome. A Roman republic was proclaimed and given a constitution very much like that of Year III. But this republic experienced great difficulty in establishing its authority over the former Papal States. During 1798 revolts in the States were endemic— they exploded in one place and were no sooner crushed than they broke out elsewhere.

First of all, in the region of Orvieto, the peasants refused to recognize the republican authorities and troops had to be dispatched there in March, 1798. Then the department of Trasimene revolted: at the end of April the insurgents besieged the administrative center, Perousa, and 130 French were killed in the city of Città di Castello in the course of this insurrection. The revolt was barely over in the department of Trasimene when it broke out in the Abruzzi in May. In July, the south of the Roman republic was aflame, especially in the region of Monte Albano. Subsequently, further south, Frosinone and Terracina revolted in their turn.

Everywhere French troops were forced to intervene. At the end of 1798 revolt flared in every direction. No doubt it did not cover a large area but bands, similar to the *chouans* of France, attacked isolated soldiers and cut French communications; insecurity prevailed throughout the Roman republic.

While French troops occupied the republic, Bonaparte had left at the head of an expeditionary corps to conquer Egypt. En route, he had landed on the island of Malta, which he occupied without much fight, owing to the treachery of some Knights of Malta of French origin, who were hostile to the Grand Master of the order.

The French installed themselves in Malta, Bonaparte leaving a garrison there while he continued on his way toward Egypt. But soon revolt broke out on the island. The insurrection began on September 2, 1798. It had a double cause: news had reached Malta of the defeat of Aboukir, where Nelson had destroyed the French fleet and thus blockaded Bonaparte's army in Egypt. And in addition the French administration, established at La Valette, had decided to obtain money by melting down the silver and gold in the churches, which irritated the Maltese. This administration had also taken other measures which displeased the populace: confiscation of Church possessions, which were then sold in the form of national properties; and raising the interest to be paid on articles deposited in pawnshops, a measure which greatly injured the interests of the poor. Finally the English, after Aboukir, established a blockade of the island so that supplies no longer arrived, signifying a famine for which the Maltese held the French responsible. The revolt of the Maltese peasants spread without let-up. From October of 1798 onwards, the French troops and the administrative cadre established at La Valette were completely blockaded. True, La Valette is an immense fortress, affording the possibility of prolonged resistance; actually, the French were to hold out for two years, but during this time all the rest of Malta was to be in the hands of the insurgents.

Bonaparte also ran into resistance in Egypt. He had been able to land at Alexandria without difficulty and after defeating the Mamelukes, he captured Cairo. Initially it looked as if the French domination would not arouse resistance on the part of the population. But suddenly on October 21, 1798, a revolt broke out in Cairo. Isolated French soldiers on the streets were murdered. The commander of the fort in Cairo, General Dupuy, a native of Toulouse, experienced great difficulty in rallying his troops to fight against the insurgents and was assassinated in the course of the military operations. Altogether 250 French soldiers were killed during the insurrection. The French replied by bombarding the quarters of the center of Cairo where the revolt had started. The insurrection calmed down, but it was to break out anew several times in this city as well as in other localities in Egypt.

So from 1796 to 1798 sporadic revolts broke out against the French in Italy and in the Mediterranean basin, but they do not seem to have been genuinely prepared. They were spontaneous outbursts, provoked either by the appearance of French troops or by certain measures taken by the French administration. These revolts were easily put down and had no serious consequences.

It was not to be the same the following year when the general war against France was resumed. It was logical that the numerous insurrectionary centers formed since 1796 against the French occupation should give the allies the idea of organizing a great counter-revolutionary movement, an idea that was to occur all the more naturally because insurrections had also broken out against French troops in northern Europe.

CHAPTER XVI

Counter-Revolutionary Activity in Northern Europe, 1795 to 1798

1 / The Insurrections in Germany

There were very few insurrections in Germany, no doubt because of the density of the military occupation there. The largest revolt broke out in 1796. During the summer of this year French troops, with Jourdan in command of the Army of the Sambre-and-Meuse, and Moreau in command of the Army of the Rhine-and-Moselle, had advanced towards central Germany in the direction of Bavaria and the Danube. But they were halted around the middle of August by the maneuvers of Archduke Charles and were forced to beat a retreat which quickly was transformed into a disaster in the wake of the general insurrection of the German peasants on the right bank of the Rhine.

The peasants had left their villages at the approach of the French army and taken refuge in the woods, where they were armed by the Austrians. They also armed themselves with whatever was to hand, searching out muskets, scythes and pitchforks, and in the course of the retreat of the French army they attacked isolated soldiers and stragglers, as well as convoys. They cut communications with the right bank of the Rhine and with France, or made it very difficult for the French to maintain them.

The generals, in particular Jourdan, took great pains to combat this insurrection. Jourdan ordered his subordinates to make "terrible warning examples," to burn villages and execute inhabitants caught bearing arms. General Moreau, for his part, wrote to the Directory that in several cantons the peasants had taken up arms at the instigation of the Austrians, and that he was taking repressive measures. But it does not appear that the French generals were able to cope with the insurrection.

One of the most curious and most discussed episodes of this revolt was the attack, by armed peasants, on the big convoy that was transporting the treasury of the Army of the Sambre-and-Meuse. This treasury consisted primarily of the product of the requisitions and taxes that had been levied on the right bank of the Rhine. The convoy was attacked in the region of Siegen, east of Cologne, by a large band of peasants. Although it was escorted by a score of soldiers, the peasants managed to seize the greater part of the money. But the charge was made that Delannoy, proprietor of the transport, and Dubreton, the chief pay commissioner, were in collusion with the peasants. The peasants are meant to have attacked the convoy at their instigation and the loot supposedly was divided among the peasants, Delannoy and Dubreton. These two men were brought before a court-martial, but the inquest was not conclusive and they were acquitted. A cloud of suspicion nonetheless hovers over the circumstances surrounding the attack.

The peasant insurrection did not spread to the left bank of the Rhine. It harassed the armies in their retreat, but could not prevent it.

2 / The Counter-Revolutionary Insurrections in Switzerland

The insurrections in Switzerland were of a more serious nature. France had intervened in Switzerland at the beginning of 1798, at the request of the Swiss patriots themselves.

The patriots of the Lausanne region, directed by Laharpe, and those of Basle, led by Pierre Ochs, had urged France to intervene in Switzerland in order to put an end to the persecutions of which they were the victims and also to emancipate "the subject districts." Switzerland in 1797 was not, in fact, a confederation formed of equal cantons; there were cantons that dominated "subject districts." Thus the canton of Berne, politically the most important, governed the district of Vaud; the inhabitants of Vaud did not possess citizenship rights. There were still other regions that were subjected to the principal cantons. Therefore the French intervention had a dual motive: protection of the patriots and emancipation of the subject districts. But the entry of French troops into Switzerland also served the political designs of Bonaparte and the French government. In fact, the occupation of Switzerland made it possible to link Paris to Milan by the most direct route, that of Simplon, which was much shorter than that of Mont-Cenis or of the Little Saint-Bernard. On the other hand, Switzerland was a strategically important country in a possible struggle against Austria; but it is debatable whether the country's neutrality would not have been more precious than its occupation.

In Switzerland the various regions were very unequally developed and the economic and social structures differed greatly. The cantons in western and northern Switzerland, particularly those of Berne, Zurich and Basle, had economic and social structures similar to those of France. On the other hand, there were regions whose structure was different. These were the Montagnard cantons, also called "primitive" cantons because they had been the first to confederate themselves around the Lake of the Four Cantons. These cantons were more "democratic" than the others in the sense that government there was exercised by general assemblies of citizens, who gathered in the public square of the administrative center of the district in order to deliberate and vote on matters affecting them. But their economy was very backward and the inhabitants very poor. There was also another factor which set these "primitive" cantons over against the larger developed cantons, such as those of Berne and Zurich. The "primitive" cantons were in the main Catholic, whereas the larger cantons, notably those of Berne and Zurich, were Protestant. Thus the opposition showed itself three ways: economically, socially and in religious terms. Moreover, the region of the "primitive" cantons was a zone where communications were extremely difficult. So conditions for possible resistance to the French varied according to the different parts of Switzerland.

In the district of Vaud, Lausanne appealed to the French, and it was the same with a part of the canton of Basle. The inhabitants of the cantons of Berne and Zurich were greatly disposed in favor of a revolution and approved the presence of French troops. In contrast, in the Montagnard regions of central Switzerland, the populace considered the ancient institutions excellent and was hostile to the French, who were considered persecutors of Catholicism. Resistance was facilitated by the difficulty of communications and by the training of the inhabitants in the handling of arms. Indeed, this was the traditional recruiting ground for the Swiss soldiers who served the sovereigns of Europe in the eighteenth century.

The underlying cause of revolt had been the French invasion, but its pretext was the constitution which the French intended to impose. In the discussions that took place in December and at the beginning of January in Paris between the members of the Directory and the Swiss patriots—

in particular, between Reubell and Merlin de Douai, both directors, and Pierre Ochs—the three men had perfected a draft of a constitution which transformed Switzerland into a republic, one and indivisible, like France. The traditional boundaries of the cantons were upset, and small cantons joined together to form large cantons so that there was no longer a marked difference in area size between them. New cantons were created out of subject districts. Finally, all these cantons were subordinated to a centralized regime, which was in marked contrast with the one it had supplanted. The Swiss Old Regime was, in fact, very federalist in character, and the cantons enjoyed a large measure of autonomy. Actually, there was no central power in Switzerland and the Diet was much more like an assembly of ambassadors of the cantons than a true parliament.

The draft constitution drawn up in Paris was publicized in Switzerland in a book with a blue cover known as the "Blue Book" and submitted to the citizens for adoption. It gave rise to many objections. The excessive centralization was criticized: Pierre Ochs himself was not greatly satisfied with it. Various other drafts were drawn up in Switzerland during February and March.

The feature common to the new drafts was a reduction in the degree of centralization and a return to a regime of a more or less federal character. One draft in particular was formulated by the canton of Basle with the participation of Pierre Ochs, who had helped draw up the Parisian draft. This, called the "Basle draft," was submitted to all the cantons for their approval concurrently with the Parisian draft. Ten cantons adopted the Basle draft, two cantons rejected it in favor of the Parisian draft, and three other cantons were undecided.

Other drafts were also published. One of them divided Switzerland into three separate republics united by an extremely vague bond. The French Directory was very undecided. It was not particularly attached to the Parisian draft, the Basle draft, or any other. But in the face of the multiplication of drafts and the uncertainty of public opinion in Switzerland it feared disturbances and finally determined to stay with the Parisian draft. On March 22, 1798, it decided to ask Switzerland to accept the Parisian draft. The commissary Lecarlier, who combined the offices of commissary to the army and commissary with the Swiss government, was dispatched by the Directory to Switzerland. His principal mission was to persuade the Swiss to accept the constitution that had been drawn up in Paris.

Immediately upon his arrival in Switzerland, Lecarlier had deputies elected according to the Constitution of Paris and they met in the small town of Aarau. The large cantons were easily persuaded to adopt the Parisian constitution, but opposition was very strong in the "primitive" cantons. Eight cantons were hostile to the constitution, six of them Catholic: a part of Unterwalden-Nidwald, the canton of Schwyz—the oldest of the "primitive" cantons—the cantons of Zug, Uri, Saint-Gall, and the region of Sargans which did not really constitute a canton. The two Protestant cantons, Glaris and Appenzell, rejected the constitution. Indeed, they rejected the whole of the "Blue Book" which they called the "infernal" book. Furthermore, they not only rejected the Parisian constitution but decided to persuade the large cantons by force likewise to reject it and made preparations to attack them.

Lecarlier and the general who commanded the French Army of Helvetia, an Alsatian, Schauembourg, tried to intervene peacefully and prevent the small cantons from attacking the larger ones. They promised the inhabitants of the small cantons that no attack would be made on the Catholic religion; on April 11, they gave the rebel cantons eleven days to accept the Parisian constitution. To compel them, an economic blockade was decreed and all communications between cantons were forbidden. It was a harsh measure inasmuch as the small cantons were very poor and lived above all on the products they imported. This meant reducing them to starvation but, perhaps, was also to force them to attack in order to escape death by slow strangulation.

· This is precisely what happened. The small cantons took the initiative for the attack. They armed their inhabitants, around 15,000 men, and aimed their offensive at the largest city of the region, Lucerne, which they occupied. The Brünig Pass that enabled Lucerne to communicate with Berne was crossed by the insurgents, who thus threatened Berne, chief communication center of the French army in Switzerland. But Schauembourg regrouped his army and attacked the insurgents on May 2, 1798. He defeated them at Morgarten, Zug was reoccupied by French troops, and Schwyz, the soul of the resistance, surrendered after a heroic struggle on May 4, 1798. Finally, on May 9, the last insurgent bands were again beaten and dispersed, after which the "primitive" cantons surrendered. They accepted the unitary constitution provided that General Schauembourg's promise that the Catholic religion would be respected was kept and that the population of the rebel cantons would not be disarmed.

Despite this submission, the resistance continued in secret. Disturbances took place constantly in the "primitive" cantons up to 1799 and even beyond; Liberty trees were cut down and functionaries of the new Helvetian republic harassed.

The agitation of the "primitive" cantons spread to another canton, the Valais, also Catholic, and also situated in part in regions where communications were difficult. Prior to 1798, the Valais, strictly speaking, did not form part of Switzerland. It was a canton "allied" with the Confederation. Nevertheless, after the entry of French troops into Switzerland, the unitary Parisian constitution had been submitted to it for approval. The inhabitants of the lower Valais, that is, of the Rhône Valley, who were more "enlightened" and had a clearer view of their interests, understood that traffic through the Valais and the Simplon Pass would increase considerably as a result of the French occupation of Lombardy so they declared themselves in favor of accepting the unitary constitution. In contrast, the inhabitants of the upper Valais, who were less affected by the increase in traffic and were more desirous of keeping their autonomy, feared that the union of Catholic Valais to a Switzerland with a Protestant majority would result only in troublesome consequences for their religion. They rose in revolt.

At the beginning of May the Montagnards of the upper Valais, armed, descended into the valley of the Rhône. They captured Sion, the capital of the Valais, and marched in the direction of Lake Léman. They also seized the town of Saint-Maurice and forced the authorities of the canton to take refuge in the outermost limits of the Vaud district.

But Schauembourg's French troops had just been liberated from their struggle against the old cantons following the surrender of Schwyz. Schauembourg regrouped them and on May 16 took the offensive in the Rhône Valley. On May 17, he captured Sion. The rebels lost more than 400 men in the course of the battle; the French resident in Valais, Mangourit, wrote to the Directory: "These fanatics fought like tigers, they died without uttering a sigh, gripping a rosary or some relic in their hands. Eight priests bit the dust." Mangourit proposed that the bishop of Sion be arrested and sent to Paris in a cage, like the bears of Berne.

On May 23 the town of Brig, an important strategic point at the base of the Simplon Pass, was occupied by the French army. This operation marks the end of the revolt of the Valais.

The Swiss émigrés in Austria—a number of aristocrats and patricians had quit their country at the approach of the French troops—had been greatly impressed by these revolts. They now figured that by providing the rebels with arms and munitions, it would be possible to drive the French out of Switzerland and re-establish the Old Regime. Two émigrés took over the leadership of this conspiracy: Steiger, formed chief magistrate of Berne, and Pancrace, abbé of Saint-Gall. They obtained English money through Wickham and received arms from the Austrians. Meanwhile, they waited for a favorable opportunity.

It presented itself in July of 1798 when a law voted by the Swiss councils on July 12 forced all Helvetic citizens to take an oath of loyalty to freedom and equality and to vow hatred of anarchy and license. Steiger and Pancrace incited the Swiss to reject the oath. In fact, most of the inhabitants of Switzerland took the oath, but once more it was in the "primitive" cantons that the opponents appeared. On August 18 the inhabitants of Schwyz and Stanz refused to take the oath and once more took up arms.

The inhabitants of Schwyz, recalling the failure of their revolt in April and May, did not persist for long in their plan. After two days they laid down their arms and went to the Helvetic authorities to ask for pardon. Their revolt ran its course without requiring armed intervention. In contrast, the inhabitants of Stanz—of the canton of Unterwalden—persisted in their insurrection. Schauembourg had recourse to the device that had already served him so well in April: he instituted an economic blockade. But now the inhabitants had reserved stocks of provisions. The harvest had been gathered and they resisted. They were offered favorable conditions of surrender which they rejected. On August 31, the Helvetic Directory sent a summons to the authorities of Stanz, giving them one week, until September 6, to surrender. But a rumor that the Austrians were coming to aid the rebels was making the rounds in the Stanz region, so the insurrection continued and it was again necessary to request aid from General Schauembourg. The French army made its way into the city without great difficulty and Schauembourg ordered the disarmament of the "primitive" cantons. The leaders of the insurrection were arrested and brought before the tribunals but given only mild sentences. The new Helvetic authorities were disposed to leniency.

The end of the insurrection of Stanz seemed to prove that thenceforth all resistance in central Switzerland had vanished. The capital of the new Helvetic republic was transferred to Lucerne, which was better situated than Berne and enjoyed the further advantage that it was wholly without a powerful patriciate under the Old Regime. The revolts simmered down and were not to be rekindled until the following year when the general war resumed.

Thus the Swiss revolts had failed by 1798. Moreover, they had all been brief. The same was to hold true for the revolts that broke out in Belgium.

3 / The Counter-Revolutionary Insurrections in Belgium

Belgium had been occupied by the French armies in 1792. Evacuated in 1793, it had been reconquered in 1794. Both occupations had been effected without encountering any serious resistance. Without question it had been difficult to implant French institutions in Belgium in 1795 and 1796, especially religious institutions. The Belgians, staunchly Catholic and very devout, had no liking for the Civil Constitution of the Clergy. But no serious difficulties appeared at that time.

The difficulties arose in 1798 when the French government wanted to subject the Belgian departments, which were an integral part of France, to obligatory military service. Up to that time there had been no question of asking the Belgians to serve obligatorily. The only Belgians in the armies of the republic were volunteers. In fact, the law which regulated military service was that of August 23, 1793. It had ordered the "mass levy of soldiers" at a time when Belgium was not occupied by the French.

But in 1798 the councils voted a law which organized universal and obligatory military service on the whole of French territory. It was the first law of this kind; General Jourdan had been its advocate, together with the deputy Delbrel. At the time of the voting of the law, however, it had been decided that provisionally the departments of the west of France, which had rebelled against the levy of 300,000 men in 1793, would be exempted from conscription. A similar exemption might have been provided for the "united" departments, that is, for Belgium, but nobody had thought of it. All the deputies were persuaded that military service would be accepted without difficulty in Belgium.

Nevertheless, as early as 1795 the commissaries Pérès and Portiez de l'Oise, commissioned to introduce the French regime into Belgium, had pointed out to the Directory the dangers of the application of military service in this region. In 1798, these recommendations had been forgotten although now the threat of a new general war was even more sharply limned on the political horizon. There was fear of a second coalition and France needed many men. Thus it was decreed, without great discussion, that the Jourdan-Delbrel law would apply in Belgium.

Immediately upon its promulgation, the commissaries of the Directory in the Belgian departments warned that the law would provoke a great ferment. Nevertheless, the Directory took no precautions along these lines in Belgium, where it had stationed only an insignificant number of soldiers. In the department of the Dyle, for example, there were only 700 men, and 150 of these 700 possessed no weapons.

Thus the insurrection that broke out in connection with the application of the Jourdan law caught the French government unprepared. This essentially peasant insurrection left a deep memory behind in Belgium, where it is still known under the name of the "War of the Peasants." It has been described in a Flemish novel by Henri Conscience which, while exaggerating the events, gives a vivid description of the revolt.

As in the Vendée, the insurrection began with the promulgation of the law of conscription. It took place in the district of Waes, on the left bank of the Escaut, between Ghent and Antwerp. The conscripts demonstrated, chopped down Liberty trees and replaced them with crosses, attacked town halls and carried off and burned all records so as to destroy the birth certificates and prevent application of the conscription law. On the same occasion, the young people emptied the public coffers and at times led the functionaries away as hostages.

On October 12, Saint-Nicolas, the principal town of the district of Waes, was occupied by the insurgents approaching Antwerp. But they could not cross the Escaut and limited themselves to beckoning to the inhabitants of Antwerp while asking them for help. If the insurrection had reached Antwerp, the situation would have been serious for the authority of France. But the revolt remained limited to the peasants. The inhabitants of Antwerp although hardly favorable to France did not budge; on the contrary, the patriots of Antwerp were requisitioned into the National Guard and it was they who were charged to pursue the rebel peasants. The National Guard of Brussels and that of Malines were also placed in readiness. The attacks of the insurgents against Audenarde and Louvain failed.

Nevertheless, on October 24 the entire east of the department of Escaut and part of the department of Dyle was in the hands of the rebels. The general in command in Brussels proclaimed a state of siege and the departmental administrations took severe measures against the insurrection.

The central administration of the department of Escaut published the following decree: "Communes not opposing the invasion of brigands shall be treated as being in a state of rebellion against the French republic and the military commands are authorized to burn the houses from which troops are fired upon and in which brigands are found hiding." The central administration ordered a "general roundup" of insurgents, with house searches. The department of Lys (whose administrative center was Bruges) took the same measures; and the department of Deux-Néthes (administrative center, Antwerp) decreed that two hostages were to be seized in each commune where a republican had been killed. The Directory of Paris placed the national guards of the departments of the north in France in readiness and formed mobile columns against the rebels.

The insurrection was countered pitilessly and crushed. In Malines, forty-one rebels were shot. Poorly armed, in open country, the rebels could not hold out. The forces of order suffered insignificant losses. As early as the end of October, within two weeks, the insurrection in the region west of the Escaut had been totally suppressed.

But at the very same time it broke out in a district that was much more wooded, and much more difficult terrain for military maneuver, in Luxembourg, which at that time formed the department of the Forêts. The commissary of the department of the Forêts signalized numerous gatherings of rebels: "They are," he said, "armed with new pikes mounted on clubs nine feet in length with parts of rifles, swords, pitchforks. They march two abreast and wear no uniforms or any distinguishing sign."

Toward the end of October the insurrection seems to have spread freely throughout Luxembourg. Only at the end of the month did the gendarmerie and the mobile columns of the National Guard begin to attack the rebels. On October 30, 1798, the rebels were attacked at Clervaux. Many of them were killed, whereas the forces of order suffered only one dead and two wounded. On October 31, there was a new clash at Stavelot, and on November 14 at Saint-Hubert. An inspector of road tolls who witnessed the battle wrote of the rebels: "Their tactic is to assemble in a mass in order to put up a resistance; immediately they are broken up and pushed back, they all make off, each one to his own home and the troop, which pursues them, finds them working peacefully in the fields or in the villages, and as soon as it moves on they assemble anew, so that they are very difficult to overtake." We recognize here the classic tactics of the Vendéans and *chouans*, which were also to be the tactics of the Spanish guerrillas during the War of Independence from 1808 to 1813.

Finally, a leader seems to have imposed his authority on the insurgents of Luxembourg, Emmanuel Rollier. On November 13 the key town of Diest was captured by the insurgents, who occupied it for three days without being disturbed. On December 4, Hasselt was occupied by 3,500 rebels, two-thirds of whom were armed. They looted the municipal archives, the public coffers and the registry offices where the sacred vessels that had been confiscated from nearby churches were kept.

But the French government and the Brussels authorities had had time to marshal enough troops under the command of General Jardon, a native of Verviers. These troops attacked the insurgents at Hasselt and slaughtered them. The survivors retreated towards Saint-Trond, pursued by the cavalry which cut down still more rebels along the route. The battle of Hasselt and the subsequent rout mark the end of the "War of the Peasants."

The terrain, however, would have been favorable in the Ardennes where the insurrection could have been prolonged for a long time. If it came to a halt at that moment, it was because the rebels did not receive arms from Germany or from England. It was difficult for them to obtain the assistance they were expecting because they were separated from Germany by the Rhineland, which was held by French troops, and they were never able to occupy the coast which faced England.

The Belgian revolt had a very precise aim: to prevent conscription. The insurgents destroyed the registries of the municipalities, hoping thereby to prevent the functioning of the conscription process. But at the same time they also destroyed the external signs of French domination, escutcheons of the republic, furniture in official buildings, public coffers. They committed acts of violence against patriots, but rarely went as far as murder; nevertheless, once can cite the murder of two municipal commissaries and a gendarme. Some rebels supposedly shouted: "Long live the Emperor!" —the German emperor—but others shouted: "Long live Louis XVIII!" which proves the desire to remain French, but under a monarchical regime. The insurgents laid the blame on those who had persecuted the Church. They freed the refractory priests, and the presence among the rebels of such priests who sometimes shouted: "Long live the Mass with three priests!"—very characteristic—was often remarked on.

This revolt, at all events, occurred at a very inauspicious time for the insurgents. General peace prevailed over the continent, negotiations were continuing at the Congress of Rastadt between the French and the Austrians. The Belgians could not possibly hope for swift assistance from abroad. Was the insurrection spontaneous, provoked or prepared? The problem has not been studied. We know that General Dumouriez, a refugee in Germany since 1793, had contacts with the Belgians, and that some Belgians had the idea of making their country into an independent republic under the presidency of Dumouriez. Several months later he was once more a subject for consideration. Had he been in contact with the leaders of the insurrection? The question has not been solved.

CHAPTER XVII

The Great Counter-Revolutionary
Assault of 1799

1 / The Insurrections of 1799

The general war between France and the great states of Europe resumed
in the spring of 1799. This was the war of the second coalition; England,
Russia and Austria had formed a new alliance against France, which
Turkey had also joined.

The allies drew up a precise plan of operations. It called for attacking
the French armies on all fronts, from Egypt to the Zuyder Zee, and
pushing them back on the metropolis. The attack was to coincide with the
outbreak of insurrections in all the occupied countries and within France
herself.

Accordingly, this plan was very broad in scope, but it was poorly
coordinated both as regards military operations proper and insurrections.
In fact, the attacks of the Austrians in Italy, of the Austrians and then the
Russians in Switzerland and of the English and Russians in Holland did
not all take place at the same time, so that the French government was
able to shift its troops from one front to another. The internal insurrections were even less well prepared, not being synchronized either with
each other or with the major offensives of foreign armies. As a result,
these movements failed for the most part. Only one succeeded because
the conditions were particularly favorable; this was the counter-revolutionary peasant insurrection in Calabria, on which we shall dwell at some
length.

The plan for insurrections of peasants against the regimes established by the French outside France and against the republic within France had not been drawn up with the precision one might expect in an assembly of delegates of the powers concerned or of the counter-revolutionary movements. Indeed, it failed for this very reason. In fact, it was only a convergence of ideas. All the insurrections were directed, almost without exception and from afar, by one man: Wickham, the English agent, formerly in Switzerland, then in Germany. But Wickham was not in direct contact with the Italian, Dutch or Swiss leaders of the counter-revolutionary movements. Each of these movements had its own organization which, moreover, was often improvised and always ill prepared; this explains the poor coordination among them. The only insurrection which succeeded was touched off in a peripheral region, Calabria. Far from the heart of France herself, this insurrection triumphed, but it could not seriously thwart the essential aim of the revolutionary movement.

2 / The Insurrections in Calabria and the Ionian Islands

Chronologically, the insurrection in Calabria is the first of all the counter-revolutionary insurrections of 1799. It began as early as February of that year, whereas the insurrections in the other countries occurred later; in Switzerland they did not start until April of 1799, in Holland and France as late as August. Thus these movements were by no means synchronized, and only a rigorous synchronism would have made them constitute a danger to France.

The insurrection in Calabria succeeded, the counter-revolution there triumphed. Why? First of all because of the very special social and economic situation in Calabria. As we have seen in the preceding chapters, southern Italy at the end of the eighteenth century was still subject to a feudal system very similar to the French feudal regime in 1789. In the greater part of the country the lords bore the title of baron and enjoyed numerous privileges. They were the landed proprietors and often their holdings were vast, the so-called *latifundia*. Most of the time these lands could not be divided by inheritance or sale; they constituted *fidei commissa*, and had to be transmitted intact to an heir designated in advance.

Although the barons were the largest landowners of the country, they paid taxes that were miniscule in proportion to their wealth, in all about 7 per cent of their incomes, whereas the peasants paid the public treasury at least 20 per cent of theirs. The lords enjoyed numerous varied feudal rights and monopolies; the peasants were obliged to use manorial services and the lords could also demand forced labor from them.

This feudal regime, however, was in the process of transformation as a result of the development and enrichment of the bourgeoisie. The bourgeoisie, still few in number, had made some great strides forward in the eighteenth century and had enriched itself, whereas the nobles had grown poorer. Many lords, when they were able to do so, had ceded their lands—sometimes in their totality—or their manorial dues to the bourgeois. As a result, the bourgeois were in a fair way to replacing the lords of old families.

Moreover, the bourgeois were employed by the lords in the capacity of intendants, collectors of manorial dues, seigniorial judges and employees. At the end of the eighteenth century, the peasantry was no longer in direct contact with the nobility. Many of the barons lived in cities, particularly Naples, in quasi-idleness, where furthermore they tried to cultivate their minds by acquainting themselves with the movement of ideas and of the Enlightenment.

Thus it was the bourgeois with whom the peasants had a face-to-face relation and the seigniorial exactions were attributed by the peasants to the bourgeois. So the peasants had no love for the bourgeois, who collected the manorial dues or brought court actions against them in order to compel them to pay those dues.

And the bourgeoisie, which kept abreast of the economic and physiocratic movement, pushed for the division of the common lands. This division, as we have seen, made it impossible for the peasant to keep a flock because from the division he received only a very tiny lot, whereas the lord grabbed the lion's share. The peasant was also in contact with the bourgeoisie in the cities when he made purchases, or when he borrowed money at interest rates that were frequently usurious.

The peasantry of southern Italy therefore was much more hostile to the bourgeoisie than to the nobility. But the bourgeoisie, although it had in part replaced the nobility, was imbued with new ideas. Many of the bourgeois had studied at the University of Naples where, in the eighteenth century, teaching chairs were occupied by remarkable men like Vico, one of the most original philosophers, or Filangieri, or Genovesi who, as we have said, was one of the first in Europe to hold a chair in political economy.

Accordingly, the Neapolitan bourgeoisie adhered to revolutionary ideas.

The peasants, totally alien to the movement of the Enlightenment and for the most part illiterate, remained hostile to the bourgeoisie and thus to the revolutionary ideas which it professed.

The development of Enlightenment, even in so remote a country where communications were extremely difficult to boot, is attested by the number of prosecutions for the holding of opinions. From 1794 to 1798, 493 Calabrians were prosecuted by the Neapolitan administration of justice for the crime of holding certain opinions, that is, for an anti-religious attitude, or for membership in a Masonic lodge. The minister of police, Medici, who had been commissioned to conduct an investigation, declared that the great majority of Calabrians were completely ignorant of the movement of ideas and of the revolutions in Europe. But a tiny minority, composed of bourgeois and nobles, kept themselves completely informed on the progress of the revolutionary movements to which they ardently adhered.

In the Kingdom of Naples the revolutionary movement surfaced on several occasions from 1790 onwards. Jacobin clubs were formed in Naples and, no doubt, in other cities; they were brutally hounded by the royal government. But in 1799, at the beginning of January, the French army, commanded by General Championnet, was approaching Naples. The king of Naples, in fact, had imprudently declared war on the French before the great European powers were ready and his army had been defeated in the environs of Rome.

On January 23, 1799, Championnet entered Naples, from which the royal family was departing precipitately in order to take refuge in Sicily. Championnet negotiated with a small group of nobles and Jacobin bourgeois who had seized power. This group, with the general's consent, formed a provisional government of twenty-five members who chose as president an Italian Jacobin called Lauberg and as secretary-general a Frenchman who had been closely allied with Robespierre in 1793, Marc-Antoine Jullien.

As soon as the republic was installed in Naples, a proclamation was sent by the provisional government to all the communes of the kingdom requesting them forthwith also to proclaim the republic, to form new municipalities elected by the inhabitants, to create national guards and to adopt the Neapolitan tricolor cockade: red, yellow and blue.

The proclamation of the provisional Neapolitan government was accepted without resistance in the great majority of the communes of southern Italy and notably in Calabria. Only Sicily lent a deaf ear to this proclamation because the king of Naples, immediately upon his arrival in Palermo, had ordered the arrest of all members of the Masonic lodges and of all those who were suspected of Jacobinism.

The king of Naples also had the time to order arrests in the extreme south of Calabria; in one night 500 persons suspected of Jacobin ideas were arrested in the region of Reggio and transported to Messina, where they were imprisoned. Thus the republic was proclaimed practically everywhere in continental Italy, except for the southern extremity of Calabria where the Jacobins had vanished from the scene.

For the peasants, the proclamation of the republic in the small villages evoked above all the idea of liberation. For them the words "Republic," "Liberty" and "Equality" signified that they would no longer have to pay any taxes, that the seigniorial regime would be immediately abolished, as well as manorial dues and forced labor on the roads. But the republican municipalities elected at that time essentially were composed of bourgeois and liberal nobles who did not understand these words in the same way. These municipalities decided that it was necessary to await new laws and that until their promulgation taxes and dues would be paid as in the past. This decision, taken nearly everywhere by the bourgeois and liberal nobles in control of the municipalities, disappointed the Calabrian peasants. However, they still did not make even rough plans for any movement hostile to the new regime.

G. Cingari has carried out a close study of the members who made up these republican municipalities.* He establishes that they were recruited essentially from the bourgeoisie, flanked at times by one or two nobles. For example, in Rossano, a village situated near the site of ancient Sibaris, the municipality was composed of a notary, a doctor, a jeweler, and a bourgeois living on his private income. In Nicastro, a large rural town south of the massif of Sila, the municipality included three liberal nobles, four of the richest bourgeois of the town, and three others who had only recently become landowners. Nowhere do we come upon a peasant in such an office.

The bourgeois who headed the municipalities wanted to maintain the feudal rights which many of them enjoyed. In Nicastro, the seven bourgeois all of whom received seigniorial dues, were in no hurry to do away with feudalism. During the fortnight that followed the proclamation of the republican government, no measure likely to attract the

* See Bibliographical Notes for this chapter—Trans.

peasants was taken: neither the abolition of unpopular taxes, nor even the reduction of these taxes, nor a partition of lands demanded by peasants who, in general, were proprietors of miniscule lots, nor redistribution of the common lands, nor abolition of feudalism. The *fidei commissa*, that is, the arrangement which obliged nobles to transmit their property *en bloc* to one of their heirs, were not abolished until January 29, but it was a long-term measure and therefore could not interest the peasants. What they needed was an immediate partition.

The feudal regime was not abolished until April 25, when the insurrection had already gained all of Calabria. Despite the absence of measures favorable to the peasantry, the rallying of the masses to the republic at the time of the proclamation of the new regime had without any question been general. Initially, only a very small number of opponents had remained faithful to the Bourbons; but the rallying of the masses lacked dimension. This might not have been the case if measures had been swiftly taken in favor of the peasants so as to improve their economic and social situation. It is characteristic that the peasants who exhibited the greatest attachment to the republican regime were the inhabitants of the "Albanian" villages. These were villages inhabited by descendants of Albanians who had arrived in Calabria in the fifteenth century when Albania had been conquered by the Turks. These villages were even more wretched than the rest; and their inhabitants saw in the proclamation of the republic a means of achieving equality with their neighbors, in consequence of which they staunchly rallied to the new regime. But these "Albanian" villages were few. In the greater part of southern Italy the peasants remained very indifferent because the republic did nothing for them in the weeks that followed the proclamation.

Accordingly, the situation was ripe for a counter-revolutionary movement. And the king of Naples, Ferdinand, who had often shown a lack of ability, nevertheless had a lucky hand when he picked the man to lead this counter-revolutionary movement, designating a native of Calabria, Cardinal Ruffo, born in fact near Cosenza. Ruffo had at first been treasurer to Pope Pius VI in Rome. He contributed to the financial reforms introduced by this Pope, but was accused of embezzlement and forced to give up his post, after which he retired to Naples. The king of Naples then appointed him superintendent of the San Leucio silk factory near the capital. Cardinal Ruffo was far more preoccupied with temporal questions than religious ones.

At the beginning of February, 1799, Ruffo was appointed vicar-general of the Kingdom of Naples and commissary-general in Calabria. He was assigned the task of setting off an insurrection against the republican regime there.

Ruffo swiftly descended on the tiny village of Pezzo on February 7, 1799. He had a hard time in rallying people to his cause during the first two days, at the end of which he had assembled eighty men, two of whom were nobles. Then he marched toward the north on the village of Scilla and appealed to the peasants to revolt against the republic.

The peasants began to make up their minds because Cardinal Ruffo promised them the lands of the nobles and bourgeois who had adhered to the new regime. To be sure, the revolt in Calabria was a counter-revolutionary insurrection, but it was also a revolt of a social character, touched off by the promise of land and the allurement of looting. Later the peasants were to say: "He who had bread and wine was considered a Jacobin." In the village of Ciro the assembled peasants shouted: "We don't want the Republic, if we have to pay like before. Long live the King, no more Republic!" On March 1, 1799, Cardinal Ruffo abolished the tax for road construction, which was detested by the peasants; he also suppressed the tax "for the maritime cordon" in all the provinces that would rally round him. And he exempted from the militia tax peasants who agreed to enroll under his orders. He abolished many other taxes, particularly the most unpopular, and suppressed a number of public offices, notably those of tax collectors and tax examiners, who were universally detested.

Thus Ruffo, after the third or fourth day of his visit to Calabria, was able to rally a great many peasants. We possess lists of these first rallies. Who were among these initial insurgents? First of all, a great number of "braccianti" or agricultural workers; then petty artisans, masons, tailors, dealers in old clothes and disbanded soldiers from the regular Neapolitan army, which had been dispersed after the entry of the French into Naples; finally, some bourgeois and some notables.

It has often been said that it was religious fanaticism which induced the peasants of Calabria to rally to the banner of Cardinal Ruffo, who had placed his army under the protection of the holy faith, whence the name "Sanfedists" given to the soldiers. A study in depth of religious problems in Calabria shows that the republicans did not touch upon religious questions at all during the six months they were in power. No doubt, they could be reproached for their collusion with the French, who were notorious for their hostility to religion and guilty also of arresting the Pope in Rome and deporting him. But the mass of Calabrians was poorly acquainted with these events which do not seem to have played any great role in the revolt. To be sure, we find convinced believers, priests and bishops in both camps—in that of the republicans as well as that of the "Sanfedists." And we likewise find unbelievers—notorious libertines—on both sides. In the opinion of Cingari, and his study is very comprehensive, there is no ground for thinking that the religious factor played a determining role in Cardinal Ruffo's recruitments of peasants. Nor did the national factor. There was no national Neapolitan movement. An Italian nationalism, of course, did arise later but it was to be set off deliberately by the Jacobins, the patriots, who were at the origin of the Risorgimento. As for dynastic loyalism, it did not exist either. Ferdinand III was the son of Don Carlos, the first of the Bourbons to rule over Naples. In the course of modern history the dynasties had succeeded one another frequently in Naples, none of them, however, arousing any profound feelings of sympathy in the populace.

The rising of the peasants had an essentially social character. It was a struggle against the rich in order to seize their properties, but a struggle that was not waged in the name of a revolutionary doctrine but obeyed a counter-revolutionary ideology, announcing the return to the "situation of former times," to the "Golden Age." In former times one was happier; in former times the peasants had more land, were better off. The movement was social although it has a counter-revolutionary political character.

By the time he had arrived 50 miles north of his point of debarcation, Cardinal Ruffo had succeeded in recruiting a troop of about 1,500 men, the vast majority of whom were peasants, with a sprinkling of nobles and above all of former officers, and some bourgeois.

When he reached Pizzo, a little further north—later to be the scene of Murat's execution—Cardinal Ruffo had 4,000 men. He continued to advance toward the north, carefully avoiding the cities, which were republican centers. At times he ran into resistance. There were villages where the republicans were in the majority, the inhabitants having sincerely rallied to the new republican regime. Paola, on the Tyrrhenian coast, was one of the towns which put up the greatest resistance. It was captured on March 9 and completely sacked. The occupation of Paola was marked by numerous murders of inhabitants reputed to be Jacobins. All the houses of the nobles and bourgeois were looted.

It was only in mid-February that the French sent columns to fight against the bands of "Sanfedists." But soon the situation in northern Italy became dangerous. An Austrian attack against the troops occupying the

Cisalpine republic appeared imminent. General MacDonald, who had succeeded General Championnet in Naples, received the order to fall back toward the plain of the Po, leaving only small garrisons in the Neapolitan fortresses. Thus MacDonald recalled all his columns and evacuated Naples, save for some elements to hold the forts. Now the coast was clear for the "Sanfedists."

They pushed forward very rapidly, aided by some English, Russian and Turkish contingents which had been landed on the Adriatic and Tyrrhenian coasts.

On May 24, all Calabria and the Puglie were reconquered. The Army of the Holy Faith arrived outside Naples: the siege of the capital lasted almost a month—from May 24 to June 19. Finally the French troops, retrenched in the forts, surrendered and signed a capitulation agreement with Cardinal Ruffo, according to the terms of which they would be repatriated to France by sea, at the same time as the Neapolitan patriots who were with them in the forts. But this capitulation agreement signed by Cardinal Ruffo in the name of the king of Naples was annulled by Admiral Nelson, conqueror of Aboukir, who had become the protector of the royal family. Nelson had arrived with his squadron in the Bay of Naples. Queen Marie-Caroline, sister of Marie-Antoinette, who was extremely hostile to revolutionaries, had asked him to show no compassion, to grant pardon to none and to denounce the capitulation agreement which, however, had been solemnly signed. Nelson agreed to the repatriation of the French troops, but he demanded that all the Neapolitans with them be handed over to the "Sanfedists." The prisoner-patriots were tried and for the most part sentenced to death and executed. This was the case, particularly, with Eleonora de Fonseca-Pimentel, the young woman who had edited *Monitore* (the principal Neapolitan newspaper published during the republican epoch) and who had been the soul of the resistance.

Naples became the scene of wholesale looting. The "Sanfedists," once masters of the city, attacked all the houses of the bourgeoisie that seemed to harbor riches, as well as the houses of the indifferent; those of persons favorable to the monarchy were looted as much as those of the Jacobins.

Thus the counter-revolution was victorious in the Kingdom of Naples and the Old Regime was restored. But calm did not return and we can say that for several years southern Italy remained in a state of great anarchy. The properties of the bourgeois and of the nobles who had taken part in the republican movement were invaded by the peasants, but the latter were not to profit from them. After a certain time, these properties were restored to the families of the former owners and ultimately the hopes of the peasants were dashed.

The "Sanfedist" movement provoked the development of brigandage throughout Calabria. This was not the first time that "brigands" had appeared in that region. Calabria is the classic land of brigandage; it develops there in every period of crisis, political or economic, but this time it was to last a long while—a hundred years.

Many homes and châteaux had been destroyed; the harvests of 1799 could not be gathered and, as a result, famine stalked the Kingdom of Naples, unleashing waves of social unrest. But we can say that the peasants did not derive the expected benefits from the "Sanfedist" movement. Looting indeed was an immediate benefit, but very soon the looted objects were sold at a low price to dealers in second-hand goods and the money the peasants received from the transactions immediately squandered. The distribution of lands alone would have been of some use to the peasants. Actually, the Bourbon government had toyed with this idea and had it proceeded along these lines, it could have consolidated the counter-revolutionary movement and the dynasty. But at the last minute, in the face of the hostility of the landowners who had remained faithful and who risked, as a result, defraying the costs of the operation, the government gave up the idea of dividing lands. Thus the counter-revolution in the Kingdom of Naples had no lasting significance. And the Bourbons, installed on the throne, were not to remain there for long since they were to be driven from it six years later. Their departure provoked no disturbance whatsoever.

The "Sanfedist" movement spread throughout the Italian peninsula and reached central Italy, notably Tuscany. In the region of Arezzo, the disturbances broke out at the beginning of May, 1799, immediately news was learned of the victories of the "Sanfedist" army in the south and of the Austro-Russian victories in the north.

On May 5, a rumor that an Austrian corps had landed at Leghorn circulated in Arezzo. The next day, May 6, a coach driven by a peasant was seen to enter the city. Beside him sat an old woman waving an imperial Austrian flag. After a wild ride through the town, the rumor touched off a general rising of the peasants of the region. Thereupon an army, similar to the Army of the Holy Faith, was formed in the region of Arezzo. It was called the Army of "Viva Maria" and at its head a council of sorts directed operations against the Jacobins. On June 28, the Army of "Viva Maria" seized Siena, massacring Jacobins and, in particular, Jews. Thirteen Jews were burned alive in the great square. The bishop, Monsignor Zondadari, requested to intervene, limited himself to the utterance: *"Furor populi, furor Dei!"*

The "Viva Marias" also vent their fury on Jansenist priests, who were arrested and manhandled. Several months went by before the movement ran its course.

At the same time, a similar insurrection broke out in the Ionian Islands, which had been occupied by the French at the time of the fall of the Republic of Venice and transformed into departments after the Treaty of Campo-Formio. The insurrection flared up in October of 1799, when the Russian fleet appeared before the islands and its admiral, Uchakov, issued proclamations in the name of the czar of Russia and the patriarch of Constantinople, calling upon the inhabitants to defend their religion.

In the island of Zante the peasants unsuccessfully tried to attack the French garrison, after which they turned against the bourgeois, whether Francophiles or no, and against the Jews. The city was looted and numerous persons massacred. On the island of Cephalonia the insurgents were able to capture the French garrison, which numbered only 300 men. In Sainte-Maure, on October 26, the rebels tore down the French flag and replaced it with the Russian colors. The bulk of the French troops, commanded by General Chabot, was stationed in Corfu. They put up a stiff resistance, but at the beginning of November the insurgents were aided by the Russians and the Turks, who blockaded the port and the fortress. After a siege of four months, the French were forced to capitulate, on March 5, 1800.

3 / The Insurrections in Switzerland, Germany and the Low Countries

Thus, in 1799, the counter-revolution scored a complete victory in southern and central Italy and in the Ionian Islands. But this victory was due above all to the absence of French troops, or to their small numbers. Until the evacuation of MacDonald's army, the "Sanfedists" had registered very slight progress. Only later was the coast clear for insurrection. A republican army had been raised by the provisional government of Naples, but it was only in the process of formation and, therefore, could not seriously intervene. There were only a handful of convinced republicans in southern Italy and the economic and social conditions were particularly favorable to insurrection. Similar conditions were to be found in Spain at the time of the great War of Independence which broke out in 1808.

The situation was different in other occupied countries in which counter-revolutionary attempts took place in 1799, that is to say, in Switzerland, Germany and Holland.

In Switzerland, however, the terrain had been well prepared. There had already been numerous insurrections in that country in 1798, as we have seen. When the war resumed, the Austrians had quite naturally been tempted to provoke revolts in regions where uprisings already had occurred, that is, in central Switzerland, the region of the Four Cantons and the Valais.

Actually, as early as the beginning of the war, acts of violence were committed against isolated French soldiers in the environs of Lucerne, Fribourg, Soleure, and in the mountains. But it was once more in the "primitive" cantons that real insurrections took place. The peasants took up arms in the cantons of Schwyz and Uri; a general insurrection broke out in the canton of Grisons; the peasants penetrated the town of Disentis, where a small French garrison was stationed; and eighty French soldiers were massacred there on May 1, 1799. Finally the upper Valais, which had already risen in revolt in 1798, took up arms again in 1799.

The Helvetic Directory appealed for help to the French army. At this time there was a large army in Switzerland because that country was an essential strategic zone between the Rhine and the Italian fronts. The French troops intervened energetically. General Soult pacified the "primitive" cantons and recaptured the town of Schwyz; General Ménard defeated the insurgents of Grisons and captured Disentis, which was razed to the ground; bloody clashes took place in the canton of Uri, particularly at Urseren. French troops behaved brutally in the Valais; many houses were burned, the insurgents who had captured Sion at the beginning of May were hurled back and defeated on the mountain passes of Simplon and Furka; many peasants were executed.

At the end of May, however, the French troops were forced to fall back toward western Switzerland under pressure from the Austrians. The Austrian troops then installed themselves in Grisons and in central Switzerland and restored the Old Regime, but the measures taken by them provoked as much discontent as the French domination. Soon the peasants were up in arms against the Austrians. Consequently, after the victory of Zurich in September, 1799, when the French regained control of these regions, the Swiss sat tight. On the whole we can say that the Swiss insurrections against the French were a total failure.

Further north, in Germany, there were but a few timid attempts at revolt. A few murders of French soldiers were noted in 1799. French functionaries wrote that in certain regions many inhabitants had left their villages to meet the Austrian troops which, however, had not yet crossed the Rhine. Marquis, the French commissary in the Rhineland, on August 5, 1799, alerted the minister of justice:

> An extreme ferment reigns in all the communes. The successes of our enemies have been so inflated that the excitement which this news engendered has gone to the heads of the people; everywhere the French name seems to be held in detestation. In several communes Liberty trees are chopped down or mutilated. Foreign gazettes circulate in great numbers, seditious placards are posted.

However, the insurrection which was brewing did not break out. First of all, because the French Army of the Rhine did not suffer new setbacks; secondly, because the counter-revolutionary organization of these regions, no doubt, was not very developed; and finally because the feudal regime there had been totally abolished, even more thoroughly than in France. The peasants could only be the losers by a return to the German Old Regime.

An insurrectional movement was also prepared in Holland. The Anglo-Russian contingents landed at the tip of Texel in August of 1799. These troops were to take the offensive in the peninsula situated between the North Sea and the Zuyder Zee, in conjunction with an attack against Arnhem by Dutch émigrés who had taken refuge in Germany, and with a general insurrection in Holland.

This plan could not be carried out. At the outset, to be sure, the Dutch admiral, Story, was forced to surrender by his sailors, who were in the great majority Orangists, that is, favorable to the Old Regime. Admiral Story was forced to hand over his vessels intact to the British. There were also several risings in the Arnhem region, but they were very quickly quelled. The bands of Dutch émigrés that had penetrated into the territory of the Batavian republic were quickly thrown back by the National Guard of Arnhem, which had been mobilized. The Dutch police launched a manhunt for the leaders of the insurrectional movement, who were arrested, tried and severely punished. Even a woman, the baroness Van

Dorth, was also sentenced to death and executed, which created a profound impression in Holland.

Nevertheless, despite appearances, the situation was perhaps more serious that it was thought. Within the Batavian Directory itself there were men who asked themselves whether it would not be better to negotiate with the prince of Orange so as to avoid massacres and a wave of destruction. Two of the members of the five-man Directory in fact began negotiations with the prince and committed themselves to his restoration on condition that he accept the Batavian constitution or, at least, the essential features of this constitution. Thus we are not dealing here with an entirely counter-revolutionary movement, since what the Batavian negotiators wanted above all was to maintain the political and social regime which had been installed in Holland since 1795. But these negotiations were soon interrupted by the successes scored by the Franco-Dutch army of General Brune, who forced the Anglo-Russian troops to surrender and re-embark.

We know that in Belgium, émigrés had been in repeated contact with General Dumouriez. They had reverted to the idea of forming an independent Belgian republic, which would have been governed by Dumouriez whose passage in Belgium in 1792 had left behind favorable memories. His return in 1799 was to coincide with an insurrectional movement. The situation would have been auspicious in May of 1799 when the English launched a sudden attack on Ostend. When they landed their troops on the Belgian coast they fancied that this operation would touch off a new insurrection of the peasants of the Campine and Ardennes. But nobody stirred in Belgium, and the English quickly returned to their ships.

We have established the total failure of the counter-revolutionary movements in Switzerland, in the Rhineland, in Belgium and in the Batavian republic. This failure was due entirely to the social and economic condition of the peasants who, in general, were satisfied with the new regime. The idea of rising in revolt filled them with a great repugnance. Nor were the military conditions any more favorable to an insurrection. The presence of large numbers of French troops ready to intervene at the least disturbance helped to maintain calm.

The counter-revolutionary uprisings in the occupied countries might have been dangerous had they been synchronized with the risings that broke out in France at the same time. Without such timing, the insurrections could be put down one after the other. This was also the case with the French insurrections of 1799.

4 / The Counter-Revolutionary Movement in France

The royalist movement in France was hard hit after 18 Fructidor. The royalist agency of Paris, sometimes called the "Factory," had been destroyed. But the principal leaders of the movement were not arrested and as early as 1798 they began to set up their networks again. The so-called "Swabian Agency" headed the royalist movements in France. The men who were particularly responsible for its operation were Précy, the general who had directed the counter-revolutionary movements in Lyons of 1793; the deputies Dandré and Imbert-Colomés, who had managed to escape police searches; and General Willot, who had been arrested the day after the *coup d'état* and deported to Guiana, from which he escaped to take refuge in Germany. Below or alongside the "Swabian Agency" there existed in Paris a "Secret Royal Council," which apparently was only set up at the beginning of 1799. This "Royal Council" was not charged with the direction of royalist movements; its function, rather, was to advise Louis XVIII. It numbered eighteen members, among whom were Royer-Collard, Montesquieu and a few personages of lesser importance. The "Secret Council" was in correspondence only with Louis XVIII. It was by definition unknown to the comte d'Artois, because Louis XVIII greatly mistrusted his brother's spirit of intrigue. The main task of the "Council" was to provide intelligence reports, whereas the "Swabian Agency" was to direct the action.

The comte d'Artois also had his own council but it was formed of characters of a much more restless type, eager for action. They included people like Hyde de Neuville, whose activity was to show itself above all under the Consulate, and the Polignacs and Bourmonts, whom we shall come upon over and over again in the royalist intrigues up to 1830.

Below these agencies were the Philanthropic Institutes, which had been able to continue although their existence had been disclosed to the government by the papers of the Paris agency after 18 Fructidor. They were reorganized in 1799.

The "Swabian Agency" had commissioned abbé de Lacombe to proceed with this reorganization. With this aim, he convoked in Lyons the leaders of the institutes of the different departments of France, in particular, the departments of the Midi. But only one came to the meeting, Dupont-Constant, the founder of the Philanthropic Institute of Bordeaux and of several institutes in the departments of southwestern France. Thus Lacombe and Dupont-Constant, by themselves, re-established the Philanthropic Institutes of the Midi.

On his return journey from Lyons to Bordeaux, Dupont-Constant passed through the principal administrative centers of the department and in each one he restored the Philanthropic Institute. He stopped among other places in Nîmes, Montpellier, Narbonne, Toulouse, Cahors and Agen.

Lacombe and Dupont-Constant had laid down new instructions for the institutes. They were to avoid any partial or premature action. They were to ally themselves with the constituted authorities in order "to prevent evil"; they were not to run afoul of any party and were to try to inspire trust so as not to be prosecuted, dispersed or destroyed before the "great day." In fact, the institutes were to hold themselves in readiness for the essential tasks of the definitive insurrection, which would expel the republicans and restore Louis XVIII to his throne. This insurrection had been planned for 1799 and was to coincide with the general offensive of the coalition against the French armies.

Dupont-Constant communicated these instructions to the leaders of the Philanthropic Institutes which he had reorganized in the Midi. The institutes began to recruit an army composed of élite companies formed of the most dependable royalists, in general former soldiers, who would be armed as the recruitment progressed. We note the existence of several "élite companies," those of Médoc and Charentes, for example.

On paper, the military organization was splendid. In reality it had little substance, as we shall see. The preparation had not been extensive.

Dupont-Constant had concerned himself, in particular, with the reorganization of the two Philanthropic Institutes which were to direct the whole movement: those of Toulouse and Bordeaux. The Bordeaux institute was practically entirely reconstituted and began to function as early as 1798. Its members organized the escape from the Rochefort prisons of a number of royalists who had been arrested after the *coup d'état* of 18 Fructidor, notably the celebrated journalist Richer-Serisy. In Nivôse, Year VI (January, 1798) the royalists of the institute of Bordeaux organized a huge demonstration against General Lannes, a native of Lectoure who was passing through Bordeaux. Death threats had been made against the general and he escaped the fate that had been held out to him only by a hairsbreadth.

At the end of 1798 and the beginning of 1799 the royalists of Bordeaux attacked the republicans anew. In his *Mémoires* Dupont-Constant has written: "We fought each other unmercifully during the summer of 1798 . . ." In Toulouse, the Philanthropic Institute had been reorganized by Dupont-Constant and Dubourg de Pourquerie, who had already founded the first institute of Bordeaux. The Toulouse institute gathered together nobles, former members of the parlements, such as the first president, de Cambon, and the councillors Fraicine, Miégeville, Raynal, etc. The royalist army in Toulouse actually numbered up to 40,000 men on paper, but the sponsors were content with adherences that were often very superficial and none too sincere. Moreover, the authorities were fully aware of the situation; as early as the summer of 1798 the commissary of the Directory in the department of Haute-Garonne wrote to the government that there were "missionaries of the philanthropic society" in the region of Toulouse. These "missionaries" conducted royalist propaganda in the countryside; they crossed the Pyrenees and moved very easily across the frontier in the neighborhood of Luchon and the Aran Valley to make contact with the increasing number of émigrés in the region. The émigrés were directed by the comte de Paulo, son of a former member of the parlement of Toulouse. Outside Toulouse, two particularly important royalist centers, Muret and Saint-Lys, were noted.

At the end of 1798 and the beginning of 1799, denunciations poured into the departmental administration of Haute-Garonne. On March 5, 1799, the commissary of Haute-Garonne wrote to the minister of police: "In this department we count 15,000 men in the Philanthropic Society. . . . All the initiated have a secret sign and a password." There were other Philanthropic Institutes in the neighboring departments, notably Gers, Hautes-Pyrénées, Basses-Pyrénées and Landes. All these institutes redoubled their activity at the beginning of 1799.

The general plan was to provoke an insurrection in the southwest, in the Vendée and in Brittany—practically half or two-thirds of France—at the precise moment that the troops of the coalition reached the French frontiers, that is to say, just when the Austro-Russia Army of Italy reached the region of Nice, the Austrians, in Switzerland, reached the Jura and, in Germany, the frontier of Alsace and the Anglo-Russian contingents landed in Holland.

This moment had been fixed for the end of August of 1799. But it was quite evident that no one had been able to give the different counter-revolutionary organizations a precise date. These organizations were only more or less ready, more or less ardent, and the counter-revolutionary movements in France in 1799 took to the field successively, instead of at one time—which would have created a very serious danger and perhaps led to the fall of the republican government. This error doomed the insurrections to failure because they could be destroyed one after the other.

5 / The Insurrection in the Southwest

The most eager and important Philanthropic Institute to enter the lists was certainly that of Toulouse. Its members had been excited to a pitch of fervency and as early as the autumn of 1798 street brawls and squabbles between royalists and republicans increased without let-up. On October 6, 1799, in Escalquens, near Toulouse, a troop of royalists attacked a detachment of gendarmes; the leader was killed and there were four wounded. Liberty trees were chopped down in the canton of Castanet in May, 1799. Shots were fired at patriots, at functionaries, at purchasers of national properties. On June 26, 1799, a republican was killed in Cintegabelle. The commissary of the canton of Castanet wrote to the departmental administration: "We cannot feign to take no notice that a Vendée in miniature is being formed in our parts." And the commissary of the department of Haute-Garonne, on July 22, 1799, wrote the minister of police: "Several republicans assassinated, the properties of a greater number burned or destroyed, Liberty trees chopped down and uprooted in more than forty communes, republican institutions neglected or held in contempt in several cantons." Such was the balance sheet of the royalist action in this department.

In the department of Ariège, the situation was similar: numerous gatherings in the mountains of émigrés, refractory priests and, above all, deserters, who were forming the troops of the insurrection, were noted. In July of 1799 there was a great gathering of deserters at Auvillar; in the department of Lot-et-Garonne, a convoy which was taking away twelve deserters was attacked between Tonneins and Marmande by the insurgents and four deserters freed. A similar incident took place in Landes.

The situation was becoming alarming, but it was not unknown to the authorities. An element that contributed greatly to the failure of the royalist reaction was the staunchly republican, indeed Jacobin, character of the Toulouse authorities. Toulouse under the Directory, in contrast to many other cities of France, was, in fact, a Jacobin stronghold. The municipality and even the departmental administration was composed, almost constantly, of republicans who at times were described as "anarchists" by the Directory because they were true Jacobins. Denunciations never ceased to pour into the Ministry of Police, nor did the demands for reinforcements.

In the other departments the authorities gave similar intelligence reports. Thus General Mauco, who commanded the troops of Bayonne, on June 23, 1799, sent the Ministry of Police a list of conspirators, pinpointing the locations of arms depots and of the general staff directing the preparation of the insurrection. His source of information was his subordinate, Brigadier-General Launay, who joined the Philanthropic Institute in order to gather intelligence and who thus had been placed in possession, by the conspirators, of the plans which he hastened to communicate to his chief. The commissary of the Directory in the Gers department also sent numerous intelligence reports and the same situation obtained in Hautes-Pyrénées.

Nevertheless the Directory did not appear to be greatly upset. No doubt it took general measures, such as the vote of the law of hostages. But in order to prevent the insurrection it would have been necessary, above all, to send large numbers of troops to the troubled districts. Now, the Directory could not do this because a very threatening situation existed on the frontiers and the first priority was to oppose the invasion. The Directory counted essentially upon the National Guard to fight a possible insurrection.

What was the aim of the insurgents? To the extent that we can reconstitute their plan, they wanted, first of all, to occupy Toulouse. They counted upon capturing the arsenal, where huge quantities of munitions, powder and muskets were stored. Once these provisions were in their hands they would be able to arm their troops, composed essentially of refractories, deserters and peasants.

It seems that the order for the insurrection was given for August 10 or 12. The government of Louis XVIII, or at any rate the "Swabian Agency," estimated that the Anglo-Russian landing in Holland and the arrival of Austrian and Russian troops on the French frontiers from the Rhine to the Mediterranean would take place on that date. In reality, this date was premature because the Anglo-Russian landing in Holland did not take place until the end of August and, further, the resistance of Genoa in Italy and the tenacity of the French troops in Switzerland prevented the Austro-Russian offensive from proceeding at the pace originally planned.

But even this date of mid-August had been anticipated by the royalists of Toulouse, who rose in revolt as early as the fourth, very much before the time fixed, whereas the royalists of Bordeaux did not think of starting their insurrection until August 15. And, as we shall see, the royalists in the Vendée and Brittany considered that they would not be ready before mid-September. Thus there was a complete lack of synchronization in the dates of the insurrections and so the victory of the republicans was facilitated.

The insurgents of the region of Toulouse had as their leader the young comte de Paulo, an émigré, but one who was ready to cross the Pyrenean frontier. Since he had not been able to command the troops from the beginning of the action, the command had been given to General Rougé. Rougé, like a great number of royalist rebels, had made his first campaign with the republican troops. He was born in Santo Domingo in 1763, had fought as a volunteer in the American War of Independence, after which he had taken up residence in the Toulouse region. In 1791 he had left as a volunteer and quickly became colonel of the 7th Battalion of Haute-Garonne. He was in the campaign of the Pyrenees, from 1793 to 1795. Immediately this campaign was over he submitted his resignation for reasons that are not completely clear to us, and began to engage in politics. He evolved toward the Right and ended up as a royalist. He was one of the active members of the Philanthropic Institute of Haute-Garonne; he stood for elections in 1799 and in Haute-Garonne these elections gave the majority to the Jacobins. The moderate minority, infiltrated by royalists, seceded. Rougé followed this minority. He had hoped that the elections would be annulled as in 1798 and that he would be able to become a deputy. But his hopes were dashed. The Jacobins were validated in 1799.

At the time of the vote of the law as hostages on July 12, Rougé quit Toulouse in order to join the underground. He grouped around him refractories and deserters and concentrated them in the regions neighboring Toulouse, as well as east of the city, around Vieille-Toulouse, in Mourvilles-Basses in the château of the comte de Villèle and in the west, around Mauvezin.

At the end of July the rebels were divided into battalions and companies. These battalions and companies were composed primarily of infantry. However, some cavalry troops were formed with horses donated by the peasants. We know of this organization because of the claims presented under the Restoration by the widows of the rebels killed in combat: in their pension claims they indicated the numbers of the units of which their husbands were members.

The rebels were to march on Toulouse and at the exact moment they came in front of the city walls, the royalists of the city were to seize the gates and open them. They would then attack the arsenal. It is estimated that the total number of rebels at that time was around 10,000 men, but only a tenth of these 10,000 were armed with muskets.

Rougé gave the attack order for August 5 in the evening, and this was the essential cause of the failure, inasmuch as Rougé was ten days ahead of the date fixed by the "Swabian Agency." Thus on August 5 the rebels came from the east, moved down the Castres and Revel roads and took up a position along the canal of the Midi. The royalists within the city were to seize the gates and launch three fire rockets as a signal to the besiegers that they could enter.

But for reasons that are still not very clear, the guard at the gates that night had been considerably increased. It has been suggested that the rebels were betrayed by abbé de Montgaillard, one of the brothers of the famous comte already discussed. The abbé was supposed to have revealed the plan for the insurrection to the commissary of the Directory. It is possible, however, that the commissary of the Directory in Toulouse, who was very well informed on the activities of the Philanthropic Institute, had obtained information elsewhere. At all events, the gates remained in the hands of the National Guard and of the troops, and the rebels inside Toulouse did not dare challenge them. No doubt they feared, in view of the state of mind of the staunchly Jacobin Toulouse authorities, that they would be worsted in the confrontation. When the three fire rockets were not launched at midnight as planned, General Rougé retreated with his troops to the hills of Pech-David, which dominated the city and constituted a very strong position.

In Toulouse the administrations, immediately apprized of the insurrectionary movement, decided to sit in permanent session. Despite the success of August 5, the news was not good. They learned that the rebels of Gers were marching toward the city, that Muret was in the hands of the insurrection and Saint-Lys had been captured. At that time the Toulouse garrison consisted only of thirty light cavalry, the gendarmerie, and the National Guard, which was not very reliable since it included royalists as well as republicans.

Nevertheless a defense committee was instantly formed, composed ex-

clusively of the most authentic Jacobins. On the basis of the law of
hostages, which had been voted several weeks earlier, the committee
decreed that all suspects were to be placed under arrest.

On August 6 and 7 the insurrection grew without pause in the environs
of Toulouse. Communications between Toulouse and Saint-Gaudens,
Castelnaudary, Revel and Auch were completely cut. On August 7
Toulouse could communicate only with Montauban, and this with great
difficulty. On August 7 a new attempt was made by the royalists inside
Toulouse to seize the guard post of the place du Salin, but this effort likewise was a fiasco. On the evening of August 7 from the tower of the
chapel of the Jacobins, the white flags of the royalists could be seen flutter-
ing over most of the villages surrounding Toulouse. In Ariège the rebels
took over the small town of Saverdun and threatened the Protestants, who
were numerous there.

But the defense committee decided to take the offensive. On August 7
and 8 the Toulousians received reinforcements coming from Tarn and
Lot, from Cahors, Montauban and Albi. On August 8 in the afternoon
the Toulouse troops, reinforced by artillery which gave them a great
superiority over the insurgents—who had none—pulled out of the city and
mounted the attack on Pech-David. But the insurgents turned towards the
Garonne, threatening to cut off the Toulousians and prevent their re-entry
into the city. The assault therefore was soon stopped and the Toulousian
troops fell back in disorder towards the Saint-Michel gate. Nevertheless
the authorities decreed a new attack for the next day, August 9. It was
absolutely necessary to eliminate the threat that hung over Toulouse as
quickly as possible. This time a plan was drawn up by General Aubugeois,
who took over command of all the troops assembled in Toulouse. Instead
of climbing directly up Pech-David Hill, these troops went around
Pouvourville and attacked the rebels who bordered the plateau of the side
nearest Toulouse from the rear. The rebels were hurled back toward the
Garonne, which they could cross only by swimming; about 200 were
killed, while the Toulousian troops suffered only 2 wounded. Pech-David
Hill thenceforth was in the hands of the republicans and Toulouse could
breathe again. The insurrection continued in the countryside, but the
threat which had hung over the city had been removed.

In Bordeaux the conspirators were not ready on August 5. However,
when news was learned of the Toulousian insurrection, some incidents of
a very sporadic character took place. Patriots were attacked on the streets

at five o'clock in the evening. On August 6 a band of thirty *muscadins* invaded the house of a republican officer and looted it, shouting death threats; during the night the streets were thronged with royalists shouting: "Down with the Jacobins!" The central bureau, which directed the administration of the city of Bordeaux, was attacked and one person on the royalist side was killed.

The garrison was placed on a combat footing, military patrols combed the city and numerous royalists were arrested. Furthermore, on the same day in Paris the Directory, following the information which it had received, ordered its commissary in the Gironde to arrest twenty-six notorious royalists. Most of these were able to flee; only one was imprisoned.

On August 7 there was also an attempt at insurrection in the department of Landes to shouts of "Long Live the King!" In Basses-Pyrénées the disturbance was concentrated in Nay and Gau particularly. In Lot-et-Garonne royalist bands marched on Agen, but they were not strong enough to capture the town.

On August 10, although Toulouse had extricated itself from immediate danger and the insurrection was not able to develop either in Bordeaux or Dax, the situation was still extremely tense. The department of Gers, save for the town of Auch, was practically in the hands of the insurgents, who had captured the towns of Lombez and of Isle-Jourdain. That part of the department of Lot nearest to Haute-Garonne had revolted. In Ariège, the mountains and even the neighboring countryside of Pamiers were held by the royalists.

Scattered efforts were made almost everywhere to fight the insurrection. In Gers, the adjutant-general Petit-Pressigny mustered his troops and the national guards, who were eager to join battle, and succeeded in capturing Gimont; communications between Auch and Toulouse were almost reestablished since the direct road was now cut only at Isle-Jourdain.

In Haute-Garonne, forces coming from Tarn retook Revel and Saint-Félix-Lauraguais; during the different clashes which took place on this occasion, the royalists lost about 100 men. In the Aude, the villages held by the royalists on the edge of Haute-Garonne were retaken by the troops come from Narbonne and Carcassonne. In the Ariège the national guards of Foix and of Pamiers, placed in readiness, took possession of the nearest villages where the royalists had raised the white flag. There they found copies of the proclamations issued by the Russian General Suvorov.

The situation, therefore, was improving little by little. On August 11, General Aubugeois decided to re-establish communications between Toulouse and Auch by launching an offensive against Isle-Jourdain. In the course of this offensive the villages situated along the route were taken by assault and numerous dwellings devastated. There were many dead: sixty inhabitants of Colomiers are supposed to have been executed by firing squads; eighty others killed. All the houses of Colomiers, without distinction, were said to have been looted. Isle-Jourdain was taken by storm. The rebels there lost 400 killed and 80 prisoners, while the republicans supposedly suffered only one fatality. The town was pillaged and many inhabitants massacred; public functionaries who had been imprisoned by the rebels were freed, to be replaced by the royalists. On August 12 at Gimont the troops of Toulouse effected their junction with a column from Auch.

At this point General Aubugeois decided to make a flank attack in an easterly direction and march from Gimont on Muret, one of the principal royalist centers of the region. On August 13, he had come before Muret, but his troops were tired. He decided to wait a day before assaulting the town which seemed to be strongly held by the royalists, and asked for reinforcements from Toulouse.

In Toulouse the number of troops was constantly increasing, the neighboring departments of Tarn and Lot having dispatched all they could muster in both soldiers and weapons. Substantial forces marched on Muret by the road extending along the river Garonne. Muret seemed to be caught between two fires and the insurgents evacuated the town on August 14.

Discord seems to have arisen among the rebels in the wake of these repeated failures. The comte de Paulo, who had joined them, maintained the arrogance and contempt towards commoners which had often been the characteristic attitude of the nobility under the Old Regime. He got along poorly with General Rougé.

The insurgents decided to retreat towards Saint-Gaudens, in the direction of the Pyrenees, so that in the event of defeat they could cross the Spanish frontier. In the course of this movement, the royalists captured the town of Carbonne, where they killed 68 republicans and took 200 prisoners.

Thereafter the insurgents continued towards Saint-Gaudens. The few republican troops stationed there considered that they could not hold the city, and fell back. The insurgents, now in control of Saint-Gaudens, also captured Montréjeau. Thus they held the outlets of the route to Spain by way of the Aran Valley and in the event of defeat, they expected to be able to seek refuge easily on the other side of the Pyrenees.

In Toulouse a general attack was organized against the insurgents; the authorities wanted to cut off their retreats towards Spain. On August 20 three columns, commanded by General Commes, the adjutant-general Barbot, and Commandant Viçose, marched on Montréjeau by three different routes. The Barbot column made a detour towards the south in order to cut off the retreat of the insurgents. Then the assault was launched against Montréjeau and the royalist army completely destroyed. The casualties were considerable and authors vary in their estimates: 1,000–2,000 dead, more than 1,000 prisoners, perhaps even 2,000. The insurgents who were able to escape the disaster of Montréjeau were reduced to very small bands which crossed the border into Spain.

The republican victory at Montréjeau put an end to the most dangerous aspect of the insurrection. Nevertheless a few royalist bands still kept the field in the department of Gers and even in Haute-Garonne; these were defeated on August 18 at Baumont-de-Lomagne and on August 22 in Gers. By August 25, all danger was eliminated. General Commes, who had been placed at the head of all the troops of the Toulouse region, demanded that the Spanish government, an ally of France, deliver into his hands all the royalists who had crossed the Pyrenees or, at least, their leaders. And he sent the governor of the Aran Valley a list of 44 names, including those of Paulo and Rougé. The governor replied that he had been able to arrest only a very few royalists and, finally, he surrendered only ten completely unknown men. In the following weeks and months, however, more than 300 insurgents were arrested along the frontier while attempting to return home. In all the insurrection seems to have resulted in at least 4,000 dead among the royalists, while the number of republican victims, except at Carbonne, was relatively small and does not seem to have gone much beyond 100.

The repression was relatively mild. It was marked first of all by placing in a state of siege all the regions which had revolted, and by numerous arrests. But the trials moved slowly; in Toulouse there were still more than 2,000 royalists in the city prisons in October. Many were freed without trial by order of the Directory; in fact in the course of the summer of 1799, the Directory had evolved in a different political direction. After first drawing close to the Jacobins, it later became fearful of being overwhelmed by them, and at the demand of the director Sieyès, Fouché, the minister of police, had closed the Manège Club in Paris. Fouché and Sieyès feared to strengthen the Jacobins of Toulouse by imparting an overly conspicuous character to the repression of the royalist movement. This is why they gave the order to free without trial all farmers who could prove that they had participated in the insurrection only under duress. Four thousand of the 6,000 insurgents arrested were freed; among these "farmers" figured large landowners such as the comte de Villèle. Those who remained in prison were held for court-martials, which passed sentence on them only after slow and long-drawn-out proceedings. Before 18 Brumaire, only eleven accused had been sentenced to death and executed. After 18 Brumaire amnesties followed and finally the military tribunals ceased their activity and most of their suspects were freed. Even returned émigrés who had been captured bearing arms and who should have been shot upon simple confirmation of their identity by virtue of the law on émigrés still in effect were freed. Refractory priests who had returned and been arrested were also freed without molestation. Some among them, however, were condemned to deportation and transferred to the island of Oléron.

What were the reasons for the failure of this insurrection? There are many. First of all, its premature date and the lack of coordination with other insurrections being prepared in France. The situation would have been different if the insurrections in Toulouse and Bordeaux had broken out on the same day. To this we must add the dissensions among the royalists and especially between nobles and commoners. General Rougé and the comte de Paulo did not get along. Finally, the tactic adopted, that of the "great war," should have been rejected following the examples of the Vendée or even of Calabria. In all the preceding insurrections it had been proved that to wage a "great war" with poorly armed peasants was tantamount to failure. What might have succeeded was guerrilla warfare, as practiced by the *chouans* in Brittany where, furthermore, the open terrain did not lend itself to such tactics. But to try to capture a city like Toulouse with several thousand insurgent peasants was to invite defeat. The sparsely wooded Garonne Valley was not suitable for guerrilla warfare; the terrain favored the republicans more than the royalists. To attack Toulouse was, moreover, to compound the difficulties because among French provincial cities at that time Toulouse was the most staunchly Jacobin, the most anti-royalist, the city that was to put up the fiercest resistance.

6 / The Insurrections in the West

The situation could have been even more serious, not only if the insurrection in Toulouse had synchronized with that in Bordeaux but if it had been linked with that in the west. The "Swabian Agency" and the council of the comte d'Artois had counted on this liaison: the insurrection in the southwest was supposed to have been linked up, by means of a revolt of the Charente departments, with the resumption of the war in the Vendée and in Brittany.

In the department of Charente-Inférieure, the rumor was circulating that the insurrection would break out on St. Bartholomew's Day, August 24. Shots had been fired at night in the countryside and all the republicans were on the alert. Calm had not been restored in the west after the pacifications which had followed Quiberon. The leaders, of course, had surrendered, but the agitation had continued to some extent everywhere —in the Vendée, in Brittany, and even in Perche, Maine and Normandy. This agitation was marked by attacks on functionaries traveling alone and also on purchasers of national properties; it even took the form of pure and simple brigandage. It was at this time that bands of stokers (*chauffeurs*) originated, whose members burned the feet of their victims in order to force them to reveal the hiding place for their valuables. The bourgeoisie had no patience with this type of agitation. Thus in 1799 the towns of the west were much more republican than they had been in 1793 and 1794. Yet the Directory, had done everything to prevent the rekindling of the insurrection. When the Jourdan-Delbrel conscription law had been voted, it decided to exempt, provisionally, the departments of the western region. But the rumor was spread that the exemption would soon be abolished and many young men who risked being subject to military service fled.

At the request of the princes, the leaders of the *chouannerie* prepared to resume the general insurrection: Georges Cadoudal in the Morbihan; Le Gris-Duval in the Côtes-du-Nord; Bourmont in Perche; and Frotté in Normandy.

The order to launch the insurrection was fixed in the departments of the west, as in the Midi, for mid-August of 1799. But the royalists of these departments were not ready. It was only in the middle of September, 1799, that 200 royalist leaders, drawn from all the departments of the west, met at the château of Jonchère and unanimously decided upon "a levy of arms and a general and simultaneous action in order to remind people of the idea of the existence of the royalist party." This meeting took place too late, one month after the failure of the insurrection in the southwest, and at a time when the peril on the frontiers was on the wane: the Anglo-Russian forces had been thrown back by General Brune in Holland and forced to surrender on October 18, 1799. The Austro-Russians had been halted in Switzerland by Masséna, who scored the victory of Zurich over them on September 26 and 27. Finally, Bonaparte himself was returning to France; on October 9 he landed in the little French Mediterranean port of Fréjus.

Thus the insurrection of the west had few chances of success. Nevertheless, it broke out and was initially marked by successful attacks against some towns: La Roche-Bernard and Redon were occupied for several hours by the *chouans*. The big city of Le Mans itself was taken by Bourmont on October 14, 1799, and occupied for four days. The *chouans* seized 200 muskets and 6 cannon; the danger seemed almost as grave as in 1793. Nantes was also occupied for several hours, on the night of October 20/21. Saint-Brieuc fell into the hands of the *chouans* during the night of October 25/26. Their leader, Mercier-La Vendée, opened the prisons, freed the royalists and seized a number of patriots who were put to death —a former deputy of the Constituent Assembly figured notably among the republicans killed. Vannes was attacked by Cadoudal, but the republicans there put up a victorious resistance.

Thus between October 15 and October 30, the *chouans* rolled up impressive initial successes. But the counter-thrust was organized very quickly by General Hédouville, who received the supreme command of the republican troops and established his headquarters in Angers. Hédouville had already served in the west under Hoche and was acquainted with methods of fighting the *chouans*. Thus he formed mobile columns which rapidly hunted down the rebels. The column commanded by General Travot crossed the Vendée and captured several large bands.

The *coup d'état* of 18 Brumaire took place at a time when the republican counter-thrust was beginning to achieve successes. The rebels were disconcerted and the *coup d'état* caused a slowing down of their operations. A few royalist leaders thought that Bonaparte perhaps intended to restore Louis XVIII. Abbé Bernier, who was in direct contact with the insurgents of the west, wrote at the end of November: "I believe that Bonaparte and Monk are very much alike." Henceforth abbé Bernier abandoned the royalist insurgents in order to effect a rapprochement with Bonaparte.

The insurrection declined during December of that year and, by

degrees, died out by itself. Already on November 24, 1799, General Hédouville in a proclamation agreed to by Bonaparte had announced the suspension of hostilities. On December 2 a truce was signed with several royalist
leaders, in the château of Angrie, near Angers. The majority of royalist
leaders showed themselves favorable to peace. On December 19 a general
armistice was proclaimed by General Hédouville and abbé Bernier moved
definitively over to the consular government.

On January 18 a royalist, d'Autichamp, who commanded the forces of
the Vendée and the left bank of the Loire, signed the peace for all the
troops under his orders. Two days later, on January 20, Chatillon concluded the peace for Maine and Anjou. Thus the pacification spread. It
was not general, of course, because there were still armed bands in Brittany
and even in the Vendée, but it became increasingly difficult for them to
hold the field. Moreover Bonaparte ordered General Brune, after the great
success he had scored over the Anglo-Russian forces, to assume command
of the French troops of the west and to transfer to this region a part of the
forces which had been under his orders in Holland. Thus the republican
troops constantly increased in strength and resistance became difficult.

On February 4, Bourmont surrendered; on February 14 it was the turn
of Cadoudal to surrender, albeit in a forced manner. Frotté, the last to
scour the countryside, was arrested on February 15 with several of his
accomplices. He was immediately brought before a court-martial which
sentenced him to death, and he was executed on the eighteenth.

Unquestionably the counter-revolutionary movement was not dead. It
continued. Bonaparte's coming to power after the *coup d'état* of 18
Brumaire had not arrested it completely. But it had lost much of its driving
force and was to take another form—that of plots, conspiracies hatched
against the very person of Bonaparte.

CHAPTER XVIII

The Successes and Failures of the Counter-Revolution
Under the Consulate

At the end of 1799 the counter-revolution triumphed in Italy, whereas in France it abated. The failure of the insurrections of 1799 and the *coup d'état* of 18 Brumaire seem to have disoriented the French counter-revolutionaries.

1 / The Triumphant Counter-Revolution:
The "Thirteen Months"

By the end of 1799 the Austrians were in control of all Italy except for Genoa and several points on the Ligurian Riviera where French troops still resisted. Indeed, they were to occupy the greater part of this region for thirteen months, during which time reaction developed in Italy. This enables us to glimpse what might have happened in France if the royalists had won similar successes there. However, this counter-revolutionary activity did not present the same features in the different regions of Italy.

In Lombardy, the Austrians settled down again as overlords, as they had been before 1796. In Piedmont, in Tuscany, in the Papal States, the Austrians wielded the preponderant influence, whereas before 1796 they ruled only through an interposed authority. Austrian troops did not penetrate the Kingdom of Naples; the reaction there was primarily the work of the Bourbon government.

The Austrians occupied all Lombardy as early as May, 1799. In Milan they issued proclamations promising peace, justice, order and the re-establishment of religion. The patriots, Lombard Jacobins, emigrated to Switzerland or France by way of Piedmont if they could. But only a minority were able to leave. The majority of the inhabitants of Lombardy acclaimed the Austrians and Russians with shouts of "Long live the Emperor! Long live Religion!" When the Austrians and Russians entered Milan, the population showered the generals with flowers; *Te Deums* were celebrated in the churches. The hunt for Jacobins began several days after the Austro-Russian military authorities had established their headquarters. Most of those who had not left were arrested; Liberty trees were cut down and numerous demonstrations took place in honor of the victors, with poems of all sorts, lapidary inscriptions, etc., composed to honor them.

It must be noted, however, that Austria did not re-establish the Old Regime. She instituted a provisional regime. The Old Regime, in fact, would have signified the separation of Lombardy, which alone was Austrian before 1796, and of Emilia, which belonged to the Pope. The Austrian government cherished the hope of preserving Emilia and Lombardy under its authority and for this reason it instituted a provisional government, composed exclusively of nobles and presided over by an imperial commissioner, count Cocastelli. This government was invested with almost unlimited powers, and took over direction of the reaction. It closed the University of Pavia, guilty of having espoused liberal ideas. It made religious practices, attendance at Sunday Mass, obligatory and re-established the feudal courts of justice which had been abolished. It even went so far as to prohibit haircuts "à la Brutus," viewed as a "sign of libertinism and perfidy." Allegedly, it even impeached in the supreme court a blackbird guilty of whistling "*ça ira*"! The imprisoned Jacobins were brought before the courts of justice on charges of high treason. All the members of the former government of the Cisalpine republic were likewise declared guilty of the same charge. As for the émigrés, their properties were confiscated, but here the Austrian government merely imitated the measures taken by the republican governments. In all, about 800 Jacobins were arrested, and nearly all of them deported to Austria and interned at Sebnitz. Thirteen were sentenced to be flogged in the public square; others were employed on public works, notably digging canals in Hungary. Only a small number were allowed to return to Lombardy at the conclusion of the Peace of Lunéville, in 1802. Censorship was reinstated. All republican books were burned in the public square, Bossuet's *Oeuvres complètes* figuring among them. Civil and political rights were withdrawn from Jews and Protestants, and the *fidei commissa* restored. On the other hand, the new taxes were maintained and even greatly increased. Whereas under the Cisalpine republic, the tax burden had been assessed at 7 lire per inhabitant it rose to 30 lire a head during the "thirteen months." All these measures but above all the increase in taxes rapidly made the Austrians unpopular in Lombardy. After four or five months, the great mass of the Lombard population had become more hostile to the Austrians than it had been to the French in 1799.

All laws voted by the Cisalpine republic were abrogated, all functionaries appointed by the Cisalpine government removed. The sale of national properties was annulled and the properties restored to their former owners. This measure affected a great number of Austrophiles who had bought such properties and the loss of their acquisitions rapidly turned them against Austria. The properties of the Church, however, were not returned; they became the property of the State—Josephism was still powerful in Austria.

The Austro-Russian army (later the Austrian army alone) lived in Lombardy as had the French army before it, that is, at the expense of the country, which it weighed down under war contributions and requisitions. The requisitions were more or less legal; but the Russians, in particular, looted the country. Cossacks dogged persons they met in the countryside and snatched their watches, an experience that remained strongly imprinted in the memory of the populace of northern Italy. These lootings probably impelled the Austrian government to request Suvorov to transfer his army to Switzerland in place of the Austrian army which was deployed there. The double movement enabled General Masséna to win the victory of Zurich but the change of the army of occupation did not restore good relations between soldiers and populace. As early as the beginning of 1800, bands of peasants took to the field, actively opposing the requisitions and war contributions levied by the Austrian army.

In Piedmont, there was a reasonable expectation that the king of Sardinia, who had ruled this country before 1798 and who, after being driven from his throne by the French, had taken refuge on the island, would return. The Austrians formally opposed this, however; the hereditary prince, the duke of Aosta, son of King Victor Emmanuel, had left Sardinia at news of the Austro-Russian victories and landed in mainland Italy, but the Austrian commissioner at Turin forbade him to return to the capital.

In Piedmont, as in Lombardy, counter-revolution was not synonymous with the restoration intact of the Old Regime. The Austrians opposed the return of the king to Turin because they cherished unmistakable hidden ambitions regarding Piedmont. Perhaps they hoped to extend their domination to all northern Italy and one day to join Piedmont to Lombardy, Emilia and Venetia under their authority.

Nevertheless, counter-revolutionary measures followed one upon the other in Piedmont, as in Lombardy. All the Jacobins who had not been able to escape were arrested. Priests who had adhered more or less overtly to the republic were imprisoned; many were in this position because a mere suspicion of "Jansenism" was enough to lead to arrest. Jews, naturally, lost their civil and political rights in Piedmont as in Lombardy. The properties of fugitives were confiscated, and fugitives were numerous because it was relatively easy to cross the Alpine mountain passes into France. In his memoirs the patriot Bongioanni tells how he crossed the Traversette Pass at a height of more than 9,850 feet in the region of Mount Viso in order to reach Dauphiné. These escapes show that there were true republicans among the populace in northern Italy who preferred exile to submission.

In Liguria, the Austrians' position was much less comfortable. The remnants of the French Army of Italy had been concentrated in Genoa. Land communications between Genoa and France were maintained up to January of 1800; they were cut only after this date and the Riviera occupied by Austrian troops. Then the vice around Genoa was drawn all the tighter, but the Austrians were not able to capture the city until June 7, 1800, seven days before the defeat they suffered not far from there at Marengo. The Austrian occupation of Genoa therefore lasted only a very short time and the counter-revolution could not prevail in Liguria.

In Tuscany, from May–June of 1799 onwards, the country was dominated by the "Sanfedists" and by "Viva Maria" bands, which chopped down Liberty trees, looted the houses of Jacobins and destroyed republican emblems. Finally, a provisional government was formed, which declared that it was acting in the name of the grand duke. But it was the Austrians, in fact, who directed this provisional government. The former senate of Florence was not reconstituted until July of 1799. At that time it decreed all kinds of counter-revolutionary measures similar to those the Austrians had taken in Lombardy and in Piedmont, notably the prohibition of short haircuts, viewed as a sign of republicanism. Patriots were arrested, hounded and imprisoned, sometimes massacred. Among the persons arrested, we must note the bishop of Pistoia, Scipion de Ricci, who had drawn attention to himself before the Revolution by his Jansenist views. On December 15, 1799, Austrian troops entered Tuscany and thenceforth the Austrians governed the country like Lombardy or Piedmont.

The situation in the Papal States was very similar to that in Tuscany. Bands of "Sanfedists" and "Viva Marias" roamed the countryside. The French garrison in Rome resisted up to midsummer of 1799, when it capitulated on condition that it could withdraw to France, accompanied by the patriots who chose to follow it. This time, unlike what had happened in Naples, this clause of the convention was observed. The French garrison from Rome landed in Marseilles, accompanied by several notable Jacobins.

A provisional government was established in Rome after the capitulation of the French garrison and took counter-revolutionary measures similar to those that had been in effect in the other regions of the peninsula. The five notaries who had recorded the proclamation of the Roman republic were arrested and exiled in perpetuity; two of the consuls of the Roman republic were arrested, imprisoned, paraded through the streets on asses and pummeled by the mob.

The last city of the Papal States to surrender was Ancona, where General Monnier put up a stiff resistance. The reaction was general after the capitulation of Ancona. In the Papal States, however, no regular government was established before the summer of 1800. In fact Pope Pius VI had been deported by the French to Siena, then to Florence, and when the Austrians resumed the war he was transported to Valence in the Rhône Valley, where he died on August 19, 1799. So the throne of St. Peter was vacant and it was necessary to convoke a conclave. In his last testament Pius VI had made provisions for the eventuality of his death in imprisonment and had expressed the wish that the conclave be held in a city situated on territory occupied by troops faithful to the Catholic religion. The Austrian government, which directed the coalition on the continent, decreed that the conclave would take place in Venice; it did not include all the cardinals because many of them found it impossible to get there. This was a very lengthy conclave, marked by sharp struggles between the different parties. Canon Leflon, in his recent book on Pius VII, has analyzed the evolution of this conclave minutely and with great finesse.* Two principal parties were opposed to each other: the Austrian party, which supposedly favored the election of a Pope devoted to the Haps-

---

* See Bibliographical Notes to this chapter—Trans.

burgs, and the Spanish party, which was hostile to it. As the government of the Consulate affirmed itself in France, the Spanish party increasingly inclined towards the prelates who were not too opposed to the Revolution. On the other hand, the Austrian government made no secret of its desire to annex all Emilia to Lombardy whereas the Spanish government, in its own name and—to the extent that it was the interpreter of the wishes of the consular government—in the name of France, opposed this possible annexation. Finally, through its representatives in Venice, Monseigneur Despuig, it ended up by supporting the candidacy of Cardinal Chiaramonti. At first Austria had been hostile to the election of Chiaramonti because, as a native of Cesena and bishop of Imola, he had numerous connections in Emilia and his opposition to the annexation of this province to Austria was predictable. Moreover, the cardinal had never taken an anti-Jacobin attitude during the period of the Cisalpine republic and on Christmas, 1797, he had even delivered a homily in which he tried to show that democracy was not incompatible with the principles of the Gospel.

The Austrian government, however, did not persist in its hostility to the election of Chiaramonti because otherwise the conclave risked remaining in session for ever. In the end it did not use its right of veto, but merely made known its bad humor. Chiaramonti was elected on March 14, 1800. The new Pope encountered all kinds of difficulties when he set out for Rome: the Austrian authorities did not lift a finger to facilitate his journey; he had to reach the Papal States by sea. Chiaramonti, now Pius VII, arrived in Rome only to learn of the victory at Marengo which completely reversed the situation in Italy. As a result, the Austrians had to evacuate the greater part of northern Italy and all of central Italy. In this region this marked the end of the reaction of the "thirteen months."

In the Kingdom of Naples, however, the reaction lasted until 1805, where it raged with extreme violence. Neapolitan patriots had been arrested en masse after the entry of the "Sanfedists" into the capital. Admiral Nelson, as we know, at the instance of Queen Marie-Caroline had nullified the capitulation convention signed by Cardinal Ruffo and the French troops, a capitulation which authorized the patriots to embark with the French to be transported to France. Instead, the patriots were brought before special tribunals and more than a hundred sentenced to death. Some illustrious people figured among these victims: Admiral Caracciolo, for example, who belonged to a great Neapolitan family, was hung from the main yard of his ship. Among the condemned sentenced to death, Mario Pagano, Ignacio Ciaia, Vincenzo Russo, Luisa Sanfelice and Eleonora

Fonseca-Pimentel, all estimable writers, should be mentioned. Numerous priests, several bishops and many nobles were also executed.

Several thousand Jacobins were imprisoned and many died of the ill-treatment meted out to them in their prisons. The reaction wiped out the Neapolitan intelligentsia: the cultured class which had made Naples the capital of the Enlightenment at the end of the eighteenth century disappeared almost entirely during the 1799 reaction. This massive massacre of the most cultivated and intelligent segment of the Neapolitan populace discredited the Bourbon dynasty of Naples. Thenceforth, it became odious to liberals of all Italy, for whom it symbolized the counter-revolution.

2 / The Failure of the Counter-Revolution in France

While in Italy the counter-revolution triumphed, in France it was arrested at one stroke. The 18 Brumaire disoriented the French royalists. Many thought that the events that had been set off in England after the death of Cromwell would now be repeated in France, that Bonaparte would prove to be the "Monk" of the French republic and restore Louis XVIII.

Some royalists, while discarding the hypothesis of a Restoration of Louis XVIII by Bonaparte, hoped that the first consul would be able to place Louis-Philippe d'Orléans on the throne of France. But Louis-Philippe, who seems to have been consulted at this time, was in the United States and showed no great eagerness to ascend the throne with Bonaparte's aid. On the contrary, he wrote to the claimant to the throne and tried to effect a rapprochement with the Bourbons.

Some French royalists felt that there was no need to precipitate matters, that Bonaparte might well restore the Bourbons but only later, when Louis XVIII had evolved and agreed to preserve on his return the principal conquests of the Revolution.

Finally, another category of royalists thought that Bonaparte would not restore the monarchy but that, all things considered, Bonaparte's regime was preferable to the republic and that they could rally to it provisionally while waiting for something better. As they put it: "One does not love Bonaparte, one prefers him," an attitude that was shared by a great many émigrés who had re-entered France at the beginning of 1800. This was the position of Chateaubriand, for example, who had returned at the advice of his friend Fontanes. The legislation on émigrés had not been abolished but it was no longer applied.

Louis XVIII also fancied that Bonaparte could play the role of "Monk," and as early as the beginning of 1800 he thought of writing the first consul to ask him to what extent he would be able to facilitate his Restoration. At that time a cartoon was making the rounds. It showed Bonaparte taking a coat smeared with a large bloodspot marked 13 Vendémiaire to a cleaner; the cleaner says to the consul handing him the coat: "I will remove it, but for no less than a Louis."

The royalists intervened with Josephine, Bonaparte's consort; with the consul Lebrun, who had been secretary to Maupeou, minister of finances to the monarchy; and with Talleyrand, in order that they might advise Bonaparte to recall Louis XVIII. They made known certain verbal promises of Louis XVIII. Bonaparte would be appointed Lord High Constable, Talleyrand receive a passport so that he could live abroad, Lebrun an important post. Finally, Louis XVIII decided to send a letter to Lebrun and another to Bonaparte. He wrote them on February 20, 1800. The letter to Lebrun includes these words: "Whatever their apparent conduct may be, men such as you, Monsieur, never inspire misgiving. You have accepted an eminent position and I am grateful to you. . . . Save France from her own passions and you will have fulfilled my heart's desire. Restore her King to her and future generations will bless your memory."

To Bonaparte personally Louis XVIII declares:

No, the victor of Lodi, of Castiglione, of Arcoli, the conqueror of Italy and of Egypt, cannot prefer a vain celebrity to glory. However, you are losing precious time; we can assure the tranquility of France. I say we because I need Bonaparte and because he could not do it without me. General, Europe is watching you, glory awaits you and I am impatient to give peace to my people.

Bonaparte received this letter but was in no hurry to reply. He declared to his entourage that he was in no way inclined to restore the monarchy. To Roederer, particularly, who had figured among the "monarchicals" and been one of his confidants at this epoch, he said: "The French can be governed only by me. I am persuaded that nobody beside myself, whether it be Louis XVIII or Louis XIV, would be able to govern France at this moment."

Meanwhile, he prepared the campaign against Austria. The successful negotiation of the Great St. Bernard Pass and the victory at Marengo, which again eliminated the Austrians from northern Italy, consolidated the consular regime in France.

Only after these events did Bonaparte decide to reply to Louis XVIII. On September 7, 1800, he wrote him as follows:

> I have received your letter, Monsieur. I thank you for the courteous things you say to me. You must not hope for your return to France; you would have to walk over one hundred thousand corpses. Sacrifice your interest to the peace and happiness of France; history will not overlook you. I am not insensible to the misfortunes of your family, and I shall contribute with pleasure to the sweetness and tranquility of your retirement.

It was an abrupt, definitive refusal. Nevertheless, Louis XVIII continued to entertain illusions, still believing that he could obtain an about-face and a Restoration from Bonaparte.

But events ran their course. The French armies continued to win victories throughout continental Europe, and at last peace was signed with Austria at Lunéville, then at Amiens with England, while religious pacification was simultaneously established as a result of the Concordat concluded between Bonaparte and Pius VII.

After all these events the entourage of Louis XVIII felt that nothing more could be done, that henceforth it was necessary to resign themselves to awaiting "The hour marked by Providence."

Bonaparte meanwhile saw his power constantly grow. The Consulate was transformed into a lifelong post. At that time Bonaparte aspired to obtain from Louis XVIII a formal renunciation of any claim to the throne. After his accession to the lifelong Consulate, he already envisioned the transformation of this dignity into that of emperor of the French. He would have liked to be in possession of Louis XVIII's abdication in order to rule over France without difficulty and without mental reservations. Bonaparte acted through the mediation of Prussia which, at that time, was on good terms with France. The king of Prussia commissioned President von Meyer, who was in Warsaw at the time, to enter into contact with Louis XVIII, who was staying there too. Bonaparte also asked the czar to put pressure on the claimant. The czar, in fact, gave a pension to Louis XVIII, who had no other means of existence; Bonaparte thought that the threat of withdrawal of this pension could induce the claimant to sign the abdication. Accordingly, von Meyer was charged to point out to the comte de Lille—as Louis XVIII was called—

that the government which desires to deal with the Bourbons is not that which has despoiled them . . . that far from having overthrown the throne, Bonaparte has avenged it, that all the parties which have desolated France have disappeared, that France is a wholly new regime, and that it is necessary that the Bourbons act quickly while their resolutions still carry some weight in the eyes of the French government.

On February 28, 1803, Louis XVIII made known his reply:

> I do not confuse Bonaparte with any of those who have preceded him. I esteem his worth, his military talents, I am grateful to him for some acts of administration, because the good one does to my people will always be dear to me. But he deceives himself if he thinks to persuade me to compromise my rights. On the contrary, he would establish them himself, could they be disputed, by the step he is taking at this very moment.

He continued by recalling his declarations of Hamm and of Verona, to which he stated that he would always remain loyal. Thus Bonaparte's move turned out to be a huge blunder. It led to the consolidation of Louis XVIII's position and to the confirmation of his claims to the throne of France. Louis XVIII's reply was not only sent to France but transmitted to all the courts of Europe. The princes of the blood royal approved it. The letter marked the definitive, total breakdown of all negotiations between Bonaparte and Louis XVIII.

The counter-revolution, therefore, continued and Louis XVIII remained the leader of the counter-revolutionary movement in France. However, the variations in Louis XVIII's attitude, the hopes that at one time had been placed in the possibility of a Restoration effected by Bonaparte, delivered a very hard blow to the counter-revolutionary movement inside France. The *chouannerie* disappeared almost totally. At the end of 1799 and the beginning of 1800, most of the leaders had ended up by signing the pacification convention. One of them, d'Andigné, went off to Paris to confer with an agent of the Bourbons, Hyde de Neuville, who was returning from England. D'Andigné and Hyde de Neuville wanted to decide the orientation thenceforth to be given to the *chouannerie* movement. They met and agreed that they should first have an interview with Bonaparte before taking a resolution. The interview took place on December 26, 1799. Bonaparte told the *chouan* leaders: "The Bourbons no longer have a chance. You have done everything you ought to have for them, you are good men, ally yourselves with the side of glory; yes, come under my banner, my government will be that of youth and spirit." And in a further elaboration, Bonaparte dwelt on the cowardice of the Bourbons, who had never set foot on the mainland to head the revolts organized in their name. He also affirmed his desire to protect the Catholic religion. "I too want good priests," he said to d'Andigné and Hyde de Neuville. "It is not that we nobles have much religion, but it is necessary for the people, and I shall re-establish it."

After this conversation, d'Andigné and Hyde de Neuville returned to Brittany and the Vendée and advised the leaders of the *chouannerie* to negotiate, which practically all of them proceeded to do. Cadoudal and Bourmont, the most reluctant, also ended up by concluding a capitulation; they agreed to come to Paris and meet there with Bonaparte. The first consul failed to convince them. Cadoudal left the interview more hostile to Bonaparte than ever, although Bonaparte had offered him the rank of division general, which he refused. Bourmont was more hesitant. Later he was to rally to Bonaparte and was to become one of the generals of the Empire, only to betray him on the eve of Waterloo.

Thus the *chouannerie* had practically vanished around the time of Marengo. But not completely. For if the great majority of the *chouans* acted out of political conviction, some of them, in the course of eight years of struggle, had ended up by practicing brigandage pure and simple. Even after the submission of the political leaders the agitation continued in the western regions. The bands of "stokers" succeeded those of *chouans*. But when it was a question of resuming the struggle in 1804, it was easy to give a political character to the disturbances in the west. As early as 1803, the police arrested some men who tried to reconstitute the *chouannerie*: a certain Lebourgeois was apprehended in Rouen; he was the bearer of messages sent by the princes, who had taken refuge in England. In these dispatches, they counseled the reconstitution of armed bands. Another *chouan*, named Picot, was also arrested upon his return from England. His papers proved that his mission was to set off an insurrection in the west of France. Both were imprisoned and were not even tried, but remained in prison until the end of the Empire, in 1814. Their arrests show the vigilance of the police. The four years of peace under the Consulate had enabled the authorities to give the police a strong structure and, thenceforth, it was to be difficult to reorganize the royalist movement in western France. Counter-revolutionary agitation in this region, without ever completely disappearing, remained slight. It was to resume on a relatively broader scale only in 1814, on the eve of the collapse of the imperial regime. The staunchest royalists were quite convinced of the impossibility of organizing new insurrections in France and therefore thought that recourse must be taken to other means of action. Hyde de Neuville, who finally refused to rally to Bonaparte, and Cadoudal believed that the principal obstacle to the Restoration was now constituted by only one man, Napoleon, and that he must be brought down.

After 1800 the counter-revolution in France took on a new look. Henceforth its aim was not to set off great counter-revolutionary revolts in certain regions of France, but to act by way of plots directed against the person of the first consul himself. The first plots were organized by Hyde de Neuville and Cadoudal. Hyde de Neuville was a very young man at the time, only twenty-four. As his name indicates, he belonged to an English family which had emigrated to France with the Stuarts. His sister was married to a deputy of the Council of Five Hundred called Larue, who had figured among the Clichyans and been deported to Guiana after 18 Fructidor. Larue had escaped and managed to reach England, and Hyde de Neuville had begun his conspiratorial activities at this time. In 1799 he was entrusted by the *chouans* with a mission to the comte d'Artois, and the prince asked him to reconstitute in Paris a royal agency with a few confederates. Several days after his interview with Bonaparte, Hyde de Neuville organized a royalist demonstration in the heart of Paris: on January 21, 1800, anniversary of the execution of Louis XVI, he affixed the king's testament on the door of the Madeleine, the façade of which had been entirely hung with black by his friends. This demonstration did not touch off any reaction; the Parisian populace was on its guard. Most of those who had staged the demonstration were arrested, sentenced to death and shot. But Hyde himself managed to escape. He then won over Cadoudal—who, as we have seen, had resented any compromise with the first consul—to the idea of a plot aiming at the assassination of Bonaparte. After Marengo, far from abandoning their scheme, Hyde de Neuville and Cadoudal thought it more pressing that the first consul be removed from the scene. The attack was preceded by a series of acts of aggression in order to set off agitation and to deflect the attention of the police. Thus Senator Clément de Ris was kidnapped by a band of royalists in Touraine, on September 25, 1800. The kidnapping of this senator was attributed to a plot by Fouché who, it was said, wanted to obtain his papers so as to be informed about the plots being hatched against Bonaparte during his absence on the campaign against Marengo. Balzac has written a novel on this theme, *Une ténébreuse affaire*. But the documents since made public show that Fouché was not the instigator of the kidnapping of Clément de Ris, which was organized by Hyde de Neuville and Cadoudal. Clément de Ris was ransomed and then left on the road, suffering no other injury. Another crime that must be attributed to the *chouans* was the assassination of the former constitutional bishop Audrein, who had voted the death of Louis XVI at the Convention. He was killed on November 19, 1800, in Brittany.

Finally, the attempt to assassinate Napoleon took place—the famous assault of rue Saint-Nicaise in Paris on December 24, 1800. Bonaparte was in his carriage on the way to the theater when an "infernal machine" exploded. At first the police could not identify the perpetrators precisely. They inferred that Jacobins or "anarchists" were guilty. In fact, the growing power of the first consul had led to the creation of a republican opposition against him. Bonaparte, without awaiting proofs, immediately decided to purge France of all remaining staunch republicans, Jacobins and "anarchists." One hundred of them who had figured in most of the Jacobin movements since 1792 were arrested and deported without trial to the Seychelles Islands in the Indian Ocean.[1] Bonaparte and his councillors seized upon the assault as the pretext for the removal from France of all those who had played a role, no matter how small, at the head of democratic movements since 1792. Although only the leaders were deported, all functionaries suspected of Jacobinism or of hostility to an authoritarian regime were ousted.

The investigation of the assault, however, continued. Soon it was established that the Jacobins had not been involved in it at all, that the authors were *chouans*, accomplices or friends of Cadoudal and Hyde de Neuville. The *chouans* Carbon and Saint-Réjeant were arrested, sentenced to death and executed on April 20, 1801. But the police could not get their hands on the real culprits, Hyde de Neuville and Cadoudal.

The repression that followed on the assault of rue Saint-Nicaise gave France a period of internal calm which coincided with the pacification abroad.

The Peace of Lunéville, the Peace of Amiens, and the Concordat put an end to the disturbances. Seemingly France was entering into a long

---

1. On this subject, see R.-C. Cobb, "Notes sur la répression contre le personnel sans-culotte de 1795 à 1801," *Ann. hist. de la Rév fr.*, 1954, pp. 23–49.

period of peace. D'Andigné and Bourmont, who without formally rallying to the first consul nevertheless had not joined with his implacable foes, were arrested and imprisoned without trial in the fortress of Besançon. This period of calm was to last until relations between France and her neighbors again became tense in 1803, resulting in a resumption of the war.

3 / *Espionage and Counter-Espionage Under the Consulate*

The intelligence services of the powers hostile to the Revolution redoubled their activity when difficulties cropped up again between France and England only a few months after the signing of the Peace of Amiens and a new war between France and Europe was once again envisaged. Bonaparte was not unaware of this activity; in particular, he knew that the two figures who had headed the counter-revolutionary services since 1790, the British consul Drake and the comte d'Antraigues, still directed them. The two cronies, however, had changed residences. They had no longer conducted operations in Italy but in Germany. D'Antraigues had set himself up in Dresden, and Drake had been appointed minister plenipotentiary to the British government in Bavaria, from where he paid frequent visits to d'Antraigues in Saxony. Bonaparte did everything he could to prevent them from continuing to damage him. In 1803 he requested the elector of Saxony to expel d'Antraigues from Dresden. The elector refused and for a time Napoleon toyed with the idea of having the count kidnapped. With this in view, he sent a French officer named Sagot to Dresden to study the conditions under which the kidnapping could be successfully carried out. But Sagot established that the comte lived in an isolated house, well defended against any attack from the outside, and that under these circumstances a kidnapping was virtually impossible. Napoleon then used other means: he unleashed against the comte d'Antraigues Montgaillard, who published his *Mémoires secrets*. These accused the comte of having sold the contents of the notorious portfolio, which thus fell into the hands of the French government, in exchange for his release in Milan in 1797. But d'Antraigues continued his activity, directing a network of spies who sent him intelligence reports from France, and communicating this information to Russia and other powers.

Drake in 1803 was still at the head of the English espionage services and it is certain that d'Antraigues passed on to him the greater part of the intelligence reports that he received. But Drake possessed other sources of information. The instructions that Drake gave to one of his agents in 1803 or 1804 were known, inasmuch as the Bonaparte government had obtained a copy of them. Drake instructed his informant to send him,

> twice a week a bulletin of all the interesting events of which the public prints do not speak, as well as of everything that happens in the ports and in the armies. . . . These bulletins must be exactly numbered, so that if one has been lost or removed, it can be easily spotted. . . . They must also, according to the nature of the news contained in them, be written in part in black ink and in part in sympathetic ink. . . . Those which are partly written in sympathetic ink will be indicated by a dot of ordinary ink dropped at random in the upper part of the first page of the letter.

What did he ask of the agents who were to draw up these bulletins? Information relative to the French policy toward Turkey and Ireland; to the military situation on the French frontiers; and to the internal situation of the country.

It was very difficult to destroy Drake because he was a clever fellow and a master in the art of espionage. So Bonaparte got the idea of discrediting him. He commissioned an agent, who was to pass himself off as an enemy of the Revolution, to enter into contact with Drake and give him false information. Méhée de La Touche, a very strange person, lent himself to the role. He had served in the police of Louis XVI and then moved to the revolutionary police. He became a secret agent of the French Ministry of Foreign Affairs in Poland and in Russia, and was also a secret agent of Danton in 1792. Later he was registrar of the Commune of Paris after August 10, at the time of the September massacres. It was he who signed the bonds of payment granted to the slayers in order to indemnify them for their "work." During the Terror he was a journalist, signing his articles "Felhémési," an anagram of his name. After Thermidor, he joined the conspiracy of Equals. Next, he appears as secretary-general of the Ministry of War, commissioned by the Directory to draw up proclamations, and then again employed by the police, in particular Fouché, after 18 Brumaire. But his advancement was too slow to suit him, so he made contact with the opponents of the consular regime, with the Jacobins and perhaps also with the royalists. At all events, he became suspect to the police. After the assault of rue Saint-Nicaise, he was placed under surveillance within France and then deported to the island of

Oléron. There he made the acquaintance of Buonarroti, who was interned on the island, and through his mediation got into contact with the members of the Secret Society of Philadelphians, whose aim was to establish a democratic regime. It seems that Méhée had thought of creating a great opposition party that would have united Jacobins and royalists alike. To this end he went to London at the beginning of 1803. He wanted to propose his plan to the comte d'Artois or to his entourage, but he was very badly received by the French émigrés in England; he was shown the door by them, as well as by the British government, and soon found himself penniless in London. In desperation he went to see the French ambassador and offered him his services. He appeared at the precise moment Bonaparte was looking for someone who could dupe Drake and create an incident which would put an end to the latter's activity. So it was agreed that Méhée would say nothing of his understanding with the French government and that he would continue to present himself as an agent of the opposition to Bonaparte. He went from London to Germany in the capacity of a royalist. He saw Drake in Munich, then returned to Strasbourg and so prepared the giant hoax designed to ruin Drake and another English agent, Spencer Smith, the English minister at Stuttgart. Méhée de La Touche had promised Drake and Spencer Smith that he would be sending them information because, as he claimed, he was well placed to obtain excellent reports. Immediately on his return to Paris, he sent a whole series of intelligence reports to Drake and Spencer Smith. Other agents also sought out these two personages, but they were all false spies acting in league with Fouché's police. This was the case with Captain Rosey, who has left the story of his mission. He was garrisoned at Strasbourg when he was commissioned to meet Drake in Munich. He presented himself to Drake as the agent of a general commanding in Alsace who would be prepared to organize the rising of four departments in eastern France to overthrow Bonaparte's government. Drake immediately gave Rosey a huge sum of money, 75,000 francs in gold. New intelligence reports were sent to Drake. They were all false, but nevertheless were faithfully transmitted to the British government. When the French police thought that this game had been going on long enough, they revealed the whole hoax in such a way as to compromise Drake and Spencer Smith irremediably in the eyes of the British government. The whole affair was exposed in a lengthy printed report drawn up by Régnier, minister of justice. The French newspapers jeered:

Mr. Drake will be punished when he comes to know that all the bulletins sent by extraordinary couriers to London, communicated to all the courts, hawked by the English ministers as far as Constantinople, of which traces are also found in the discussions of Parliament, were fabricated and contained nothing which was either true or likely, and that before being sent to him they were communicated to agents of the Paris police. The latter blushed upon reading them and could not overcome their surprise at seeing these fables, woven so casually, utterly charm Mr. Drake and serve as a foundation for the hopes and calculations of the British Cabinet.

After the publication of this report, Drake and Spencer's activities were put paid to. Totally discredited, they were summarily recalled.

D'Antraigues, however, continued his activities. It had proved impossible to assassinate, kidnap or compromise him and he had numerous correspondents in Paris: relatives, friends, compatriots, his uncle, de Barral, bishop of Troyes; the arch chancellor Cambacérès, a native of Montpellier, whom he had known in his youth; General Suchet, brother of one of his former purveyors of silks; General Mathieu Dumas, who had been one of the two Clichyan leaders under the Directory; one of his friends from the village of d'Antraigues; Méjan, secretary-general of the prefecture of the Seine; sons of former domestics of his relatives, such as Duclos or Delmas; and above all, two people who sent the most interesting reports of all, but who are known only as the "Ami de Paris" and the "Amie de Paris." These two personages have remained a mystery and until now no attempt to establish their identity has been successful. The "Ami de Paris" provided intelligence reports of great value, many incontestably very useful to the enemy. D'Antraigues forwarded these reports to the Russian government via Prince Czartoriski. The bulletins sent by d'Antraigues to Russia were read by Léonce Pingaud in the Saint Petersburg and Moscow archives. Since then it has been impossible to obtain a microfilm of them and because there is no complete photographic copy of these bulletins, it is difficult to make a critical study of them or to formulate valid hypotheses as to the author's identity. But the "Ami de Paris," like Vannelet formerly under the Directory, gives all sorts of biographical information about himself. These reports warrant the supposition that his career was very similar to that of Vannelet and so it has been asked whether the "Ami de Paris" may not be the same person as Vannelet. The "Ami de Paris" claims to have made his fortune in the military administration; like Vannelet, he is very rich, has a capital of 2 million and is an informant for foreign powers only because of his love of peace, not in order to get money out of them. He says that he has the confidence of Talleyrand, minister for foreign affairs, and that he is closely linked with a clerk of this ministry, Durand de Mareuil, son of a receiver-general of tolls and for a long time in service at the ministry. Like Vannelet, the "Ami de Paris" states that he was formerly a partisan of the Revolution but that he broke with the revolutionaries after the execution of Louis XVI and that he yearns for the restoration of the claimant, on condition that the latter grants France a constitutional regime. He claims to have known d'Antraigues since 1772, that is, from the time the comte was twenty-one years old. Moreover, he is considerably preoccupied with d'Antraigues's mother who, after having emigrated, had returned to France. The "Ami de Paris" transmitted intelligence reports of uneven value, but some were of capital importance. For example, a memorandum by Talleyrand on the constitution of the kingdom of Italy, and the correspondence exchanged between General Hédouville, French minister to St. Petersburg, and the minister for foreign affairs. The latter documents were vital to Russia, since they made her privy to the French ambassador's reports on Russia to the French government. The "Ami" sent many extracts from dispatches addressed to the French government by its agents abroad, and also reports on the struggle being waged against the royalists within France. He died suddenly in the summer of 1804, bequeathing 50,000 francs to d'Antraigues, which he said was only a restitution because the comte's father had lent him this sum, which had helped him to make his fortune, and he was happy to pay it back to the son.

The "fils de l'Ami" continued the correspondence. In his first letter he says that he is "better situated than his father to know men and to observe events." He too is rich and asks for no remuneration. He has many highly placed relatives and friends in France, especially in Languedoc and Dauphiné. The "fils de l'Ami" sent intelligence reports as valuable as those of his father; memoranda on Bavaria, Saxony, and one particularly vital document: the plan of the naval campaign of 1805, which indeed was to lead to the French disaster at Trafalgar. It is debatable to what extent the transmission of this plan to the Russian government and thence to the British government contributed to facilitating Nelson's victory. The "fils" also transmitted details of the strength of the French army at the beginning of the campaign of 1805, another immensely valuable piece of information which, however, did not prevent the French from winning victories constantly, above all at Austerlitz. The correspondence ceased the moment war was resumed on the continent, in the autumn of 1805.

As for the "Amie de Paris," we know that she was a former mistress of d'Antraigues, before 1789. When the comte emigrated, she remained in Versailles, married in 1790 and shortly thereafter became a widow. At that time she resumed her correspondence with d'Antraigues. In 1803 she was still living in Paris, in contact with milieux that were very close to Bonaparte and Josephine. Her letters are full of information of no great military or political value, on the life of the first consul and the doings of Josephine. They are drawing room anecdotes, gossip and tittle-tattle, less important than the reports transmitted by the "Ami de Paris."

Who was the "Ami de Paris"? Immediately after the publication of Léonce Pingaud's book, which revealed the "Ami's" extraordinary activity, some historians, notably Chuquet, proposed to identify him with the Darus. The father, Noël Daru, had, in fact, been secretary-general of the intendancy of Languedoc, in Montpellier, before the Revolution. And his son, Pierre, after having been pay commissioner of wars, became secretary-general of the Ministry of War and then intendant-general of the grand army, minister of the war administration, and later member of the Académie française. Many historians have accepted this identification, hastily established by Chuquet, and concluded that the Darus were traitors. Admittedly there is one disturbing coincidence: Noël Daru died in 1804, almost the very moment when the "Ami de Paris" dies in d'Antraigues's correspondence and is replaced by his son. However, many other items of information contained in the letters make this identification hypothetical. Thus, Noël Daru had never been a purveyor to the armies nor a pay commissioner of wars; and even if he was rich, it is difficult, even if one takes into account all the elements of his fortune, to think that in 1804 he possessed a capital of 2 million francs. The Darus are very important in literary history because they were cousins of Stendhal, who had lived with them at the end of 1799 and the beginning of 1800. In his works Stendhal discussed the Darus—whom he did not like very much although they were the source of his career—at length. His cousin, Pierre Daru, got him into the war administration and obtained a job for him that he maintained until the end of the Empire. Nothing in Stendhal's numerous allusions to them warrants an accusation of treason against the Darus.

On the other hand, we cannot deny certain disturbing coincidences. It is possible that the case of the "Ami de Paris" is like that of Vannelet, that he was a fictitious person, invented either by a Parisian spy or by d'Antraigues himself out of different elements of existing people. This would have enabled him to give greater verisimilitude and weight to the reports addressed to the foreign courts, and consequently to obtain larger remuneration for them.

Whatever the identity of the "Ami," it is no less a fact that d'Antraigues transmitted to Russia and England intelligence reports of the first rank which greatly harmed Bonaparte's policy. Bonaparte tried very hard to reduce this espionage. He succeeded in part by discrediting Drake, but he could not put an end to the activity of d'Antraigues. Nevertheless, the false spies sent to Drake, and the correspondence which they maintained with the English agent, enabled the French government to learn of the existence of new plots being hatched against the very person of Bonaparte.

4 / *The Cadoudal-Pichegru-Moreau Plot*

The plots revived in 1803 when relations between France and England once more became tense.

At the heart of these plots the figure of the comte d'Artois is unmistakable. Much more restless and imprudent than his brother, he wanted the disappearance of Bonaparte, whom he thought the principal obstacle to a Restoration. The plots were also facilitated by the enigmatic attitude of General Moreau. Already in 1796 and 1797 Moreau had showed an attitude that was, at the least, suspect. We have described the liaisons maintained with the émigrés during the famous Bavarian retreat. We have also seen under what strange conditions Moreau had withheld the correspondence of the Austrian General Klinglin with Pichegru, instead of transmitting it to the French government. There is little doubt that Moreau had royalist sympathies. Under the Consulate it had been thought, wrongly it seems, that Moreau was a republican. His father had been guillotined during the Terror, and Moreau had always been favorable to the royalists; it had been so in 1796 and 1797, and in 1803, as we shall see, and it was to be so again in 1813 when Moreau resumed service in the coalition against Napoleon.

Despite this, in 1803 Moreau enjoyed a fine reputation. He was the general who, after Bonaparte, had won the greatest victory. In December, 1800, in fact, he had defeated the Austrians at Hohenlinden and so forced them to negotiate.

Now, Moreau, the most brilliant general of France after Napoleon, resented the first consul and adopted an unseemly attitude toward him, to which his family contributed. Several days after Hohenlinden, Moreau had married the daughter of Mme Hulot, a Creole like Josephine. The Hulot and Tascher de La Pagerie families had been separated for a long time by all kinds of petty quarrels, which dated back to the time of their residence in the Antilles.

Mlle Hulot, now Mme Moreau, showed herself very jealous of Josephine. One day she refused an invitation to dine at the Tuileries. Josephine decided that she would never invite her again, and a split took place between the Moreaus and the Bonapartes. Mme Hulot "mère," having come to pay a call on Josephine, was asked to wait in the ante-chamber. She rose and left. At the death of General Leclerc, brother-in-law of Bonaparte, all the wives of the generals present in Paris went into mourning save Mme Moreau. On another occasion General Moreau, invited to a grand ball at the Ministry of War, went there in ordinary dress, which created a scandal.

These petty wrangles increasingly separated Moreau from Bonaparte. Thus Moreau became the man towards whom all the conspirators looked. Now two of them—Hyde de Neuville and Cadoudal—decided to revive the plot which had failed at the time of the assault of rue Saint-Nicaise. They were in England at the beginning of 1803, where they saw the comte d'Artois and told him that it would be easy to kidnap Bonaparte and then assassinate him. This would touch off a general insurrection in France, but it would be absolutely necessary to guide it along the proper lines, which required that a Bourbon enter France, take over the direction of the revolt and be ready to reserve the throne for Louis XVIII.

Cadoudal thought of kidnapping Bonaparte, using several *chouans* when the first consul was traveling on the road leading from Saint-Cloud to Paris. Pichegru and Moreau would then declare themselves for the Bourbons. Pichegru was living in England; he had arrived there after having escaped from Guiana, where he had been deported at the time of 18 Fructidor. After the success of the coup projected by Cadoudal, a Bourbon would arrive in France, be appointed lieutenant-general of the kingdom and bring about the Restoration.

D'Artois supposedly promised to come himself, but his promise was not formal. The correspondence exchanged between Drake and the false spies, delegated by Bonaparte, noted this plot without naming the participants or detailing the circumstances, and spoke above all—and this is very important—of the possible arrival in France of a prince of the House of Bourbon, who would then take over direction of the conspiracy.

The organization of the conspiracy began. A royalist named Charles d'Hozier set himself up in Paris and summoned several *chouans*, some of whom had participated in the assault of rue Saint-Nicaise. These men were to kidnap Bonaparte later; the British government lent them a helping hand in the form of £1 million.

On August 30, 1803, Cadoudal himself arrived in Paris. He took all sorts of precautions to avoid arrest; changing lodgings every night. The *chouans* knew that a "great leader" had arrived from England, and they passed this on to Méhée de La Touche, who was still in contact with them. Thanks to Méhée, the police got their hands on a letter which proved to them that Cadoudal had returned to Paris; they also came into possession of another letter which mentioned that a prince of the House of Bourbon would soon be arriving on French soil to head the insurrection. The police thereupon redoubled their energies and looked everywhere for Cadoudal. Mobile columns were again launched in Brittany and the Vendée to see whether, by chance, he had taken refuge in the west, but the troops failed to capture him.

Finally on January 16, 1804, Pichegru landed in France clandestinely, with his long-standing friends Lajolais, Major Rusillion, the aide-de-camp of d'Artois and Jules de Polignac, future prime minister of 1830. D'Artois had refused to come himself. When Cadoudal learned this he exclaimed: "All is lost!" Nevertheless, plans for the conspiracy were continued.

On January 28, 1804, Pichegru and Moreau met on the boulevard de la Madeleine, in the presence of Cadoudal. As usual, Moreau showed himself hesitant and shifty. He said that he could not help the conspirators in any way, but that if Bonaparte was brought down, it was probable that the senate would appeal to him and appoint him consul. He also said that Pichegru could not hope to obtain an important position in France because a charge of treason would be hanging over him; he would first of all have to be judged by a court-martial, which no doubt would acquit him. At all events, when the subject of the Restoration of Louis XVIII was brought up, Moreau showed great reticence. Cadoudal had the impression that Moreau intended to be the principal beneficiary of the plot, and he left in a fury.

One of Cadoudal's friends was arrested at that very moment and revealed the principal *chouan* hideouts in Paris. On February 8, a servant of Cadoudal's was apprehended in his turn. Under torture, he revealed his master's hideout in even greater detail. A wave of arrests ensued, the police managing to close an increasingly tighter net around the leaders of the conspiracy. The authorities were fully acquainted with the respective roles of Pichegru, Moreau and Lajolais, and also learned of the interview of January 28 on the boulevard de la Madeleine between Moreau and Pichegru. The first consul, in possession of these incriminating documents, ordered the arrest of Moreau on February 15, 1804; he was imprisoned in the Temple.

Following Moreau's arrest, most of the *chouans* who were in Paris were also seized, but the police could not get their hands on Cadoudal. A law promulgated on February 27 declared the concealment of Cadoudal and his accomplices a capital crime and denunciations multiplied. Polignac and the marquis de Rivière were arrested on March 4; Major Rusillion on the sixth. Cadoudal was hunted down, his place of refuge surrounded on March 9; he escaped, killing a policeman, but was pursued. A veritable manhunt was organized in the Latin Quarter where he was hiding and he was finally arrested near the crossroads at the Odéon. He was immediately locked up in the Temple. Interrogated, he confessed, saying that he wanted to kidnap the first consul in order to restore Louis XVIII; but he exonerated Moreau. In his confession he even accused Moreau of being the cause of the failure of the conspiracy because of his desire to replace the first consul and his refusal to work for the Restoration of the claimant to the throne.

5 / The Execution of the duc d'Enghien

The last accomplices of Cadoudal were arrested at the end of March, but in their interrogations one disclosure above all impressed Bonaparte: that of the imminent arrival of a prince of the House of Bourbon. Bonaparte, as we have seen, had tried to obtain from Louis XVIII a formal renunciation of the throne. He was extremely disturbed upon learning that a Bourbon was to come to France. Who could this prince be? He proceeded to solve the mystery by process of elimination. Louis XVIII? That was hardly likely, inasmuch as he was in Warsaw. His nephew the duc d'Angoulême? Equally unlikely, inasmuch as he too lived in Poland. The comte d'Artois or his second son, the duc de Berry? Both were settled in England, with the Condés. Only one prince of the House of Bourbon resided near France: the duc d'Enghien.

The duc d'Enghien, son of the last Condé, lived in fact in Ettenheim, a small village in the duchy of Baden about 9 miles from the French frontier, with his mistress, Charlotte de Rohan-Rochefort, niece of the notorious cardinal of Rohan. Méhée de La Touche, in a report sent from Strasbourg, had drawn the attention of the police to the scheming of the duke, who kept up a steady correspondence with the enemies, with the émigrés and with the royalists inside France. Furthermore, a report from the Strasbourg gendarmerie—fake, in fact—signalized that General Dumouriez had come to Ettenheim. The prefect spoke of very important gatherings of émigrés around this village—also partly false.

Simultaneously with these reports Bonaparte received Drake's letters, which referred to the arrival in France of a Bourbon prince. Bonaparte now no longer doubted that it was the duc d'Enghien who had been designated to take over leadership of the conspiracy. Accordingly, he decided to have him kidnapped from the duchy of Baden. This was of course contrary to international law: a government could not arrest an individual on the territory of a foreign state in time of peace. But Bonaparte was pushed to the act by two of his ministers, Fouché and Talleyrand, the former because he did not want Bonaparte to enter into an agreement with the royalists. Fouché, previously a member of the Convention and a regicide, was unhappy over the anti-Jacobin reaction which had followed the assault of rue Saint-Nicaise. He wanted relations between Bonaparte and the royalists definitively severed, as they had been between himself and the royalists. As for Talleyrand, he aspired to consolidate his position at the Ministry of Foreign Affairs by appearing indispensable.

On March 10, Bonaparte called a council of government in which figured Cambacérès, Lebrun, Talleyrand, Chief Justice Régnier and Fouché. This council concluded that the duc d'Enghien was guilty and decided he must be abducted regardless of the consequences that might ensue. Fouché closed the council by declaring that the kidnapping and the sentence that followed would show the whole world clearly that Bonaparte had no intention of playing "Monk."

Orders were immediately given for kidnapping the duc. An expedition of gendarmes, under the command of General Ordener, left for the frontier. On March 14 it reached Strasbourg and crossed the Rhine at night. On the morning of the fifteenth the duc d'Enghien's house was surrounded and the duke carried off to Strasbourg without anyone telling him the reason why.

At first there were only mild protests in Germany against this violation of international law. The duc d'Enghien himself did not doubt that he

would be released very soon. But by March 16 Bonaparte had decided to
have him shot without even a hearing. It was a true vendetta, Corsican
style. On March 20, the first consul made the following resolution:

> The ci-devant duc d'Enghien, accused of bearing arms against the
> republic, of having been and being still in the pay of England and of
> being a party to conspiracies directed against the internal and external
> security of the republic, will be brought before a military commission
> composed of seven members, appointed by the governor-general of
> Paris, Murat, which will meet in Vincennes.

Bonaparte himself formulated the list of questions to be submitted to
the prince and the following question figured in this list: "Have you borne
arms against your country?" Bonaparte stated specifically that if the duc
responded to this question in the affirmative, the death sentence would be
automatically applied without any discussion, in conformity to the law.

The duc d'Enghien was transferred in a post-chaise, driven at high speed,
from Strasbourg to Vincennes, where he arrived on March 20 at eleven
o'clock in the evening. The military commission met at midnight. The
duc, utterly bewildered and with no inkling of the horror in store, insisted
upon seeing Bonaparte. He thought that if he spoke to Bonaparte he could
easily exonerate himself. But the members of the commission, at the order
of the first consul himself, refused his request. In reply to the fateful
question, the duc stated that he had borne arms against France and
acknowledged having received money from England. Thenceforth his
condemnation was no longer in doubt. The commission unanimously declared him guilty and he was sentenced to death in conformity to a law
voted by the Convention which specified that any émigré seized on French
territory was liable to this punishment. In fact, the duc d'Enghien had not
been arrested on French territory and the law was not applicable to him.

General Savary, commissioned to see that the prescriptions of the first
consul were carried out to the letter, ordered an immediate execution of
the sentence. At two o'clock in the morning, and in violation of the law
specifying that death sentences were to be carried out only after sunrise,
the duc d'Enghien was executed in the dungeons of the château of
Vincennes. When news of the assassination was learned—for it was a
veritable assassination—someone said: "It's worse than a crime, it's a
blunder."

Nevertheless, the trial of the conspirators continued. On April 16,
Pichegru was found dead in his cell. What had happened? Had he com-

mitted suicide, or been killed to prevent him from talking? Had somebody wanted to prevent him from revealing the names of other accomplices? To this day complete uncertainty hangs over the circumstances of Piche-gru's death. His accomplices did not appear before the court of assizes but before an exceptional tribunal, judging without a jury and without appeal. The judges had been specially chosen. The trial lasted from May 28 to June 10. Moreau was sentenced to two years imprisonment, a mild punishment; Bonaparte went into a fit of rage upon learning of it. But could he have Moreau, one of the most prestigious generals that France had seen since 1789, shot? Moreover, Bonaparte was surrounded by people who beseeched him to pardon Moreau. Finally, he decided to commute the sentence to lifelong banishment. It was thus that Moreau left for the United States, from which he was to return in 1813, only to meet death in the battle of Leipzig, killed by a French bullet.

Cadoudal, Armand de Polignac, d'Hozier, and sixteen other accused were sentenced to death. But here too there were numerous intercessions on their behalf. The members of the former nobility, who had returned from the emigration in considerable force, had already found friends in the new court that was being formed. In the face of the supplications addressed to him, Bonaparte judged that the execution of the duc d'Eng-hien sufficed as a warning. He pardoned seven of those sentenced to death belonging to the nobility, notably Polignac, Rivière and d'Hozier. In contrast, the commoners were all guillotined on June 24, 1804. Actually the pardoned nobles were kept in prison and owed their deliverance only to the Restoration in 1814.

The condemnation of these conspirators and the execution of the duc d'Enghien had enormous repercussions in France and in Europe. Bonaparte realized it and after the execution of the duc, declared: "At least they will see what we are capable of and, henceforth, I hope they will leave us in peace. I am the statesman, I am the French Revolution. I repeat it and I will maintain it."

The Austrian ambassador in Paris, Cobenzl, wrote to the minister: "Your Excellency cannot imagine the profound consternation that reigns here now. I doubt that the consternation produced by the sentencing of Louis XVI could have equaled it." The royalists were horror-stricken and furious with the first consul. Chateaubriand ostentatiously handed in his resignation as embassy secretary. Bonaparte explained that he had considered having the duc d'Enghien executed publicly so as not to compromise other royalists who would have shown themselves at the time, and he added: "I will not consent to negotiate with England until she turns out the Bourbons as Louis XIV turned out the Stuarts. The prince of Baden did not hesitate to deliver the duc d'Enghien to me . . ."

The courts of Europe were horrified by the execution of the duc; nevertheless, they did not dare to react. The duke of Würtemberg sent his felicitations to Bonaparte and congratulated him on having escaped a plot. The duke of Baden expelled from his territories all the émigrés who had taken up residence there. The German emperor maintained a prudent silence. The king of Prussia, although very hostile to Bonaparte, expressed to the first consul his desire "that he uproot the horrible, savage, scheme against his person." For a moment the czar toyed with the idea of breaking off diplomatic relations with France, but he did not do so and limited himself to ordering his court to go into mourning. Pope Pius VII declared himself "grieved." Charles IV of Spain, a Bourbon, hence a relative of the duc d'Enghien, approved the execution and his prime minister, Godoy, said to the ambassador of France: "When one has bad blood, it must be spilled." Upon learning of this utterance, Louis XVIII returned to his cousin in Spain the collar of the Golden Fleece which he had received from him.

Louis XVIII maintained a very dignified attitude. He had clearly understood that the execution of the duc d'Enghien marked the definitive rupture between Bonaparte and the Bourbons, so he seized upon this act as a pretext to reaffirm his claim to the throne of France before all Europe. Once more he encountered great difficulties in doing so, because none of the princes of Europe would permit him to publish a proclamation on their territory. In order to draw up a proclamation, Louis XVIII had to remove himself in a ship to the middle of the Baltic Sea. This proclamation, known as the Calmar Proclamation, contains notably these words: "Frenchmen, in the middle of the Baltic Sea, in the face and under the protection of heaven, fortified by the presence of our brother, of that of the duc d'Angoulême, our nephew, with the assent of the princes of the blood royal, we swear that we shall never give up our rights." Nevertheless, Louis XVIII, in the same proclamation, later spoke of a general amnesty for Frenchmen who had not taken part in the Revolution, to which he had never before referred. He promised to maintain in their rank and office all officers and functionaries, and he guaranteed, which was also new, to all proprietors possession of the national properties they had been able to acquire. Thus the proclamation of Calmar marks a step forward in the direction of the Revolution, compared to the proclamations of Hamm and Verona.

Louis XVIII sent his proclamation to all the sovereigns of Europe; none replied. Thereupon he addressed them in a letter to show them that by acting in this manner they were denying the very principle they represented, that of legitimacy.

In fact, although the Revolution continued under another form, that of the imperial military dictatorship—at this time Napoleon assumed the title of Emperor of the French—the counter-revolution also continued. Drake, of course, had been placed in a position where he could do no more harm; but d'Antraigues sent as many intelligence reports as before to the foreign powers. And the counter-revolution was to continue until its victory in 1814 over the Revolution, masked under the mantle of military dictatorship.

CONCLUSION

Two conclusions emerge at the end of this study: the relatively minor influence of doctrine on counter-revolutionary action; and the almost complete failure of this action in 1804, the year in which the study ends.

Most of the counter-revolutionary movements just studied have, in fact, appeared either as spontaneous movements, reflexes of peasant masses before some decision or counter-revolutionary action, or as enterprises launched without great concern as to what would be done in the event of their successful outcome. It is characteristic that the theorists of the counter-revolution held themselves aloof from such action. No doubt, Joseph de Maistre indirectly aided the struggle against France in 1793, and Chateaubriand participated in the campaign of 1792, but both wrote their great works only afterwards. As for the comte d'Antraigues, his theoretical studies predated the time he took over direction of the espionage networks of the counter-revolution. For all these doctrinaires the consequence of this divorce between theory and action was a striking lack of contact with reality. Most of the counter-revolutionary insurrections, as we have seen, were peasant revolts. It would have been logical to exploit the peasant discontent, the resentment of the peasantry against the bourgeoisie, in order to extend the counter-revolutionary insurrections. For that, it would have been necessary in addition to give a large place to economic and social elements in the doctrines of the counter-revolution. But the counter-revolutionary theorists paid no attention to these problems. Their attention was focused, above all, on the political and religious aspects; they did not understand that by satisfying the basic demands of the peasants they could have won them over to their side and forged a solid and lasting alliance with them.

If the counter-revolutionary theories had little influence on the counter-revolutionary movements, the cause doubtless also lies in their diversities. The leaders of the action—the pretender to the throne, the émigrés, the governments at war with France—thought purely and simply of the restoration of the Old Regime. On the other hand, most of the counter-revolutionary theories proposed more or less profound reforms, from the theocrats, de Bonald and de Maistre, to the "monarchicals," Mallet du Pan and, at this time at least, Chateaubriand. "Monarchicals" and absolutists fought against the Revolution with the mental reservation that, in the event of victory, they would establish a regime conforming to the doctrine they preferred. But these doctrinal differences impaired the unity of the counter-revolutionary movements and often were the cause of their failure.

Of all the counter-revolutionary doctrines we have reviewed, only that of Burke enjoyed great popularity at the time. But Burke's work, precisely because of its content, encouraged passive resistance rather than active struggle. Burke's *Reflections* arrested the revolutionary movement which was spreading rapidly in England, and slowed it down in the United States and Germany. But it had little effect in France, Switzerland or Italy, and seems hardly to have been appreciated by the French émigrés. It is quite paradoxical that the great counter-revolutionary doctrines published from 1789 to 1804 did not begin to be known until after the victory of the counter-revolution in 1814. At that time they dominated counter-revolutionary thought in France and abroad—until the end of the nineteenth century and the publication of the works of Charles Maurras. Thus the counter-revolutionary doctrines themselves had a long-term rather than a short-term influence. They acted on the thought and deeds of the counter-revolutionaries of the nineteenth century much more than on the ideas of the leaders of insurrections in the period running from 1792 to 1804. And this is one of the causes of the failure of these counter-revolutionary movements.

But there were also other causes. In the first place, the military power of revolutionary France. The year 1799 can be considered as a kind of prefiguration of 1814. But in 1799, although Bonaparte was absent during the essential struggles, the republic triumphed; whereas in 1814 France, although ruled by him, suffered defeat. The fact is that in 1799 the French armies were still animated by the revolutionary ardor which had enabled them to repel the invasions of 1792 and 1794 and to win the great victories of 1796. The patriots of the sister republics, although disappointed by the policy of the Directory, still believe in France. The Italian patriots thought that a victory would lead to the rapid unification of their country; those of Holland that it would consolidate the new regime by liberating their country from the presence of French armies. The Rhineland patriots were still partisans of annexation to France, and those of Switzerland believed in the existence of a Helvetian republic, one and indivisible. All helped France unreservedly and with all their might, and so aided the victory of the republican armies. In 1814 this was no longer the case. Ten more years of war, of mourning, of heavy financial burdens, of political disappointments and a burdensome military dictatorship to boot, which masked the introduction or continuance of the principal conquests of the Revolution, had discouraged Frenchmen and foreigners alike. The enthusiasm discernible in 1799 had disappeared. This facilitated the victory of counter-revolution.

But in 1814 the counter-revolutionary coalition was also more coherent and broader than in 1799. In 1799 liberal England, Josephist Austria, a Russia ruled by a capricious czar prone to quick changes of attitude, Turkey mistrustful of Russia and England, the Kingdom of Naples, and Louis XVIII, faithful to the principles of traditional absolutism, all got on together very poorly. In 1814, their viewpoints and aims were to be closer to each other and they were to be aided by Prussia and Sweden, who had been neutral in 1799, and by Spain, who had been an ally of France in 1799. The coalition at that time was to be directed by a centralized general staff, which was to range peoples against France in the name of the great revolutionary ideas the French themselves had sowed in all Europe. Finally, in 1814, the attacks against France were to be co-ordinated.

One of the principal causes of the failure of the counter-revolution in the period under review, and particularly in 1799, lies in fact in the lack of synchronization of the attacks launched against France. The republic was attacked successively, not simultaneously, in Italy, Switzerland, Holland, the interior, the southwest and then in the Vendée and Brittany. Each time it had been able to muster up all its forces to hurl back these assaults.

Although the Empire consolidated the work of the Revolution, it also cemented the forces of the counter-revolution and enabled it to triumph in 1814. But the counter-revolution that imposed itself in power at that time bore only a distant resemblance to the counter-revolution of 1804. It had to appropriate many of the ideas and principles of the Revolution.

It was to install lasting regimes only to the extent that these regimes accepted the essentials of what had been wrought by the Revolution. But when it was to attempt to restore more or less total absolutism in Italy and Germany, it was to lead only to the creation of ephemeral regimes that were to be swiftly swept away in the first decades of the nineteenth century.

BIBLIOGRAPHICAL NOTES

CHAPTER II

On the May 5, 1789, meeting of the Estates General, see the important work published under the direction of Georges Lefebvre, *Recueil de documents relatifs aux séances des Etats généraux, mai–juin 1789*, Vol. I, Paris, 1953. The royal session of June 23, 1789, has been studied by Armand Brette, "La Séance royale du 23 juin 1789," *La Révolution française* (1891–92), Vols. 22 and 23. See also Pierre Caron, "La Tentative de contre-révolution, juin–juillet 1789," *Revue d'Histoire moderne et contemporaine*, 1904. On the whole of this counter-revolutionary attempt, see the synthesis by Georges Lefebvre, *Quatre-Vingt-Neuf*, Paris, 1939.

On the counter-revolutionaries whose ideas are analyzed in this chapter, see Léonce Pingaud, *Un agent secret sous la Révolution et l'Empire*, 2nd ed. Paris, 1894; Siegfried Riemer, *Die Staatsanschauung des Grafen d'Antraigues in seiner Denkschrift über die Generalstände*, Berlin, 1934; J. Brugerette, *Le Comte de Montlosier et son temps, 1755–1831*, Aurillac, 1931; A. Ricard, *L'Abbé Maury*, Paris, 1887; and Marcel Chapron, *Mirabeau-Tonneau*, Paris, 1956.

One can find much information not only on the eloquence but also on the ideas of the counter-revolutionary deputies in the classic work by Alphonse Aulard, *L'Eloquence parlementaire pendant la Révolution, les orateurs de l'Assemblée constituante*, Paris, 1880.

CHAPTER III

Of the authors studied in this chapter, only Rivarol has been the subject of important works: André Le Breton, *Rivarol, sa vie, ses idées, son talent*,

Paris, 1895; L. Latzarus, *La Vie paresseuse de Rivarol*, Paris, 1926; V.-H. Debidour, *Ecrits politiques et littéraires de Rivarol*, Paris, 1956. The *Mémoires du comte Ferrand* appeared in the publications of the Société d'Histoire contemporaine in 1897.

On the other writers dealt with here, see Beik, *The French Revolution Seen from the Right*, as well as M. Ferraz, *Histoire de la philosophie en France au XIXe siècle, internationalisme et ultramontanisme*, Paris, 1880, and L. Dimier, *Les Maîtres de la contre-révolution au XIXe siècle*, Paris, 1907.

CHAPTER IV

Sources: *Burke's Works*, Bohn Standard Library, 5 vols., London, 1875–79; *Réflexions sur la Révolution de France*, by the Right Honourable Edmund Burke, French translation, 1790; new translation, Paris, 1912; Prior *Burke's Life*, London, 1826, new edition, 1872; Ross J. F. Hoffmann and P. Levack, *Burke's Politics, Selected Writings on Reform, Revolution and War*, New York, 1949.

General bibliography: B. H. Murray, *Edmund Burke*, Oxford, 1931; Sir Philip Magnus, *Burke*, London, 1939; Alfred Cobban, *Edmund Burke and the Revolt Against the XVIIIth Century*, London, 1929; new edition, 1960, and *The Debate on the French Revolution, 1789–1800*, London, 1950; E. Halévy, *La Formation du radicalisme philosophique*, Vol. II, Paris, 1901; E. Barker, "E. Burke et la Révolution française," *Revue philosophique* (Sept.–Dec., 1939), pp. 129–160; Thomas W. Copeland, *Our Eminent Friend Edmund Burke, Six Essays*, New Haven, Conn., 1949; S. Maccoby, *English Radicalism, 1785–1832*, London, 1955; J. Voisine, *J.-J. Rousseau en Angleterre à l'époque romantique*, Paris, 1956; S. Skalweit, *Edmund Burke und Frankreich*, Cologne, 1956; C. Parkin, *The Moral Basis of Burke's Political Thought*, Cambridge, 1956; R. R. Palmer, *The Age of the Democratic Revolution*, Princeton, N.J., 1959; P. Mantoux, "A qui furent adressées 'Les Réflexions sur la Révolution de France' de Burke?," *La Révolution française*, 1932, pp. 5–15; H. V. F. Somerset, "Le Correspondant français à qui Burke adressa ses 'Réflexions sur la Révolution de France,'" *Annales historiques de la Révolution française*, 1951, pp. 360–373; J. Godechot, "Une première critique des 'Réflexions sur la Révolution de France' de Burke," *Ann. hist. de la Rév. fr.*, 1955, pp. 217–227; Hans A. Schmitt and John C. Waston, Jr., "Ten Letters to Edmund Burke from the French Translator of the Reflections on the Revolution in France," *Journal of Modern History*, 1952, pp. 406–423, and 1953, pp. 49–61; Louis Gottschalk, "Reflections on Burke's Reflections on the French Revolution," *Proceedings of the American*

Philosophical Society, Vol. 100 (October, 1956), pp. 417–429; J.-J. Chevallier, *Les Grandes Oeuvres politiques*, Paris, 1949, pp. 187–217, "Les Réflexions . . ." de Burke. This chapter was of very great service to me.

CHAPTER V*

Sources: the principal works of Mallet du Pan, *Considérations sur la nature de la Révolution de France et sur les causes qui en prolongèrent la durée*, London and Brussels, 1793 (three French editions; one German edition, Berlin, 1794; an Italian edition, Cosmopoli, 1797; an American edition, New York, 1795); *Correspondance politique pour servir à l'histoire du républicanisme français*, Hamburg, 1796, 2nd ed. in French, London, 1796; *Essai historique sur la destruction de la ligue et de la liberté helvétique*, London, 1798; *Mémoires et Correspondance de Mallet du Pan, pour servir à l'histoire de la Révolution française*, 2 vols., Paris, 1851; *Correspondance inédite de Mallet du Pan avec la cour de Vienne, 1794–1798*, 2 vols., Paris, 1884 (with a preface by Hippolyte Taine).

Works: M. Moeckli-Cellier, *La Révolution française et les écrivains suisses romands*, Neuchâtel and Paris, 1931; N. Matteucci, *J. Mallet du Pan* (in Italian), Naples, 1957, and "Mallet du Pan, Genevois et Européen," *Bulletin de la Société d'Histoire et d'Archéologie de Genève*, Vol. XI, 1957, pp. 153–168.

CHAPTER VI

General bibliography: Sainte-Beuve, *Joseph de Maistre* and *Louis de Bonald* reproduced in *Les Grands Ecrivains français par Sainte-Beuve*, edited by Maurice Allem, Vol. I, Paris, 1930, pp. 1–163 and 210–232; F. Baldensperger, *Le Mouvement des idées dans l'émigration française*, 2 vols., Paris, 1923–24; D. Bagge, *Les Idées politiques en France sous la Restauration*, Paris, 1952, pp. 191–213; Beik, *The French Revolution Seen from the Right*, pp. 62–71 and 73–82; J.-J. Chevallier, *Les idées politiques de Joseph de Maistre* (unpublished lectures); M. Prélot, *Histoire des idées politiques*, Paris, 1959; Jean Touchard, *Histoire des idées politiques*, Vol. II, Paris, 1959.

On Joseph de Maistre: *Les Considérations sur la France*, edited by R. Johannet and F. Vermale, Paris, 1936; G. Cogordan, *Joseph de Maistre*, Paris, 1894, 2nd ed., 1922; A. Omodeo, *Un reazionario, il conte J. de Maistre*, Bari, 1939; E. Dermenghem, *Joseph de Maistre, mystique*, Paris, 1944; F. Bayle, *Les idées politiques de J. de Maistre*, law thesis, Lyons, 1944; P. R. Rohden, *Joseph de Maistre als politischer theoretiker. Ein*

---

* This chapter was published as an article in *Information historique*, 1959, pp. 8–15.

Beitrag zur Geschichte des Konservativen Staats-Gedankens in Frankreich, Munich, 1950; J. C. Murray, "The Political Thought of Joseph de Maistre," *Review of Politics* (January, 1949), pp. 63–86.

On Louis de Bonald: H. Moulinié, *De Bonald*, Paris, 1915; R. Mauduit, *Les Conceptions politiques et sociales de Bonald*, Paris, 1913, less satisfactory than the work by Moulinié).

CHAPTER VII

General bibliography: J. Droz, *L'Allemagne et la Révolution française*, Paris, 1949; F. Valjavec, *Die Entstehung der politischen Strömungen in Deutschland*, Munich, 1951; M. Boucher, *La Révolution de 1789 vue par les écrivains allemands, ses contemporains*, Paris, 1954; M. Rouché, *La Philosophie de l'histoire de Herder*, Strasbourg, 1940; V. Brunauer, *J. Möser*, Berlin, 1933; P. Klassen, *J. Möser*, Frankfurt, 1936; F. Braune, "Edmund Burke in Deutschland," *Heidelberger Abhandlungen zur mittleren und neueren Geschichte*, Vol. 50, 1917; R. Lessing, *Rehberg und die französischen Revolution*, Fribourg, 1910; E. Weniger, *Rehberg und Stein*, Göttingen, 1921; E. Guglia, *Friedrich von Gentz*, Vienna, 1901; A. Robinet de Cléry, *Un diplomate d'il y a cent ans, Frederic de Gentz*, Paris, 1917; P. F. Reiff, *Friedrich Gentz, An Opponent of the French Revolution*, Urbana, Ill., 1912.

CHAPTER VIII

General bibliography: Prélot, *Histoire des idées politiques*; Touchard, *Histoire des idées politiques*; Beik, *The French Revolution Seen from the Right*; Baldensperger, *Le Mouvement des idées dans l'émigration*; Sainte-Beuve, *Chateaubriand et son groupe littéraire sous l'Empire*, edited by Maurice Allem, Paris, 1948; H. Bérenger, *Chateaubriand*, Paris, 1930; *Chateaubriand, le livre de centenaire*, Paris, 1949; P.-André Vincent, *Les Idées politiques de Chateaubriand*, law thesis, Montpellier, 1936; A. Cassagne, *La Vie politique de François de Chateaubriand*, Paris, 1911; B. Chenot, "La Pensée politique de Chateaubriand," *Le Mercure de France* (August, 1950), pp. 687–702; André Maurois, *Chateaubriand*, Paris, 1946.

Although they concern the period of the Restoration, the reader is also referred to the two following works: M.-J. Durry, *La Vieillesse de Chateaubriand*, 2 vols., Paris, 1933, and E. Beau de Loménie, *La Carrière politique de Chateaubriand, de 1814 à 1830*, 2 vols., Paris, 1929.

CHAPTER IX

There are numerous works on the emigration; the essential ones are cited here: D. Greer, *The Incidence of the Emigration During the French*

Revolution, Cambridge, Mass., 1951, summarized by J. Vidalenc in *Information historique*, 1953, pp. 1–9; Forneron, *Histoire générale des émigrés*, Paris, 1884–85; E. Daudet, *Histoire de l'émigration pendant la Révolution française*, 3 vols., Paris, 1904–07 (Vol. I, 1789–97; Vol. II, 1797–1800; Vol. III, 1800–14); Baldensperger, *Le Mouvement des idées dans l'émigration*; E. Vingtrinier, *La Contre-révolution*, 2 vols., Paris, 1924–25; M. Bouloiseau, *Le Séquestre et la vente des biens des émigrés dans le district de Rouen*, Paris, 1937; M. Bouloiseau and G. Lefebvre, "L'Emigration et les milieux populaires, émigration, paniques, embauchage," *Ann. hist. de la Rév. fr.*, 1959, pp. 110–126; G. Sangnier, *Les émigrés du Pas-de-Calais pendant la Révolution*, Blangermont, 1959; M. Weiner, *The French Exiles, 1789–1815*, London, 1960.

CHAPTER X

The work which first posed the question of intelligence networks is the official British publication, *The Manuscripts of J. B. Fortescue, Esq. Preserved at Dropmore*, Vols. II and III, London, 1894. The same year saw the appearance of the second edition of the book by Léonce Pingaud, *Un agent secret sous la Révolution et l'Empire, le comte d'Antraigues*. See the reviews published of this book by Alphonse Aulard, *La Rév, fr.*, 1897, Vol. XXXII, p. 121; Clapham, *English Historical Review*, 1897, Vol. XII, p. 67; and Glagau, *Historische Zeitschrift*, 1897, Vol. LXXVIII, p. 217. The problem was taken up again later by A. Mathiez, *Etudes robespierristes*, 1918, Vol. II, pp. 138–224, then by J. Godechot, "Le Directoire vu de Londres," *Ann. hist. de la Rév. fr.*, 1949, pp. 311–366, and 1950, p. 1–27; A. Ollivier, *Saint-Just ou la force des choses*, Paris, 1954; H. Mitchell, "Francis Drake and the Comte d'Antraigues, a Study of the Dropmore Bulletins," *Bulletin of the Institute of Historical Research*, 1956, pp. 123–144; J. Bessand-Massenet, *La Vie de conspirateur*, Paris, 1956; J. de Grandsaignes, "Enquête sur les bulletins de Dropmore," *Ann. hist. de la Rév. fr.*, 1957, pp. 213–237; H. Mitchell, "Vendémiaire, a Reevaluation," *Journal of Modern History*, 1958, Vol. XXX, pp. 191–202; A. Rufer, "En complément des 'Dropmore Papers,' " *Ann. hist. de la Rév. fr.*, 1958, no. 4, pp. 14–43; J. de Grandsaignes, J. Godechot and M. Reinhard, "A propos de Vannelet et des 'Dropmore Papers,' " *ibid.*, 1958, no. 5, pp. 1–20; J. Godechot, "Le Comte d'Antraigues et ses mystérieux correspondants méridionaux," XXXth and XXXIst Congrès de sociétés savantes du Rousillon et de Provence, Beaucaire, 1957, Montpellier, 1959; J. Godechot and J. de Grandsaignes, "Essai d'identification de quelques correspondants du comte d'Antraigues," *Bull. de la Soc. d'Hist. mod.*, 1959, pp. 5–9.

The sources for the history of the insurrections in the west are both numerous and widely scattered. Some are preserved in the French archives, others are found abroad, above all in Great Britain where they have not yet been utilized by historians as they should be. But many *Mémoires* dealing with the insurrections in the west have been published. They can be divided into two categories, those written by royalists, and those from republicans. Among the former those of Mme de La Rochejacquelein, Poirier de Beauvais, Lucas Champonnière, Le Bouvier, d'Andigné, Rochecotte and Puisaye should be noted; among the latter, those of generals Grouchy, Hugo, Kléber, and of Rouget de Lisle, Benaben, Choudieu, Philippeaux and Larevellière-Lépeaux. Numerous letters have also been published, in particular those of the royalists Charette, Stofflet, Puisaye and d'Autichamp.

The number of works devoted to insurrections in the west of France is also considerable. Among the most important we shall cite those by C.-L. Chassin, *La Préparation de la guerre de Vendeé*, 3 vols., 1892; *La Vendée patriote*, 4 vols., 1893–95; *Les Pacifications de l'Ouest*, 3 vols., 1893–99; *Tables générales*, 1900. This work tends to favor the republicans. On the other hand, E. Gabory, *La Révolution et la Vendée*, 3 vols., Paris, 1925–28, is pro-royalist. The following two works try to be impartial: L. Dubreuil, *Histoire des insurrections de l'Ouest*, 2 vols., Paris, 1929–30, and G. Walter, *La Guerre de Vendée*, Paris, 1953. Finally, see Charles Tilly, "Civil constitution and counter-revolution in Southern Anjou," *French Historical Studies*, 1959, pp. 172–199. On one precise point, the La Rouairie conspiracy believed to be at the origin of the insurrections in the west, consult Daudet, *Histoire des conspirations royalistes du Midi*, and G. Lenotre, *Le Marquis de La Rouairie et la conjuration bretonne*, *1790–1793*, Paris, 1910, and *Le Vrai Chevalier de Maison-Rouge. Le baron de Batz*, Paris, 1911. See also A. Mathiez, *La Révolution et les étrangers*, Paris, 1918, and A. Goodwin, "Counter-Revolution in Brittany: The Royalist Conspiracy of the Marquis de la Rouërie, 1791–1793," *Bulletin of the John Rylands Library*, 1957, pp. 326–355.

CHAPTER XII

The Midi: Daudet, *Histoire des conspirations royalistes du Midi sous la Révolution*; abbé Jolivet, *La Révolution dans l'Ardèche*, 1930; M. Lecoq, *La Contre-révolution dans le Midi (1790–1798)*, Paris, 1932.

Lyons: C. Riffaterre, "Le Mouvement antijacobin et antiparisien à Lyon et dans le Rhône-et-Loire en 1793," *Annales de la Faculté des Lettres de Lyon*, 1912, Vol. I; 1928, Vol. II; E. Herriot, *Lyon n'est plus,*

4 vols., Paris, 1937–40; A. Kleinclausz, *Histoire de Lyon (1595–1814)*, Vol. II (by L. Dubois and F. Dutacq), Lyons, 1948; R. Fuoc, *La Réaction thermidorienne à Lyon*, Lyons, 1957; R. Trénard, *Lyon, de l'Encyclopédie au préromantisme, histoire sociale des idées*, 2 vols., Paris, 1958.

Provence: G. Guibal, *Le Fédéralisme en Provence en 1793*, Paris, 1908; O. Havard, *Histoire de la Révolution dans les ports de guerre*, 2 vols., 1912 (Vol. I, Toulon); P. Cottin, *Toulon et les Anglais en 1793*, Paris, 1898.

CHAPTER XIII

General bibliography: see the works of Dubreuil, Gabory and Daudet cited in the previous chapters; A. Mathiez, *La Réaction thermidorienne*, Paris, 1929; G. Lefebvre, *Les Thermidoriens*, Paris, 1937; Käre D. Tønnesson, *La Défaite des sans-culottes*, Paris and Oslo, 1958; Fuoc, *La Réaction thermidorienne à Lyon*; T. de Closmadeuc, *Quiberon*, Paris, 1898; E. Gabory, *L'Angleterre et la Vendée*, 2 vols., Paris, 1930–31; H. Zivy, *Le 13 vendémiaire*, Paris, 1898 (Bibl. de la Faculté des Lettres de Paris); G. Rudé, "Les sans-culottes parisiens et les journées de vendémiaire an IV," *Ann. hist. de la Rév. fr.*, 1959, pp. 332–346.

For detailed studies see P. Vaillandet, "Les Débuts de la Terreur blanche en Vaucluse," *Ann. hist. de la Rév. fr.*, 1928, pp. 109–127, and "Le Procès des juges de la Commission révolutionnaire d'Orange," *Ann. hist. de la Rév. fr.*, 1929, pp. 137–163; E. Courcelle, "La Réaction thermidorienne dans le district de Melun," *Ann. hist. de la Rév. fr.*, 1930, pp. 113–128, 252–261, 329–350, 443–453; and E. Poupé, "La Répression de la révolte terroriste de Toulon," *Bull. du Com. des Travaux historiques*, 1924.

CHAPTER XIV

General bibliography: G. Caudrillier, *La Trahison de Pichegru et les intrigues royalistes dans l'Est avant fructidor*, Paris, 1908; A. Mathiez, *Le Directoire*, Paris, 1934; J. Godechot, *La Propagande royaliste aux armées sous le Directoire*, Paris, 1933, and *Les Commissaires aux armées sous la Directoire*, 2 vols., Paris, 1937; G. Lefebvre, *Le Directoire*, 3 vols., Paris, 1928; J. Godechot, "Moreau et les papiers de Klinglin," *Ann. hist. de la Rév. fr.*, 1932, and "Le Directoire vu de Londres," *ibid.*, 1949 and 1950; G. Caudrillier, *L'Association royaliste de l'Institut philanthropique à Bordeaux*, Paris, 1908; Bessand-Massenet, *La Vie de conspirateur*; H. Guillemin, *Benjamin Constant muscadin*, Paris, 1958; M. Reinhard, *Le Grand Carnot*, 2 vols., Paris, 1949–52; J. Suratteau, "Les Elections de l'an IV et les opérations de l'assemblée électorale de France," *Ann. hist. de la Rév. fr.*, 1951, 1952, and 1955, and "Les Elections de l'an V," *ibid.*, 1958.

CHAPTER XV

General bibliography: E. Rota, *Le Origini del Risorgimento*, 2 vols., Milan, 1938; G. Candeloro, *Storia dell'Italia moderna*, Vol. I, Milan, 1956; G. Lumbroso, *I moti popolari contro i Francesi alla fine del secolo XVIII (1796–1800)*, Florence, 1932; Maurice Vaussard, *Jansénisme et Gallicanisme aux origines religieuses du Risorgimento*, Paris, 1959; J. Leflon, *Pie VII*, Vol. I, Paris, 1958; R. Dufourcq, *Le Régime jacobin en Italie: la République romaine*, Paris, 1900; V. E. Giuntella, *La Giacobina Republica romana*, Rome, 1950.

On Malta: J. Godechot, *Histoire de Malte*, Paris, 1952, with bibliography.

On Egypt: F. Charles-Roux, *Bonaparte gouverneur d'Egypte*, Paris, 1936.

CHAPTER XVI

General works: Daudet, *Histoire de l'émigration*, Vol. II, 1908.

Germany: P. Sagnac, *Le Rhin français, pendant la Révolution et l'Empire*, Paris, 1917.

Switzerland: Dierauer, *Histoire de la Confédération suisse*, Lausanne, 1910–29; *Dictionnaire historique et géographique de la Suisse*, the article on the Helvetian Republic by A. Rufer, Berne, 1927; M. Salamin, *Histoire politique du Valais sous la république helvétique*, Sion, 1957; J. Godechot, *Les Commissaires aux armées*, Vol. II, Paris, 1938.

Belgium: H. Pirenne, *Histoire de Belgique*, Vol. III, new edition, 1958; P. Verhaegen, *La Belgique sous la domination française*, Vol. II, Brussels, 1935; Lanzac de Laborie, *La Domination française en Belgique*, Vol. I, Paris, 1895; A. Orts, *La Guerre des paysans (1798–1799)*, Brussels, 1863; Victor Pierre, *La Terreur sous le Directoire*, Paris, 1887.

CHAPTER XVII

On Italy: See the works cited in the preceding chapter, and also *La Reconquista del regno di Napoli, Lettere del Cardinal Ruffo, del Re, della Regina e del ministro Acton*, edited with a preface by B. Croce, Bari, 1943; R. Bouvier and A. Laffargue, *La Vie napolitaine au XVIIIe siècle*, Paris, 1956; Harold Acton, *The Bourbons of Naples*, London, 1956; G. Cingari, *Giacobini e Sanfedisti in Calabria nel 1799*, Messina, 1799.

On the Ionian Islands: Rodocanachi, *Bonaparte et les îles Ioniennes*, Paris, 1899.

On Germany, Switzerland and Belgium: See the works cited in the previous chapter. For the Batavian republic: L. Legrand, *La Révolution française en Hollande*, Paris, 1899; H. T. Colenbrander, *De Bataavsche Republiek*, Amsterdam, 1908.

On France: Caudrillier, *L'Association royaliste de l'Institut philanthropique de Bordeaux*; Dubreuil, *Histoire des insurrections de l'Ouest*, Vol. II, 1930; Marcel Reinhard, *Le Département de la Sarthe sous le régime directorial*, Paris, 1935; abbé Joseph Lacouture, *Le Mouvement royaliste dans le Sud-Ouest*, Hossegor, 1932; T. de Hansey, *Contribution à l'histoire de l'insurrection de thermidor an VII dans l'Ariège*, Foix, 1936; Jean Beyssi, "Le Parti jacobin à Toulouse sous le Directoire," *Ann. hist. de la Rév. fr.*, 1950, pp. 28–54; Philippe Wolff, *Histoire de Toulouse*, Toulouse, 1958; R. Langeron, *Royer-Collard*, Paris, 1956.

CHAPTER XVIII

General bibliography: L. Madelin, *Histoire du Consulat et de l'Empire*, Vols. III and IV, Paris, 1938 and 1939; J. Thiry, *L'Avènement de Napoléon*, Paris, 1959; E. Gabory, *Napoléon et la Vendée*, Paris, 1915; E. d'Hauterive, *La Police secrète du Premier Empire*, 2 vols., Paris, 1908; Welschinger, *Le Duc d'Enghien*, Paris, 1888, 2nd ed., 1913; Marcel Dupont, *Le Tragique Destin du duc d'Enghien*, Paris, 1938; B. Melchior-Bonnet, *Le Duc d'Enghien*, Paris, 1954; G. de Cadoudal, *G. de Cadoudal et la chouannerie*, Paris, 1887; G. Caudrillier, "Le Complot de l'an XII," *Rev. hist.*, 1900–1902, Vols. 75, 78 and 79; E. Picard, *Bonaparte ét Moreau*, Paris, 1905; E. d'Hauterive, *Napoléon et sa police*, Paris, 1943, and *La Contre-police royaliste en 1800*, Paris, 1931; J. Leflon, *Etienne-Alexandre Bernier, évêque d'Orléans et l'application du Concordat*, 2 vols., Paris, 1938.

On Italy: See Candeloro, *Storia dell'Italia moderna*, Vol. I, 1956; F. Bongioanni, *Mémoires d'un jacobin (1799)*, Turin, 1958; and Leflon, *Pie VII*, Vol. I, 1958.

Index